Modernity, Tradition, and Indian Women

Modernity, Tradition, and Indian Women

U. Kalpagam

BLOOMSBURY
NEW DELHI • LONDON • OXFORD • NEW YORK • SYDNEY

BLOOMSBURY INDIA
Bloomsbury Publishing India Pvt. Ltd
Second Floor, LSC Building No. 4, DDA Complex, Pocket C–6&7,
Vasant Kunj, New Delhi 110070

BLOOMSBURY, BLOOMSBURY ACADEMIC INDIA and the Diana logo are trademarks of Bloomsbury Publishing Plc

First published in India 2025

This edition published with permission from Bloomsbury Publishing Plc, 50 Bedford Square, London, WC1B3DP, UK

British Library Cataloguing in Publication Information Available
Library of Congress Cataloging-in-Publication Data

ISBN: 978-93-69521-13-5

For sale in the Indian subcontinent only

Printed and bound in India by Replika Press Pvt. Ltd

To find out more about our authors and books
visit www.bloomsbury.com and sign up for our newsletters

Contents

Preface

Every Indian, over the course of their lifetime, faces numerous instances of resolving their existential dilemma of how much of modernity to adopt and how much of traditional values and cultural practices to retain. Inhabiting modernity is, after all not that easy as it may seem. Especially for women, this dilemma is entwined with the patriarchal cultural ideologies that socialize them in the fulfillment of certain social and familial norms that constrain their ability to access freedoms to construct their modern selves in their desired ways. Each of the chapters in the book explores this dilemma that confronts women in their private sphere relating to issues of marriage practices, religion, clothing, and consumption. These studies are based on ethnographic fieldwork conducted among women both in north and south India and were done when I was a serving professor. Earlier versions of some of the chapters have been published in journals and edited volumes. The journals are *Economic and Political Weekly*, *Indian Journal of Gender Studies,* and *Nivedini.* A few have also been published in edited volumes (Sarai/CSDS Readers 3—*Shaping Technologies* and 7—*Frontiers*) and in *Marriage and Migration* edited by P. Uberoi and R. Palriwala. I am thankful to all the editors for their suggestions and comments that improved the earlier versions, and to all individuals and institutions that have supported my research. For the preponderance of references to cultural anthropology, I am, as always, indebted to Rayna Rapp for providing the opportunity many years ago to immerse myself in studies of cultural anthropology. An anonymous reader of the manuscript for Lexington Books provided helpful suggestions to improve the text in certain places and I offer my thanks to her as well. I thank Mark Lopez, my editor, his assistant Madeline Jenkins, and the production team at Lexington Books for facilitating a smooth transition of the manuscript to the printed book.

Introduction

The Conundrum of Tradition and Modernity

Culture is intrinsic to human living and is a product of human imagination, creativity, and external conditions. It consists of beliefs, language and communication, and everyday practices of living. As such, there can be no individual without a culture. Culture, though, is not static and does change over time both due to collective volition or even involuntarily brought about by changes on account of historically developing modes of livelihood, cultural influences through interaction with other alien groups by war and conquest or migration, and in contemporary times through modernity, capitalist development and globalization. Not only does each individual has a culture and lives within a culture, but culture also constructs their self and constitutes their subjectivity. No doubt individuals are involved in the creation and construction of culture while living their cultural lives through belief systems and everyday practices, constantly reproducing that culture. Many of the belief systems have been long enduring, such as religion and so has caste stratification in Indian society, which is also a product of belief systems, archaic social division of labor, and everyday practices.

While individuals live in a culture and, for the most part, seem comfortable carrying on their pursuits in life, they also at times find cultural norms and practices to be constraining rather than enabling. This happens when cultural ideas and practices are intertwined with forces of social domination, leading to sociocultural domination of some groups of people over others that stifle and hinder their life pursuits. Also, ideas of modernity that spread around the world through Western colonization established a hierarchy of cultural values that privileged Western cultural values, especially regarding individualism and reason or rationality, while simultaneously belittling non-Western cultures. Equally, ideas and practices of modernity expand the imagination, creativity, desire for freedom, and opportunities of individuals, which some find incompatible with their cultural norms and practices, thus stifling their pursuits. They seek to change or modify these norms even as they attempt to incorporate ideas and practices of modernity.

These contending forces of old and new ideas and values set societies in constant cultural tensions and even conflicts. Even modern Western societies experience cultural tension generated by societal changes through technological and other features of modernization. Such is the case in the United States with the debate on Free Choice over Abortion that has long been opposed by certain Christian groups, even as these societies are introducing legal changes to the traditional conception of marriage as heterosexual unions initiated through social activism. There is today a growing concern that Afghanistan under Taliban rule will roll back some of the freedoms affecting women's and girls' lives through the enforcement of strict Sharia laws. Many Islamic societies also try to hold back the influence of Western modernity on their societies through constant modifications and re-adaptations of the Sharia law under their differing political systems of governance.

This is an outcome of a growing resentment toward the increasing influence and absorption of Western cultural ideas and values around the world that different societies seek to navigate to counteract some of these tendencies through sociopolitical means, be it in China, India, or Nigeria. Many social and political actors in these societies are apprehensive that their core cultural values are threatened by Western influence, even as many others, including men in these societies and especially women and girls, minorities, and others would seemingly like to break free from some cultural values and practices that bind and shackle them in their pursuit of modern life.

In India, cultural issues and their impact and influence on women's lives have been part of public debates since early colonial times, often resulting in contested debates by nationalists among themselves and with the colonialists. The encounter with Western modernity through the colonial state and missionary influences caused social reformers and social reform movements to find ways to navigate through new ideas of modernity impacting cultural life, and the lives of women and girls as well as of men. Ironically, these ideas of modernity based on reason and modern science privileged the value of human dignity even when colonial rule at its core value and everyday practices were at variance with the value of human dignity in the governance of the colonized, as colonialism carried the burden of its civilizing mission.

History textbooks are replete with information on the colonial civilizing mission, such as the role of Christian missionaries in deprecating the "heathen" practices to promote Christian conversions, the role played by Rammohan Roy in the abolition of Sati and in the founding of the *Brahmo Samaj* that sought to reshape *Sanatan Dharam* in the image of monotheistic Christianity in the early nineteenth century, followed in the later decades by other reforms such as widow remarriage by Ishwar Chandra Vidyasagar, the abolition of child marriage and the Age of Consent Bill as well as contests among nationalist leaders themselves, exemplified by the rhetoric of leaders like Bal Gangadhar Tilak, as to the extent to which such social reforms and cultural change should be encouraged in a society that was being influenced by modern Western education.

The nationalist negotiation with colonial modernity gave rise to the possibility of selective appropriation of Western modernity without disrupting the essential features of the spiritual culture of India in the construction of the national culture. While accepting the project of modernization in the public realm, nationalism asserted its spiritual superiority to the West. This has resulted in the conundrum of modernity and tradition that continues in the contemporary life of the nation and its women. Late nineteenth-century nationalist crafting of the emerging middle-class women as "modern" with access to modern education and freedom to participate in the public realm had their domestic life redefined by new norms of patriarchy. While studies on middle-class women in colonial India have highlighted the ways they were drawn into the modernizing life worlds through education that drew many women into the fold of the nationalist movement from the latter half of the nineteenth century, there is not much written about the contemporary context of how women negotiate between the contending forces of modernity and tradition in their attempts to construct themselves as modern women in their private and intimate spheres as an ongoing everyday feature of their lives in India.

The conundrum of tradition and modernity in self-construction is an ongoing and seemingly never-ending puzzle for all individuals in modern India, irrespective of caste, class, and religion. This conundrum offers women, especially, the option to live abiding by social and cultural norms that may also seem to constrain them by setting limits on their aspirations and achievements in some spheres or expanding their potentialities for better human flourishing through accessing modern freedoms. These choices come with associated costs, as in an attempt to expand one's capacity for flourishing, one may have to forgo the cultural securities of norm-governed life as embedded practices in a life quest, or break free from constraining social disciplines with certain consequences. Nor are there any guarantees that modern freedoms would necessarily promote the human flourishing that one desires, as individuals' life goals and the possibilities for the successful attainment of one's goals do differ.

In modernizing societies, people are socialized in varying degrees to selectively accept modern trends of thought, practices, and lifestyles. It is not always the case that the selective appropriation of modernity and the traditions to be retained is a puzzle that makes choice difficult. In the middle-class family setting in the metropolitan city of Chennai where I grew up, I celebrated my birthday twice a year—the English birthday based on the Gregorian calendar system and the Tamil birthday based on the Tamil calendar system. This was never experienced as a choice puzzle, and as a child, I looked forward to both. But there are many other issues, both in one's growing and adult life, when the choice between traditional and modern lifestyles and values poses a puzzle that is negotiated by each individual through varying degrees of resistance and acquiescence. Matters relating to clothing and dress and the choice of one's life partner are usually fraught with tension in the negotiation between modernity and tradition.

This book explores how women resolve the conundrum of tradition and modernity through studies based on fieldwork in North and South India relating to women's marriage aspirations and choices, religiosity in the modern urban context, clothing and lifestyle choices, and as consumer-subjects in the global economy. The expansion of zones of freedom in the private sphere of women's lives through attempts at changing patriarchal attitudes embedded in cultural ideologies that frame the everyday lives of women could resolve the conundrum to some extent, enabling women to flourish in their capabilities and endeavors.

Scholars and students often go by popular understandings of modernity and tradition that obliterate the historicity of modernity in the West, the difference between modernization and modernity, the spread of modernity, and the modernization of non-Western societies. Popular understandings of tradition also view tradition as immutable, fixed, and unchanging which could as a matter of fact be invented or change over time. The conundrum of tradition and modernity in India and other non-Western societies is primarily due to attempts at retaining the essence of one's cultural authenticity even as cultural practices change, whereas in the modern Western world, authenticity is the expression of one's true self arising out of one's own self-construction by choice.

The notion of "modernity" emerges in European Enlightenment thought and in more clarity in the post-Enlightenment and later European thought. Colonial encounters with Western modernity and the projects of modernization in the non-Western world questioned the universality of Western modernity, leading to the conceptual development of "Alternate" modernity and "Multiple modernities." In the constructions of modernity everywhere, the role of tradition is constantly interrogated. The concept of tradition is explained here with a view to clarify that it is not necessarily a fixed and unchanging practice or principle from the past but could also undergo changes. As modernity connects the present to the future, tradition connects the present to the past. Both pose a conundrum in the search for origins and the construction of the self in modernizing non-Western contexts, raising the question of the authenticity of the "nation" and the "modern."

The remaining sections seek to clarify these issues of modernity, tradition, and authenticity. It is not necessary for readers to read these theoretical sections very intently on their first reading. After gleaning through them swiftly, the reader could move on to the other chapters and then come back again to read these parts for greater clarity.

MODERNITY AND ITS VARIANTS

Historian Chakrabarty (2002) has noted that modernity is easy to inhabit but difficult to define. There is an overwhelming consensus that since the European Enlightenment, modernity signifies the rule of institutions founded on Reason and Rationality, suggesting that institutions of both the premodern European contexts and all other non-Western contexts were outside its ambit. Taylor (2001) has indicated two theories of modernity: one is a "cultural" theory of modernity and another is "a-cultural" theory of modernity. The "a-cultural" theory conceives of modernity as the growth of reason, such as scientific consciousness, instrumental rationality, the decline of superstitions, and the development of a secular outlook, along with accompanying economic changes such as industrialization, urbanization, and modern education. Being culture-neutral, this theory makes possible the transmission of these features of modernity originating in Europe to be transposed anywhere else in the world. With each culture having a language and a set of practices around specific understandings of personhood, social relations, virtue and vice, and body, mind and soul, a "cultural" theory of modernity, according to Taylor, refers to transformations in the West on account of a rise of new culture. By and large, the "a-cultural" view of modernity as the rise and spread of reason, rationality, and progress has gained dominance. Unarguably, the spread of reason and rationality in European contexts entailed not merely the eradication of superstitions but also a radical and complete rupture with premodern ways of knowing and the knowledges through such epistemologies. Concomitantly, modernity is associated with increasing self-reflexivity and social transformation through functional differentiation of institutions, disenchantment of religion and secularization of society, and the public sphere. These contributed to the development of individualism, liberalism, democracy, and capitalism. With these quintessential features, modernity also came to be considered as exclusively Western or European in origin.

Recently, scholars of Western modernity have sought to understand transformations of modernity over time by comparing the current state of society with its state prior to, roughly, the 1960s, in what is termed "successive modernities." Scholars of "successive modernities" such as Beck, Giddens, Bauman, and Touraine, while pointing to novel challenges created by the transformation of modernity, present a simplified picture of the past modernity with inadequate consideration of the historicity of modern social configurations (Wagner, 2011). For Beck (1986), it was first simple modernity followed by reflexive modernity, while for Giddens (1990), it was institutional reflexivity that followed the earlier modernity. For Bauman, the earlier modernity had solid features such as legislation, order-production, and elimination of ambivalence, whereas the succeeding one had liquid characteristics, preferring to call it "liquid modernity" rather than "postmodern." Drawing inspiration from Koselleck, Wagner has noted that the search for the dynamics of succession within modernity leads to a reassessment of the notions of crisis and critique and the link between them. Touraine (1995), while being cautious of periodization, makes distinction between the subjectivizing and rationalizing features of modernity, suggesting that rationalization has long been dominant in modernity but is being challenged recently by a rising concern with subjectivation. While all these writings are underpinned by a normative agenda, the evaluation of the two periods of modernity differs across the authors nor are they easily interpretable as progress or regress either (Wagner, 2011).

Scholars of modernity's successive transformations, like Bauman do not consider postmodernity as part of the succession and prefer to name the contemporary phase differently, for they believe that postmodern scholars, in emphasizing critique of foundationalism and difference, do not provide an adequate framework to analyze social change and agency. But the postmodern concerns of the collapse of meta-narratives and the certitudes of modernity in an increasingly globalized world of technologies, with capacities to render much of human work redundant, and the planetary spread of modernity's destruction of environments and climate change are still relevant to the understanding of the transformations of modernity.

The progress of modernity within "successive modernities" based on principled critique of crisis, can be measured by the extent to which emerging sociopolitical problems are solved in accordance with modernity's normative commitments. The dual principle of individual and collective autonomy is taken as the starting point of the normative political philosophy of modernity. Although there is some debate about the relation between the two aspects of the principle of autonomy, much of political theory considers this principle as a possible universalist accomplishment derived from the ideas of liberty and equality. The increase in individual autonomy has been a key commitment of European modernity from at least the sixteenth century onward, even though it spread only gradually through society (Taylor, 1989).

Modernity's normative commitment has recently been enriched by adding a theory of justice for universally grounding some commitment to the redistribution of resources (Rawls, 1971). While critiquing the universalist procedural approach, scholars have argued for historically situating such proceduralist approaches. Honneth (1997) criticizes Habermas's limitation to the liberal state as the sole institutional embodiment and defender of individual autonomy. Noting that human beings need recognition not merely in the legal sense, but also recognition for their contribution to the collectivity and recognition as a particular human being in private life, he notes that in addition to rights, human beings need love and respect. For Honneth, recognition is a prerequisite for individual autonomy. Also, in his view, normative theory should no longer construct a neutral standpoint to work out principles of justice, but rather reconstruct those principles from the historical processes of recognition in which they are always already effective as norms of mutual respect and consideration. He also notes that a reconstructive theory of justice becomes helpless where social relations are ethically entirely destroyed and demoralized.

Scholars writing about modernity from various disciplines of philosophy, history, political science, sociology, and anthropology such as Marx, Weber, Parsons, Giddens, Taylor, Habermas, Foucault, Berman, Lash, Blumenberg, Koselleck, Eisenstadt, Beck, and others have largely focused on modernity instilling aspirations of freedom and rights in the public domain, neglecting the private sphere and the sphere of intimacy, with the exception of some scholars in gender studies and a few writing on Indian modernity such as Partha Chatterjee, Dipesh Chakrabarty, and Arjun Appadurai.

In an attempt to explain how modernities are constructed in various national and cultural sites, Gaonkar (2001) provides the most comprehensive explication of Western modernity. Noting the need to relook at the distinction between societal modernization and cultural modernity, he noted that societal modernization has two aspects that worked in harmonious tandem, namely cognitive transformation leading to the spread of reason and rationality, and social transformation leading to industrialization, urbanization, market economy, and a bureaucratic state. These developments also resulted in a new subject who was set free from traditional constraints to pursue his own private ends motivated by acquisitiveness and this-worldly concerns. Cultural modernity emerged in the West in opposition to middle-class conformism and the pursuit of money that stifled creativity and imagination, emerging first in the aesthetic realm and then carried forward in the popular media.

By the middle of the nineteenth century, cultural modernity in the West began to focus on self-exploration and self-realization using imagination as its ally, while reason was viewed as a constraint. The aesthetic of the self emerged in the capitalist context of constant change and deadening routine wherein the modern self was made and remade, a fact that scholars of modernity like Marx, Weber, Baudelaire, Simmel, and others sought to grapple with. In the midst of all the continuous changes, only the vortex of "everyday life" endured, which Baudelaire and others sought to give aesthetic expression to. For Baudelaire, everyday life was concrete, fragmentary, and immediate in presence, though in constant flux, but wants to also grasp the "classic" in the modern that is fleeting. Habermas (1983, 4) notes, "The emphatically modern document no longer borrows this power of being a classic from the authority of a past epoch; instead, a modern work becomes a classic because it has once been authentically modern." Prior to Baudelaire, the term "modern" designated a consciousness of having made the transition from the old to the new, where the old representing antiquity and tradition follows the modern to remind and instruct, which with the spread of Enlightenment reason also enables the "modern" to free itself from the spell of tradition.

This, Gaonkar (2001) notes, is a double-edged gesture, for tradition is being deprived of its mediating function while the modern renounces its claim to instruct the future. Everything turns to the present, which has broken out of the continuum of history and is caught in a never-ending process of internal ruptures and fragmentation. The other side of flux and novelty is the routinization and standardization of economy and society, which follow societal modernization, giving rise to a pervasive sense of alienation and despair among people. If the dark side of Weber's societal modernity is the alienation and despair of being caught in the iron cage, the dark side of Baudelaire's cultural modernity is the descent of the self into narcissistic self-absorption and hedonism.

The solutions to the dilemmas of modernity, in particular the ways of minimizing the dark side effects, are varied depending on how these sides are conceived and connected. Habermas, for instance, is critical of Weber's instrumental rationality and is committed to rehabilitating the project of modernity in which reason is an agency with many forms and voices. But Foucault is pessimistic about such rehabilitation as reason is enmeshed with power in his accounts of disciplinary society emerging from Enlightenment reason. For Foucault, reason, knowledge, and truth are constituted by and constitutive of power. Even in his later writings, when Foucault shifts the focus of his investigations from the technologies of subjectification associated with modern institutions to practices of freedom and the arts of self-formation in everyday life, he continues to think of reason in terms of power and strategy.

For Foucault, modernity is not an epoch but an attitude, a mode of relating to contemporary reality, which appears Baudelairian. Foucault finds in Kant's (1784) text "What Is Enlightenment?" a new way of posing the question of modernity. For Foucault, modernity entails both a form of relationship to the present and to oneself and "not in the longitudinal relation to the Ancients, but in what might be called a 'sagital' relation to one's own present" (Foucault, 1994, 141). He notes:

> The deliberate attitude of modernity is tied to an indispensable asceticism. To be modern is not to accept oneself as one is in the flux of the passing moments; but it is to take oneself as the object of a complex and difficult elaboration: what Baudelaire in the vocabulary of his day, calls dandysme. (Foucault, 1997, 311)

The care of the self as the practice of freedom also involves complex relationships with others. One who masters himself through self-knowledge is capable of properly exercising power over others and thus taking his rightful place in the city or the household or any other congregation. For Foucault, the significance of the Enlightenment is to subscribe to "a philosophical ethos that could be described as a permanent critique of our historical era" (Foucault, 1997, 312).

ALTERNATE AND MULTIPLE MODERNITIES

For quite some time, sociologists and others have been grappling with the term "modernity," questioning its singularity and its hegemonic association with Western modernity. They have proposed conceptual variations to capture its space-time dynamics such as "multiple modernities," "alternative modernities," "vernacular modernities," and "global modernity." This section engages with this literature in order to understand what would possibly be a relevant characterization of modernity for contemporary India. It is virtually impossible to abandon the Western discourse on modernity while thinking of alternative modernities.

Modernity has traveled from the West to the rest of the world not only in terms of cultural forms, social practices, and institutional arrangements but also as a form of discourse that interrogates the present. That questioning of the present taking place at every national and cultural site, whether in vernacular or in cosmopolitan idioms, cannot escape the legacy of Western discourse on modernity. But Gaonkar does not consider how the construction of alternate modernities in different national and cultural contexts selectively draws and retains, even if modified its prior civilizational values and its local cultural and social practices in the changing contexts of modernity.

Classical sociological thinkers (Spencer, Marx, Weber, Durkheim, Simmel, and Parsons) conceptualize modernization as an interlinked process of structural differentiation, cultural rationalization and personal individualization, and modernity as a culture-neutral, universally applicable model that posits a break with tradition as the process unfolds everywhere. Multiple modernists reject this conceptualization for its incapacity to capture the immense social, political, and cultural diversity exhibited by the modern age and seek to pluralize the concept of modernity.

One of the primary themes of the new approach is the role of non-Western traditions in the creation of diverse forms of modernity. Interaction with the Western model has been a component of all modernizing processes and patterns, but non-Western forms have been co-determined by the encounter with local civilizational settings. It follows equally, however, that the civilizational factor is as operative in the Western case as all others.

Schmidt (2006) rejects the notion of "multiple modernities" and favors the phrase "varieties of modernity." He points out that Parsons, like other modernization theorists, explicitly stated that there could be "[great] variations within the modern type of society" (Parsons, 1977, 228) and that many such variations would probably emerge as a result of the global trend toward completion of this type of society. Parsons' theory of modernity is embedded in a more encompassing theory of the general action systems comprising four subsystems—the social system, the cultural system, the personality system, and the behavioral organism. As his theory of modernity did not engage with the subsystem of the behavioral organism, it did not consider the likely behavioral changes in individuals as a consequence of cultural flows. He did argue, though, that upon modernization the personality system becomes increasingly achievement-oriented, aware of its own individuality, and empathetic; and that modernization leads to rationalization, value generalization, and the diffusion of secular norms in the cultural sphere. But functional differentiation was the foremost structural characteristic of modern society. Parsons identified four universals that he believed were crucial both for the breakthrough and ultimate consolidation of modernity, namely money and market systems in the economy, democracy in the political realm, the rule of law and equality before the law in the legal system, and bureaucratic organization of public and private institutions (Parsons, 1964). While Parsons mentions the diffusion of secular norms in the cultural sphere, he does not deal with cultural modernity and self-reconstruction in the Baudelairian sense.

The multiple modernities approach rejects the idea that modernity entails a complete break with tradition, which it finds misleading both in relation to the Western model and the non-Western experiences. It foregrounds civilizational particularities and their lasting impact, arguing that different civilizational legacies, both cultural and institutional, give rise to multiple modernities. Eisenstadt and Arnason (2001b) pioneered the multiple modernities approach and see civilizations as macro-historical, macro-social, and macro-cultural combinations of "cultural visions of the world" and "regulative frameworks of social life" (Eisenstadt, 2000a, 2000b, 1). Whereas for Eisenstadt (2000a, 2000b) civilization theory forms the primary perspectival reference point for the idea of multiple modernities; Arnason (2001a) provided a systematic legitimation of civilizational theory as the framework for sociological analysis.

All modernizing processes entail interaction with Western modernity and are co-determined by local civilizational contexts. Following through this argument, it has been argued, as the recent works on the anthropology of colonialism have done, that ideas from colonial contexts moved to European centers of power as well in the construction of European modernity. More interestingly, Western modernity and its own prior civilizational contexts have come to be reexamined, as in Touraine's (1995) *Critique of Modernity*.

Whereas modernity for modernization theorists was primarily defined with respect to structural and institutional factors, the multiple modernities approach stresses the constitutive role of cultural orientations and structures of consciousness while avoiding all forms of cultural determinism. By insisting on the autonomy of culture and the openness of cultural frameworks to reinterpretation in changing social and historical contexts, both Eisenstadt and Arnason share a hermeneutical understanding of culture and its role in social life. While for both, the core cultural orientations of modernity are open to multiple interpretations, Arnason emphasizes hermeneutics of the self-understanding of modernity as an essential complement to historical and structural analysis. Such self-understanding of modernity conceives of modernity as internally conflictual and fraught with tensions operative at both cultural and social levels. This perspective identifies new conceptions of human agency, wherein the resolution of the conflict of interpretations is interpreted as reflexivity and expressivity on the one side, and rational mastery and control on the other, as the central core of cultural modernity.

The ways in which "Axial Age" civilizational contexts provide "cultural visions of the world" and "regulative frameworks of social life" are explained in the *Tanner Lectures on Human Values* by Eisenstadt (1990). In these civilizations that crystallized from 500 BC to the first century of the Christian era, conceptions of a basic tension between the transcendental and mundane orders emerged and were institutionalized in many parts of the world. The given mundane order was perceived in these civilizations as incomplete and inferior, and the attempts were "to reconstruct the mundane world-human personality and the sociopolitical and economic order according to the appropriate transcendental vision, to the principles of the higher metaphysical or ethical order" (Eisenstadt, 1990, 448). He further notes that one of the central aspects of these civilizations was the development of the potential questioning of their own basic premises, which is indicative of a high degree of reflexivity, focused on the basic premises of the social and cultural order, and on individual adherence to the given social and moral order.

More interestingly, there were attempts to restructure human personality and motivate human action with transcendental goals. Eisenstadt notes:

> Thus in these societies or civilizations, personal identity was taken beyond the definition of man in terms of the primordial givens of human existence, and beyond the various technical needs of daily activities, and constructed around the central mode or modes of human action through which the tensions between the transcendental and the mundane orders are resolved. Such purely personal virtues as courage and interpersonal ones as solidarity and mutual help were taken out of their primordial framework and combined, in different dialectical modes, with the attributes of resolution of the tension between the transcendental and the mundane orders, thus generating a new level of internal tensions in the structuring of the personality. (Eisenstadt, 1990, 448)

He also noted that the types of social organization that develop in different civilizations emerge from a variety of contingent constellations, economic and political trends, and ecological conditions—even as they relate to religious tenets or beliefs, basic civilizational premises, and their institutional implications and carriers (Eisenstadt, 1990, 502). The recognition of the spread of modernity, Eisenstadt suggests, has to be viewed as the crystallization of a new type of civilization which, by combining economic, political, and ideological aspects and forces, has a much more intense impact on the societies to which it spread than any before. As it seeks to undermine the symbolic and institutional premises of the societies incorporated into them, it calls for them to respond and open up new options and possibilities (Eisenstadt, 1990, 502). Such restructuring on account of civilizational encounters with the civilization of modernity could also result in some irreplaceable loss to the modernizing civilization. As Ricoeur in his book *History and Truth* notes:

> The phenomenon of universalization, while being an advancement of mankind, at the same time constitutes a sort of subtle destruction, not only of traditional cultures, which might not be an irreparable wrong, but also of what I shall call for the time being the creative nucleus of great cultures, that nucleus on the basis of which we interpret life, what I shall call in advance the ethical and mythical nucleus of mankind. (Ricoeur, 1965, 276)

The core of modernity for Eisenstadt is the crystallization and development of a mode or modes of interpretation of the world, or of a distinct social imaginaire, indeed of the ontological vision, of a distinct cultural program, combined with the development of a set or sets of new institutional formations—the central core of both cultural program and institutional formations being an unprecedented openness and uncertainty.

As modernity expanded throughout the world, it gave rise to continually changing cultural and institutional patterns as different responses to the challenges and possibilities inherent in the core characteristics of the premises of modernity. The history of modernity is therefore best seen as a story of continual development and formation, constitution and reconstitution of a multiplicity of cultural programs of modernity and of distinctively modern institutional patterns, and of different self-conceptions of societies as modern—of multiple modernities.

The strength of multiple modernities approach of Eisenstadt is that it foregrounds the civilizational context, the tensions of the chasm presented by the transcendental and mundane orders in Axial Age civilizations leading to the structuring of human personality with moral concerns and transcendental goals, the selective appropriation and reconstitution of modernity's cultural programs in modernizing societies, and the role of elites in effecting choices. Eisenstadt has been criticized for an almost exclusive focus on Axial Age civilizations in explaining multiple modernities, ignoring the constraints imposed by the colonial contexts on modernizing societies, overlooking the contexts of contemporary globalization, and above all, conceding to the hegemony of Western modernity.

TRADITION, CHANGE, MODERNITY, AND SUBJECTS

Touraine's view of the central cultural orientations of modernity also converges with that of the multiple modernities approach. For Touraine (1995), like Eisenstadt and Arnason, the emergence of the subject and new conceptions of agency associated with it are the defining features of modernity. For Touraine, the cultural orientations of modernity are always embodied in social practices and institutions, and he sees the defining tension of modernity as one between both principles and processes.

Focus shifts in modernity studies from the social to the cultural field, and from a general theory of society to a particular critique of modernity, resulted in an approach that gives prominence to traditions which, Touraine argues, played a central role in the Western model of modernity. In his book *Critique of Modernity*, Touraine analyzes the social forms, conflicts, and logics of modernity through an elucidation of the self-interpretations of modernity as analyzed in the developments, transformations, and specific combinations of concrete traditions; traditions that are not undifferentiated, conflict-free, or have a deterministic relationship to modernity. His analysis brings to the fore the selective, and often conflictual, reactivations of concrete cultural traditions as they are reinterpreted in the light of new historical circumstances.

Touraine's elucidation of successive self-images of modernity through the analytical prism of rationalization and subjectivation uncovers the traditional sources of both the dominant rationalist conception of modernity and an alternative modernity which it suppressed. The breakthrough to modernity meant the destruction of the correspondence between a divine subject and a natural order, but rationalist—and especially historicist—self-understandings of modernity reasserted the idea of unity in the idea of a world unified by reason. According to Touraine, although the Enlightenment saw itself as a break with tradition, its idea that reason was the basis for a correspondence between the liberty of the individual, the organization of society and rational mastery was ultimately an attempt to preserve the traditional idea of the unity of humankind and the universe (Touraine, 1995, 23). On this view, the Enlightenment struggle against Christianity was a transition from a dualistic view of the world to a unified conception of man and world, which subordinated subjectivity to the idea of a rational order.

The dominant rationalist conception of modernity is, therefore, a selective reactivation of traditions that gives rise to a unified worldview and subordinates the subject to reason. It is a one-sided and unbalanced expression of the cultural constituents of modernity, as this selective relationship with tradition obscured the part of Western tradition that embodied a non-rationalist conception of the subject and a mode of thought based on a dualism of reason and subjectivity. For Touraine, a renewal of its latent other half is the key to a more adequate realization of modernity's potentials. For Touraine, modernity is to be a dialogue between Reason and Subject. Touraine's account of the co-determination of modernity by tradition undermines the idea of modernity as culture-neutral and brings to light the civilizational specificities underlying the putatively universal model.

In every national and cultural site where modernity constructs itself, it simultaneously opens up a dialogue between Reason and Subject. Touraine notes:

> The Subject can only be constituted by the integration of its two contradictory components in a cultural project which is capable of uniting the choice for modernity with the intention to conserve the past. This integration is only possible if we give a central importance to the personal assertion of the individual as a Subject. The assertion of the singularity of each actor can alone make possible the combination of instrumentality with value-orientations. Such a combination would not be possible if it should be reduced to the clash of two value systems. On the contrary, it becomes possible when the modern world is seen as a set of means or instruments which have their own function, while a culture is defined as a system of ends. (Touraine, 2002, 393)

Noting from Eisenstadt that Axial Age civilizations provide the "cultural visions of the world" and the "regulative frameworks of social life" as they attempt to transform the deficient mundane world-human personality to a higher metaphysical and ethical one by motivating human actions with transcendental goals, their encounters with Western modernity would necessarily entail a dialogue between Reason and Subject, especially as some of these civilizations had strong traditions and precedents of questioning and self-reflexivity by collectives of orthodoxies and heterodoxies. Cultural and social practices, traditions and norms governing the conduct of groups and individuals, which were themselves dynamic, differentiated, and changing, provided the moral compass to restructure personality.

When Foucault elaborates on his practices of freedom and the arts of self-formation in everyday life, he suggests an attitude of a "sagital relation to one's own present"; for modernity, he argues, entails both a form of relationship to the present and to oneself. For Foucault, the deliberate attitude of modernity entails a "this-worldly asceticism," not "other-worldly asceticism," for to be modern is not to accept oneself as one is in the flux of the passing moment but to take oneself as the object of a complex and difficult elaboration. The mastery through self-knowledge as an art of self-formation in everyday life that Foucault suggests refers to the use of reason in controlling the ego from succumbing to pressures of culture and desire.

MacIntyre's (1981) philosophical history of the ideas of virtues and morals from Aristotelian thought to the modernity of Nietzsche and Sartre helps us to better understand what lacks in Foucault's "sagital" relation to one's present. In the Aristotelian framework, what constitutes the good for man is a complete human life lived at its best, and the exercise of virtues is a necessary and central part of such a life, not a mere means to secure such a life, although the virtues are unavailable to slaves or to barbarians. In the Kantian framework, wherein Foucault situates himself, modern liberalism, by separating law from morality, lets individuals to seek their own good, whereas in the Aristotelian framework, the individual is identified and constituted in and through certain roles, which bind the individual to the communities in and through which alone human goods are to be attained; an individual therefore confronts the world as a member of a family, a household, a clan, a tribe, a city, a nation, or a kingdom. For Aristotle, the telos of life is not something to be achieved at some future point, but in the way one's whole life is constructed. The good life, which is the telos, culminates for the medieval in the contemplation of the divine as the good life moves to a climax. Virtues are those qualities which enable men to survive evils on their historical journey.

This premodern concept of virtues has the concomitant concept of selfhood, where the unity of the self resides in the unity of a narrative linking birth to life to death as narrative beginning to middle to end. MacIntyre observes that it would not be surprising if this premodern conception of the self still remained an unacknowledged presence in many modern Western ways of thinking and acting, which correct conceptual insights about human actions and selfhood would show that it is natural to think of the self in a narrative mode.

To think of the self in a narrative mode, behavior cannot be characterized independently of intentions, and intentions cannot be characterized independently of the settings which make those intentions intelligible both to agents themselves and to others. A social setting may be an institution, a practice, or a milieu of some other human kind. For MacIntyre, each setting has a history within which the histories of individual agents are to be situated, for without the setting and its changes through time, the history of the individual agent and his changes through time will be unintelligible. In writing the narrative history of individuals, behavior can be characterized adequately only when one knows what the longer and longest-term intentions invoked are and how the shorter-term intentions are related to the longer.

Individuals live their lives, both individually and in relationships with each other, with certain conceptions of a possible shared future. There is no present that is not informed by some image of some future and which always presents itself in the form of a telos—or of a variety of ends or goals. MacIntyre notes that the narratives that individuals live out have both an unpredictable and a partially teleological character. If the narrative of individual and social lives is to continue intelligibly, there will always be some constraints on how the story can continue, and within those constraints, there are numerous ways that it can continue.

Man is basically a teller of stories that aspire to truth and becomes so through history. Every society has therefore its stock of stories, and mythology being one such. For MacIntyre, as the self inhabits a character whose unity is given as the unity of a character, there is no way of founding identity on the psychological continuity or discontinuity of the self.

MacIntyre notes that to be the subject of a narrative that runs from one's birth to one's death is to be accountable for the actions and experiences which compose a narratable life. The other aspect of narrative selfhood is one who can always ask others for an account and put others to the question, as the narrative of anyone's life is part of an interlocking set of narratives. This asking for and giving of accounts itself plays an important part in constituting narratives. Thus, the unity of an individual life is the unity of a narrative embodied in a single life.

In every action, asking the two questions of what is good for oneself and what is good for humanity and attempting to provide the answers in deeds and words will provide moral life with its unity. The unity of a human life is the unity of a narrative quest. Quests can sometimes fail for many reasons. But the only criteria for success or failure in a human life as a whole are the criteria of success or failure in a narrated or to-be-narrated quest.

Virtues are to be understood as those dispositions which will not only sustain practices and enable one to achieve the goods internal to practices but which will also sustain one in the relevant kind of quest for the good.

The catalog of virtues will include the virtues required to sustain the kind of households and the kind of political communities in which men and women can seek the good together and the virtues necessary for philosophical inquiry about the character of the good.

One will never be able to seek the good or exercise the virtues only qua (as an) individual. This is partly because living the good life concretely varies from circumstance to circumstance, even when it is one and the same conception of the good life and one and the same set of virtues that are being embodied in a human life. But it is not just that different individuals live in different social circumstances; it is also that everyone approaches their own circumstances as bearers of a particular social identity.

One inherits from the past of one's family, and other social associations such as caste, tribe, ethnicity, and nationality, a variety of debts, inheritances, rightful expectations, and obligations. These constitute the given of one's life, one's moral starting point, which gives each life its own moral particularity, although it does not entail that the self has to accept the moral limitations of the particularity of those forms of community. Only in moving forward from such particularity can the search for the good and for the universal begin, as particularity can never be just dropped or obliterated. Within a tradition, the pursuit of goods extends through generations, sometimes through many generations.

Traditions can degenerate, decay, and disappear and the reason being the lack of exercise of the relevant virtues. MacIntyre notes:

> The virtues find their point and purpose not only in sustaining those relationships necessary if the variety of goods internal to practices are to be achieved and not only in sustaining the form of an individual life in which that individual may seek out his or her good as the good of his or her whole life, but also in sustaining those traditions which provide both practices and individual lives with their necessary historical context. (MacIntyre, 1981, 223)

To recognize this requires the virtue of having an adequate sense of the traditions to which one belongs or which confront one, which is the kind of capacity for judgment the agent possesses in knowing how to select among the relevant stack of maxims and how to apply them in particular situations. The choice between rival goods in a tragic situation differs from the modern choice between incommensurable moral premises in that both of the alternative courses of action in the choice between rival goods which confront the individual have to be recognized as leading to some authentic and substantial good. For MacIntyre, the notion of escaping from it into a realm of entirely universal maxims, whether in its Kantian form or in modern analytical moral philosophies, is an illusion with painful consequences. He notes, "The individualism of modernity could of course find no use for the notion of tradition within its own conceptual scheme except as an adversary notion" (MacIntyre, 1981, 222).

MacIntyre's ideas of a human life as a narrative unity and the concept of a practice with goods internal to itself are alien to individualist modern culture. The kind of work done by the vast majority of the inhabitants of the modern world cannot be understood in terms of the nature of a practice with goods internal to itself. The means-end relationships embodied, for the most part, in such work are necessarily external to the goods and have consequently been expelled from the realm of practices with goods internal to themselves.

Once virtues have been severed from their traditional context in the modern period, it opened up a new way to understand them as dispositions related to the psychology of the newly invented "individual." Some of the virtues could be understood as expressions of the natural passions of the individual, or some could be understood as dispositions necessary to curb and limit the destructive effect of some of those same natural passions. Morality came to be understood as offering a solution to the problems posed by human egoism, with morality being largely equated with altruism.

MacIntyre's ideas of a human life as a narrative unity and a narratable life require that in every action, one must ask the two questions of "what is good for oneself" and "what is good for humanity," as attempting to provide the answers to these two questions in deeds and words will provide moral life with its unity, which is the authentic life that would restore the unity of a human life as the unity of a narrative quest.

AUTHENTICITY, TRADITION, AND MODERNITY

The emergence of "authenticity," with its numerous understandings, as a virtue in modern life is explained here, drawing from Varga and Guignon (2014). The seventeenth and eighteenth centuries of Europe saw a cultural change with the emergence of a new ideal when human beings came to be seen as "individuals" and not as placeholders in systems of social relations. Simultaneously, society came to be seen as an aggregate of individual human beings, as the result of a "social contract" (Trilling, 1972). Being human was understood as being unique and distinctive, even when it violated social norms. Taylor has noted that there was at the same time an increasing awareness of what he calls "inwardness" or "internal space," resulting in a distinction between one's private and unique individuality and one's public self (Taylor, 1989, 1991). Accompanying these changes, there was also a shift in the conceptions used in judging others and oneself. Concepts like sincerity and honor became obsolete and lost normative appeal as the older social order of hierarchies crumbled. In its place emerged a relatively new concept of authenticity, understood as being true to oneself for one's own benefit. Whereas earlier, the moral advice to be authentic recommended that one should be true to oneself in order to be true to others, as a means to the end of successful social relations, in contemporary thinking, authenticity as a virtue refers to a way of acting that is choice-worthy in itself (Ferrara, 1993; Varga, 2011a, 2011b).

The modern ethic of authenticity acknowledges the value of the ethic of autonomy that shapes modern moral thought. The idea of autonomy emphasizes the individual's self-governing abilities, free from diverse cultural and social pressures. Each individual is to follow those norms that one can will on the basis of rational reflection. Both authenticity and autonomy should strive to lead one's life according to one's own reasons and motives, relying on one's capacity to follow self-imposed guidelines. Both require that one has the ability to put one's own behavior under reflexive scrutiny and make it dependent on self-determined goals (Honneth, 1994).

The ethic of authenticity also introduced the idea that there are motives, desires, and commitments that sometimes outweigh the restrictions of rational reflection. Besides leading an autonomous life, guided by one's own, nonconstrained reasons and motives, authenticity requires that these motives and reasons should be expressive of one's self-identity. Under Kantian autonomy, one can lead an autonomous life, even if it fails to express a person's self-understanding. Hence, some argue that authenticity demands more than is necessary for autonomy, for even if a person acknowledges that aspects of her identity contradict her self-conception, she might still be autonomous.

In sum, the ideal of authenticity does not object to the importance of the self-given law but disagrees that full freedom consists in making and following such a law. For it is about how this law fits with the wholeness of a person's life, and how or whether it expresses who the person is. The idea of autonomy represents a counter-position to an ethic that is solely concerned with strict adherence to social norms. However, authenticity goes beyond autonomy by holding that an individual's feelings and deepest desires can outweigh both the outcome of rational deliberation in making decisions and the willingness to immerse oneself into the reigning norms and values of society. Authenticity thus becomes an implicitly critical concept, often calling into question the reigning social order and public opinion.

The ideal of authenticity emerged in the Western world together with a distinctively modern conception of the self. Rousseau argued that the orientation toward life that should guide the conduct one chooses should come from a source within the individual. This led to questions about inwardness, self-reflection, and introspection. Suppressing one's deepest motivations has the potential for self-alienation. Rousseau also argued that with the emergence of a competitive public sphere, the ability to turn inward is increasingly compromised as competitive relations require instrumental role-playing that ultimately destroys the immanent moral understanding within humans. Rousseau thus externalizes the origins of societal evil and alienation from the original nature of man. Such a conception of the self is akin to the tradition of "religious individualism" that centers religious life on the individual and stresses the importance of inwardness and the introspective examination of one's inner motives, intentions, and conscience.

Some have argued in favor of abandoning the ideal of authenticity because it builds on confused assumptions about the self. Yet others worry that the ideal of authenticity, with its focus on one's own inner feelings and attitudes, may breed a self-centered preoccupation with oneself that is antisocial and destructive of altruism and compassion toward others. But Taylor is of the view that authenticity does not amount to egoism or self-absorption. On the contrary, by turning inward and accessing the "true" self, one is simultaneously led toward a deeper engagement with the social world. Taylor describes the trajectory of the project of authenticity as "inward and upward" (Taylor, 1989, 419–455).

Thinkers such as Nietzsche and Freud have questioned the conception of human nature, especially the "inner" nature, as being fundamentally good, as it could include forces of violence, disorder, and unreason as well as tendencies toward beneficence and altruism. An ethic based primarily on the ideal of authenticity is, for them untenable.

Yet others have questioned the conception of the self that underlies the idea of authenticity, as it is built on dichotomies like conformity versus independence, individual versus society, or inner-directedness versus other-directedness. The assumption that the individual is separate from the environment is, for them absurd as it erodes the bond between the individual and the community, which ultimately is the source of the authentic self.

Investigating the characteristics of the modern subject of inwardness, Foucault (1980, 58–60) observes that looking inward to monitor one's interior life and to tell certain "truths" about oneself has become part of contemporary Western cultural life, reaching from religious contexts to psychological therapy. The distinction between true and false interiority has led to new possibilities as inner states, motivations, and feelings are now increasingly thought of as objectifiable and malleable in different contexts. Foucault maintained that contemporary Western societies were witnessing a crisis, not only of authenticity but also of the whole idea of the subject in its temporary historically contingent constitution. Foucault clearly opposed the idea of a hidden authentic self. Rather than searching for a hidden true self, one should attempt to shape one's life as a work of art, proceeding without recourse to any fixed rules or permanent truths in a process of unending becoming (Foucault, 1988,

49). It appears that the term "authenticity" can refer only to whatever feels right at some particular moment.

Heidegger's *Being and Time* introduces the conception of "ownedness" as the most fully realized human form of life. For Heidegger, human being is a "relation of being," a relation that obtains between what one is at any moment (the immediacy of the concrete present as it has evolved) and what one can and will be as the temporally extended unfolding or happening of life into an open realm of possibilities. To the extent that all of one's actions contribute to realizing an overarching project or set of projects, one's active life can be seen as embodying a life project of some sort. Existence has a directedness or purposiveness that imparts a degree of connection to one's life stories. Such a life plan results from one's competence in being members of a historical culture that one has learned growing up in a shared world. Heidegger suggests that in average everydayness, one is as a rule adrift, acting as one of the "herd" or "crowd," and there is something deeply problematic about this, as one fails to own up to who one is, and one is not really the author of one's own life. To the extent that one's life is unowned or disowned, existence is inauthentic, not one's own.

There are two senses of freedom in Heidegger's account of human existence. One is freedom in the humdrum sense of doing what one chooses to do under ordinary conditions, a freedom that could be interpreted in an agent-libertarian way. The second is freedom in an ethically more robust sense wherein one is capable of "choosing to choose a kind of being-one's-self" through its ongoing constitution of that identity for the sake of which it exists (Heidegger, 1962 [1927], 314). For Heidegger, the "true self" is an ongoing narrative construction; the composition of one's own autobiography through one's concrete ways of acting over the course of a life as a whole. Authenticity is regarded as an executive virtue that provides the condition for the possibility of being a moral agent. Such a life is not necessarily opposed to an ethical and socially engaged existence.

For Sartre, there are no transcendent values that exist antecedently to humans, as all values are generated by human interactions in situations (Sartre, 1992a [1943], 796). Freedom is absolute to the extent that each person decides the significance of the constraints. According to Simone de Beauvoir, Sartre's conception of the human being as "engaged freedom" also implies that willing one's own freedom necessarily involves willing the freedom of all humans. In achieving one's own freedom, freedom must also will "an open future, by seeking to extend itself by means of the freedom of others" (Beauvoir, 1948, 60). The point here is that a dedication to freedom will open unrestricted range of possibilities to all.

In *The Ethics of Authenticity* and in *Sources of the Self*, Taylor makes a case for retaining the concept of authenticity (and the practices associated with it) on the grounds that the original and undistorted idea of authenticity contains an important element of self-transcendence (Taylor, 1991, 15). While in modernism, the turn inward still contained a self-transcending moment, the critical point where the ideal of authenticity becomes flattened is by a certain form of "self-determining freedom" that also contains elements of inwardness and unconventionality (Taylor, 1991, 38). Self-determining freedom is the idea that one is free to decide for oneself what concerns one, rather than being shaped by external influences. It demands that one break free of all external impositions and decide for oneself alone (Taylor, 1991, 27). Not only is self-determining freedom not a necessary part of authenticity, it is also counterproductive because its self-centeredness flattens the meanings of lives and fragments identities.

For Taylor, the process of articulating an identity involves adopting a relationship to the good or to what is important, which is connected to one's membership in a language community (Taylor, 1989, 34–35). As whatever is important for one must connect to an intersubjective notion of the good, wherefrom a good part of its normative force emanates. In this sense, authenticity simply requires maintaining bonds to collective questions of worth that point beyond one's own preferences. Thus, not only does one need the recognition of concrete others in order to form one's identity, but one must also (critically) engage with a common vocabulary of shared value orientations.

Ferrara (1998) suggests reconstructing contemporary understandings of normativity through the reformulation of "well-being" (*eudaimonia*) as the normative ideal of authenticity. Such a move can ground a new ideal of universal validity ultimately linked with the model of exemplary uniqueness or enlightening singularity. Authenticity would then be characterized by the self-congruency of an individual, collective or symbolic identity, and would provide a new universal validity that does not build on the generalizable but rather on the exemplary. Ferrara draws his ideas from Simmel's idea of an individual law as an instructive example of such anti-generalizing universalism, and which he claims is better suited to the pluralist contexts of modern societies.

Guignon (2004) aims to identify the manner in which authenticity can be understood as being at the same time a personal and irreducible social virtue. The social embodiment of virtues suggests that authenticity, like many other character ideals, carries with it an obligation to contribute to the maintenance and well-being of a particular type of social organization and way of life (Guignon, 2008, 2004). Questioning the ethical value of authenticity, Golomb (1995) maintains that there is no reason to suppose that it is any better or any more valuable to be authentic than to act inauthentically.

This overview of the modern virtue of authenticity linked to the modern conception of selfhood emphasizes the importance of being true to one's self. All viewpoints underline the importance of freedom, with some suggesting that the demand for freedom by one ought to extend to the demand for freedom for all similarly situated. Some have objected to self-determining freedom that is fully delinked from bonds to the community. Yet others have noted that authenticity as virtue entails self-transcendence as it needs to connect to an intersubjective notion of good in order to appropriate the values that make up one's collective horizon. Excepting Kierkegaard, Heidegger, and to an extent Taylor, most of the modern conceptions of virtue are devoid of one's life project over a lifetime with certain goals of moral goods to be attained. All are of the view that there is no antecedently given human nature and that virtues have to be cultivated by one in the act of living.

It appears that MacIntyre's approach in restoring the unity of a human life as the unity of a narrative quest by seeking both what is good for oneself and what is good for humanity in every action encompasses many of these viewpoints such as the inwardness of the modern self, self-determining freedom within limits, bonding with community, intersubjective notion of good, and one's life as a narratable life project. This approach seems more tenable in the contexts of multiple modernities than Foucault's suggestion that one should attempt to shape one's life as a work of art, proceeding without recourse to any fixed rules or permanent truths in a process of unending becoming.

Modernity in Axial Age civilizations like India has unique civilizational features that have a lasting impact in the form of "living traditions" that provide "cultural visions of the world" and "regulative frameworks of social life" (Eisenstadt, 2000a, 2000b, 1). The conception of selfhood in multiple modernities contexts necessitates that the practices of freedom by the modernizing subject be attuned not only to the relationship to the present and to oneself but at the same time also cultivate an attitude or ethos of a permanent critique of the present historical era to the inherited cultural visions of the world and its regulative frameworks of social life. It is through an ongoing engagement with both the modern present and its living traditions that the authentic modern self can be shaped in these situations by restoring the unity of a narratable life with the unity of a narrative quest.

Thus far we have dealt with the authenticity of person or self, but authenticity is often a term that is used in characterizing tradition, culture, or even goods. The English word "authenticity" has been derived from the Greek word "*authentes*" meaning author. It indicates a person who scripts his or her own life story, who rules or is the master, that is, a person who is in charge of the self. This requires following a self-directed course in life, rather than passively submitting to external pressures or blind obedience to the demands and expectations of others. The *Chambers Concise Dictionary* (1992) lists the meaning of "authentic" as "genuine, authoritative, true, and of established credibility," while in the *Oxford Advanced Learner's Dictionary* (2004) "authentic" means "known to be real and genuine and not a copy; true and accurate; made to be exactly the same as original."

Understanding authenticity as it relates to tradition, culture, and goods is necessary to better grasp modernity's impacts on life forms and its endless possibilities of change and choices in the future.

CULTURE, TRADITION, AND AUTHENTICITY

It is difficult to characterize a culture as authentic or inauthentic as cultures are not bounded, and cultural change comes about through contacts with other cultures. Cultures are composed of traditions, customs and habits, and while all these do change over time, traditions are more likely to remain stable even as cultural changes under pressures of modernity are ubiquitous. Traditions are closely aligned with the construction of the authentic self. Contrary to the ideas of authenticity under Western modernity discussed earlier, traditions are seen as constitutive of authentic self in most non-Western societies. Being true to one's self in non-modern and non-Western contexts is not to let experiences succumb to immediacy and the unintegrated succession of fleeting sensations but to ground experiences in a moral order drawing meaning and values provided by tradition.

According to Gross (1992), "tradition" refers to a set of practices, a constellation of beliefs, or a mode of thinking that exists in the present but was inherited from the past. Examples of tradition, when they are active in the present even though they originated in the past, could be a set of observances, a collection of doctrines or teachings, a particular type of behavior, a way of thinking about the world or oneself, a way of regarding others, or interpreting reality. However, artifacts, symbols, or images passed down through the centuries, or institutions that survive from a long time are not considered traditions but may serve as conduits of traditional attitudes or patterns of conduct.

Gross provides a clear explication of the characteristics, continuity, and change in traditions. A tradition requires the prior existence of something else, which is then imitated or repeated. Every tradition has an element of the prescriptive, and being prescriptive also makes it authoritative. Any tradition, to be authentic needs to satisfy three conditions. First, it must link together consecutively at least three generations (two transmissions) while there is no limit to the maximum. Second, a tradition, in conveying a sense of the past in the present, must also carry a certain amount of spiritual or moral prestige. Third, a tradition must convey a sense of continuity between the past and the present. It has to give one a feeling that it has been sequentially passed down through time, which upon receiving, makes one feel part of something continuous, as if one were a link in a chain stretching back in time.

Sometimes traditions may appear to be radically discontinuous, disappearing and then reappearing. Sometimes they do end in one form, say as practices, but continue as beliefs. Reconversion from belief to practice is also possible. Traditional modes of behavior may be converted into ideas and teachings and handed down to generations, strongly affirmed as values, even when they are not simultaneously embodied in conduct.

The difference between tradition and custom is blurred, as customs bring the past to the present and preserve a sense of community. But customs mostly involve superficial modes of behavior and are not heavily invested with value as traditions are. Most traditions, unlike customs, have their own discourses that explain them and their meaning, indicating that they have been raised to reflexivity. Tradition can also change into a custom with changes in weightage assigned to the value invested in it. When a long-established custom is consciously reassessed and in the process raised to a higher level of importance, it can become a tradition. When tradition becomes routinized, its moral authority could wear down after a long period of time.

Gross has also noted that tradition can change as it adapts to situations, as the totality of relations that encompasses a receiving generation is never exactly the same totality that was taken for granted by the transmitting one. As social and cultural changes occur, the ways of confronting and organizing experiences also change. As experiences change, so do modes of perception, including perceptions of what a tradition is and means. The medium of transmission of tradition can also bring changes in tradition. Oral transmission leads to tacit knowledge and becomes an integral part of one's natural attitude, but written transmission removes the immediacy and intimacy that come with oral tradition and can be interpreted in various ways.

Tradition defined values, established continuities, and codified patterns of behavior. In premodern times, the assumption was that value itself was created by supernatural beings at some remote point in time and became the fount of meaning. Tradition provided central categories through which the world could be understood and the order that could stabilize social existence. By connecting one with ancestors whose heritage had to be preserved, tradition fortified ties with the community that shared the traditions, gave people a sense of belonging, and fostered certain mental dispositions. With social life differentiating, multitudes of traditions began to operate in different spheres. But wherever the allegiance given to tradition became a matter of choice, both the authority of tradition itself and its hold on people diminished.

Western modernity dislodged most traditions. For the sixteenth-century philosopher Francis Bacon, the hold of tradition on the human mind had to be broken if life is to be apprehended freshly. There was no limit to humanity's capacity for creative action once a stance of empirical openness toward life was adopted. Rationalism also emerged around the early seventeenth century, asserting that what one can know with certainty is discovered only through reason and not through sense experience, and hence reason had no need for tradition. For the Enlightenment, tradition was a negative force and had to be dissolved altogether, as prejudices, superstitions, and errors transmitted across generations hindered human creativity. The authority of tradition based on the premise that there was inherent value in repeating what had gone before had to satisfy criteria of rationality. Kant (1784) famously wrote, "Enlightenment is man's emergence from his self-imposed immaturity." Wherever the past rules, mankind as a whole is prevented from becoming mature. Human beings lose their autonomy and fail to develop according to their highest capacities. Kant's solution was that people must learn to rely on their own understanding and their reason, not what is handed down in authority, including the authority of tradition. Bentham noted in 1824 that the past by modern standards was full of abuses and imperfections and was much inferior to the present, and therefore it would be wrong to idolize older traditional wisdom under the name of the wisdom of our ancestors. It was more preferable to embrace the present exclusively in order to forge new values and prescriptions in line with modern conditions.

From 1850 onward, though substantial pockets of tradition in the West survived, it was viewed through the lenses of modernity and as a result, it was stripped of its power to bind social life into an organic whole. From the 1880s, it was taken for granted that whatever authentic subjectivity one had was hidden beneath the debris of convention. There was presumed to be something like an outer self (rational, status-oriented, shaped by social roles) which invariably obscured or denied an inner self (always vital, spontaneous, creative). It was every individual's responsibility to liberate one's true self from imprisonment by the false one.

Non-Western societies, particularly the Axial Age civilizations, hold the view that without tradition, the texture of social life is disrupted, leaving people with nothing but an impoverished feeling of immediacy. A genuine ethical existence is thought to be impossible, as morality cannot be forged anew by every generation based on the exigencies of the moment. For a true moral order to exist, there must be continuous ethical language and a legacy of moral ideals which shape and interpret action, and actively help to produce moral behavior.

AUTHENTICITY OF OBJECTS

The rise of authenticity in response to modernization is not limited to the self and culture alone but has extended to organizations, communities, and objects as well. As the modern world in the contemporary phase of capitalism is witnessing an explosion of newer and newer objects, it is not surprising that authenticity is attributed to objects and entities. Authenticity verification processes have therefore spawned a whole array of regulatory norms and mechanisms such as identity documents, GI tags, trademarks, brands, and laws to protect against identity thefts of persons and objects in the increasingly globalized world of contemporary capitalism.

The literature on marketing has identified characteristics of authenticity in objects such as consistency between an entity's internal values and its external expressions, conformity of an entity to the norms of its social category, and connection between an entity and a person, place, or time as claimed. In the case of consistency, the referent is the entity itself, and as to whether it is true to itself. Brand authenticity in the sense of consistency emphasizes notions of "faithfulness," "truth," "consistency," "sincerity," and "trust." Authenticity as conformity means the extent an entity conforms to the social category to which it has been assigned or that it has claimed for itself. Here, the focus is on the classification of entities by external audiences engaging in a perceptual organizing and sensemaking process, and the referent is the social category. Entities refer not to the good but to the production enterprise that operates within the context of existing categories, and audiences make authenticity attributions on the basis of conformity to norms and expectations inherent in those categories. Authenticity as connection means whether an entity is authentic to the extent that it is connected to a person, place, or time as claimed. Rooted in psychological essentialism and semiotics, the authenticity attribution here can also be found outside of the entity as a specific person, place, or time. Focused mostly on the authenticity of objects, the referent in this case is the point of connection (Lehman et al., 2019).

Authenticity references the intangible and involves a verification process that asks whether an entity aligns with a specific referent, revealing whether a person is consistent with her true self, whether a producer conforms to its social category, or whether an object connects to a specific person, place, or time. Authentication thus resembles a truth-seeking process. However, authenticity refers to that which is intangible and seemingly unstable as the essence that makes an object authentic is, by definition unobservable and dependent on spatio-temporal proximity. Moreover, categories and boundaries are elusive and evolve, and this is further compounded by questions of objective versus subjective cues. Resting on such shifting qualities, it is doubtful whether any entity can actually ever be truly authentic. Baudrillard (1983) has suggested that if human experience is so reliant on the subjective perception of a system of signs and symbols, then reality itself is just a simulation. Perhaps authenticity too is similar. It is simply a series of changing perceptions of signs and symbols represented in the mind as a compelling truth, but where "imagination demands the real thing and, to attain it, must fabricate the absolute fake" (Eco, 1986, 8). Through authentication processes, individuals test an entity against a referent and, in doing so, perhaps "simulation threatens the difference between the 'true' and the 'false,' the 'real' and the 'imaginary'" (Baudrillard, 1994, 3). Maybe authenticity is merely imagined fantasy, but whatever it is, it produces a range of important and very real outcomes for organizations and their various stakeholders. There is an important though subtle difference between being authentic and brand authenticity. As authenticity is part of the ongoing search for meaning and belonging in life, the symbolic resources of brands have come to offer transformations so that self-actualizing consumers can enact their true selves.

FRAMEWORK OF THE BOOK

The following chapters examine notions of "modernity," "tradition," and "authenticity" as they have evolved in contemporary India and their effects on women's lives, focusing on the opportunities and constraints in accessing greater freedom in their private lives. The manner in which the conundrum of modernity and tradition plays out in women's everyday lives, from consumption choices to the more life-changing decisions such as choice of marriage partners and the practice of religion, is examined for a cross-section of women through fieldwork in different contexts. The fieldwork-based chapters also present the methodology of the study, which varies for each study. Additionally, all interviewed persons' names have been anonymized and are referred to with pseudonyms as in chapters 2 and 4, or the names were dropped altogether as in chapter 3.

Chapter 1 accepts the framework of "multiple modernities" as the more appropriate one to understand the construction and experience of women's modernity in India. It examines the nationalist negotiation of colonial modernity and highlights crucial aspects of the domesticity debate in Bengal in the nineteenth century that linked the "nation" and "women" to the spiritual domain as social and economic changes were taking place. Although this debate was not replicated in other regional contexts such as Madras on account of differences in the political context, it nevertheless set in process the progressive acceptance of the nationalist resolution of the women question outlined in a canonical form by Chatterjee (1990 [1989]). It thus explains how the nation today is animated by two meta-narratives—the civilizational meta-narrative and the constitutional meta-narrative—that provide resources for varied constructions of gender ideology. At the familial level, women have access to gender scripts to shape their self. The gender script of socialization or societal gender scripts socialized women and men, from their childhood onward, around cultural and social norms and expectations that enable them and their families in the attainment of social status and in marking out their life quest encoded with the desired virtues. At the same time, women can script their own modernity by accessing and negotiating freedom within their families for the attainment of status through modernity. This chapter provides the overarching theoretical framework in understanding how women resolve the conundrum of tradition and modernity in various aspects of their everyday lives, making their life a continuous quest for both progress and virtue.

Chapter 2 deals with the issue of marriage norms and rural women's aspirations as marriage by choice is increasingly being cognized as a category between "arranged" marriage and "love" marriage without the constraint of caste. It explores the aspirations of women and young girls regarding changes in marriage practices, highlighting how patriarchy, customs, and traditions operate in the form of social disciplines that constrain women's lives, and women's perceptions of these social disciplines as they attempt to carve out spaces of freedom. Most women and young girls, however, seek to access greater freedom in life through education and a move into urban areas while leaving the task of arranging marriages to parental responsibility.

Chapter 3 explores, through women's narratives, the marriage aspirations of urban young women and their perceptions of the constraints or otherwise within their families in making their choices. Interviews with educated women of diverse castes provide insights into how new cultural ideas in the sphere of intimacy and marriage are shaping the aspirations of young women. The contradictory pulls of status attainment through gender performance of traditional ideology versus status attainment through performance of modernity are evident across all castes, which is resolved through combining some modifications in traditional gender ideology and in the performance of modernity.

Chapter 4 explores diasporic matrimonial arrangements among the Tamil people, focusing especially on the Tamil Brahmins, as in recent years diasporic marriage alliances have increased on account of a large number of working professionals migrating to the United States and elsewhere. It focuses on the search for suitable partners and the kinds of social expectations that currently prevail. While diasporic matrimonial opportunities have certainly opened up new avenues for Brahmin women to move into the modern world, the matrimonial strategies deployed and accepted still reflect gender asymmetries in spite of the changes in the nature of arranged marriage. Current trends in diasporic marriage alliances among all social groups also reveal interesting facts about sociocultural changes.

Chapter 5 locates women in the contemporary landscape of Hindu religiosity in Chennai city in Tamil Nadu, which various indicators mark as a rising flourish of religiosity in recent years. It explores how women negotiate between tradition and modernity alongside this religious flourish and whether the increase in women's piety is a pointer to a possibly more regressive move of fulfilling patriarchal norms. It examines how women's expression of religiosity and their religious dispositions accord with the project to refashion selves into modern subjects. Insights on these issues are drawn through an understanding of the forms of piety across social groups, the process of sanskritization, the portrayal of religiosity in the modern media, and the recent lifestyle changes in the urban life of the city.

Chapter 6 explores issues of tradition and modernity in clothing and dress. It examines how clothing styles have been changing in the city of Chennai, known for long as a traditional city that is presently undergoing a makeover into a global city. The intense global and regional cultural flows in the domain of fashion and clothing are evident in the marked increase in the variety of clothing, an expansion of individual choice, and a market-induced democratization of clothing styles. Individual women's choice of clothing is circumscribed by ideas of modernity and norms of modesty that are in constant flux. Also, the cultural politics of the male gaze over female bodies play themselves out in women's clothing conventions and choices that are distinctive to this culture and determined by age, yet represents a more universal predicament across cultures. Women demonstrate through clothing their social identity and selfhood by constantly negotiating between modernity, tradition, and the changing social norms of modesty.

Chapter 7 deals with the construction of women as consumer subjects, as the ever-increasing range of commodities under capitalism requires the simultaneous production of consumer-subjects. Advertising is a terrain of producing women as consumer-subjects, one where cultural and capitalist patriarchies operate in tandem. The contending pulls of tradition and modernity in the construction of women as consumer-subjects are evident, while also reinforcing their roles in the domestic sphere. It also reveals the power of kitchen gadgets in the constitution of Brahmin women's caste and gender subjectivity as consumer-subjects conditioned by cultural patriarchy. Consumerism propelled by globalization has witnessed both the rise of "brand aura" with Western goods and "aura busting" through counterfeiting. This section of the chapter deals with counterfeit consciousness and expands the ideas of authenticity to both persons and the material sphere of modernity.

Chapter 8 seeks to draw within the fold of feminist theory and politics the individual acts of acquiescence and resistance women perform in their everyday lives. Drawing upon Pierre Bourdieu's ideas about habitus and doxa to explain women's internalization of patriarchy and subordinate status, as well as their ways of overcoming it, the chapter explores why a majority of women do not identify themselves as feminist. The ways they can manage (or not) to bring the experience of their subordination from the field of doxa to the field of opinion, a precondition for feminist politics, are examined. Understanding women's experiences and invoking the entire range of human relations that constitute such experiences is essential for feminist theory.

Chapter 1

Modernity, Nation, and Women

The onset of colonial modernity in the early nineteenth century set rolling the conundrum of tradition and modernity since then. Puzzling questions of whether to follow traditional beliefs and practices, how to retain or recuperate the authentic self that provides the cultural and moral mooring, how to appropriate features of modernity into one's life selectively, and the ways to mix and match the two when both tradition and modernity are not fixed and unchanging are constantly resolved by individuals in their self-construction in the daily lives of the nation. As the multiple modernities approach indicates the foregrounding of civilizational consciousness in the construction of some non-Western modernities, the construction of Indian modernity deeply entwines both civilizational awareness and consciousness as well as the ideals of the Indian Constitution. Indeed, Das (1994) noted some time ago that all institutions in India have a double articulation in tradition and modernity.

The ways in which this double articulation is sought to be realized both in the nation and in the family, within which women chart their life quest, need to be examined. Women seek to make their lives meaningful by negotiating with the social and cultural norms and expectations and by navigating through the expanding or constrained set of capabilities that modernity offers women in their self-construction. Three issues are analyzed here, namely, the nationalist resolution of the women question, the meta-narratives of the nation that constitute the spirit or the vital principles that animate the nation, and the gender scripts of socialization and modernity that women script for a meaningful life characterized by unity, wholeness, and a quest.

WOMEN, COLONIAL MODERNITY, AND NATIONALIST NEGOTIATIONS

Historians still debate the onset of modernity in India. While for some the "early modern" period pre-dates the colonial period, for others the first encounter with modernity was Western modernity during the colonial period, generally referred to as colonial modernity. The European encounter with eighteenth- and nineteenth-century India was marked by heightened criticism of the religion, customs, and traditions of India as colonial officials and missionaries embarked on their tasks of producing knowledge of India. While the European perception of the polytheism of the Hindu religion set them on the missionary agenda of Christian conversion, they at the same time sought to eradicate many religious practices, deeming them as "barbaric." Such criticism of polytheism prompted self-reflection by Bengali intellectuals like Ram Mohan Roy and his group of *Brahmo Samaj* members who sought to reconstruct a monotheistic Hinduism along Christian lines in the early decades of the nineteenth century, but the *Brahmo* movement in urban Bengal petered out by the mid-1840s.

For most knowledgeable Hindus of that time, the colonial missionary criticism of polytheism and the *Brahmo Samaj* response must have seemed unwarranted, for the monism of Hinduism had been the subject of philosophical discourse since the ninth century onward with Sankara's exposition of *Advaita* philosophy, which provided clarity to the insights of the *Upanishads* that were composed just before the Christian era. Sankara's *Advaita* was challenged by his contemporaries and others like Mandana Misra, Madhavacharya, and Ramanuja and even today there are those whose faith is based on *Advaita* and others whose faith is based on *Vishistadvaita* and *Dvaita* philosophies. The Hindu monism of *Advaita* philosophy proclaims the individual soul and the universal soul to be one.

The unsettling nature of European criticism of Hindu religious beliefs and practices was to such an extent that even the remarkable effort of the translation of the *Rig Veda* by the British/German Orientalist philosopher Max Mueller was done with the aim of initiating a Hindu Reformation that is comparable to the Christian Reformation. In 1866 Mueller wrote, "India is much riper for Christianity than Rome or Greece were at the time of St. Paul" (Mueller, 1902, 191). Through a Hindu Reformation, Mueller hoped "the old mischief of Indian priestcraft could be overthrown and the way opened for the entrance of simple Christian teaching" (Mueller, 1902, 191). In 1868 Mueller wrote to the Secretary of State for India,

> India has been conquered once, but India must be conquered again, and that second conquest should be a conquest by education. Much has been done for

> education of late, but if the funds were tripled and quadrupled, that would hardly be enough (. . .) By encouraging a study of their own ancient literature, as part of their education, a national feeling of pride and self-respect will be reawakened among those who influence the large masses of the people. A new national literature may spring up, impregnated with Western ideas, yet retaining its native spirit and character. . . . A new national literature will bring with it a new national life, and new moral vigor. (Mueller, 1902, 357–358)

A monotheistic Hindu Reformation movement promoting the values and practices based on the belief in the infallible authority of the *Vedas* was indeed founded in the 1870s by Dayananda Saraswathi, called the *Arya Samaj*, that included proselytization of Hinduism to enable reconversion to the Hindu faith and continues even in present times as a worldwide organization.

An early effort at reforming social practices by colonial administrators was the abolition of *Sati* (widow burning on the funeral pyre of the husband) with the *Bengal Sati Regulation XVII OF 1829,* for which Christian missionaries and Hindu reformers under the leadership of Ram Mohan Roy campaigned. This subsequently led to other social reforms which the Indians themselves initiated and participated in, such as widow remarriage, the abolition of child marriage and increasing the age at marriage, women's education, improving the status of untouchables, the eradication of superstition, and the promotion and diffusion of scientific knowledge. All such reform initiatives had two contending factions—the conservatives and the liberals. While the conservatives, in general supported changes that were in consonance with the scriptures and traditions held for long, the liberals were more open to new ideas drawn from European Enlightenment thought and practices as well.

Clearly, the colonialists found the status and condition of Indian women to be appalling, especially since they perceived it to have scriptural sanction, even as the status and condition of lower-caste and lower-class women, who are generally outside the purview of scriptural sanctions and interpretive authority of the priesthood, must have been equally, if not worse. The colonialists' concern with women's status was more on account of the fact that they believed practices derived from scriptural sanctions became so degraded that the priesthood and upper-caste men victimized the women.

After the 1857 rebellion, when governance was transferred from the East India Company to the British Crown with the 1858 "Queen's Proclamation" stating there would be no interference in the religious affairs of Indians, the social reform movement accelerated under the initiative of the nationalists—both conservative and liberal. This happened at a time of significant changes in the political economy, such as increased industrialization, urbanization, development of railways, public works and urban sanitation, and increased urban employment for Indians in the secondary and tertiary sectors. In fact, the "Queen's Proclamation" had also assured eligible Indians of employment in government posts. From about the 1870s, more and more women acquired education at both school and university levels in vernacular and English. By the end of the nineteenth century, women began to be employed in factories, schools, and a few other urban jobs. Along with the revamping of colonial administration, these changes clearly set in process the colonial modernization agenda.

Such changes as salaried employment opportunities in the colonial administration for the educated upper-caste men created the conditions for the emergence of a bourgeois urban middle class. Family life was bound to be affected, and as Bengali writers at that time pointed out, the women of the new middle class were able to afford servants and enjoy more leisure. This set in considerable anxiety as to the kind of lifestyle modernity these women would choose as they were living in the midst of European women missionaries, wives of British colonial administrators, and the Anglo-Indian women of mixed race.

The concern with domesticity, as revealed in the colonial administrators' claims of their difficulties in gaining knowledge of the domestic life and customs of the people, was part of their civilizational critique of India. The domesticity debate in Bengal and elsewhere linked domestic life to national improvement in the scale of civilizational ranking. The debates in the vernacular public sphere simultaneously developed an understanding among the writers of what could be publicly narrated about the private or domestic sphere and therefore did not tell much of the lives actually lived by the women, and were presented mostly in the new genres of Western modernity such as autobiographies, novels, diaries, and letters.

Chakrabarty notes that male and female nationalist writers engaged in debates in the vernacular public sphere of colonial Bengal to shape Bengali public opinion on the kind of lifestyle modernity that would be appropriate for the newly emerging middle class, as they were "haunted by the fear of looking unoriginal" (Chakrabarty, 1993, 1). According to him, nationalist writings subsumed "the question of difference within a search for essences, origins, authenticities, which, however, have to be amenable to global-European constructions of modernity so that the quintessentially nationalist claim of being 'different yet modern' can appear valid" (Chakrabarty, 1993, 1).

Discussing the issue of domesticity in colonial Bengal, he notes that English education brought a certain waywardness among young men who began to neglect their family duties, especially since the British idea of friendship and the Victorian patriarchal ideal of companionate marriage began to captivate them. In order to counteract such waywardness among women, the colonial construct of the Indian home as being disorderly and dirty served Bengali writings to project the Victorian virtues of "discipline," "routine," and "order" as objects of desire in domestic arrangements. Such improvements in domestic arrangements were possible only with obedience to the husband or father in the family, thus linking domesticity and civilizational ranking to patriarchal order.

As nationalism evolved, the construction of the "new woman" and the domestic sphere became an integral part of the national project. The modern educated housewife was linked to the older patriarchal imagination of the mythical divine figure of the Hindu goddess Lakshmi who signified abundance, wealth, beauty, and prosperity. Chakrabarty notes that the invocation of the Lakshmi ideal was not a contest of tradition versus modernity, for the modern Lakshmi was to be produced through proper education and would acquire a virtuous self by adopting a disposition free from jealousies. This virtuous "new woman" was also expected to fulfill all her domestic duties without neglecting the household tasks and was referred to as "Grihalakshmi." Her freedom, Chakrabarty notes, would not be the Western one of being self-indulgent and selfish but freedom in the Indian sense of being free from the ego, and one who could serve and obey voluntarily.

The female self of the Bengali upper castes was visualized as a part of the *kula*, the conception of the patriarchal, patrilineal, and patrilocal extended family, and tied to a mytho-religious idea of time rather than to the temporality of secular history. Often prefixed with *Gotra* in conversation, the *kula* is the three generations of ancestors along the patrilineal line of an extended family that is verifiable through the memory of the living generations in ancestor worship rituals. It could also, in some places refer to a *jati* community. It is an integral part of the categories with which the upper-caste Hindu patriarchal ideologies of women's role and status are constituted, as well of the new domesticity of the Bengali modern that was instituted in the context of a growing colonial public sphere.

In an interesting reading of the neologism "Grihalakshmi," Chakrabarty highlights the opposition between two articulations of the domestic and the civil-political that Bengali modernity entailed in public narratives of the social life of the family. One way was to subordinate domesticity and personhood to the project of the citizen-subject and the goals of the civil-political sphere, which was seen as the site of work for the acquisition of improvement and happiness based on the European idea of progress predicated on the consciousness of the present state being unhappy, which was to be overcome within a historicized future. The other was to imagine a connection between the domestic and a mytho-religious social—often equated with "community" or the "nation"—whereby the colonial civil society itself became a constraint whose coercive nature was to be tolerated but never enjoyed (Chakrabarty, 1993, 24–25).

According to Chakrabarty, discipline in public and personal life called for a dislodgment of the self from the mytho-religious time of the *kula* and its insertion into the historical narrative of freedom/happiness. Chakrabarty observes that the Bengali modern, to the extent that s/he was the subject of this fable, was the embodiment of this unhappy consciousness struggling to transform itself (Chakrabarty, 1993, 21), as the expression "Grihalakshmi" draws on ideas of personhood that do not owe their existence to the bourgeois projects that European imperialism brought to India. The ideology of the auspicious "Grihalakshmi," intimately tied to the concern for the well-being of the *kula,* is much more than the bourgeois project of educating women to allow them into the modern public sphere without denying that it may have entailed patriarchal oppressions.

In sum, Chakrabarty notes,

> the Bengali modern-implicated in the structures and relationships of power that produce the social-justice narratives of the public sphere—oppressions produced by and productive of the categories of class, gender, nation, state, ethnicity, etc.—is constituted by tensions that relate to each other asymptotically. There cannot therefore be any one, unitary history of its becoming. Questions of this history/modernity have to be situated within a recognition of its not-oneness. (Chakrabarty, 1993, 25)

He also notes that no adequate critique of this modernity can be mounted from within secular-historicist narratives alone as these are "incapable of re-presencing what is not secular-historicist, except in an anthropologizing mode" (Chakrabarty, 1993, 26).

The colonial civilizing discourse deemed the entire body of scriptural canons and ritual practices as being oppressive to its women, for by rationalizing patriarchal atrocities within a framework of religious doctrine, it made them appear to both perpetrators and sufferers alike as "the necessary marks of right conduct" (Chatterjee, 1989, 622). The nationalist response in the latter half of the nineteenth century was to defend the cultural traditions from the onslaught of colonial modernity. As Chatterjee noted, Indian nationalists in the late nineteenth century argued that it was not only undesirable to imitate the West on any matter other than the material aspects of life, but it was unnecessary to do so as in the spiritual domain India was superior to the West.

While nationalists accepted the modernization agenda, Western modernity and its cultural influence were to be restrained and selective. According to Chatterjee, while construing the nationalist project of constituting a national culture, they made the binary distinction of material and spiritual spheres, which was condensed into an ideologically more powerful distinction between the "outer" and the "inner," where the "outer" signified material life that is external while the "inner" signified that which is within each self, the spiritual. So long as the spiritual distinctiveness and its cultural practices were protected, the changes in the "outer" material sphere could be accommodated. This "inner" and "outer" distinction was then easily transposed to the Domestic and Public realms in which women were tasked with the role of defending the spiritual or cultural realm even as it allowed them to participate in the material sphere outside the domestic realm. Women could participate in activities in the public realm once the essential femininity of women was fixed in terms of certain culturally visible and spiritual qualities such as their dress, eating habits, social demeanor, and religiosity (Chatterjee, 1989).

The home was considered the principal site for expressing the spiritual quality of the national culture, and women must take the main responsibility for protecting and nurturing this quality. While the social role of women had the responsibility of spiritual virtues considered as "feminine virtues" in the domestic sphere, men's responsibility was material/masculine virtues. Nationalists therefore held the view that there would have to be "a marked difference in the degree and manner of westernization of women, as distinct from men, in the modern world of the nation" (Chatterjee, 1989, 627).

Chatterjee (1989) notes that the central ideological strength of the nationalist resolution of the women's question was that the "new woman" of nationalist ideology was given a status of cultural superiority to both the westernized women as well as the common women of the lower classes, as it marked her newly acquired freedom to attain, through her own efforts, a superior national culture. This also installed a new patriarchy on middle-class women by setting up norms of comportment and behavior to distinguish themselves from the colonial *memsahibs* (the white women and Anglo-Indian wives of white colonial rulers) and the vast majority of poor working women.

This nationalist negotiation with colonial modernity gave rise to the possibility of selective appropriation of Western modernity without disrupting the essential features of the spiritual culture of India in the construction of the national culture. Changes necessitated in the internal contexts of the home were often reasoned as necessities of modern life through the exercise of interpretive freedom of tradition. But the content of the resolution was always consistent with the system of dichotomies of "inner and outer," "domestic and public," and "material and spiritual" of the nationalist project.

At the same time, this new patriarchy of the emerging new middle class ushered through a negotiated colonial modernity was layered onto the pre-existing cultural patriarchies that varied across regions and ethnic and caste communities. Cultural patriarchies refer to all those cultural practices and social norms of caste relations governing social interactions that ensured male dominance and women's suppression, confining women to the domestic sphere with limited access and activities outside the home. These cultural practices and norms that evolved over the long historical past in communities were often justified as religiously sanctioned, and there were diverse religious and cultural traditions that were under the influence of the sanskritization process over a long period. Writing of the colonial civilizing mission of women, Gayatri Spivak notes, "Between patriarchy and imperialism, subject constitution and object formation, the figure of the woman disappears, not into a pristine nothingness, but into a violent shuttling which is the displaced figuration of the 'third-world woman' caught between tradition and modernization" (Spivak, 1988, 306).

Chakrabarty astutely observes,

> while nationalist thought mobilizes for its own ends the cultural field of difference, its resolutions, whether of the "woman question" or of the "nation," are inherently unstable as the differences are too heterodox for the nationalist project of modernity to contain them. Even in these public narratives of domesticity and personhood, there were possibilities of other maneuvers to look far beyond the patriarchy of the Bengali modern. (Chakrabarty, 1993, 1)

While Bengali nationalism's focus was on the modern self-fashioning of upper-caste women, nationalist thought elsewhere in the country was more inclusive and perhaps even less focused on domesticity in women's self-fashioning. In the Madras Presidency, the Tamil poet Subramanya Bharati wrote a poem in 1908 titled *Pudhumai Penn* or "New Woman," expressing his idea of a modern woman who would be a leader and a lawmaker and above all, "a free, independent, and fully realized human being" (Sundara Rajan, 2017). The translated poem below in Rajasri Blog (2021) reads:

She walks with her head held high
And looks straight ahead,
She is fearless because of her integrity,
She is confident because of her intelligence and wisdom,
The righteous women will not become weak,
Despite being humiliated by the darkness of ignorance,
Despite being ashamed without any knowledge,
She fights and abolishes this slavery and that reflects her virtue,
Did you listen to this modern women's words?

Bharati's nationalism was an inclusive one that advocated social and gender equality and was against casteism. His poems emerged at a time when caste politics was rising among the Tamils who were dissatisfied with the Brahmins securing a disproportionate share of employment in colonial administration and thus formed an association, the "Madras Dravidian Association," to contest the issue. This set the stage for the non-Brahmin movement leading to the formation of the "Justice Party" in 1917 that for some time, allied with the colonial power and then subsequently transformed into the Dravidian movement guided by rationalist views. By foregrounding social justice and women's equality, it ushered in the "self-respect" movement that established equality in marriage, a new non-religious way of conducting marriage based on self-respect, and countered the hierarchy and inequities of the caste system. Bharathidasan, the rationalist writer and poet much influenced by Subramanya Bharati, was a leading figure of the Dravidian movement who wrote on women's liberation and caste injustices.

Between 1920 and 1950, there were a number of periodicals published in the Madras region by women and for women, and there were at least thirty women editors. Appearing before the discourse of women's empowerment, these magazines provided different perspectives, as each had its own agenda on issues such as girls' education, marriage reforms, and women in society and family. Some of the magazines were *Sindhamani* (1923), *Tamizhimadhu* (1926), *Thamizh Magal* (1926), *Grihalakshmi* (1936), *Madhar Marumanam* (1936), *Mangai* (1946), *Pudhumai Penn* (1947), *Magalir Kural, Sakkaravarthini, Penn Viduthalai*, and *Penniyakural*. There were also many community journals representing the views of their communities as caste politics evolved with the census classification and enumeration of castes. Some of the community journals were *Vishwakarmam* (1913), *Nadarkula Mithran* (1919), *Vaisiyan* (1923), *Yadhavamithran* (1929), *Gramini Kulam* (1936), and *Chettiar Kula Mithiran (*1935).

In this milieu, Tamil nationalist writers did not link education and domesticity, nor did they mobilize in the vernacular public sphere a discourse of domesticity under colonial modernity to resolve the question of "women" and the "nation" in the way the nationalist writers of Bengal seem to have done.

Much like in Bengal, women's education spread in the Madras Presidency from the 1870s onwards, and as elsewhere, "Home science" was a subject taught to women to gain skills in modern home management. As in Bengal, goddess Lakshmi is worshipped by the Tamil sanskritized Hindus in her eight manifestations called Ashtalakshmi (Adi Lakshmi, Dhana Lakshmi, Dhanya Lakshmi, Gaja Lakshmi, Santana Lakshmi, Dhairya Lakshmi, Vijaya Lakshmi, and Vidya Lakshmi) that does not include the neologism "Grihalakshmi." Each manifestation represents a source of wealth such as spirituality, material wealth, agriculture, royalty, knowledge, courage, progeny, and victory. Marital status was considered auspicious as the bride, personified as goddess Lakshmi, would be the harbinger of prosperity and goodness in the family. Although Lakshmi was widely worshipped, Tamil nationalist writers did not cast a Lakshmi ideology to construct a Tamil modernity and to institute a new patriarchy as in upper-class Bengali society.

Both colonial capitalist modernity and anti-colonial nationalist modernity demarcated two realms—the domestic and the public realm. Chatterjee (1989) argues that it was in the public realm of material life that anti-colonial modernity desired to effect changes through reason and science, and this was a realm open to both men and women to participate in to bring those desired changes. The domestic sphere was the realm of intimacy, emotion, and spiritual life that was to be defended from modernity, and it was left to the women to protect that realm. Notwithstanding criticisms from feminist scholars who do not agree with this sharp distinction between the private and public realms and have indeed shown that colonial rule was marked by many legal and juridical interventions in the sphere of marriage, it is clear that the project of nationalist modernity followed an uneven path of progress not only across the rural/urban, caste or genders divide but between the private and public realms as well.

Reverberations and Consequences

The neologism "Grihalakshmi" did not remain confined to Bengal alone. In the course of time, it spread to other regions in southern India, and its meaning, disassociated from the nationalist project, was stabilized as "good wife" and harbinger of multidimensional "prosperity," which included spirituality to portray women's roles in the domestic sphere. "Grihalakshmi" (the Educated Wife) appealed to the cinema world as a Hindi film of that name was first screened in 1934, portraying an educated, steadfast wife going through humiliation at the hands of her husband but continuing to stay with him. In a 1938 Telugu language film "Gruhalakshmi," the steadfast wife loses her mental balance as well as her trust in God and justice after her husband falls for the seduction of a prostitute and becomes alcoholic. The 1955 Tamil film "Gruhalakshmi" (Prosperous Housewife) was a Tamil version of the 1938 Telugu film by the same producer. The 1967 comedy film "Gruhalakshmi" in the Telugu language, which was also remade as a Tamil film in 1975, narrates the story of a young married couple trying to escape the shackles of the girl's father-in-law, who is an orthodox disciplinarian. Their honeymoon escapade runs into a series of problems, and unable to pay their hotel bills due to wallet theft, they return home. The girl tells her father-in-law, in the presence of her family members, that it was his strict discipline that caused all the chaos, making the elderly man realize that there are limits to the exercise of discipline by family elders in young adults' lives. A 2019 "Grihalakshmi" film is an advocacy film for *Sahaj Yoga* meditation, where a mother hopes to choose a perfect bride for her son. Confronted with a choice between two sisters, one of whom is glamorous and another whose inner self is awakened through meditation, she decides in favor of the one who practices meditation. In striking contrast to the "Grihalakshmi" films, the Tamil film *Pudhumai Penn* (1984), bearing the same title as Bharati's famous poem, sought to convey ideas of women empowerment through a female protagonist who endures unimaginable harassment and torture from her husband but ultimately exercises her freedom to live an independent life on her own.

However, the "Grihalakshmi" of the films is not the same as imagined in the Bengali nationalist project, who was tasked with defending the spiritual/Domestic realm from the incursions of Western modernity, even as it freed her to participate in the outer or public world through education and employment. In these films, the "Grihalakshmi," even as she performs her domestic roles as a wife, also signifying virtue-change in the transition to modernity. From being the devoted wife in the earliest film, which is in striking contrast to the protagonist of the Tamil film *Pudhumai Penn* (1984) discussed earlier, she in a later film loses trust in both God and justice. Then, in later one questions the excesses of parental guidance and discipline, and yet another one on the virtue of inner self-awakening through meditative practice.

Apart from films, "Grihalakshmi" is also the name of a widely circulated fortnightly magazine for women in the Malayalam language, published from Kerala since 1979, with a Hindi edition as well. There was also a magazine by the same name in Tamil as early as 1936. Recently, the governments of Karnataka, Telangana, and Rajasthan have even introduced "Grihalakshmi" schemes to provide financial assistance to poor women. The Karnataka scheme explicitly targets females who are heads of households, and surprisingly even a deposit is made every month to the Goddess Chamundeshwari temple in Mysuru.

Similarly, Bharati's poems, especially *Pudhumai Penn* has, since the country's independence if not even earlier, been on the curriculum of Tamil-medium schools, playing an important role in the self-fashioning of girls as modern women that is delinked from issues of domesticity. As being free from ignorance and empowered through education was the theme of Bharati's poem, a *Pudhumai Penn* Scheme to provide financial support for higher education to girls from government schools was even launched recently in Tamil Nadu.

Although colonial capitalist patriarchy was constructed in different societies that had varying traditional pre-colonial conditions, some in which traditional patriarchies were stronger, like India and Sri Lanka, while in others it was weak, like Burma (Myanmar) and Kenya, over time, the development of capitalist industrialization transformed all societies in a similar direction. This transformation tended to the devaluation of women's work, a greater burden of housework and care work, and a lack of public childcare support. Such a common tendency was due to the gender ideologies that were introduced through colonial rule that sought to implement the European notion of the ideal family, characterized by the male breadwinner and the dependent woman. This notion had only evolved in Europe's recent historical past.

Debates on domesticity and the delineation of public and domestic spheres in the colonial context of India and the nationalist responses to it suggest that nationalism reworked the colonial gender ideologies to its advantage even as it left unchallenged the subordination of women in the domestic sphere and their dependent status, which had implications for their roles and outcomes in the public domain as well. Not only was there wage discrimination in practice despite the laws of wage equality, but women were also invisible and had to be made visible in development policy and practice. As Das observes, "Norms of masculinity in Indian society emphasize not only men's authority over women but also their responsibility to ensure the economic well-being of the family. Women's labor is always considered secondary" (Das, 1994, 57).

The colonial gender ideology of the dependent woman in India not only affected women in the economic sphere but also in the social sphere. The conjoint workings of cultural and capitalist patriarchy have devalued women across the spectrum of caste and class, and have caused the gradual shift from bride price to dowry. Women being considered "Grihalakshmi" matters little in the matrimonial market for the bride-takers who, despite having access to her work in the home and perhaps even control over her earnings if she works outside, set high dowry expectations based on the nature of the boy's employment. Moreover, the cultural idea of the feminine virtue of spirituality and women's responsibility to defend the spiritual life in the domestic realm are widely interpreted to signify that a family's honor depends on women's actions, giving men the power to control women, resulting in the widespread phenomenon of male dominance across all castes and social classes.

In the trajectory of Indian women's modernity from the late nineteenth century and continuing till the present, there have been ongoing controversies about the application of the home/world, spiritual/material, feminine/masculine dichotomies in the everyday matters of women like dress, food, manners, education, her role in organizing life at home, and her role outside the home in the context of modern social and economic changes.

META-NARRATIVES OF THE NATION

Meta-narratives of the nation animate the nation in the present time by constituting the vital principles of the national community and the virtues of the individual that guide the moral conduct of the people. It includes the stories both mythological and historical, from the past, especially in the Axial Age civilizations. It also includes the narratives of the nation's Constitution that are constantly being made in the making of the nation to fulfill its goals and people's aspirations.

A "meta-narrative" is an overarching account or interpretation of events and circumstances that provides a pattern or structure for people's beliefs and gives meaning to their experiences. For instance, religions like Hinduism provide stories that have an overarching narrative about how one should live one's life. The term is widely used in Literary Studies and is described as a "narrative about narratives of historical meaning, experience or knowledge, which offers a society legitimation through the anticipated completion of a (as yet unrealized) master idea" (Childers and Hentzi, 1995, 186). Some have noted that a meta-narrative is "a story about a story, encompassing and explaining other 'little stories' within conceptual models that assemble the little stories into a whole to provide formulaic expectations of certain cultural codes" (Stephens and McCallum, 1998). Others have referred to meta-narratives as "recurrent skeletal stories, belonging to cultures and individuals that play a powerful role in questions of identity, value, and the understanding of life" (Abbott, 2008, 236).

Since Jean-François Lyotard highlighted the increasing skepticism toward the totalizing nature of meta-narratives and their reliance on some form of transcendent and universal truth, postmodernism has preferred localized narratives around a single event, building a repertoire of a multiplicity of theoretical standpoints around which progressive politics could be grounded rather than a totalizing one. Needless to say, Lyotard only expressed skepticism over narratives that have marked modernity, which

> like myths, have the goal of legitimating social and political institutions and practices, law, ethics, ways of thinking. Unlike myths, however, they look for legitimacy not in an original founding act but in a future to be accomplished, that is, in an idea to be realized. (Lyotard, 1986, 29)

The spirit of India today is animated by two meta-narratives, namely the civilizational meta-narrative and the constitutional meta-narrative. These two meta-narratives offer the nation its legitimation through the anticipated completion of a master idea, which in the case of the civilizational meta-narrative is the constant signification of virtues that would enable individuals in their life's moral quest as members of society and nation, thereby making narratable lives accountable to themselves and to society. This is a never-to-be-completed task as newer generations become members of the nation. The constitutional meta-narrative is an assurance guarantee that the social contract of the people with the nation will always be fulfilled. In a democratic state, it would ensure that democracy prevails in law-making and governance, and most importantly ensure justice, liberty, and rights to the people.

Civilizational meta-narrative is not a single authored narrative document, but what has been drawn over a long period of existence in popular memory, beliefs, and cultural practices that, though varied carry certain common unifying principles that govern moral conduct. Whereas the Constitution of India is a written document that is constantly revised through amendments, the constitutional meta-narrative draws both from the Constitution of India as well as from legislation, governance practices and outcomes, judicial discourses, rulings and judgments and highlights through contested debates in the public sphere, the extent of fulfillment of the constitutional principles of justice, liberty, equality, fraternity, and the ever-shifting modernist goal of progress. The constitutional meta-narratives provide constant and continuing legitimation to the nation-state, as this will be an ever-incomplete project of the nation.

Civilizational Meta-narratives of the Nation and Women

Civilizational meta-narratives of India are those narratives that historically the people of the Indic civilization heard, predominantly through oral sources, at different times that conveyed to them a set of virtues to guide their everyday conduct. It is by now well accepted that while the Vedic system evolved, providing an interlinked understanding of the origins of the cosmos, universe and all beings, there also prevailed simultaneously, since a long time ago, beliefs about the dark, unknown forces of nature that could disrupt life, with fears of these dark forces leading to the appeasement of the primordial energy represented as *Sakti* that at some later point in time took the anthropomorphic form of the mother-goddess. These narratives of *Sakthi,* even today highlight her power and the need to not arouse her anger, for she could cause destruction and misery through natural disasters, disease and epidemics, incursions by evil spirits, and predators both non-human and human into habitats. But there is no clear delineation of virtues and moral conduct in these narratives of *Sakti*.

The early Vedic period systematized a set of practices in the four Vedas (*Rigveda, Samaveda, Yajurveda,* and *Atharvaveda*) and the *Brahmanas* indicated the conduct of Vedic rituals as necessary for the reproduction of the entire interlinked system of cosmos, universe, and beings. There were very few Gods in the Vedic pantheon, and these were considered celestial beings. The Vedic texts clearly specify women's roles and actions in the various rituals that householders perform and those that kings occasionally performed. These Vedic rituals only indicated right practices toward the goal of reproduction in the broadest sense and continue to this day in the Vedic practices of Hindu marriage consecration, with some variations across regions and caste communities. As the Vedic invocations in Sanskrit were for a very long time transmitted only orally and were codified in writing much later, this must have resulted in accretions over time.

Initially, it brought together the keepers of the Vedas—the Brahmins—and the Kshatriya caste of rulers as the consecration of kingship was performed by Brahmins. As the caste system evolved over time, it also brought other castes within its fold.

The Vedic system also propounded the concept of *Varnashrama Dharma* that defined duties and responsibilities based on their *varna* (social class/caste) and *ashrama* (stage of life) as a framework of moral and ethical living. The later Vedic period witnessed the development of the *Upanishads,* which are texts that explain the concept of Vedas, enabling individuals to engage on a personal and spiritual level. These texts are constitutive of *Sanatana Dharma,* the duties enjoined for all, which later was called as "Hinduism," the religion of the people living beyond the Indus River. *Sanatana Dharma* seems to have developed alongside Jainism and Buddhism. Jainism claims that the precepts of Jainism are eternal and that Mahavir, the founder of Jainism in the sixth century BCE, was preceded by twenty-three preceptors. Buddhism was founded by Gautama Buddha also around the same time.

The post-Vedic period was followed by the period of the Puranas, during which the epic poems *Ramayana* and *Mahabharata* were composed. These epics were set in the mythical time frames of *Treta Yuga* and *Dwapara Yuga*, where each *Yuga*'s duration, though varying is for many hundreds of thousands of years, establishing the traditions of *Sanatana Dharma* as stretching far back into antiquity. These two epics are lessons on leading a virtuous life, the victory of good over evil, and establishing a desirable virtuous social order and rule. By characterizing protagonists from all four *varnas*, these epics sought to make themselves relevant for all social classes.

All three (*Sanatana Dharma*, *Jaina Dharam*, and *Buddha Dharam*) are known as Dharmic religions with important differences in their understandings of the attainment of soul's liberation, with emphasis by Jains on non-violence, and the Buddhist belief on human suffering and its rejection of the caste system of *Sanatana Dharma*. The propagation and cultivation of virtues were part of all the Dharmic religions, and with the spread of Jainism and Buddhism in the country, there were struggles to establish the supremacy of *Sanatana Dharma* in the early centuries of the Christian era. As part of this struggle for supremacy, large-scale temple building was undertaken, especially in southern India, with a temple legend called *Sthala Purana* being presented for each temple. These were virtue-stories in the life of the central God and Goddess to whom the temple was dedicated that were meant as virtue-lessons to guide the moral conduct of individuals. Most villages in southern India had a big temple, and these *Sthala Puranas*, as well as the stories of *Ramayana* and *Mahabharata*, and stories of *Upanishads,* formed part of the storytelling cultures in villages and temples in southern India and elsewhere in the subcontinent for many centuries.

Hobsbawm (1983, 9) has noted that traditions, whether consciously invented or not, serve diverse social functions. According to him, they seem to belong to three overlapping types: those establishing or symbolizing social cohesion or the membership of groups, real or artificial communities; those establishing or legitimizing institutions, status, or relations of authority; and those whose main purpose was socialization, the inculcation of belief systems, values, and conventions of behavior.

For the most part, the storytelling cultures served the purpose of inculcating beliefs, value systems, and establishing conventions of behavior. Most of these virtue-stories of Hindu temples relate to the fantasy lives of the Hindu Gods (*Trimurti*) Brahma, Vishnu, and Siva that aim to establish social order, and so were centered on the conjugal family, chastity, and devotion on the part of women that could be construed through a modernist lens as patriarchal compositions. Through a textual reading of selected Hindu scriptural literature, it has been argued that in these texts women are in fact treated equally (Padia, 2020). But patriarchal cultures can evolve through familial strategies of socialization and control to produce the desired woman of virtues.

Telling stories is an open-ended exercise on the part of the narrator as there could be additions, deletions, and contextual innovations. While the narrator could provide interpretive nuances grounded in local contexts, allowing for creative deviations from the so-called "original," it also leaves much to the hermeneutic capability of the listener to comprehend and internalize the values. As Richman (1991) and several others have shown, there are over three hundred retellings or versions of *Ramayana* as also the many oral traditions, each presenting and emphasizing different male and female role models as paragons of virtue. There are even versions of the epic Ramayana among many Muslim communities in India. Not to forget that in Tamil versions, the anti-hero Ravana is not seen as an embodiment of evil as in North India; he being a Shiv-*bakht* and the dominance of Saivism in the southern region is notable. Only in recent times has the culture of such storytelling declined and been overtaken by the new media of films and television, with story lines being constantly revised to suit the changing times. It has been reported that in the television renderings of the epic *Ramayana*, the viewers expressed disappointment with deviations from what they thought was the original storyline. In children's storybooks on Hindu mythology, it has been noted that there has been a tendency to foreground social harmony and the unity of the nation while erasing the social fault lines of social inequities (Babb, 1995).

Civilizational meta-narratives of the nation are, for the most part, constructed by individuals themselves from the cultural resources available to them, their past experiences of their traditions, and their socialization in a particular culture within their families when they reside in the political communities of kingdoms and of the nation. As such, there can be many civilizational meta-narratives, as these are imagined by individuals, and no one person's imagined civilizational meta-narrative has hegemonic status, be it Hindu, Christian, Muslim, Jain, or Buddhist. Individuals need to imagine their civilizational meta-narrative of the nation both in order to draw meaning to their life, authenticate their cultural practices, and to feel secure in their cultural identities in the community, society, and nation.

Analogous to the "Grihalakshmi" (the goddess of prosperity at home), Bengali nationalists created the figure of the *Bharat Mata* (mother of the nation), a nationalist personification drawing from the spiritual significance of the mother goddess seen as the primordial energy of creation and reproduction of the universe. The idea first came up in a Bengali play by Kiran Chandra Banerjee in 1873 dealing with the eighteenth-century Bengal famine, and then figured as a salutation to the mother goddess in Bankim Chandra Chattopadhyay, and a few years later, the iconography emerged in painting and by 1930 became well accepted in the popular imagination of eastern India. In 1934, the *Bharat Mata Mandir* (temple) was opened in Banaras (now Varanasi), thus deifying her in a city of great spiritual significance to Hindus. The project of reforming Hinduism thus culminated in spiritualizing the nation, enabling the conscious creation of the civilizational meta-narrative of the nation. An invocation of *Bharat Mata* written by Bankim Chandra Chattopadhyay has become the national song, usually performed as an inaugural song at national and state events.

States can also construct a civilizational meta-narrative of the nation to promote values such as individual and collective virtues like fraternity, non-violence, and peace. The Asoka Chakra or *Dharmachakra* in the Indian national flag represents Buddha's teaching on suffering and overcoming it through awareness, which is considered a universal virtue that should be present in every human being and is also found in other *Dharmic* religions. States can also selectively draw from tradition or invent them to establish or symbolize social cohesion or the membership of groups, real or artificial communities, or for establishing or legitimizing institutions, status, or relations of authority.

Parekh (2008) recounts that the national motto *Satyameva Jayate,* meaning "Truth alone triumphs," is from the Hindu scripture *Mundaka Upanishad,* the colors of the national flag symbolize religious pluralism, and the national anthem sacralizes the territory and seeks the blessings of the architect *Vidatha,* which could be interpreted as a transcendental deity, local deity *Bharatbhagyavidhata* (the male counterpart of *Bharat Mata*) or in a secular sense of *Vidatha* or architect. While nineteenth-century nationalists sought to distinguish Indian civilization from Western civilization by marking out its spiritual dimension as the essence of Indian civilization, the goal and politics of the latest Hindutva formation is building a "nation capable, successful, beautiful, and divine India," as stated by Modi at the inaugural event of the Ram Mandir in Ayodhya, considered by many as an important ritual of cultural reawakening and the beginning of the reconstruction of *Bharatvarsh*.

One of the reasons for the state's invocation of cultural symbols drawn from *Dharmic* religions, no doubt arguable, can be understood from Shils (1958) who pointed out that the art of the politics of liberty requires the matrix of the traditional outlook to be left unimpaired, as liberty is sustained by both the traditions of liberty and traditions which flourish outside the sphere of political liberty. He is of the view that traditional receptiveness, which is one of the ultimate pillars of freedom in society, can never be supplanted by either calculation, reason, or power.

Mystics and Hindu saints, some of whom were educated in Europe and subsequently even participated in the nationalist movement before their spiritual turn, also contributed to the production of the civilizational meta-narratives of the nation. They highlighted an Indian perspective on authenticity that attends to the complexities of the multilayered structure of being, a holistic view present in diverse schools of Indian philosophy. It is inspired by an understanding of transcendence which encompasses various domains of life and is rooted in a deep awareness of an implicit and underlying continuity and connectedness across various life forms throughout the universe. The authentic choice in the Indian thought system toward the realization of the true self and liberation maintains that striving to be authentic enhances and facilitates self-expansion/self-transcendence by emphasizing the notion of self as a ground for existence. Within this paradigm, a search for the true or authentic self is held to be the prime goal of human life.

Leading an authentic life implies striving for a relationship with one's true self (brahman) and realizing all the possibilities of our true nature. Authenticity, therefore, becomes the realization of our oneness with the transcendent and cosmic Divine, and with all beings. The nationalist mystic Sri Aurobindo observed that to arrive at freedom, mastery, and perfection, one has to get back to the real self and soul within and arrive thereby at one's own true relations with one's own and with universal nature. For him, becoming authentic is the psychic's coming to the front, which is the true original conscience in us, deeper than the constructed and conventional conscience of the moralist (Aurobindo, 1970, 226). The authentic person perceives their true self to be one with the Transcendent and no longer takes their constructed individuality as anything more than a formation for world experience. Leading an authentic life will result in the transformation of ordinariness to extraordinariness (Sharad, 2010).

The Indian conception also recognizes the power of the cultural and social dimensions of one's existence, and the necessity of a continuous negotiation between the inner world and the outer world as integral to the very process of living. Striking a balance between the personal and the sociocultural remains at the heart of authenticity, and the locus of authenticity appears in the dialectic between the inner and outer. Authenticity is therefore not about consistency in behavior, but about congruence and correspondence between the inner (self) and outer (behavior). Leading an authentic life, therefore, means moving beyond the boundaries of the ego. Choice and responsibility define authenticity, as to be authentic is to be autonomous. While there can be an external, moral order guiding one's actions, or it can be self-created morality, with internalized social values, the emphasis of authentic living is on the location of the agency within the individual, who chooses how to author one's own life (Sharad, 2010).

It is interesting that all these mystics and saints present the ideal woman as the mythological figures of Sita, Savitri, Damayanti, and Draupadi who embody virtues of purity, chastity, and fidelity. Sri Aurobindo wrote an epic poem, *Savitri: A Legend and a Symbol.* Gandhi too believed that a woman must be pure, firm, and controlled and projected these mythological figures as the ideal womanhood.

While the mystics and saints provided guidance for an authentic life in the context of an Indian modernity that is rooted in the moral values of Indian culture, there were other nationalists who constructed their civilizational meta-narratives of the nation that were explicitly linked to the cultural and political project of the nation. Gandhi constructed his ideal of a united India based on *Sarva Dharma Sambhav* (all religions are equal), where Hindus would rule the unified India by virtue of their numerical superiority and took up the issues of temple entry of Dalits and inter-dining of castes. Veer Savarkar, a nationalist who suffered incarceration in the Andaman cellular jail by the colonial authorities, based his conception of united India on the idea of *Hindu Rashtra,* where his inclusive definition of Hindu included others of Indic religions such as Jains, Sikhs, and Buddhists but excluded Muslims and Christians by defining a citizen to be one who considers India to be both *pitribhumi* (ancestral land) and *punyabhumi* (holy land). Contemporary political renderings of the Savarkar ideal of a united India claim that all Muslims and Christians have Hindu ancestry in some historical past, and it would therefore also not be far-fetched to claim that the churches and mosques where the Christians and Muslims worship make India a holy land, even if they go on religious pilgrimages to Mecca and the Vatican.

Savarkar's essay "Seven Shackles of the Society" (1931) mentioned the fetters of Hindu society that must be abandoned in the construction of Indian modernity. These are Vedic monopoly (restricting access of Vedic knowledge and rituals exclusively to the Brahmin community), occupational bondage (advocates that one's profession should not be determined by caste and birth but chosen based on individual aptitude and skills), social exclusion of

Dalits, losing caste status upon foreign travel or crossing oceans, opposing restrictions on reconversions to Hinduism, prohibition of intercaste dining, and restrictions on intercaste marriages. While modernity in contemporary India is witnessing a significant dilution of these fetters, there is hardly any discourse in the public sphere of making caste (both *varna* and *jati*) itself an individual choice and instituting processes, both religious and constitutional, for such conversions as well. Pathways to caste (both *varna* and *jati*) conversion among Hindus through a constitutional process could lead to the abolition of the caste system eventually in the long run. Once caste as choice is legislated, the modalities of positive discrimination could be worked out within the framework of the Constitution through deliberative processes. In the state of Tamil Nadu, it is now possible to get a "No Caste and No Religion" certificate from the government to avoid specifying those details on applications by individual choice.

The headline event in the latest construction of the civilizational meta-narrative of the nation is the recent inauguration of the Ram Temple in Ayodhya. Lord Ram, known as *Maryada Purushottam,* is now installed as the national icon of the embodiment of public virtues. His reign in the *Treta Yuga* as King of Ayodhya was considered an ideal one of virtuous rule, a desire that has since remained as the civilization's collective aspiration expressed as *Ram Rajya*. For women, it signifies the same emphasis on purity and chastity, for according to the epic *Ramayana*, Lord Ram succumbed to social pressure of suspicions over his wife Sita's chastity and sent away a pregnant Sita to the forest upon her return from Sri Lanka, having been abducted by Ravana and rescued by Hanuman, the Monkey God. Upon hearing of Sita's death in the forest, Lord Ram then drowns himself in the river. Today, one of the worst forms of oppression that poor women face in India is the perennial accusations of a woman's infidelity by the husband, often resulting in domestic violence whether in a drunken or non-drunken state (Das, 1994). Women are therefore never free from patriarchal dominance and social pressure as they are always subjected to suspicion as a mode of power exercised upon them. The asymmetry in the virtue expectations of women and men leads to situations where virtue expectations from women are translated into cultural and social norms that in many ways strengthen patriarchal dominance in the intimate familial sphere to uphold these norms, while there are no such constraints on men arising from the virtue expectations of men.

The implications of all these civilizational meta-narratives of the nation regarding women falls back on the notion that women's primary role is in the domestic sphere, tasked to defend spiritual values even as they can participate in the life of the nation outside their home through employment and other activities. But such freedom for women to move outside their homes is limited as they still need patriarchal assent from their husbands for participation outside. Women's autonomy is thereby restricted. A former judge of the Indian Supreme Court has observed that even Mahatma Gandhi was unable to see women as an equal participants in production but saw them as an embodiment of sacrifice and suffering. Gandhi thought that women should not pursue a vocation independent of their husbands and that care of the family and concerns of the household would keep them fully occupied, although he greatly inspired women to participate in the freedom movement and gave them the dignity and confidence to be able to take up issues of women's equality subsequently (Reddy, 2008, 116).

Nagarathna, another Supreme Court judge, recently addressed the complexities within the institution of marriage, family dynamics, and the imperative need for inclusivity in the legal realm by emphasizing the importance of rectifying existing gender biases, particularly within professional domains and household dynamics. Calling for the importance of dismantling condescending attitudes within marriages, she also urged for the preservation of the institutions of family and matrimony. She advocated for a more nuanced understanding between spouses and to challenge the perception of a wife as the one who sacrifices her career for family welfare (Times Now Digital, January 5, 2024).

Not only does the civilizational vision of womanhood get replicated in customs, cultural practices, cultural and social norms, and gender ideologies, but it also plays a constraining role in the democratic project of India as we shall presently analyze. There have been resistances to the project of spiritualizing the nation, most notably in the Dravidian movement in Tamil Nadu that set its project on the principles of rationalism and opposed superstitions, the caste system, and the unequal status of women, and remains today the dominant force in the politics of the southern state of Tamil Nadu.

Constitutional Meta-narratives of the Nation and Women

The Constitution of India is a moral document embodying an ethical vision and is also an assemblage of state-formative practices. Constitutional meta-narratives of the nation would therefore be an overarching narrative of the ethical dimensions of national life that is enjoined upon all citizens as the project of the nation and citizenship moves toward its unending telos of progress. Being a modern Constitution for a modern nation, it draws on the ideas of European Enlightenment, of Reason and universal morality based on Kantian ethics, and the Republican values of the French Revolution. It therefore enjoins citizens with duties, and the state to ensure the Rights of the citizens as specified in the Constitution.

The Preamble of the Indian Constitution sets the ethical principles of the nation by declaring the nation to be a "Sovereign Socialist Secular

Democratic Republic committed to Justice, Liberty, Equality, and Fraternity of the people." The two ideals "Socialist" and "Secular" that were not in the Constitution adopted in 1950 but added through the 42nd Amendment to the Constitution were removed recently.

One needs to draw out the normative potential of the Constitution to construct a coherent vision of society and polity envisioned by the framers of the Constitution that would likely emerge from the interpretation of the key concepts of the Indian Constitution and an adequate grasp of the structure of the ideals of the Constitution. Bhargava notes, "There is, then, a pressing need to excavate the moral values embedded in the Constitution, to bring out their connections, and to identify the coherent and not-so-coherent ethical values contained in it" (Bhargava, 2008, 9). According to him, such an exercise would enable the evaluation of its multiple propositional content and arbitrate between contesting interpretations of the many core values on which the Indian polity is supposedly based.

The Indian Constitution was designed to break the shackles of traditional social hierarchies and grant freedom, equality, and justice to all. Like in all other Constitutions, value conflict is endemic to it, as an unambiguous specification of one ordered set of values is impossible. However, it is arguable whether the refusal of the framers of the Constitution to give well-delineated criteria for the settlement of moral conflicts is the strength of the Indian Constitution, as Bhargava suggests. (Bhargava, 2008, 28)

Baxi suggests a move away from the analysis of the Constitution to an anthropological analysis of the notion of "constitutional formation" that would factor into the analysis the "mass of heterogenous constitution generative, sustaining, defying, and denying practices, and the order of expectations and experiences" (Baxi, 2008, 96). While constitutional formations are "tradition-constituted" and "tradition-constitutive," Baxi notes, the "constituted" tradition only refers to the European Enlightenment and its derivatives and remnants, ignoring the role of the traditions of non-European Enlightenment.

While much of the rights, procedures of state formation, and the laws adjudicated by the judiciary are no doubt based on ideals and comparative past experiences, there are important features drawn from Indian traditions pertaining to property inheritance and marriage laws affecting women that are part of the personal laws of different religious communities as stipulated in the Constitution. Moreover, even the country's name in the beginning of the Constitution as "India, that is Bharat" allows for the civilizational values reflected in traditions and customs to figure in the interpretive adjudications of the judiciary, making juridical statements of constitutional validity not entirely based on Enlightenment reason and morality but drawn from religion-based virtue ethics.

A spate of recent judicial decisions that affect women's lives is discussed to highlight the ways tradition and cultural norms are factored into such decisions.

In February 2024, the Supreme Court of India adjudicated on a petition filed by a forty-four-year-old single woman who challenged the surrogacy law that defines an "intending person" eligible to access surrogacy as "an Indian woman who is a widow or divorcee between the age of 35 years and 45 years" as being discriminatory and violative of the basic human rights of an individual to found a family. Noting that it is a norm in India to become a mother within the institution of marriage, the Supreme Court observed that the institution of marriage could not be thrown out of the window and claimed to be speaking from the point of view of the child's welfare. Addressing the petitioner's lawyer, the Supreme Court said,

> Your client preferred to remain single. We are also concerned about the institution of marriage. We are not like the West where many children do not know about their fathers and mothers. We do not want children roaming here without knowing about their fathers and mothers.

The Delhi High Court in January 2024 rejected a challenge to the constitutionality of Section 5(v) of the Hindu Marriage Act, 1955 (HMA), which prohibits marriage between two Hindus if they are *sapindas* of each other—"unless the custom or usage governing each of them permits of a marriage between the two." A *sapinda* marriage is one between individuals who are related to each other within a certain degree of closeness. *Sapinda* relationships for the purposes of the Hindu Marriage Act are defined in Section 3(f)(ii) of the Act as follows,

> Two persons are said to be *sapindas* of each other if one is a lineal ascendant of the other within the limits of *sapinda* relationship, or if they have a common lineal ascendant who is within the limits of *sapinda* relationship with reference to each of them.

Under the provisions of the Act, on the mother's side, a Hindu individual cannot marry anyone who is within three generations of them in the "line of ascent." On the father's side, this prohibition applies to anyone within five generations of the individual.

In striking down the petition, the court noted, "If the choice of a partner in a marriage is left unregulated, incestuous relationship may gain legitimacy." Here again is a case of the judiciary upholding tradition and cultural norms.

The idea of the Constitution's founders not providing criteria for resolving moral conflicts is sometimes mooted as being its strength. Beteille (2008) explained that while it would be a mistake to deny the moral basis of the obligations of family, kinship, and community, the moral basis of these obligations is different from the basis of constitutional morality. This implies that in citizens' appeals to law, it is constitutional morality that will prevail over societal morality. The fundamental tenet of constitutional morality is that one should uphold the provisions of the Indian Constitution and refrain from acting arbitrarily in a way that would undermine the fundamentals of the rule of law. Also, it would be necessary to create traditions in order to uphold the integrity of such morality.

However, the Constitution of India does not define "constitutional morality." Constitutional morality was first proposed in the nineteenth century by British Classicist George Grote. According to him, "constitutional morality" represents the country's "ultimate respect for the forms of the Constitution." That basically means both freedom and self-imposed restraint can coexist. B. R. Ambedkar, credited with drafting the Constitution, first used the term "constitutional morality" in an Indian context during a parliamentary debate on November 4, 1948. He quoted Grote as saying that constitutional morality was not a "natural spirit" and that Indians "have yet to learn it." Ambedkar used this persuasive argument to emphasize that courts should not apply constitutional morality to invalidate laws or government actions. In his view, constitutional morality meant effective coordination between conflicting interests of different peoples and administrative cooperation to resolve those issues or conflicts amicably or as far as possible in a friendly manner.

Constitutional morality encompasses the idea that the Constitution of a country should not only be a legal document but also a moral one that reflects the moral and ethical values of a society, such as the rule of law, equality, justice, freedom, and human dignity. It also involves the protection of individual rights and freedoms, and the obligation of the state to uphold these rights. It helps to create a moral and legal framework that can guide the actions of the state and its citizens and ensures that the Constitution remains relevant and in tune with the changing values and needs of society over time.

In the present times, constitutional morality consists of two main aspects, namely a resuscitation of the "Basic Structure Doctrine" and a critique of popular and social morality. The "Basic Structure Doctrine" is a common-law legal doctrine that asserts that the Constitution of a sovereign state has certain characteristics that cannot be erased by its legislature. This meaning was employed in the first instance in *Naz Foundation v. Government of the NCT (National Capital Territory) of Delhi* in 2010. In this form, a precedent was set for the courts to disregard societal norms, stigmas, and limitations while assessing the actions of the state. In this case, the Court considered the ideal of upholding the constitutional principles rather than society's perception regarding the legitimacy of same-sex relationships when deliberating upon the issue of decriminalizing homosexuality, which was then a criminal offense under Section 377 of the Indian Penal Code (IPC).

The two judicial decisions presented above (the Surrogacy case and the *Sapinda* marriage case) indicate that these are "tradition-sustaining" decisions upholding societal morality as constitutional morality. In another case relating to the entry of women in the *Sabarimalai* temple that had in recent decades barred the entry of women in the menstruating ages, the judicial conclusion based on the principle of constitutional morality resulted in two divergent opinions, with one in favor of women's entry by prioritizing the principle of equality and the other in favor of restricted entry by prioritizing the freedom of religious groups and sects to practice their religion.

Prioritizing the principle of equality, Justice Chandrachud clarified that individual dignity can be achieved only by reckoning individual liberty as a natural right. Such individual dignity postulates equality between persons irrespective of sex, age, and status. Therefore, freedom from discrimination, equal protection of the law for all, and protection against the arbitrariness of authority ought to be the founding principles governing constitutional notions of morality. Only by firmly rooting constitutional morality in the fundamental postulates of human liberty, equality, fraternity, and dignity can justice be secured in all its dimensions for the individual citizen. In the public law conversations between religion and morality, it is this overarching sense of constitutional morality that has to prevail. Therefore, freedom of religion and the freedom to manage the affairs of a religious denomination are subject to and must yield to these fundamental notions of constitutional morality. Where a conflict arises, the quest for human dignity, liberty, and equality must prevail (2019).

He went on to add: "A claim for the exclusion of women from religious worship, even if it be founded in religious text, is subordinate to the constitutional values of liberty, dignity and equality. Exclusionary practices are contrary to constitutional morality" (2019).

The dissenting Justice Indu Malhotra, however, had a different view even if she is a woman. Acknowledging that equality and non-discrimination are certainly one facet of constitutional morality, she noted that a balance is required to be struck between the principles of equality and non-discrimination on the one hand, and the protection of the cherished liberties of faith, belief, and worship guaranteed in the Constitution to persons of all religions in a secular polity to ensure that the religious beliefs of none are obliterated or undermined (2019).

While ensuring the paramount importance of human dignity and prioritizing the principle of equality to achieve the dignity of women is a significant achievement in judicial precept and precedence, it still remains a contested one, as it is not written down as a fixed principle in the Constitution to prioritize equality over all other principles in all spheres.

Justice Dipak Misra noted, "The magnitude and sweep of constitutional morality is not confined to the provisions and literal text which a constitution contains, rather it embraces within itself virtues of a wide magnitude that ushers in a pluralistic and inclusive society" (Hindustan Times, October 5, 2018).

Whether these publicly announced goals of constitutional morality through judicial decisions usher in an inclusive pluralism or not, it does raise normative constitutional expectations by leaps and bounds. Baxi (2008) notes that in the passage from normative constitutional expectations to lived constitutional experience, there is enormous human violation and tragedy, especially in actually existing constitutionalism that does not orient legitimation of state conduct to popular expectations. Also, enormous anterior expectations developed as a consequence of the nationalist movement, and so the idea of citizenship in the Constitution was not limited to the conduct of governance but was extensive to include all interactions and everyday transactions in society and economy.

Every day there are reports of horrific violence against women and Dalits. In parts of Tamil Nadu, forms of humiliation such as the double tumbler system for serving tea to Dalits are prevalent. Recently, two women from the Gounder community were arrested for serving tea in coconut shells to Dalit women, which, even if it is environmentally sustainable, becomes discriminatory when Dalits alone are served in this way (The Times of India, February 11, 2024).

Moreover, as Baxi (2008) noted, there has been for decades "constitutional immiserization of the masses," as most of the welfare and development measures affecting the large majority of the people were placed in the non-justiciable section of the *Directive Principles of State Policy* of the Constitution. Baxi notes that the fairy tales and horror stories pose numerous challenges to any master narrative of Indian constitutionalism as no narrative can be privileged as each destroys the hegemonic position of the other (Baxi, 2008).

Like the civilizational meta-narrative of the nation being constructed by individuals and collectives, so too the constitutional meta-narrative needs to include the meanings of constitutionalism of individuals and groups and their practices, whose aspirations for change may not be in conformity with the meanings and interpretations of law persons. Baxi observes,

> The theory effect not only fails to archive the plurality and multiplicity of practices of representation generated by a whole variety of lawpersons, but also more importantly, obscures from view the perspective of non-lawpersons, people bearing the weight of the constitutional practices that they often seek to shed or overthrow. How may we grasp different types of citizen interpretative practices that insist on a redirection of the production of constitutional meanings? May we include within this range militant forms of insurgent citizen interpretation?

> How may we grasp forms of meaning that strategize confrontation between expectations and experience of constitutionality against the constitution itself? How may we observe and relate the impact of citizen interpretive practices with native official ones? May one, then, with appropriate caution, speak of the "dominant" and "subaltern" practices of constitutional theory? (Baxi, 2008, 99)

He further noted that ethnography of constitutionalism in all its protean senses is still to emerge.

The possibility of constructing such ethnographies has been flagged off by Kalpana Kannabiran (2021) in the concept and politics of "Constitution-as-Commons" by drawing from the literature on "constructed cultural commons" that deals with the formation of communities to produce and sustain cultural resources. It has been used in legal analysis by scholars (Madison, Frischman, and Strandburg, and Daniels and Hudson) though they do not set their arguments within an insurgent perspective. Foucault's (1980, 81) call for an "insurrection of subjugated knowledges" in an attempt to redeem subjugated practices and recover subjugated subjects has motivated Kannabiran's construction that attempts to initiate ethnographies as suggested by Baxi. Adding to Baxi's "constitutional formation" comprising "a mass of heterogenous constitution generative, sustaining, defying, and denying practices, and the order of expectations and experiences" (Baxi, 2008, 95), Kannabiran introduces the idea of the Constitution being silenced through practices of juridicalization that reinstate responsibilization as the sign of citizenship. She suggests ethnographies of "constitution-as-commons" by drawing from the experiences of annihilation, occupation, carcerality, and crimes against humanity of the collectives of Dalits, Muslims, Adivasis or tribal populations, the multiplicity of their resistance to the rule by maiming, as also the archives of resistance they draw upon (Kannabiran, 2021, 233). She calls this "an insurgency to wrest citizenship from the jaws of enclosure, through a radical crafting of the contours of the Constitution-as-Commons" (Kannabiran, 2021, 233).

She explains that this idea resurrects the moral economy of the constitution and its ethical foundations immersed in empathy (fraternity) evident in the work of Ambedkar. Whereas the idea of "constitutional morality" introduced by Ambedkar has now become a guideline for judicial decisions, this idea of "Constitution-as-Commons" foregrounds the Constitution as an irreducible ethical framework, asserts the need for the indivisibility of the Constitution, and claims free and unfettered access to the Constitution and its protections, just like a "public good."

The preamble (in letter and spirit) of the Constitution is not perceived here as the ideals of the nation that the state facilitates in its attainment but as "the anthem of resistance" for citizens that anchors the understanding of the Constitution as redefining "constitutional communities" through engagement with popular constitutionalism (Kannabiran, 2021). This would enable, according to her, the inscription of decolonial visions of dignity, autonomy, self-determination, birthright, and justice in the constitution-as-commons.

The constitutional meta-narrative of the nation is therefore the distillation of hope from the Constitution's text, the visions of the framers, the discourses of "constitutional formation" or constitutionalism, the judicial discourses and practices of constitutional morality, and the decolonial visions articulated by "constitutional communities" in the constitutional "commons." This is the hope of realizing the ideals of justice, liberty, equality, and fraternity for each citizen found in the ever-present gap between constitutional "expectations" and constitutional "experiences" that both the state and its citizen-subjects in both public and private domains seek to keep alive, aligning with modernity's project of looking forward. All the possible constructions of the constitutional meta-narratives of the nation drawn from these multiple resources of inspiration and aspiration involve the dignity, equality, liberty, and fraternity of all women at all sectional and intersectional social positionings.

GENDER SCRIPTS

The concept of "Gender Scripts" developed by Davies differs from socialization in that it implies "the individual's ability to write and rewrite her own lines; to perform differently in different programs in public and in private; to experience with different parts within the same play; and free to add, edit, and forget" (Davies, 1987, 88). The person socialized through gender scripts is not a passive object, but instead, the self is constituted in an ongoing fashion.

Two types of scripts are used to constantly create the reality of the social world. First, there are societal-type scripts, which are ascribed statuses inherited by virtue of one's membership to a particular category, such as sex, age, race, caste, and class (Davies, 1987, 96). These scripts vary across time and place with the changes in traditions and cultural practices. Secondly, there are personal scripts that can be called "identity work," which are actively created by the individual in relation to the social world. One's personal script "indicates where the person stands in relation to what he or she perceives to be going on" (Davies, 1987, 96).

The value of a script metaphor of identity and social life is that individuals are viewed as complex beings who adjust, adapt, and actively shape the world in which they are located. As Davies notes, there is not one reality but "multiple realities which make up the hundreds of miniature dramas of our everyday lives" (Davies, 1987, 97).

Drawn from semiotics and performance theory, gender scripts refer to the encoding of cultural constructs of gender and gender ideologies in the everyday performance and practices of gendered subjects. For women and girls, it is a process of socialization that embeds gender roles and expectations of the conduct of women, men and thereby constructs their gender identities. Understanding gender scripts is therefore crucial to unraveling the status of women in society and how that status could be changed. Personal gender scripts authored by individuals express their desire for change or otherwise in keeping with their aspirations of modernity.

Societal gender scripts are authored by authorizing powers such as the family, community, social institutions, and, to an extent by the state. Patriarchal power operates through these scripts in the construction of women and girls as gendered subjects of male dominance. Societal gender scripts are not immutable and do change slowly over time. As modernity changes traditional ways of life, societal gender scripts are likely to be rewritten as patriarchy reinvents itself with changes in roles and expectations. However, the stability of marriage and reproductive roles of women implies that societal gender scripts governed by culture and tradition are unlikely to change in keeping pace with socioeconomic changes. In India, both societal gender scripts and personal gender scripts draw from both civilizational meta-narratives and constitutional meta-narratives.

Civilizational Meta-narrative, Tradition, and Societal Gender Scripts

Societal gender scripts embody the gender ideologies in the discourses and practices of socialization of females and males in families right from their childhood. In the structurally differentiated Indian society comprising various religious groups, caste groups wherein the fourfold *varna* enfolds the numerous subcastes of *jati*, indigenous or Adivasi groups, all further classified based on ethnicities, the socialization discourses and practices are bound to differ substantively even within overarching gender ideologies of patriarchy. These discourses and practices are usually justified as religiously sanctioned cultural practices that are constitutive of the civilizational meta narrative of desired virtues that set the telos of an individual's moral life. The concept of *Varnashrama Dharma* in Hindu Vedic thought defines the duties and responsibilities of individuals based on their *varna* (social class) and *ashrama* (stage of life), thereby providing a moral and ethical framework for leading a balanced and purposeful life. The norms of modern ethical life based on the principles of equality and universalizability would be considered antithetical to this religion-based ethics of differentiated duties and responsibilities, but it plays a very significant role in the discourses and practices of socialization within families.

Such caste-gender socialization entails the cultivation of dispositions and comportment invoking cultural frameworks and patriarchal ideologies. Gender scripts of socialization within *jati* groups give insights into the simultaneous construction of one's caste-gender identity as well as the construction of "others," and the discourses and practices in the cultivation of appropriate comportment in dealings with others. It also give insights into the extent to which each *varna* and *jati* disallows "the ordinary and everyday as sites for realizing and affirming their being," for it plays a role in women's lives in terms of marriage norms and individual choice (Thirumal et al., 2024, 298).

This has led to the practice of marriage within endogamous groups of *jati* and proscription within the Brahmin caste of marriage within a lineage (*gotra*) that is imaginatively constructed to its origins from seven Vedic *rishis* (sages) and their progeny. Given the occupation-based grouping of *jatis* in ancient times that evolved over time with societal development of division of labor in settled agrarian communities, highly graded notions of purity and pollution evolved alongside, restricting social intercourse between *varnas* and between *jatis*. Over time, a number of *jatis* were deemed "untouchable" castes and socially placed outside the fourfold *varna* group of Brahmin, Kshatriya, Vaishya, and Shudra. There are multiple interpretations for their evolution, such as intermarriage between high-caste and low-caste people and their progeny being segregated, as also the subjugation of indigenous groups with the evolution of settlements of agrarian communities who were prevented from integrating fully in the settlements (Gupta, 1996).

Hindu understandings of pollution are based on celestial and biological events. The planetary event of a solar and lunar eclipse is marked as a period of pollution for both gods and humans, both requiring purification after the eclipse period. Similarly, the period after death is considered a period of pollution for the family and the extended members of the family along the patrilineal descent. Women are subjected to periods of pollution during menstruation and the postpartum period, where the time period could vary between *jati* groups. Socializing young girls in the family to observe the period of menstrual pollution, especially in upper-caste families with all the associated restrictions on movement and touch, is a significant factor in the differential gender socialization of boys and girls. As part of this, girls are also socialized to take on responsibilities for household chores like cooking and serving food for the family when mothers have to observe menstrual seclusion. The boys of the "twice-born" castes, which exclude the Shudra caste, go through a spiritual initiation ceremony that Brahmins call *Upanayanam* that confers on them the sacred duties of maintaining the patrilineal lineage and the authority to perform such rituals for its maintenance, the most important being the rituals upon the death of parents and *Shrardham* done annually marking their death date.

Given the Vedic understanding of the unity of Cosmos, Universe, and Beings, time periods are also classified as auspicious and inauspicious as the positions of the celestial bodies of planets, sun, moon, and stars and their movements are deemed to have good and ill effects on persons, and on event and action outcomes. This has led to varying methods of astrological readings and predictions that are classified as Vedic science. The trust in Hindu astronomy that has successfully specified the date, time, and place of eclipses since ancient times has also bolstered the Hindu belief in astrological predictions. The casting of horoscopes for an individual based on the celestial positions at the time of birth, horoscope matching to find perfect partners for marriage, and the practice of arranged marriage evolve out of this belief in astrology and the Vedic duties and responsibilities assigned to parents to settle the marriage of their children. Girls and boys are socialized and prepared for their marriage and marital roles based on the appropriateness of arranged marriage, with the family being responsible for finding the proper match.

The differential socialization of boys and girls based on cultural norms and expectations has resulted in the habitus and the formation of dispositions that accept an unquestioned and unchallenged patriarchy as the appropriate form of norm-abiding life. While many of the cultural norms of Vedic practices were, in the early periods, confined only to the keepers of the Vedas, who were the Brahmins, it spread to other groups as the caste system evolved. It also set in the sanskritization process as an ongoing process, bringing more and more groups with varying beliefs on the primordial divine force into the Vedic fold, with the emulation and adoption of some of the Vedic rituals progressively and gradually setting a patriarchal mindset in conjugal roles and expectations.

Girls are therefore socialized in their parental home for marriage and their life in their marital home, with emphasis on devotion to their husband and his family. One of the conjugal roles and expectations that has come up recently for adjudication before the Courts of Law pertains to the role and expectations of the daughter-in-law to care for her parents-in-law. The Delhi High Court noted in August 2023, while granting divorce to a man, that a woman's "persistent insistence" on living separately from her in-laws without justification is an act of cruelty. It found her reason to live separately "whimsical" and noted that the son has a moral and legal obligation to take care of his parents when they grow old, and if his wife attempts to deviate from the custom, she must have some justifiable reason. Comparing to Western standards, the Court observed,

> In India, generally people do not subscribe to the Western thought where, upon getting married or attaining majority, the son gets separated from the family.

> In normal circumstances, the wife is expected to be a part of the family of the husband after her marriage. (The Times of India, August 25, 2023)

In January 2024, the Jharkhand High Court observed the same in a similar case of the wife's insistence to live separately, noting that "serving elderly mothers-in-law or grandmothers-in-law is both a cultural practice and an obligation for women in India" (Upadhyay, 2024).

The Calcutta High Court ruled in October 2023 that no girl can be forced to stop caring for her parents while disposing of a complaint filed by her husband. The judge noted that taking care of one's parents is an emotional and loving act, and no force in the world can stop a child from doing it, nor can the child be forced to do it if he or she does not want to. This ruling overlooked arguments of duty, custom, cultural norms, and expectations, making it a non-binding act of love applicable to both males and females. The Supreme Court had, in 2023 ruled against a father who disinherited his daughter from his property because she had married of her choice and against his wishes. His contention was that as it would only be his son who would take care of him in his old age, he had disinherited his daughter. The Supreme Court rejected his argument, stating that such patriarchal notions have no place in modern society and emphasized that all children, regardless of gender, have a moral and legal obligation to take care of their parents in their old age.

Noting that gender equality is a fundamental right, the Supreme Court also ruled that courts should avoid making patriarchal remarks and should not further the notion that only male children will assist parents in their old age. While this promotes gender equality, it still does not resolve the issue of the cultural norm and obligations of daughters-in-law to take care of parents-in-law, and restraining the son and daughter-in-law from setting up an independent household, with negative effects on the career prospects of the daughter-in-law who is bound to serve her in-laws.

Thus far, the cultural practices that have arisen as traditions drawing from the notions of virtue and duties specified in Hindu scriptures and their effects on gender socialization by way of scripting roles, obligations, and expectations have been examined for their influence in the formation of patriarchal gender ideologies embodied in the habitus and the formation of appropriate dispositions through socialization.

It also needs to be noted that cultural beliefs and practices vary between groups. Susan Wadley (1991 [1980]) explains that the cultural belief among the Tamils is that women have powers to control and alter events, and so she is feared and her blessings are sought. But in order to control and direct her powers, the dominant ideology states that a woman has to be constrained and controlled by her male kin. Women who are controlled by men are held in higher esteem than single women or widows. Despite regional differences in gender conceptions, it may not be far-fetched to assume that similar processes happen across all religious and ethnic groups, with some variations perhaps in matrilineal societies in Kerala and Northeast India, as studies have shown that patriarchal gender ideologies are weaker in these societies even as they are changing.

Modernity, Aspirations, and Personal Gender Scripts

The key commitments of Western modernity are the principles of autonomy drawn from the ideals of liberty and equality, and also justice. With modern education and development, women and men in India are drawn toward the Western cultural modernity's ideal of self-exploration and self-realization using one's imagination. As Western modernity replaced the older virtues of sincerity and honor with authenticity, it increasingly came to be understood to refer to a way of acting that is choice-worthy in itself. It is therefore not surprising that younger generations under the influence of Western modernity would desire to craft their modern self that they deem authentic by exercising their choice, as they believe they have developed self-reflexivity to assess their choices.

Being authentic or true to one's self in the context of multiple modernities like India, however, is not to let one's experiences succumb to immediacy and fleeting sensations but to ground experiences in a moral order drawing meaning and values provided by its traditions. The demands of traditions, cultural practices, gender ideologies, and socialization in families are oriented to curtailing the self-determining freedom of both young women and men such that while modern lifestyles and modern aspirations are deemed desirable and coveted, they are simultaneously rooted in moral values inspired by the *Dharmic* duties and responsibilities, and modern constitutional values, not necessarily of freedom and equality in the private sphere, but the public virtue of civility in life outside the home with some concern for social justice. This allows free intermingling of castes and religions in all public spaces like roads, buses, railways, educational institutions, hospitals, offices, temples, and all other institutions as a citizen's right that cannot be curtailed, but importantly retains caste socialization within homes that is outside of the state's purview. Caste has by and large lost its civic status in national society but has private status in the intimate sphere of family and public status in the State and Constitution that seek to do away with the inequalities of the caste system to usher in social justice.

This sets a conundrum for young women and men who choose to marry outside their caste as it pitches tradition-based family moral values, social honor, parental duties and children's obligation to parents against modernity's values of freedom and autonomy. This is the most significant domain today where women seek freedom in various degrees from tradition-bound practices. Young women may script their lives accessing some degree of freedom and agency in the choice of marriage partners in both "arranged" and "love" marriages, and parents may or may not accede to children's demands as explained in the three chapters that follow this. There is increasing evidence that arranged marriages with greater parental responsibility and exercise of some agency in granting consent to parental choice is still the dominant form of marriage. Families are increasingly also more open to accepting girls' choice of their marriage partners if it is within the same caste. The severity of gender and caste socialization within families constrains young girls to seek more freedom in forming cross-sex friendships and accessing freedom to make their own choice. Even if modernity's influence through education and media may bring in more liberal gender socialization in families, there is also increasing moral policing at the societal level caused by patriarchal anxieties over declining morals under the influence of Western modernity. Women struggling to expand their freedom of choice have to contend with these counteracting forces.

The earlier section provided instances of women seeking to set up households independently from their in-laws, and the courts' decisions varied from upholding customs and obligatory duties to questioning the patriarchal mindsets of elders in resisting the move. In these instances, women script their lives from an accommodative stance to strategic negotiations to achieve their ends, with fewer elders taking the matter to court. Some working women turn the situation to their advantage, as the in-laws provide additional help in running the household. A contentious and evolving issue is the question of bearing children in marriage. With the age at marriage increasing and more women employed in professions, who also face discriminatory practices at work, such as losing jobs on account of pregnancy, they put off their decision to have children. An elderly parent recently approached the court claiming that he has a right to become a grandparent and that it was obligatory for his son to give him a grandchild. He demanded his son repay him all the expenses of his upbringing and education if he failed to give him a grandchild.

Fifty years ago, the norm in middle-class families was to educate girls until they got their undergraduate degree in Arts or Science, with a few women opting for engineering courses. Parents either did not have the resources to educate girls beyond this or were moreover anxious that with more education, they would be unable to find a groom for their daughters. Fears of highly educated women not being not good housewives reflected the patriarchal mindset of the time, which has in present times, with more women becoming professionally qualified, pushing up the bar for the minimum educational level of middle-class women. Many young women in the past who tried to cross this bar for higher education always had to do it with some strategizing and struggle, with their illiterate and uneducated mothers helping them overcome patriarchal obstacles. Today, young middle-class women can script their educational aspirations to a great extent without much patriarchal resistance in urban India.

Edward Shils (1958) notes that in the antinomy of tradition and liberty, it has come to be widely regarded that the expansion of individual freedom is incompatible with the maintenance of tradition. Shils is of the view that tradition is an encouragement to incipient individuality rather than its enemy, as it is a stimulant to moral judgment and self-discipline and establishes contact between the recipient and the sacred values of one's life in society. Socialization of girls and young women in the family based on societal gender scripts seeks to achieve this, although societal and group pressures are likely to exacerbate such socialization into strict disciplinary regimes. The extent to which young women can aspire for freedom is no doubt the result of their exposure to a modern outlook and modern lifestyles based on their education and interaction with the world outside their homes. However, the extent to which they can negotiate and access greater freedom on aspects such as the choice of marriage partner is dependent on the extent to which the elders in the family have been able to cognize, appreciate, and draw from the values of modernity and integrate them into the gender socialization process. Parental opposition to granting the freedom to daughters to freely make their own choices is also because they feel young minds are likely to be swayed by fleeting moments that would be inimical to the long-term goals of one's life quest. But it could also be stretched far to become an ideology of traditionalism, where strict conformity to traditional outlook and practices and a heightened sensitivity to the opinions and pressures of the community can stifle all attempts by young women to negotiate freedoms.

However, young women's participation in the public domains through education and employment, along with their acquisition of dispositions of both self-restraint and freedom through rational conduct in the public domain, is more likely to enhance their capabilities to negotiate and access more freedom to script their personal life in their intimate private sphere. For young women to script their own aspirations of modernity and freedoms, where self-determined freedom is also grounded in the moral values of a life-as-quest, it is necessary to open up opportunities for their participation in the public domain for all social classes, drawing on the constitutional principles of dignity, justice, equality, and liberty.

Chapter 2

Marriage Norms, Choice, and Aspirations of Rural Women

Modernity for rural women is the possibility of aspirations for change in their private lives more than in public life. State-supported transformative agendas of modernity focus more on the public sphere and on changing subjectivities in the public life of rural women as citizens, workers, rights-bearing individuals, subject and agents of participatory development and political processes. Modern law and legislation on marriages do recognize free choice marriage, but the weight of custom and tradition associated with the reproduction of the caste system works severely against it. Yet, the conditions of modernity such as law and rights, changes in the political economy, and the emergence of urban cultures at marked variance from rural cultures have no doubt a bearing on the possibility of aspirations for change in private lives. It is the private life, the sphere of intimacy and emotion, that rural women aspire most to offer better and more choices. But such aspirations remain for many a subversive and hidden desire, as analysis of women's folk songs indicates their longings to be free from oppressive customs, practices, and disciplines of rural life.

In the present time, many rural women in North India aspire for an alternate modernity, recasting their subjectivity in the direction of choice and freedom in their emotional lives. However, caste endogamy and village exogamy still remain, and are likely to remain into the indefinite future, as constitutive features of rural matrimonial alliances. Marriage and kinship rules in regions and among castes specify marriage within endogamous caste groups as the norm, with many other restrictions and taboos overlaid, such as prohibition of marriages within the same or other prohibited *gotra/got* (clan/lineages) within a caste group called *biradari,* and of village exogamy (Chowdhry, 2004a, 2007; Uberoi, 1994). Any transgression of the norm is perceived as a violation of customarily delineated social disciplines that are constitutive features of caste socialization (Dube, 1996; Chowdhry, 2007). In examining the implications of the metaphor of the seed and earth in biological reproduction in various cultures, Dube (1986) highlighted its importance in the boundary maintenance of different castes and its role in the assignment of patrilineal descent, with the attendant implications on the control over women's sexuality, property, and rights. Particularly in parts of Rajasthan, Haryana, and western Uttar Pradesh, these marriage prohibitory rules are sometimes interwoven with an enlarged notion of incest taboo based on notions of fictive kinship (Raheja, 1988; Lambert, 1997) and village brotherhood known as *bhaichara* that results in punitive measures for transgressions, such as social ostracism and expulsion of family and kin from the village—sometimes even resulting in honor killings, which are not found elsewhere with such frequency (Chowdhry, 2004b). Although caste endogamy may appear to be a stable marriage norm, it is, in practice, quite contingent due to the shifting circles of endogamy, as the permissible *jati* groups for marriage alliances keep changing, and due to the preference for hypergamous marriage in some instances (Abraham, 2014). It is also contingent in its enforcement, as it varies over time and circumstances.

Kinship and marriage rules, caste and class boundaries, multiple and intersecting patriarchies that regulate forms of desire are thus organized into strategies and tactical positions constituting social disciplines, which by regulating everyday social interactions are as much instrumentalities of self and "other" construction as they are of caste and class socialization. The majority of women in rural North India still abide by these social norms and acquiesce to the social disciplines of village life. For the few who select their own spouses overlooking these norms, in what is called "love marriage," the change in marriage practice reflects the aspirations for change by these women who have to negotiate between freedom and choice, social disciplines, patriarchal securities and domination, honor and shame, tradition and intergenerational mobility. Based on ethnographic fieldwork among women of different castes of Lahurpur village in Allahabad (Prayagraj) district, this chapter explores how women abide by the social disciplines or negotiate to create more spaces of freedom to exercise choice and agency both for themselves and as an intergenerational strategy toward greater freedom and mobility. It presents women's narratives of marriage practices and their desires to map a trajectory of an alternative modernity for rural women that encompass their private realm as well.

SOCIAL EVILS IN MARRIAGE PRACTICES

Numerous cases are reported regularly in newspapers of young couples in love who, having eloped or married against the wishes of their families and village society, are either killed or commit suicide under threat because these are considered illicit intercaste unions and incur the wrath of family and village society. Mody (2003) notes,

> The murders of young women and men, who have married by choice or across caste barriers, often go unnoticed. There are no names, not even statistics. Many are not investigated because the community closes ranks, apparently making it impossible to find out what really happened.

Although eastern Uttar Pradesh does not record as many killings, both abduction and rape of minor rural girls happen quite frequently. Informal discussions with knowledgeable lawyers handling cases of abduction indicate that it is quite common in eastern Uttar Pradesh, although it is difficult to obtain consolidated statistics either of the abduction and rape of minor rural girls or the instances of young women eloping with their lovers, who often are pursued relentlessly or ostracized. Often the cases of young women asserting their choice of partners are also charged as cases of abduction. Women's groups allege that agents of the state, like the police and the courts, abet in this kind of patriarchal-feudal repression.

Caste Endogamy

As elsewhere in the country, intercaste marriages are not encouraged here, and the lives of young rural girls are governed by social disciplines of the village that monitor intercaste interactions among the young of various castes (Chowdhry, 2007). For the individual, these social disciplines operate at the level of caste socialization, which produces a *doxic* submission to the social order of arranged marriages following principles of village exogamy and caste endogamy. Chowdhry (2007) has also observed that, ironically, while some youth breach the norm of caste endogamy, the youth are also the ones who seriously denounce intercaste marriages and appear more complicit rather than rebels of the social norms, having been socialized to the *doxic* submission of within-caste marriage. Beneath the caste tension and violence in the villages lies much libidinal politics. Forbidden love attracts wrath and vengeance because it tries to break barriers that maintain the separation and hierarchies of caste. Intercaste marriages, more than any other action, blur the boundaries of caste and shake its foundations, for the reproduction of the caste system requires the maintenance of these boundaries.

A greater understanding of the feudal shaping of patriarchal values is necessary to unravel the particularities of this process as a regional phenomenon, even as a more general exploration of patriarchal norms and dominance would throw more light on intergenerational tensions and young women's subordination. The bizarre notion of honor or *izzat* depends rather heavily on a code of conduct for women.

> Modesty, obedience, and duty define good conduct. A woman's failure to live within the prescribed code results in loss of honor to her family. Exercising choice and breaching the caste barrier are extreme violations of the code and apparently are good grounds for murder or at a minimum, the forcible dissolution of marriage. Mody (2003)

There is indeed much anthropological literature on the notion of honor or *izzat* in rural North India that governs social and sexual relations and distinguishes between the intertwined *biradari* honor and village honor, sometimes known as *gaon ki nak* (the village nose) or *aika* (village unity), which rests solely on the behavior of women (Lambert, 1997; Chowdhry, 2004a, 2007).

Bought Brides

Despite strict enforcement of cultural norms to protect honor, feudal oppression and patriarchal values allow men to treat women and girls as sexual objects devoid of any will. Young girls are sometimes forced into an inappropriate sexual match as a way to redeem parents from debt. But selling daughters is not just restricted to children. Nor is this exactly what is customarily called "bride price" that may have over time transformed into the dowry. The phenomenon refers to one in which when a family for some reason cannot get a bride for their boy, they actually buy a bride from a poorer family that is in dire poverty. This is referred to as "bought brides" (Jeffery and Jeffery, 1996, 6). Blanchet (2005) has highlighted the sale of Bangladeshi girls as wives to men in Uttar Pradesh. These are long-distance and cross-caste purchases of brides through middlemen. Even in eastern Uttar Pradesh and Bihar, this kind of transaction does exist (Chaudhry and Mohan, 2011). These are new forms of commercial transactions mediated through middlemen, just like labor contractors bringing in interstate migrant workers. The reasons for this kind of transaction arise on account of the boy's bad reputation in the village, his prior marital status, or extreme poverty, as well as the scarcity of brides within the region to meet the demands of such persons, perhaps due to low sex ratios in the region. Meanwhile, the reasons for the sale of brides across regions are due to the poverty of the families and their inability to meet the dowry demands of local men. Some Pasi (a Scheduled Caste) women in Lahurpur village near Allahabad also revealed this phenomenon in a few instances during my fieldwork.

Dowry

Dowry still remains in place in rural matrimonial transactions, and almost all social classes find dowry demands a burden to settle their daughters. For the last few decades, dowry inflation in rural areas has been reported (Rao, 1993). Dowry harassment by in-laws and husbands often leads to deaths of girls in their marital homes or they are sent back by their in-laws to their natal homes, causing anguish and loss of honor to the girl's family (Bloch and Rao, 2000). This burden strikes deeper as girl children are seen as a burden, resulting in their neglect, female feticide, and the resultant low sex ratios in the aggregate. In situations of extreme poverty such as drought and famine conditions, or the recent Covid upheaval and loss of work opportunities, when families find it difficult to even feed their children, they marry off young underage girls, perhaps for low or no dowry, to anomalous matches such as older, disabled, or widowed men.

Although people are aware of such anomalous matches, they remain quite inflexible regarding conventional marriage norms and rarely seem to negotiate or seize the interstices of flexibility and freedom. They rigidly abide to marriage norms that entail normalizing caste and class boundaries through social disciplines in everyday conduct.

These issues are explored through interviews conducted in the village of Lahurpur in October 2004. Although twenty years have passed since the fieldwork, the findings are still relevant in present times. Despite the visible signs of neoliberal prosperity in urban India, changes in rural villages of eastern Uttar Pradesh are still not discernible, as development is still urban-oriented with only a slow trickle down to the villages. Moreover, cultural norms and caste disciplines remain, more or less, stable for long periods. Through interviews with a cross-section of women and girls in the village, we reconstruct women's narratives of their views on marriage by choice and traditional social norms. The analysis provides a revealing picture of their experience of lived constraints and their aspirations, which, though common to all women, are still, marked by differences of caste and class.

THE STUDY VILLAGE AND FIELDWORK

Lahurpur was classified as a village at the 2001 census. But as per the 2011 census it is denoted as a town consisting of an agricultural settlement a mile away from the main highway, engaged in agriculture and consisting mainly of Hindu households of the Kurmi caste as the dominant landowners. Muslims, who comprise 28.46 percent of the population, are engaged in trades and household industries like Beedi rolling and live abutting the national highway, almost a mile away from the agricultural settlement.

At the 2011 census, there were 687 households with a total population of 4,406, of whom Hindus made up 70.72 percent. There were 365 Scheduled Caste people, all of them staying in the Dalit settlement, which, though part of the agricultural settlement, had a different access lane to the hamlet. The literacy rate in Lahurpur was 78.03 percent, well above the state average, with female literacy at 69.52 percent.

Lahurpur village was selected for the study as my institute librarian was from the village and knew both the village headman and the elected female panchayat leader and introduced me to obtain their permission to enter the village for my research work. Outsiders from the village, especially for such purposes as interviews, are advised to approach the village elders, for their reference elicits greater cooperation. Interestingly, although the Hindus dominated the village, the village *Pradhan*, a young Muslim woman, was elected to the reserved seat that was made possible by the 73rd constitutional amendment in 1992 that ensured reservation for women in the three-tiered Panchayati Raj institutions (democratically elected governing bodies in rural India). She was first approached to grant permission to conduct research in the village and was also interviewed even though she lived in the bazaar area outside the village. With the help of the village headman, the *Zilla Parishad* member, who gave us the demographic and economic arrangement of the different street lanes in the village, it was ensured that women of all castes in the village were interviewed. Interviews were conducted both in the agricultural settlement and with Muslims living away from them.

This was a short ethnographic endeavor as we sought voluntary interviewees without drawing a random sample. Guided by a set of leading questions, about twenty interviews covering a cross-section of the castes in the village were conducted over a period of a week. The interviews were conducted in a way to let the women speak freely on the issue; sometimes they were alone and at times with other family members. A group discussion in the Dalit hamlet was also conducted. Most interviews lasted between thirty minutes to an hour. While the interviews were not recorded and transcribed, copious notes were taken while interviewing to help in the construction of the narrative.

The village is inhabited mainly by Kurmi Singraur, the landowning OBC caste (administrative classification "Other Backward Classes") of the village, although the average size of the holding is only about 2 hectares or so. In the state of Uttar Pradesh, the Kurmis, along with three other backward castes, namely, the Yadavs, Lodhas, and Gujars, benefited from the first wave of land reforms in the 1950s that conferred ownership rights on erstwhile tenants through the *zamindari* abolition laws. These four backward castes, which had controlled only 6 percent of *zamindari* rights, came later to control about 20 percent of the land (Jain, 1996). While there are other castes too in Lahurpur, they are neither numerically nor economically as dominant as the Kurmi

Singraur. The few Scheduled Caste (Pasi) families work on the fields of the landowning groups and live apart from the rest, although in proximity.

The women of Lahurpur could thus be grouped as follows. Women of the well-off landowning Kurmi caste do not work in the fields but do household work as well as cattle tending. Most of the households, except among the very poor Pasi, own at least one milch buffalo, and so tending cattle is an important component of women's work. Some women of Kurmi households who are not that well-off do assist in the fieldwork along with their husbands, which is mostly in the nature of cutting and gathering the straw and bringing it from the field to their homes for the cattle. Women of other service castes, such as Vishwakarma or Gupta, do work from their homes like carpentry, and some are just homemakers. Pasi and Khatik women, who are Dalits, work as field laborers for Kurmi landowners for kind wages whenever work is available, either in this village or the adjoining villages. Some Muslim women are engaged in home-based work like beedi rolling or tailoring. Unlike a few men, no woman goes out to work in the bazaar area or the city of Allahabad (Prayagraj). However, the proximity to the city has made city life an integral part of their imagined mobilities to a better and freer life.

The ethnographic fieldwork conducted in the village comprised mainly of individual interviews in a family/household setting, which meant that other female members around also partook in the discussions with the exception of two interviews done in the field by the roadside, as well as unstructured, spontaneous, and informal group discussions in neighborhoods where a good number of a single caste, either the Kurmi*s* or the Dalits, assembled together. Our informants in such a setting could not be purposively or randomly selected but were left largely to the voluntary initiatives of women and girls. There was much enthusiasm and eagerness to participate and talk to me and my research assistant, although the same cannot be said of the discussion with the Dalit group, who felt disappointed; some left the discussion rather abruptly as we had nothing tangible to provide them or even an honorarium for their interview. Women's narratives are presented here by caste groups as they highlight the caste-wise differences in attitudes, opportunities, and constraints that women and young girls face.

Narratives of Kurmi Women

Narratives of Kurmi women and girls were collected from four situational contexts. In the village, the *Zilla Parishad* member was clearly the dominant family with his big *pucca* house (sturdy house built with bricks and cement) in the village center and surrounded by three or four smaller *pucca* houses. This cluster of houses is the well-off Kurmi households in which the women do not work in the fields. One woman, out of the three families of well-off

Kurmis in this cluster who was interviewed, was living as a nucleated but joint household in a big house in which three brothers and their families lived in separate portions of the house. Some of the women in this household did field work during the peak season. This was a household that had once seen better times and now lives in strained economic conditions. Another adjacent Kurmi neighborhood where the families were not as well-off as indicated by smaller non-*pucca* houses and where the women did much field work and cattle tending—participated in a focus-group discussion that combined individual interviews with women who either spoke up on their own or were coaxed to do so both by the group and by the interviewers. This was a large group of nearly twenty women, old and young, as well as girls. The third set of interviews was conducted in another part of the village, in which a young Kurmi woman seated outside her house cleaning mustard seeds showed an interest in participating. While she and her daughter were interviewed, her two Kurmi neighbors joined in and gave their interviews as well. One well-off Kurmi woman was interviewed at the field site, for although she was well-off as indicated by their landholding size, she, being much older, was accustomed to a certain amount of field work, mainly bundling and carrying the straw. The cross-section of Kurmi women whom we interviewed thus covers both the well-off and the not-so-well-off ones and included old, middle-aged and young married women, young unmarried women, married daughters and daughters-in-law of the village, and a few young boys who were onlookers.

Women from Well-off Families. Tara and Shivkali belong to the dominant Kurmi household that also appears to command a lot of respect in the village, residing in the big house in the village center. Tara is forty years old and the wife of the *Zilla Parishad* member from the village, who, in his conversations with us, indicated the kind of social change he has witnessed in the village over the years. But his notion of the village is exclusive of the Pasi settlement, although the Pasis themselves were inclined to participate in the interview only after we had indicated to them that we had taken the permission of the *Zilla Parishad* member. According to him, the most remarkable change is that the literacy and educational levels of females have made quantum jumps in every age-generational cohort, and at present most Kurmi households send their girls to school at least until school completion. Such varying levels of literacy and education across generations were evident in his own household. All of Tara's children reside and study in Allahabad (Prayagraj) city, where one of her sisters-in-law lives. She does not work in the fields but does the household work. She got married when she was nineteen years old and married according to her parents' wishes. She says that nobody in her family has ever married against their parents' wishes. As her children are too young, she says, she has not thought about their marriage yet, but if they like to marry by choice, she would think about it then, although the final decision would rest with her husband. She admits that marriage in her community has become quite expensive as groom's parents ask for too much dowry, but she has never heard of dowry deaths in this village. She feels that with the passage of time, girls are becoming independent and the outlook of the villagers toward girls has changed because everyone is getting educated. People can no longer suppress girls as they used to; now they can decide for themselves and make their own decisions.

Shivkali is Tara's mother-in-law. She got married when she was barely five years old and says that she has been taking *ghunghat* (the Hindu mode of veiling in this region) since she was young. She is past seventy years and still feels shy and takes a long *ghunghat* when any stranger visits her house. Although she expects her daughter-in-law to cover her head in front of men and strangers, her *ghunghat* is not as long as that of her mother-in-law. Chowdhry (1993) argues that *ghunghat* in Haryana is central to *dehati* (rural) culture and that it exerts a most cogent control over women in terms of their interactions and behavior in the private and public realms. It is therefore an indicator of patriarchal control as much as it is a symbol of *dehati* culture. If the same is true for Lahurpur village, then we can suppose that Tara experiences less patriarchal control than what her mother-in-law experienced and the patriarchal values she has internalized. Shivkali too feels that as people are getting educated, they are marrying by choice as their expectations have increased and they also want a well-educated life partner who can converse freely with people.

As we talk to Shivkali and Tara, Manju, their young neighbor, walks freely in and out, at times participating and at times joking in the conversation. Manju is the only daughter of another well-off Kurmi family who lives in an adjacent single-storied *pucca* house. Manju is twenty-four years old and has completed her undergraduate course in science from Allahabad University. She says she is looking for a job and does not want to marry until she is financially independent. She gets irritated when villagers interfere in each other's lives. She says she is free to choose her husband, but she wants to marry according to her parents' choice as she is not confident in her own choice. However, she wants to meet the boy before getting married. The intergenerational differences in outlook toward marriage may constrain and determine her destiny. Her grandmother would like Manju to marry someone who has lots of land and stays in a village, whereas she wants to marry a city lad. Her grandmother and mother oppose love marriages and feel that children should marry according to their parents' choice and in the same caste. Manju says that people in her community are marrying by choice and people are also accepting them happily.

For women like Tara, Manju, Shivkali, and others, marriage by choice means marrying someone of the same or an acceptable caste, but one in which the person who is marrying makes the choice of the partner, rather than his/her parents. This is not quite the same as intercaste love marriages.

Among the Kurmi, it was observed that despite the mothers' overriding concern about the welfare of their daughters, they are not free to adopt a liberal attitude or encourage their daughters in matters concerning marriage, as it rests largely with the man and the elders of the family's kin group. Phulabo Singh, whose house too is at the center of the village, was it appears relatively well-off in earlier times compared to the present. They also own land as well as a tractor and some buffaloes. Phulabo Singh feels if her daughters ever want to marry by choice, she would agree to it only if the boy is of the same caste. If her daughter ever wants to marry into a different caste, she would talk to her and try to change her mind. But if she still insist on marrying him, then she will consult her relatives and follow their suggestions. Phulabo is aware of how social change has caused flexibility in the caste groupings for marriage. She notes that Kurmi Singraur have now have started marrying their children into other castes such as Sachan, Patel, and Chandel (i.e., hypergamous marriages), but not to other inferior castes like Yadav or Bhartiya (SCs), or higher castes like Varma and Shukla, meaning the Brahmins. Phulabo Singh's husband is a graduate of Allahabad University, who regrets even now that he is not in any "service" job (i.e., government jobs). He wants to marry his daughters to boys living in the village because he feels that his daughters will not be able to adapt to the ways of the town. Clearly, Phulabo Singh appears as a mother with very little voice in her family matters. Just as we were taking leave of her, she called us back and told us in a low tone that she does not want anything for herself but prays every day that her daughters get educated, become financially independent, and lead a more comfortable and easy life than her.

Viewing societal changes through Savita's eyes is insightful. She is another Kurmi woman in the village, over seventy years of age, from a prosperous household owning 100 bigha of land and other assets. She was working alongside her husband in their field, setting the straw properly to be bundled when we interviewed her. Savita says that during her time, girls were married to people who had lots of land and property. Servicemen were not preferred, as only those men who were poor and did not have enough land did service work. This was the reason nobody was permitted to study and do a job. Now, she says, times have changed, and the overwhelming majority of the younger generation are studying and looking for a job. She says now young people do not want to stay in the village. Boys who are not studying are the ones who want to settle in villages and look after the crops and fields, whereas those who are studying want to move out of the village and do a job.

She also admits that life in the village is quite difficult compared to towns. At her younger son's marriage, the bride's father provided her son with a job in exchange for his daughter. She admitted that among the Thakur, dowry is prevalent, and a marriage is quite expensive. Many of the Kurmis, especially the well-off ones, identified themselves as Thakur in their conversations, a sign of aspiration for upward caste mobility.

Savita got married when she was barely twelve or thirteen years old, but *gauna* (consummation) took place after she was eighteen or nineteen years old. Being from a conservative family, she had to follow strict rules and norms set by the elders. Women were not allowed to dine with their husbands or talk to them in front of elders. They were also not allowed to wash their hair in front of their husbands (they used to wash their hair in the open because there were no bathrooms then), and she herself has followed these rules to date. She considers that marrying off the children is the sole right of the parents and that the children should not go against their parents' wishes. She admits that girls in her community have restricted freedom and can never marry by choice. They are also not allowed to have a job as the village folk jeer that the parents are eating from their daughter's income.

By urban standards of living, none of these well-off Kurmi households are on a comparable level. Only the *Zilla Parishad* member's household had furniture like a sofa set and dining table, and the furniture was also not in the women's wing of the house, suggesting that only male members and city guests used them, just as we too had been given the reception there. But the household itself functioned in a very rustic mode with a few buffaloes in the front yard of the house. Aspiring for urban mobility and an urban lifestyle for their daughters was therefore not surprising. They have also realized that such aspirations can be actualized only by educating the girls. As a consequence, there appears to be an intergenerational slackening of patriarchal controls.

Not-so-well-off Kurmis. Among the not-so-well-off Kurmis, the aspiration for urban mobility also requires that the young girls themselves show active agency, as is evident from Seema's narration in the focus-group discussion. Seema is clearly the brightest and most articulate, perhaps even a role model for many young girls in her community. Being a daughter of the village, she was not expected to veil her head like the other married women and was visiting her natal home on account of her father's recent death when he was struck by lightning. She is twenty-three years old and had done her graduation from a college in Allahabad studying Medieval History, Politics, and Hindi. The popularity of such subjects among the youth in the village clearly suggests the need for ways of promoting both science and vocational education among them. She commuted to college every day from the village to the city and is now pursuing her master's program from Kanpur University as a private candidate. She is married and stays in Delhi with her husband. She says that her family, especially her grandmother, would have opposed her if she would have wanted to marry someone of her choice. So, she happily agreed to marry by her parents' choice. While she always wanted to get a job first and marry afterward, her parents did not agree to it, and she had to marry. These days, young men from villages who have jobs in urban areas and are marrying a girl from a village do want the girl to be a graduate. And just about every young girl in the village dreams of such an urban lad. Seema says that if someone marries by choice, they lose all the relatives and are left all alone as both families disown them. People are against love marriages or intercaste marriages to such an extent that the whole community boycotts the family where any such case occurs. Due to societal pressures, one is not able to convey his/her feelings and agrees to marry according to their parents' choice. Also, she says men are not that reliable and they make false promises, and that is why girls stay away from all these things. She noted cases when girls took poison and died when their boyfriends did not marry them. She says that generally, Kurmi parents of the village fix their daughters' marriages after seeing the property and lands of the prospective groom.

Anuradha and her mother Manorati are from the not-so-well-off Kurmis whom we interviewed along with Anuradha's friend Priyanka. Anuradha is pursuing her BA degree course and seems to think that girls have become independent and are making their own decisions. While her parents would not mind her marrying someone of her choice if the boy is of the same caste, she will have no guts to decline if her parents bring any marriage proposal. She wants to marry someone who is from a village but has a service job in the town. Her neighbor and friend Priyanka, who is fourteen years old, also wants to marry a person who has a permanent service job and lots of land in the village. She feels that a girl should be financially independent and only then marry, and that she should not be dependent on her husband for everything. She wants to marry into a household that has no purdah system and is confident that her parents would bring good proposals for her. She feels that one should marry according to their parents' choice only because no parent would throw their daughters in the pond "*talaab main nahin phekenge.*" Priyanka is in high school and wants to graduate from Allahabad University. Anuradha's mother Manorati, an attractive woman in her early thirties, is clearly disgusted with village life, especially her frequent quarrels with her mother-in-law over the sharing of household and cattle-tending work. She wants to marry her daughters in town because she feels that in a village a woman has to lead a very difficult life. She says that if a girl has an affair, then she is called *awara* (loafer). She admits that today girls are marrying according to their choice and parents have also become liberated, in the sense that they are also taking their daughter's opinion before marrying them. But at the time of her marriage, the girl's opinion was not taken. Manorati feels that television has a huge impact on the younger generation, which is visible in their clothes and body language.

Being from the not-so-well-off Kurmi households and yet being influenced by social changes affecting their caste, many Kurmi mothers think of their daughters' education and sons' marriages in more instrumental ways than those from the well-off Kurmi families. One such mother, Kusum, says she is educating her daughters so that when they get a job, they can help her financially. She says that nowadays people ask for a huge amount of dowry, and that is why people prefer having fewer children. She, however, thinks that marriage is essential and everybody should marry. Observing that it will take a long time to change people's perspectives on love marriages, she says they will never ever likely marry their children to the Harijans. Another Kurmi mother, Sushila Devi, has three school-going sons. Her husband has a medical store and 20 *bighas of* land. Although she herself never went to school because she never liked studying, she wants well-educated daughters-in-law. She says that she will not let her sons marry according to their choice. Uma is from a slightly financially well-off Kurmi family. She says that she would not ask for dowry in her son's marriage but confesses that deep down in her heart she wishes that the bride's parents, of their own accord, give a handsome dowry.

The views of the Kurmi women suggest that this is a caste group in transition. Over time, there is the possibility that women of this caste group will grant more freedom to the young girls, as even now the mothers yearn for a better future for their daughters, to be away from the village and acquire more education. But for the moment, the younger generation of women would prefer the security of abiding by traditional social norms rather than face risks in their personal lives. Many of the young girls are hoping to move out of the village to towns after marriage. What is very clear from both the young and the old is that they now cognize a category of "marriage by choice within the same caste" that is betwixt the "arranged marriage" and "love matches unconstrained by caste."

Narratives of Women of Other Castes

Unlike the Kurmi*s* and the Dalits of the village, whose settlements are marked and identifiable, the households of the other castes in the village are dispersed. Walking through the village, we asked women seated in front of their homes if they were non-Kurmis and if they would be interested in being interviewed. We were able to identify two such families, one of the Gupta (Vaishya) caste and another of the Vishwakarma caste. These two families do not own or work any agricultural land, although they own their houses; the *Guptas* have a small *pucca* house, and the Vishwakarma family has a non-*pucca* tiled house, both ancestral properties.

Gupta Caste. Shyam Dulari Gupta is forty years old and is living in her husband's ancestral home. Her father-in-law was an oil monger who used to sell oil in the village in exchange for mustard seeds. Their family business ended after his death, and her husband worked as a plumber for some years. They have no land from where they could earn any income and have only one earning member who manages to earn a few hundred rupees a month. A mother of six children, she wants her youngest daughter to get a job and stand on her own legs but regrets that the atmosphere of the village is not conducive for girls to move freely. So, she could not send her to continue her studies after high school but has encouraged her to take some professional courses like painting and tailoring. She had married her elder daughter when they were facing financial problems and had no money to give for dowry. She still regrets that they had to marry her to a casual laborer who remains unemployed most of the time. As she married her elder daughter in a hurry when she was only eighteen, she has decided to marry her second daughter after the age of twenty. But she says that times have changed, and people ask for an unreasonable amount of dowry. She observes, "These days men who have good jobs do not demand much in comparison to those who do not do anything." She agrees that society is male dominated and though she is permitted to give her views and suggestions, they are not given much importance in her household. On marrying her daughter to someone of her choice, she says that she will only agree if the boy is of the same caste and has a "service" job, implying permanent salaried employment. Rita, her younger daughter, says that if she marries outside her caste, then people will say that the girl is not under her parent's control or the girl is shameless, as she has no consideration for her parent's reputation. She admits that the social norms of the village have not permitted the girls to make decisions for themselves. Her family, however, has however given her the freedom to easily confide in them if she ever wants to marry someone of her choice. If her parents do not agree to it, she will leave the person and marry whomever her parents want her to marry.

Vishwakarma Caste. Gulabkali is a fifty-year-old mother who has been quite successful in marrying her three daughters to perfect grooms whom she says are "*goolar ke phool*" (sycamore flowers). One of her sons works in Mumbai in a private company and sends money regularly. Her sons also help pursue their family business of making furniture and accessories needed in a wedding ceremony. Gulabkali's husband works in Grameen Bank in Rai Bareilly and comes home only on weekends. She confesses that her mother was not at all happy with the idea of her marrying a man who was dark, but her father forced her to marry him. She is elated at the fact that the proposals for her daughters came from the groom's side only and she did not find any difficulty in searching for them or marrying her daughters, as there were no dowry demands then. She herself is against dowry and says that she did not take anything in her son's marriage; instead, she had spent lavishly on the marriage. Now she is facing problems in fixing the marriage of her younger daughter as people are asking for unreasonable dowry. She says that she will not marry her daughter in a hurry but will wait until she finds a handsome and understanding groom for her daughter. She has educated her daughters well up to the high-school level and feels that a girl should marry only after she is financially independent. On their freedom to choose their life partner, she says that if her daughter likes to marry according to her choice, then she will not have any problem if the boy is of the same caste and has a permanent job. She feels that girls should never do anything which would spoil their parents' repute. She says that if her daughter elopes with someone and marries him and does not come back, then she will have no problem. But if she comes back, then she will kill her, for after committing such a heinous crime, she will not make a pickle of her daughter and keep her in the jar ("*achar banake seeshi main nahin rakhenge.*") Clearly, this utterance by the mother indicates familial violence as punishment for transgression that must have been part of the girls' socialization so as to instill fear and obedience in them as suggested by Raval et al. (2010). She says that her eyes have been damaged twice due to smoke from the mud *chulha* (stove), but she is not able to buy a cooking gas for herself as the cylinder is very expensive and she still has the responsibility of settling the youngest daughter. Vandana, Gulabkali's youngest daughter, has studied till high school in the village and has never been to the nearby town of Allahabad. She, too, like the other young girls, wants to marry someone who has a family in the village but stays in the city and has a permanent job. She also wants her mother to give her a cooking gas at marriage because she does not like cooking on the mud *chulha*. She admits that her parents have given her enough liberty and she can easily confide in them if she ever likes someone.

From these narratives, it appears that non-Kurmi mothers are not only prepared to grant more freedom to their daughters, they would also like them to be economically independent. The constraints they experience are not merely on account of poor economic circumstances but also the social constraints of upper-caste intimidation that do not allow them to go far in granting more liberty to their daughters, thereby restricting their opportunities. Both mothers of the Gupta and the Vishwakarma families highlighted the not-so-conducive atmosphere in the village that indicates societal pressures and constraints at the village level affecting women and girls of various castes differently.

Narratives of Muslim Women

Lahurpur village has very few Muslim households within the village, as the village just adjoining is predominantly of Muslims and Dalits. The few

Muslim households of Lahurpur reside outside the village in a *Mohalla* in the bazaar area on Hanuman Ganj, which for *Panchayat* jurisdictional purposes is part of Lahurpur village. The present *Pradhan* of the village is a Muslim woman elected on a reserved seat whom we first approached to seek permission to do the village fieldwork. This also gave us an opportunity to interview her in her household setup. Another elderly Muslim whom we interviewed was a chance encounter, as she was resting by the wayside and seemed eager to talk to us, from whom we obtained the most fascinating life story.

Ansari-Muslim

Shaheen, the village *Pradhan,* is Ansari-Muslim by caste and has been married since she was eighteen years old. Her husband owns a footwear store in the bazaar area, and it is at his instigation that she stood for the election and won the *Panchayat* seat. She is a clear example of a proxy *Pradhan* whose husband acts on her behalf. She is thirty-five years old and the mother of four children. One of her relatives had fixed her marriage. Shaheen says she did not even see her husband before marrying. She observes that *Ansari* do not marry outside their caste, and if someone marries outside their caste, then he/she is socially boycotted by the villagers of the same caste. Shaheen says that people have married by choice outside their religion but they have converted to Islam before marrying. She observed that girls in her community are not allowed to move freely. They stay at home and do household work, and they also have to follow the *purdah* (veiling) system rigidly. She says that inspired by television, children are defying their parents and marrying on their own, and she does not let her children watch television. Rashid and Rizwan, her nephews studying in high school, when questioned about their freedom to choose their spouse, confide that they have freedom up to certain limits. They say if they ever want to marry by choice outside their caste, they will negotiate with their parents and are confident that their parents would agree to it. But they quickly added that should their parents not agree, they would abide by their parents' advice. Although dowry is not prevalent in their community, the girls' parents themselves give everything like furniture, electrical gadgets, utensils, and so on. Shaheen earns about five hundred rupees a month rolling beedis. Just adjoining her house is a tailoring class teaching Muslim girls of the *Mohalla* who seemed shy to answer our questions but quite determined to make a livelihood.

Muslim Sheikh

Johra is a seventy-year-old Muslim Sheikh and still has a glitter in her eyes when she tells us of her earlier days. She had a small family of three children, two daughters and a son. Her husband used to earn enough by printing saris, and she led a happy life. Though she had twelve children, nine of them died due to some ailment, and only three survived. With their meager savings, Johra and her husband also managed to construct a house. All her children are educated up to high school. Johra says that her husband used to love his daughters more than his son. He used to fulfill all their demands. Soon her sunny days ended, and their life changed when her elder daughter, when she was barely eighteen years old, eloped and married her uncle who was then already married. For four years, they looked for their daughter but got no information about her. Johra's husband lost his mental balance and died. Johra says that her daughter was very innocent and simple but the villagers coaxed and helped her to run away. She says that if she had known about her daughter's intentions, she would have married her to him, rather than let her elope. She married her younger daughter at the very young age of thirteen years to a distant relative, scared that she too would follow in her sister's footsteps. Johra says that in her community, one can marry within the family (i.e., a married man with a family), but *nikah* (marriage contract) takes place with the parents' consent only. As times have changed, children prefer to marry by choice, as they do not like the proposals brought by their parents. In her community as well, people have started taking dowry though *mehr* (bride wealth obligation paid by the groom) is compulsory in the marriage. She herself had given dowry in her younger daughter's marriage. Now she is a frail and poor widow living on alms.

These narratives of Muslim women suggest that they lead more circumscribed lives with greater social and family disciplines. The fear that mothers in the village express about the moral climate being not conducive and their daughters coming under bad influences is borne out by the fact that village members themselves could guide the girls in immoral ways, contrary to social disciplines. Social disciplines regulating interactions and family discipline by way of constant moral policing are the reality of the lived constraints of young Muslim girls. Although the women are coaxed to access opportunities for political positions, they do not show enthusiasm for girls' education as a way of mobility to urban lifestyles in the way the Hindu women and girls in the village do. Shaheen was too reticent in the interview despite holding a political post and had to be coaxed to answer our questions even in the presence of her husband.

Dalit Women's Narratives

The Dalit settlement in the village has a separate access path from the road leading to the village, and they all seemed to use only this separate path, although their huts adjoin some of the Kurmi houses. The *Anganwadi* (preschool child center) worker, who is a Kurmi woman with a postgraduate degree, lives close to the Dalit settlement and relates to them well. It was in front of her house that we had the group discussion with Dalit women. As the Dalits are well aware of their growing political clout in the state's politics, they expected that we would help them leverage some gains. A Pasi family that got a small plot of land allotted under a family planning beneficiary scheme during an earlier stint of Bahujan Samaj Party (BSP) rule in the state was now facing threat of eviction by the Kurmis in the village, as they were seen to be occupying land of prime value near the bazaar area, and they requested our help to approach the District Magistrate. Much to our disappointment, the group discussion wound up after a short while as they lost interest when there were no immediate benefits in sight for them. Dalit women's narratives describe more of their problems arising out of their poverty condition.

Shanno is a thirty-year-old Pasi woman. Both her husband and she work in others' fields and manage to earn 500–600 rupees per month. Her husband gets 3–4 kg of wheat or any grain every day for working ten hours a day. Shanno works day and night to make both ends meet but still cannot provide her children with two meals, education, and clothes. She has three sons and also had a daughter who died a month after her birth. Married when she was twenty years old, her father had fixed the marriage. She is happy with her marriage and feels that her husband is quite understanding and caring. Her only discontentment is that she is not able to build a house. She lives on rent in a small hut made of mud and straw. She is against love marriages and says that one should marry according to parents' choice, and children who marry against their parents' wishes are disloyal. Shanno explained that when a poor Dalit is not able to find a bride, they would buy one from an even poorer family from Bihar or elsewhere, clearly indicating that singleness for both men and women is an unviable survival option for poor Dalits.

Geeta is a thirty-year-old poor Pasi woman who makes bricks with her husband and gets 3 kg of wheat for ten hours of work, while her husband gets 50 rupees per day. She has three sons and a daughter. Being poor, she sends her children to government school; although, she said that no teaching takes place in government schools. If her children are educated and want to marry by choice, she will have no problem with whom they have chosen, although she married according to her parents' choice.

Shanti is a khatik, another Dalit caste. She does not remember her age, but it seems she is past eighty. The hut is in a guava orchard that her son has taken on lease and pays 14,000 rupees every year to the owner. They have no permanent dwelling and keep wandering from place to place. She has four sons and three daughters. Her husband died twenty years ago. She married off her youngest daughter to a dumb man two years ago because she did not have enough to give as dowry in her marriage. She regrets that she has spoiled her daughter's life, who has never been to school and deeply regrets it now. Her daughter's husband is a laborer and earns 40 rupees a day. She has a three-month-old daughter who she says she will educate to become financially independent. Her husband beats her and does not give her food, but she cannot leave him as she has nowhere to go. She says that if her mother would have had money, her life would have been different. She thinks that a girl is born only to face miseries and serve the males.

Clearly, Dalit women seem to think that only by moving out of poverty and acquiring education is it possible to have more freedom in their personal lives.

TRADITION AND MARRIAGE BY CHOICE

Ethnographic research in this village revealed that across caste groups, young girls and women still preferred marriages to be arranged by parents. Both parents and daughters felt it was the moral obligation and duty of the parents to do so. Women felt that dowry demands have increased across the board and that over time it has become more difficult for them to find suitable matches for their daughters. Although over the years, girls have become more educated and generally have higher educational attainments than women of the older generation, it has not changed marriage practices or made them economically independent. What it has surely done is allow women to give freedom to their daughters and sons "up to a certain limit" as most put it. They also felt the need to consider the opinions of their daughters in the choice of a partner and in some cases, made them rethink the kind of relationships they would maintain with their daughters-in-law. However, women overwhelmingly felt that the husbands would have the final say in the choice of their children's spouses. Almost all of the mothers hoped that their daughters' lives would be better than theirs and hoped that they would not be burdened with the rigors of toil that village life ordained. Mothers who, on account of poverty, could only settle their daughters with poor matches felt overwhelmingly guilty doing so.

Jeffery and Jeffery (1996) note of rural Bijnor, which is probably true of most rural North India,

> Settling children in marriage was an important parental obligation. It should not and could not be left to the children themselves. Indeed, in rural Bijnor, it was inappropriate for the bride and the groom either to be asked their opinion or to speak up during the marriage negotiations. Parents with adolescent children would be roundly criticized if they failed to execute their duties in a timely and careful fashion. But doing so often seemed a heavy responsibility. There would be urgency but also fear that excessive haste could result in mistakes, especially

> during the delicate negotiations when arranging a marriage with virtual strangers. (Jeffery and Jeffery, 1996, 98)

Both among Muslims and Hindus, the increase in dowry and other expectations has caused problems in finding grooms. Bringing up daughters so that they do not go astray and finding a suitable match for them are indeed big burdens for parents. What is interesting to note is that the women are aware of the problem but do not seem to think of ways to circumvent the problems as when they say that "times are bad" or "the moral climate" is not conducive. If by empowerment we understand autonomy, the ability to assert choice and exercise agency, the ability to understand social-structural constraints and yet not feel compelled to be constrained by them but to think of ways of exercising freedom and living life freely, then it is clear that for these women who understand the issues, the domain of freedom needs to be enlarged both socially and psychologically. This requires cognizance of their perceptions of how social disciplines shape their lives.

PERCEPTIONS OF SOCIAL DISCIPLINES

For the women of Lahurpur, the reproduction of the caste-gender system means the internalization of the social disciplines of village life, of which veiling, or taking the *ghunghat,* is an essential aspect (Chowdhry, 1993). Married women are expected to wear the end of the sari as a veil to cover their heads and faces, and the modes of veiling differ according to the nature of the encounter with the "Other." In general, the greater the perception of the person as a stranger, the more fully they are expected to cover their head and face. Unmarried girls are socialized to take on the veil when they get married and move to their marital village. A few women whom we met did not take on the veil, and when asked, reported that they were visiting their parental home in the village, what is referred to as *maika* and hence enjoyed a reprieve from veiling that they otherwise observe in their marital village.

Let us examine how women and young girls of Lahurpur perceive the social disciplines that bind them in the reproduction of the caste-gender system.

Shaheen, the Muslim woman and village Pradhan, attends only few *gram panchayat* meetings. She says that if her presence in the meeting is required, only then she goes for the meeting. According to her, girls in her community are not allowed to move freely. Shaheen's case illustrates how her community's curtailment of girls' freedom to move about freely continues into their adult life even when they hold an elected public office.

Younger women of the well-off Kurmi households perceive social disciplines as an imposition that is still difficult for them to shake off, despite the social changes affecting their caste and class. Tara, the wife of the *Zilla Parishad* member, says her husband gets angry when she does not take *ghunghat* when they go out. She would like her daughter to marry in the city as there is no purdah system in cities. Tara pointed out the discrimination she suffers as her sisters-in-law in Allahabad wear *salwar* suits, which she cannot wear in the village. Given a chance, she would also like to live in Allahabad. Shivkali, her mother-in-law, feels that girls should necessarily cover their heads in front of their elders to show respect and save themselves from evil men. She gets offended when her daughter-in-law does not cover her head while performing household chores, as one should also cover the head while cooking to prevent hair from falling into the food. Tara initially found it difficult to cover her head but has become accustomed to it. Manju's parents have not imposed any restrictions on her, and she is free to go anywhere and wear anything. She admits, however, that other girls in the village are not as free and have many restrictions imposed upon them. Her friend, Renu Singh, is never allowed to step out of her house besides going to college and has never seen or been to her fields. Although she has completed her BA degree, she is not allowed to look for a job. Manju's family has a house in Allahabad, but she stays in the village with her parents as they do not want her to live in the city.

Unlike Manju's parents, Seema's parents are not that well-off and have much less land, though they belong to the Kurmi caste. She says her husband is very supportive, and she frankly admits that she is freer in her husband's house in Delhi than in her parents' house, as in Delhi she can wear *salwar* suits and jeans, and her husband does not object to it. With education, urban living, and freedom, Seema exuded confidence that was apparent, for she clearly dominated the focus group meeting.

Wadley (2000) has argued that the body is the locus of social control, and female bodies are impressed with prevailing historical forms of selfhood, desire, and femininity. In opposing veiling, young girls are resisting the selfhood imposed upon them through social disciplines exercised over their bodies. They want to use clothing as a marker of identity in which they would control their bodies through their choice of clothing as markers of self-identity (Wadley, 2008).

Anuradha, a young Kurmi girl from a not-so-well-off family, complains that in the village, a girl does not enjoy her childhood. She is forced to do all the household work and attend to her younger brothers and sisters. She laments that girls are not able to enjoy their lives as boys do. Boys can roam freely and do whatever they want compared to girls who have so many restrictions. She told us that all her friends, including her, have been cooking since they were seven years old.

Mothers feel that if their daughters were to be educated and become financially independent, then they would be able to access freedom in their lives, making their lives immensely better than theirs, and most women want that for their daughters. While for the women of the dominant Kurmi Singraur caste, it was matter of changing their attitudes, for the women of the other castes in the village, sending their daughters for higher studies or for a job is a social challenge as the atmosphere of the village is not conducive for girls to move freely. Young girls like Vandana of the Vishwakarma caste feel that one should not stay in the village as there are no opportunities for one's growth.

There is a clear-cut boundary among different castes in the village. While at social events like marriages they visit each other's houses, only men of both communities eat together in each other's places. It is the tradition that women of different castes do not dine together. Priyanka, a fourteen-year-old Kurmi girl, made astute observations of village social relations as she says that in the village there is a rigid system of caste groupism. Different castes stay together. People of low caste do not mix freely with people of high caste, and so people of different castes cannot even think of marrying each other. She feels that a girl should be financially independent and then marry.

Women take the *ghungha*t before family and village elders even when personal and social relations are otherwise friction-ridden. Even as Gulabkali of the Vishwakarma caste was telling me how and why she and her husband had severed all relations with her father-in-law on account of a property dispute, her daughter announced in a whispering tone that her father-in-law was going to pass by the adjacent house. Gulabkali immediately took the ends of her sari and covered her head. This is the behavior of a woman nearly sixty years of age. Even *Dalits* practice veiling in the village. Sumitra, a married Pasi woman, says that it is compulsory to take *ghunghat* in front of elders, whether they feel free with it or not, though she does not do so in her maternal house. That married women often exercise the privilege of the village daughter to remove the veil while visiting the natal village, and that they otherwise wear it, is itself an indication of their longing to get rid of it and of it being an imposition that they dislike.

Sushila Devi, a Kurmi mother of three school-going sons, reflects on the kind of relations she would maintain with her future daughters-in-law. She opposes *purdah* (veiling) and says that she would ask her daughters-in-law to cover their heads only in front of their father-in-law. She would try to have friendly relations with them and would not mind if they wear *salwar* suits. She says that they have to work hard in the fields. Her father-in-law never lets her take rest, and if she does not work, he asks her to go back to her *maika* or her maternal house. She notes that daughters-in-law are freer than daughters. They can move about freely and can talk to anybody because they have their husband's support, whereas daughters have restrictions on their movement and on conversing with strangers. She feels that a girl leads a more comfortable and unrestricted life in her husband's house as compared to her parent's house.

Jeffery and Jeffery (1996) note the nature of family discipline embedded in early socialization in the villages they studied:

> Throughout a girl's childhood, her parents would prepare her for her inevitable marriage. . . . She would learn to be circumspect in how she dressed and taught to cover her head to signal her bashfulness [*sharm*] and respect for her seniors. Her compliance was likely to be fragile, however, and it would have to be constantly constructed and enforced through her elders' strenuous discipline. . . . Through constant reiterations about the demeanor of women who had been married into her natal village, through watching how young married women conducted themselves, she would come to understand the difference between being a "daughter of the village" and a "bride of the village." (Jeffery and Jeffery, 1996, 6–7)

NORM VIOLATION AND CONSEQUENCES

Caste and gender socialization within rural families are indeed very strict, as the consequences of violating caste disciplines and social norms have serious repercussions for the families and individuals involved. For centuries the boundaries of caste and the reproduction of the caste structure and the social relations it entails have been maintained by caste panchayats and village panchayats, which were informal regulatory bodies that traditionally governed the everyday conduct of individuals and communities in villages. This included marriage and family matters managed by the caste panchayats that existed in all villages for each *jati* (subcastes) and that expanded to the larger circle of several nearby villages to form a higher body. As Hindu marriage rules in North India stipulate village as well as *Gotra* or lineage and *Khap* exogamy alongside caste endogamy, one of the roles of caste panchayats, among several other roles, was to police marriage alliances to ensure that caste and other norms were followed and, importantly, to monitor women's sexuality so that intercaste liaisons were not formed to breach caste norms. This form of policing enforced caste loyalties that maintained the reproduction of the caste structure. In contemporary times, the role of these caste panchayats has expanded from the surveillance of individuals and families to enforce caste loyalties to the bio-politics of caste, with its integration into the modern state's democratic politics of rights and entitlements that also requires the enforcement of caste loyalties (Ingole, 2019).

These traditional caste panchayats were not elected bodies and consisted solely of men considered the leading men of that caste in the village. This ensured the perpetual reproduction of patriarchal power, especially as they regulated and adjudicated issues relating to marriage and separation. Ethnographic evidence indicates that marital disputes brought before the caste panchayat are more likely to favor men than women, as they exercise patriarchal power in dispute settlement (Cohn, 1965; Moore, 1993). Moreover, when such disputes are brought for resolution to the caste panchayat, there is a significant loss of honor for the family that deters women from doing so. In certain instances, caste panchayats could penalize individuals and families with social ostracism and ex-communication. Although in present times state laws prevent such forms of punishment, they still continue to exist among groups in many villages. Enforcing the cultural codes of caste and honor in the context of intercaste liaisons often results in violence inflicted on the young couple by family and community. Although such violence accompanying intercaste liaisons is prevalent in most parts of the country, horrific acts of violence are reported from regions where *Khap* Panchayats are active, as in Haryana, western Uttar Pradesh, and parts of Rajasthan (Chowdhry, 1997). Despite modern state law and the state legal structures of adjudication, the informal system of traditional mechanisms for enforcing social and caste norms is still prevalent. Gender scripts of socialization within families are inscribed with these cultural codes of caste and honor, which in everyday life become the social disciplines that govern young women and men who are well aware of the consequences of norm violation.

RETHINKING RURAL WOMEN'S MODERNITY

The ethnographic findings suggest that rural women perceive modernity in terms of freedom, choice, agency, and autonomy in their private lives. The expression of that freedom is perceived at the moment as the overcoming of constraints in their mobility, freedom to take up jobs, freedom in choice and style of clothing, being given voice to dissent on parental choice of life partner, and freedom to marry by choice within the caste group. For the older women and mothers, such modernity is cherished and desired for their daughters, in terms of a freer life in urban settings without much of a change in their own lifestyles in the villages.

The paradox of a freer life for daughters with those of their prospective daughters-in-law who are to marry into the villages was apparent. Not many were ready to articulate choices and freedom for them, except just one woman who said she would maintain a better relationship with her daughter-in-law than what perhaps she had herself received as one. Many of the younger mothers complained of receiving severe treatment from the mother-in-law or father-in-law, especially regarding their expectations of work. Even so, all of them did expect their prospective daughters-in-law to do hard work as was required in the village setting. Even the young high school boys, some of whom we interviewed, wanted their wives to take on the veil, wear saris rather than *salwar* suits, and abide by the social disciplines of the village. To our surprise, though, we did find a number of married women, both young and middle-aged, wearing lipstick during the day even when they were engaged in home-based tasks like cleaning mustard seeds, which has now become an everyday cosmetic wear like puffing their faces with talcum powder. This suggests that while social disciplines have remained the same, the social norms and expectations of femininity and beauty have changed. By and large, the women are tied down to drudgery and routine housework and tending to cattle.

Contrary to the general expectation, rural women do not perceive modernity in terms of becoming rights-bearing citizens, participating in decision-making in the Panchayats or Self-Help Groups (SHGs), or having a voice in development planning at the village level, although they are increasingly brought within the fold of participatory development. But they do perceive modernity in terms of overcoming feudal-patriarchal mindsets that restrict their freedom in their private lives and decision-making in their households. For the very poor *Dalit* women, such freedom in their personal lives, though important and much desired, was also accompanied by the expectation of state measures to mitigate their poverty and efforts to overcome caste dominance. It is for the very poor rural women that modernity in the public sphere, such as state's development measures and affirmative actions, was a necessary condition, but even for them modernity in the private sphere of a more equal treatment in their intimate relations was important. It was their general feeling that such freedom could be more easily accessible in the urban environment than in the village setting.

Modernity is generally understood to entail changes in the realms of polity, society, economy, and the self. In the realm of polity, the modern state, unlike premodern states, effects a contract between the ruler and the governed that confers on those governed certain rights as citizens within the framework of a nation-state. In the sphere of society, the nature of social relations governed by customs and traditions is gradually displaced and dis-embedded into more contractual relations, and many thinkers view "society" itself as a construction of modernity that displaced the earlier notion of "community." Economic relations are similarly transformed into more and more market relations. By effecting all these changes, modernity also reconstructs "personhood" with the emergence of "individuals" exercising free will and reason. However, it is important to note that in rural India there are two levels of affiliation, namely citizenship of states and membership of communities, that are negotiated by individuals in the plural regulatory system of formal law and informal adjudicating systems that Cohn (1965) characterized as "lawyers' law" and "local law-ways." Despite the constitutional setup of democratic decentralization of governance through elected village panchayats, the traditional caste panchayats in villages still continue, making the interaction of modernity and tradition more complex as notions of justice and rights are not just in the realm of the state but are appropriated by caste panchayats and other non-state adjudicating fora in the name of religion, caste, culture, and history. As scholars have noted, the governance of polity and governance of community overlaps powerfully to regulate sexuality and normalize the politics of honor, and so "the claims of citizenship in the realm of the domestic sphere must be understood in the interstices of the relationship between law, violence and governance" (Baxi, Rai, and Ali, 2006, 1242). Recently, family courts or *Nari Adalats* have been set up as Alternate Dispute Resolution (ADR) entities where non-state agencies assist women in distress to resolve marital and family disputes by way of counseling outside of the state legal structures, but these are not widespread in rural areas and neither are they free from the influence of patriarchal cultural values (Vatuk, 2013).

By exploring the aspirations of women and young girls to changes in marriage practices, this ethnographic study sought to understand how patriarchy, customs, and traditions operate in the form of social disciplines that constrain young women's lives and how they perceive these social disciplines and attempt to carve out spaces of freedom. Most young women seek to access greater freedom in life through education and a move into urban areas while leaving the parental responsibility of arranging marriages intact, yet granting them some choice and more agency in partner selection. In this analysis of women's aspirations and marriage norms, we witness women's attempts to reconstruct their personhood/self, whereby they seek to exercise free will by overcoming the binds of custom and tradition. The nationalist resolution of keeping colonial modernity out of the domestic and private sphere, while assigning urban middle-class women the task of protecting the culture and spiritual life in the domestic sphere, as highlighted by Chatterjee (1994), has clearly inhibited the spread in the private sphere of the values of modernity, namely freedom and equality, thereby subjecting rural women to cultural norms of patriarchy in their intimate lives.

Chapter 3

Marriage Aspirations and Choice among Urban Women

As young urban women have greater exposure to contemporary global trends in fashion, and ideas about friendship and intimacy, marriage patterns and practices seem to be changing faster in metropolitan centers and at a slower pace in smaller towns. In metropolitan cities, girls are more attuned to ideas from current global cultural flows, being active participants in adapting them in the spheres of work, education, lifestyles, and fashion. In smaller towns, girls aspire to rise from their small-town social status to join their globalized sisters in metropolitan cities, influenced by television and other media, much like rural women aspire through marriage to move out from their villages to the cities.

Marriage issues that serve as markers for urban women to position themselves on the scale of tradition and modernity are mainly preferences for arranged marriage or love marriage, parents' attitudes toward mate selection, dowry, the importance of horoscope matching, freedom to socialize with male friends and/or having boyfriends, intercaste marriage, orientation to employment before and after marriage, and the importance of financial independence before and after marriage. The issue of "arranged" versus "love" marriage itself encompasses many of the issues of freedom and choice noted above, as the latter is perceived by the youth as giving them greater freedom from some binding duties and responsibilities toward parents-in-law, irrespective of being in nuclear or joint-family settings. Precisely for these reasons of greater freedom for young couples, elders in the family see such marriages as transgressive behaviors needing curtailment, and arranged marriages are perceived by them to offer greater securities, social and psychological, to both the young couple and the elders in the family.

Sociological studies have recently focused on "arranged" versus "love" marriage, as many working women in metropolitan cities choose their partners while at work or through dating apps and exercise their choice to live as couples either within or outside of marriage (Banerji, Martin, and Desai, 2008). Netting (2010) has empirically substantiated the claim made by Appadurai (1996b) that as the Western-inspired ideal of romantic love encounters Indian family values, Indian upper-middle-class youth respond by generating hybrid goals and systems of mate selection by linking imagination to hope and using their voice within their families to win recognition and support for their choice.

Interreligious marriages, especially between Hindu and Muslim couples, acquire strong political overtones such as the "Love Jihad" controversies, and intercaste marriages of Dalit and non-Dalits lead not infrequently to violent caste clashes (Das, 2010; Pathak, 2014; Rao, 2015; Iwanek, 2016; Ahuja and Ostermann, 2016). Whereas earlier sociological literature was concerned with marriage and kinship, recent works have also focused on sexuality and sexual politics (Menon, 2009; Legg and Roy, 2013). For most women and men in India, sexuality is primarily expressed within marriage, which is more than sexuality with its emphasis on the reproduction of family, lineage, and culture. Reproduction is not merely a sexual contract but is also part of religion with scriptural sanctions.

The divergent pulls of tradition and modernity impact aspects of marriage, sexuality, and reproduction. As smaller towns come under the cultural influence of modernizing globalization, young girls and their families seek to reconstruct their conceptions of "arranged" marriage, attempting to reconcile traditions with their current expectations in the choice of their marriage partners. Of interest to explore is the extent of "choice" girls seek or desire in choosing their partners, their views on dowry, expectations of their partners' desirable qualities, and how much of freedom they seek both before and after marriage regarding their career and employment. Additionally, it is important to examine the extent girls would seem both interested and capable of crossing the bounds of tradition regarding dowry, love marriage, intercaste and interreligious marriage, and their awareness of the consequences of such transgressions both from their family and social circles. Equally interesting to explore is how educated women see marriage in purely individualistic terms of their own self-interest and future, and of not being a burden on their parents beyond their college education, or whether they see it as an important part of family decision and strategy to vindicate the honor of their families and to enhance, not jeopardize the family's social standing. Sharangapani (2010) has noted that her informants perceived themselves through multiple registers not only as individuals with goals and desires but also as members of families and extended kinship networks, suggesting that identity is a fluid site of contradictions of intersecting discourses for specific objectives.

CONTEMPORARY PERSPECTIVES ON URBAN WOMEN AND MARRIAGE

Today, the vast majority of marriages in India are termed "arranged." But its opposition to the category of "love marriage" is a simplified polarization that cannot mirror social change. This has prompted scholars to suggest that the dichotomy between "arranged" and "love" marriage requires rethinking, as with new lifestyles and social realities, notions regarding marriage, love, and gender roles are constantly being reworked in society.

"Arranged marriage" involves parents and family elders in choice and decision-making in marriage as it is within endogamous caste (*jati*) groups according to cultural norms. Among the Brahmins, it entailed prohibition of *sagotra* marriages (marriage within the same *gotra*) and these rules also vary between the Dravidian norms of kinship and marriage in South India and the rules of North Indian society, where in some regions intra-village choice of partners is prohibited as an incest taboo. Recently, there has been active intervention by young girls and boys in planning their marriages in conjunction with their parents in terms of consent to the choice of partner based on attributes, and yet fulfilling to a large extent the cultural rules on mate selection, whether horoscope matching is done or not. Matrimonial websites also enable this form of active intervention in planning one's marriage.

Emphasizing that the term "agency" as the capacity to act is better than the term "choice" that seems to connote a consumerist viewpoint, scholars have noted that many women do not associate arranged marriage with a lack of agency (Sharangpani, 2010). However, "choice" does not always connote a consumerist viewpoint; rather, it indicates the desire to make their own choice even if they do not have the freedom to do so and hence lack agency or the capacity to act. The desire to make one's choice precedes the ability to act, and such desire could be the effect of various social factors leading to increased self-awareness of gaining autonomy over all aspects of one's life.

Increasingly young women in metropolitan cities are moving beyond the conventional love-versus-arranged marriage dichotomy to focus instead on achieving specific goals like intimacy, equality, and personal choice by using both systems either separately, simultaneously, or in creative combinations (Netting, 2010). The introduction of online matchmaking services has prompted a general shift toward more individualistic patterns of partner search, while simultaneously maintaining and even reinforcing traditional criteria and requirements (Titzmann, 2013). However, marriages are still overwhelmingly termed "arranged," as opposed to "love marriage," which also implies within-caste marriage, while love marriage could be either within or outside of one's caste, religion, ethnicity, or nationality.

Many matrimonial profile descriptions suggest that societal expectations are influenced by the image of a new "Indian Woman," who is confident and takes her own decisions but stays culturally rooted. This prompts the matrimonial site users to harmonize social expectations with their personal intentions. Despite the influence of modernity and global culture on the urban middle class, there is still a persistent male preference for modesty and femininity, with young men preferring family-oriented, "simple" wives who "respect elders," as seen in matrimonial advertisements. Marriage decisions still remain largely within the purview of the family, as only less than 5 percent of all female respondents of the *Indian Human Development Survey* (2005) stated they had a primary role in choosing their husbands, while 62 percent felt they were consulted in the choice (Banerji, Martin, and Desai, 2008).

The emerging middle class has become a factor in the increase of intercaste marriages, with openness to such marriages rooted in a desire for upward mobility (Ahuja and Ostermann, 2016). Among Scheduled Caste individuals, interest in intermarriage increases with income while the opposite is true of the upper castes. Despite the legalization of intercaste marriages some fifty years ago, new intermarried couples are still threatened with violence by their own families and communities. Interreligious marriages, especially Hindu-Muslim marriages, are marked by heightened societal anxiety that does restrain young women from making such a choice. Changes in sexual cultures ushered in by contemporary processes of globalization include an increase in live-in couples of both sexes who postpone their marriage as well as an increase in same-sex couples living together in metropolitan cities. Professional women are also known to restate a normative sexuality in negotiating the pressures of an excessively materialist culture and changing sexual freedoms, although the demands of preserving tradition in the face of globalized modernity are not exclusive to women alone (Radhakrishnan, 2011; Derne, 2005).

GENDER SCRIPTS AND MARRIAGE

Gender scripts in India reflect both "culture-in-action" and "status-in-action" (Desai and Andrist, 2010). Marriage is part of the societal gender scripts propagated primarily by the family and community. Societal gender scripts that emphasize segregation between men and women and value girls' "decorous" and "modest" behavior are also associated with early marriage. Modernity could bring in counter-gender scripts wherein women aspiring to be educated and employed rewrite their personal gender scripts in favor of such aspirations, which would likely see families retaining power over marriage decisions only partly or none at all. Desai and Andrist note that Indian families are increasingly torn in two directions: status attainment through gender performance being constructed as part of a traditional ideology that a modern society must transcend, or status attainment through the performance of modernity.

Through the narratives of women, we examine the ways girls and their families in a non-metropolitan city, not fully engulfed by global cultural flows, navigate the conflicting pulls of status attainment through gender performance constructed as part of a traditional gender ideology or status attainment through the performance of modernity, and the ways girls seek to write their personal gender scripts of marriage, accommodating in varying degrees the values and expectations of both tradition and modernity.

METHODOLOGY OF THE PRESENT STUDY

The study explores young women's preferences for "arranged" or "love marriage," their perceptions of constraints set by their families in making their choices, the opportunities they expect with higher education and employment, their choices of marriage partners, and the freedoms they wish to access both before and after marriage. Twenty young women of diverse castes (*jati*s), mostly above fifteen years of age or close to being married, many either with engineering or management education and a few with work experience, were interviewed in Allahabad (Prayagraj) in 2010. Parents present during the interviews were also interviewed.

These in-depth interviews were conducted to understand how new cultural ideas in the sphere of intimacy and marriage are shaping the aspirations of young women in small towns. Twenty respondents may be a small sample size for a statistical study of qualitative variables but are quite sufficient for an ethnographic study to generate insights by gathering individual life stories and experiences. The sample, though not random, covered a cross-section of the upper and middle castes with none from the Scheduled Castes and one from the Scheduled Tribe. Among the respondents were Brahmins (3), Thakur/Rajput (3), Kayastha (4), Bania/Vaishya (4), OBCs (3—one each from Yadav-Ahir, Patel-Kewat, and Pal castes), Punjabi Khatri (1), Punjabi Sikh (1), and Bengali Scheduled Tribe (1). (The number within brackets indicates the number of respondents in each caste group.)

Some pointers on the dynamics of sociocultural change can also be discerned as responses of different castes in the sample enable a better understanding of how caste-gender socialization of girls in families varies, and their perceptions of social norms and social disciplines that girls and families may feel compelled to abide by. This provides insight into the extent to which girls have the freedom to write their own personal gender scripts on marriage expectations and partner choice.

The narrative accounts of the respondents that were written as field notes were processed in terms of the extent of parental choice of mates, the process of finding a match for an arranged marriage, views on dowry, the girls' views on love marriage, the parents' views on love marriage, the freedoms available to girls and whether they are permitted to have boyfriends, the preferred marriage age, and whether girls have restrictions before and after marriage to pursue employment and careers. These dimensions are generally considered good indicators of whether one is modern or otherwise in matters of matrimony in India. Grouping these narrative responses by castes provides pointers on the gender-caste socialization of girls and their efforts to break free from such caste-gender patriarchal constraints to script their modern lives. The narratives are discussed in the alphabetical order of the castes and do not represent the caste hierarchy.

PARENTAL CHOICE OF MATE

Analysis to discern patterns of choice behavior within and across caste groups indicates that many young women would only marry based on the parental choice of a boy from the same caste, although the reasons given differed.

The Baniya community consists of subcastes such as Agarwal, Kesharwani, and Gupta, with variations in their caste status. The Guptas could be upper castes or Other Backward Classes (OBCs) meriting positive discrimination under the law, depending on their traditional occupations. A girl from the Agarwal subcaste, a higher caste among the Baniya, pursuing postgraduate studies, said that being a large extended family, they usually find a boy from within the family itself. A girl from the Kesharwani subcaste pursuing an engineering degree has decided to marry another engineer, her neighbor from the same subcaste, his mother being a distant relative of her mother. Her mother, too, had married based on her choice, a man who used to tutor her and of the same caste. She has also consented to her son choosing his coworker as his spouse from outside their caste. A girl of the Gupta subcaste pursuing a management course has her batch mate as a boyfriend and looks forward to marrying him. Although his parents know of their relationship and have accepted her as their prospective daughter-in-law, her parents are unaware of it and she does not know if they will accept him as he is from another caste. She hopes to convince her parents and only marry after obtaining their permission. One can discern here a greater freedom for girls among the lower subcastes than those from the higher Agarwal subcaste to choose their partners.

Brahmins considered to top the caste hierarchy abide far more strictly by their caste rules of caste endogamy and non-*sagotra* marriage. Marriage to non-Brahmin caste members is very uncommon. A Brahmin girl preparing to join an engineering course said that although marriage was not on the cards right then, she will marry according to her parents' choice only because her parents would never accept her choice. Her mother too remarked that she would turn her children out of her home if they wanted to marry someone of their choice, as it is a "parental right" to settle the children and those who marry by their choice do not have good company, do not respect their parents' sentiments, and are selfish. Another Brahmin girl thought that it is her mother's right to find her partner as her father had died, and she would never do anything to hurt her mother. Her mother too candidly remarked that elders, generally parents, decide about their children's marriage without even discussing it with them. She was of the view that children are too immature to take this big step. If her children ever wanted to marry someone who is educated and well-settled in life, then she would consider the alliance only if the boy is of the same caste. A girl who had completed an engineering course and had a job offer clearly preferred an arranged marriage, and her mother too was confident that she would not marry according to her choice as she was a simple girl who knew her father was very conservative. While her father said he would consider it if she had found for herself a well-settled boy of the same caste, he indicated that he was actively looking out for a match for her in the same IT industry so that she could continue her career even after her marriage. All the Brahmin girls indicate they prefer arranged marriage within the caste. Both parents and girls are of the view that it is the sole right of parents to arrange their daughters' marriages. Despite this strong bond of tradition, they are very liberal about girls' education as two of the respondents have aspired for engineering education and hope to pursue their careers.

The Kayastha caste, perceived as culturally more advanced and forward-looking, held administrative positions in pre-colonial administrations in North India and were early participants of colonial modernity as well. A Kayastha girl who completed a dual master's degree and had joined a Call Center in Delhi confided that a Sikh boy in her office had indeed proposed to her, but she rejected it as she feared that her father would call her back from Delhi and then confine her in the house as he was both strict and conservative. She had to leave her job to take care of her father after her mother died. Another girl pursuing an Engineering degree had found herself a boyfriend from among her classmates, a forward-looking Brahmin from the southern state of Andhra Pradesh. Although she desired to marry him, there were not only caste but also linguistic, ethnic, and regional cultural differences between them, and she was well aware of the likely opposition from both families. They plan to get married only when their parents agree, however late it may be, but her parents have different marriage expectations for her. Her mother does not think that she will marry by her choice, and if she does, she would prefer the boy to be of the same caste, as marrying outside the caste would earn the ire of the elders in the family. Her father is also rigid about caste, as he stated forthrightly that if she wants to marry someone of her choice outside the caste, he will not accept it even if the boy is good. He felt that children who marry against the wishes of their parents forget the sacrifices of the parents in bringing them up and create embarrassment for them. A Bengali Kayastha girl in a management program wants to marry her boyfriend from the Gupta caste and is hoping that neither parent would object to it, although she is certain that her relatives would object and would likely put pressure on her parents. She thinks that parents should not object if children want to marry someone of their choice just because of the caste, as even marriages within the same caste can sometimes fail. A Bengali Kayastha girl pursuing a course in Biotechnology hopes to continue with a doctoral program and only upon completion would she like to marry. Her parents, however, will not mind if she marries according to her choice as they also had a "love marriage," but she would like to marry according to her parents' wishes as she is not confident about her choice. Moreover, she thinks that it is her father's task to find a boy for her. Her father has even told her several times that if she likes a boy, she should tell him so he could go to the boy's house and talk to his father. Her younger sister has a Brahmin boyfriend, her coworker in a software company, and they have plans to get married, although she has not disclosed it to anyone, not even her parents, as she fears disclosing it would jeopardize her sister's marriage prospects, as the sisters would likely be perceived as not being of not good character. It is evident from the above profiles that the Kayastha caste values girls' higher education. Whereas the Uttar Pradesh Kayastha parents are more conservative and want their daughters to marry within their caste, the Bengali Kayastha girls are hoping for a more liberal stance from their parents to make their own choice of partners.

Rajputs belong to Kshatriya caste and have historically been the ruling class of kings and their warrior kinsmen. Given their martial culture, it is generally believed that patriarchal dominance is widely prevalent among them, though they too have begun to give importance to girls' higher education in recent times. A Rajput girl pursuing an MBA degree wants to marry according to her choice but with the consent of her parents, though she has no boyfriend. Another girl, preparing to join medical school was fairly certain that she wanted to marry only after finishing her medical studies and getting an MD, though she already had a boyfriend from the Bania caste whom she was hoping to marry. She confided that she never wants to marry a Rajput because they do not respect women. Her mother will not object if her children want to marry on their own but prefers that the boy be of the same caste and well-settled. A girl who had completed her doctoral degree is against arranged marriage, where a girl has to compromise a lot. Though she did not say that she had a boyfriend, she was certain that she will only marry according to her choice. Her parents are very rigid about caste and would be offended if she marries outside the caste, as they fear that relatives would speak ill of them; they also think that it will be difficult for her to adjust to a family of a different caste culture. For her, though, caste is not important, and she would not verify the caste of the person if she happens to like someone. There is clearly a preference for the Rajput girls to seek partners outside of their caste on account of their perceptions of patriarchal dominance, although it is not certain that they would be able to do so precisely for the same reason, as in general, Rajput fathers are quite particular about marrying their daughters within their caste only.

Two Yadav sisters of the Ahir subcaste (OBC), who had just completed their schooling, were in for a shock when their father took them to a village in the neighboring state of Bihar purportedly for a cousin's wedding. Upon reaching there, they found that one of the sisters was going to be married off to a boy still studying, with the consummation of the marriage to take place four years later. Neither the girl nor their mother had been consulted or even informed. The two sisters were hoping to become teachers after their graduation. The unmarried sister remarked that even though times have changed, male dominance still continues. A girl of the Patel-Kewat caste, just completing school, says that she would marry according to her parents' choice as she could never think of marrying according to her own choice. Another pursuing her doctoral research from the Pal caste has not thought of marriage yet, but thinks that arranged marriages are better as parents take all the responsibility. In love marriages parents do not help if something goes wrong, as they say that it was the girl's own choice. She, like many others, is afraid of her father; if she ever has a boyfriend and her father comes to know about it, he will turn her out of the house. Her mother, though is lenient and may accept her boyfriend, but her father is rigid about caste. It is evident that among the OBC castes, girls prefer to marry within their caste according to their parents' choice as they face more restrictions and have less freedom, even as their families feel a greater pressure of caste conformity and social disapproval.

A Punjabi Khatri girl completing a management course was hoping to join a bank as she had specialized in Finance. She confessed that she had many male friends, and some of them had even proposed to her, but she has not thought about marrying yet for she wanted to work for a couple of years before doing so. She would like to marry within her caste only, as Punjabi boys are tall and macho besides being good looking. It is good to marry within familiar families as there is less chance of being deceived. Her mother stated that if her daughter wanted to marry someone of her choice, she and her husband would not object to it if the boy was good, well-settled, decent, and well-educated. A Sikh girl also pursuing management education said she would abide by her parents' choice as it is very difficult to find grooms in their community who are pure vegetarians, although her parents are very broadminded and will not object if she marries by her choice so long as the boy is not a Muslim.

A Bengali tribal girl was of the view that marriage burdened women more and made them compromise a lot. But she will marry only according to her parents' wishes, although her mother thinks she is quite mature to make her own decisions, and neither she nor her husband will have any objection.

Overwhelmingly and across castes, the respondents preferred parental choice of partners, with many parents insisting it is their right to settle children. Children also think it is the parents' responsibility to find partners for them. Many parents would be liberal enough to consider and accept a girl's choice if only the boy is of the same caste, while girls too prefer parental choice with the girl's consent. Hardly anyone stated that they were anxious to find a partner of their choice.

FINDING A MATCH FOR AN ARRANGED MARRIAGE

Finding an appropriate match for a girl or boy for an arranged marriage entails first collecting a list of prospective candidates through various sources, then scanning according to certain parameters such as wealth, income, social status, family background, the matching of horoscopes, the girl's accomplishments of which beauty is an important factor, the boy's accomplishments such as education and employment, his habits of partying and drinking, and the dowry and wedding expectations. Once the two families agree on these, only then do the boy and girl usually meet, and these days with the availability of online video communication they may first meet online. These processes such as horoscope matching, consulting astrologers and priests, or letting online conversations between the boy and the girl could vary across castes and families.

Modernity's influence on arranged marriages lies primarily in two aspects namely the matching of horoscopes in consultation with an astrologer, and whether and how long the girl and the boy are allowed to meet prior to their marriage. Whereas in earlier times, the girl and the boy only met at the auspicious moment of marriage, this is not the case in present times. Increasingly, many families are also skipping the matching of horoscopes and just letting the girl and boy decide if they are compatible when all other parameters are approved by the two parties.

A Gupta girl of Bania caste was of the view that it is not very difficult to find a groom in her family as marriages are settled within the extended family only. The Kesharwani are not very rigid about horoscope matching and only check the horoscope for any significant *dosha* or ill-effect caused by the mis-positioning of the astrological elements, and there are also many Kesharwani families in town to make the choice easier. An Agarwal girl observed that alliances in her family are found through relatives and friends and not through newspapers and matrimonial sites, and being a large family, it is possible to get a suitable alliance from the extended family itself. Horoscope matching is the first step after approval of the photos of the girl and the boy, and her parents, being rigid about it, got the children's horoscopes made when they were very young. All the Bania caste respondents said that prospective partners are sourced within the larger extended family through relatives or friends and avoid advertisements through the matrimonial sites. While horoscopes get greater scrutiny among the higher caste Bania like Agarwal, they are not altogether ignored by the others of the Bania group.

A Brahmin girl observed that marriages in her family are mostly settled through a family priest, who brings suitable alliances and mediates between the families. Parents make the decision, and children's consent is hardly taken. Usually, one informs the priest of how much one would be able to spend on the marriage and their preferences for the alliance, and the priest then brings alliances according to the defined parameters. When asked whether she has asked her daughter about her preference for marriage, her mother replied that she does not speak much. The daughter trusts her mother to act in her best interest, and the mother is also confident her daughter will abide by her choice. There has never been a love marriage in their family. They start looking for alliances mostly when the children have completed eighteen years, and matching horoscopes is very important. Another Brahmin girl, who prefers arranged marriage to love marriage, stated that her uncle has placed an advertisement for her marriage on *Shaadi.com* (a matrimonial site). Responses do come, but he discusses them only with her father. Although she is not interested in marriage, she will marry only for her parents' sake because they are worried about her, and only after her marriage is settled will her parents look out for a partner for her younger sister. Her mother stated that they have asked their relatives to suggest suitable alliances as good responses are hard to come by through newspaper advertisements. Moreover, advertisement channels would entail screening families and prospective candidates who are total strangers, and they prefer to deal with those already familiar to them. Horoscope matching is mandatory before proceeding with the alliance, as observed by her and other Brahmin respondents. Another mother noted that no marriage takes place in their family without consulting the family priest. With traditional methods of sourcing marriage partners and with parents considering it their right to fix their children's marriage, girls have much less scope to make their own choice, although their consent to an alliance is not altogether overlooked.

Among the Rajput, the binds of tradition vary across families. While one Rajput girl noted that her parents would agree to an alliance only after the horoscope matches and if the boy is of the same caste, another said that horoscope matching is not done in their family. A Rajput mother observed that horoscope matching is done before taking an alliance for further consideration, although she would be willing to accept if the daughter chose on her own as long as he belonged to the same caste. They, too, prefer not to advertise in newspapers but to look for prospective ones through a mediator, relative, or friend. Sometimes fathers and uncles place advertisements in newspaper and on matrimonial sites but do not discuss anything with the girl. Many castes do not make or match horoscopes and also do not have *gotra* (lineage name) assigned to them, as these practices had long remained exclusively Brahmanical or upper-caste ones that have slowly permeated into many caste groups.

The father of a Kayastha girl has been searching for a groom for three years but has been unable to find one. She has even overheard her father asking people to suggest suitable boys from other castes as the marriage was getting delayed, and if the boy is educated and well-settled, he would marry his daughter to him. She observed that when her parents were searching for a groom for her elder sister and could not find one for years, their neighbors would suggest boys from other castes, which offended her parents so much that they even severed relations with them. Her elder sister had placed an advertisement on *shaadi.com* and does the follow-up after getting her approval. Her father also goes through advertisements in newspapers. Her father does not give much importance to horoscopes but has to oblige when the groom's parents ask for it; he did not match the horoscopes of his son and daughter-in-law. He thinks horoscope matching is all rubbish, as whether one's marriage works or not depends on one's destiny. The mother had a contrary view on horoscope matching and would only consider an alliance if the horoscopes matched.

While matching of horoscopes is prevalent among the UP Kayasthas, it is not so among the Bengali Kayasthas for whom it is optional. It is evident that the binds of tradition are observed only when it is possible to do so and are not followed otherwise. Even parents are prepared to change their preference for within-caste marriage when they are unable to find a partner.

Enmeshed in social power relations with other castes, both the binds of tradition and patriarchal dominance in OBC caste families seem to mark the experience of young girls on marriage matters. Horoscope matching is mostly not done, nor do they have their horoscopes made. Among some lower castes with meager resources, fathers are in a haste to marry off the girls to unburden themselves, and peer pressure increases as well with delayed marriage. Girls therefore have very limited freedom to rewrite their personal gender scripts toward greater freedom.

The mother of a Punjabi Khatri girl said that horoscope matching is not done by them, and they did not ask for the horoscope of their daughter-in-law, nor did her parents ask for it. A Sikh girl said they do not search for grooms through newspapers or matrimonial sites but only through friends and relatives, as proposals from known families are reliable. A Bengali girl of Scheduled Tribe said her parents have not started actively searching for a groom and only follow up on suggestions made by relatives or friends.

In general, exercising the option to place advertisements in newspapers or online matrimonial sites and follow-up requires families to overcome their inhibitions about going public over marriage and family details to strangers, as these were always held to be private matters within the family. But the increasing number of newspaper pages devoted to matrimonial advertisements, as well as the popularity of some of the online sites, suggests that many view these as efficient channels. When the responses are numerous, it makes selection more time-efficient compared to an occasional single suggestion brought in by friends, relatives, or family priests.

VIEWS ON DOWRY

Sociological literature has highlighted the increase in dowry in India over the years, both in levels and spread, by converting bride-price prevalent in many communities to dowry. Dowry amounts are determined by the asset-linked social status of the groom's family, the level of the boy's education, and his employment and income. It still persists in other forms as well despite its legal prohibition, as the rise of neoliberal consumerism ushered in ostentatious "Bollywood-style" weddings with the bride's family bearing the expenses (Kapur, 2009). Women's perspectives on dowry explored here highlight its prevalence in different castes and the ways young women seek to contest and resist it in scripting their modernity

The Baniya community, having greater cash flow in their hands due to their business involvement than the salaried middle class, is predisposed to spend more on dowry and weddings. A Gupta girl whose marriage was fixed based on her choice and subsequently canceled noted, "I am against dowry but I know my father will give me everything without the groom's family even asking for it." Her mother too observed, "We are always ready to give dowry if we get a well-settled guy. We start to save as soon as a girl child is born in our family." Her father noted, "I will give whatever I can, even a car.

I have only two daughters and I have saved enough for their future. Though her in-laws have not demanded anything I will give whatever I can." Another Gupta girl, when asked whether she will marry her boyfriend if his parents ask for dowry, said, "No Way." She is against dowry and says she herself is the dowry for anyone who marries her. Although her father had given a good amount of dowry in her sister's marriage, she will not marry someone who asks for dowry. A Kesharwani mother observed that while there is dowry, the amount to be given is decided beforehand, which they will give whether they ask or not. They had not asked anything from their daughter-in-law's parents for her son had a "love marriage" outside of their caste, and anyway, her son was well-placed. A girl of the Agarwal caste noted that there is no dowry in her family. It is evident that Baniya girls, like many educated girls, are not in favor of dowry, while their parents do not mind giving dowry and at times are willing to forgo taking dowry for their son.

Dowry among the UP Brahmins, though not as high as among the business communities, could still be a burden for the girl's parents as they are mostly of the salaried class, with some still owning land in their ancestral village. A Brahmin girl being brought up by her widowed mother says her mother will not be able to give much dowry as she has too many liabilities but will give whatever she can. She does not want her mother to take loans for her marriage as it will add to her tensions. Her mother supports the family with incomes from the insurance money she got after her husband's death, some past savings, monthly help from her parents, and the produce from her lands. Her mother says she will give as much as it is possible within her means. While she will not be able to give a car, she will give appliances like a television, refrigerator, and washing machine that will make her daughter's daily chores easy. She can only spend half a million rupees on each daughter's wedding. An engineering graduate noted that people demand too much dowry, and her mother observed that because of excessive dowry it is very hard to find a suitable groom and also very difficult to find one if the girl crosses the age of twenty-five. Once, a boy's father demanded one million rupees in cash and a car because the boy was employed in a nationalized bank. Her father observed, "These days groom's parents ask for cash and a car too. They do not give any importance to girl's education."

As noted earlier, Brahmins in general are bound strongly to tradition and caste norms even as their modernized outlook has paved the way to encourage their daughters to pursue higher education and employment. The contradictory pulls of status attainment through gender performance of traditional ideology versus status attainment through performance of modernity, and the ways in which girls and families navigate and negotiate between the two, is discernible among them. Their strong preference for within-caste marriage, dowry payment to a limited extent, arranged marriage with the girl's consent, freedom for girls in their pursuit of education and careers, limiting social interaction with boys, and the parental hope that their investment in their daughter's education would not go waste and that her marital family would permit her to continue her career are pointers that the pull of status attainment are resolved in favor of combining both gender performance through a modified traditional gender ideology and the performance of modernity.

Dowry is widely prevalent among the Kayastha caste, and it is very difficult for a girl to get married without giving dowry, as those who do not take dowry are quite negligible. A Kayastha girl pointed out that for both of her sisters' marriages, her father had given a good amount of dowry, both in cash and kind. The dowry taken in her brother's marriage was much less in comparison to what was given to the daughters. As her father is now retired, he will not be able to give much dowry for her, as he has to keep some savings for his old age too. However, he would give everything he can if the groom's parents do not demand much. Her father observed, "if a daughter goes to a good home, then all the troubles of the parents are gone." Another Kayastha girl hopes to marry her boyfriend from a Telugu Brahmin family but knows there would be problems as there is too much dowry expectation in his family. Her boyfriend's father had spent 20 million rupees on his sister's wedding, and she thinks they would expect the same from her family as well. As her parents always hoped to get her married to an IAS (Indian Administrative Service) officer, her father would be able to give 10 million rupees as dowry. The prevalence of dowry among the Kayastha and fathers' viewing daughters as liabilities, along with their eagerness to fulfill dowry expectations to get their dream-grooms and ensure their daughter's happy marital life, suggest that they seek status attainment primarily through gender performance of traditional ideology. Despite girls being highly educated, they are unable to script their marriage without dowry as they too are caught in the same bind. However, sociocultural changes seem to have affected the Bengali Kayastha differently. While there is no system of dowry among the Bengali Kayastha, the girl's parents still have to give gold jewelry to their daughter that costs a huge amount. Although the boy's parents do not ask for dowry in the form of cash or a car, they seek educated and professionally qualified girls as working wives who could share in the expenses of the household. They do expect parents to provide security for their daughters through gold and education and are also more open to marrying outside their caste. In this case, societal gender scripts are modified with modernity such that parents seek status enhancement through the performance of modernity by modifying some traditions.

The OBC castes also give and take dowry. As the boys' education and employment prospects become good, dowry expectations also rise. Girls question the dowry demand, stating that parental investment in their education should be considered as dowry. A fourteen-year-old girl belonging to the Patel-Kewat caste opined that it is difficult to find grooms as everybody wants a beautiful bride and dowry too, and she does not mind if her parents have to give dowry in her marriage. Another girl of the Pal caste is against dowry and would only marry someone who accepts her without dowry. For the OBC castes, both channels of status attainment, either through gender performance of traditional ideology or through the performance of modernity, pose significant challenges to be surmounted.

Among the Rajput, dowry is widespread and quite high, signifying the patriarchal dominance in this caste group. However, educated Rajput girls do take a stance against dowry, increasingly conscious that educational investment is a form of dowry. A respondent pursuing an MBA degree says she is against dowry and will not marry if someone asks for it. Another girl observed that it is very difficult to find an appropriate match for girls and no marriage in her family has been conducted without dowry. She does not want to marry within her caste because of the dowry or marry anyone who asks for dowry. Another observed that a guy who asks for cash and electronic goods has no right to marry as he is incapable of shouldering the responsibility of marriage. Her parents neither took dowry in her brother's marriage nor gave one in her sister's marriage. A Punjabi Sikh girl noted there is no dowry in her family and that parents give according to their wishes. While dowry may be common in a particular community, it is still possible for families to negotiate marriage without dowry through mutual consent, although it is not clear to what extent the anti-dowry stance of many of the respondent girls is actually realized in practice.

GIRLS' VIEWS ON LOVE MARRIAGES

While many of the girls preferred arranged marriages, some expressed their desires for a "love marriage" as they already had a lover or boyfriend whom they hoped to marry. Many of them thought there would be disapproval from their parents and elders in the family if they chose partners outside their caste. For yet others, love marriage seemed unproblematic if either their parents had a love marriage or if there were others in the family who had so married.

A Gupta girl said that her marriage is settled and the boy is of her choice, he being a Punjabi Khatri. She claimed it was love at first sight. Although her father did not initially approve it as he did not want to marry her into a house from where they have taken a daughter-in-law, he did come around and so did the elders as he was from an affluent and good family. However, the marriage was canceled as the boy felt that the girl's father was imposing too many restrictions on his choices in life. Another girl was of the view that love marriages are increasing because girls are getting educated and think they are mature enough to decide for their life. She has a boyfriend whom she hopes to marry after convincing her parents. A girl of the Kesharwani caste noted that her parents are not very rigid about caste as they have agreed to her brother's marriage to a Kayastha girl. But had the girl been of some lower caste, they would never have agreed to the marriage. Her mother also married by her choice, and her grandparents did not object as her father was of the same caste. Love marriages are getting popular as girls want to marry someone who is more a friend than a husband, a companionate marriage, and parents also do not mind if the choice of their children is good. A girl of the Agarwal caste says that because of cultural differences between castes, she would prefer to marry within her caste only. Although love marriages have increased, she says not all are successful as girls do not compromise. She also felt that girls are taking undue advantage of the freedom given by their parents. Parental objection to intercaste love marriages among the Baniyas is mitigated to some extent by the affluent status of the chosen partner and by caste hypergamy.

Brahmin girls seem to be editing their personal gender script in the construction of their modern self by their desires for higher education and career even as they seem to abide by the social gender script of gender performance based on tradition. All three Brahmin girls in the sample responded that they would never marry according to their choice. In their view, love marriages have increased in recent times due to coeducation, as boys and girls interact with each other, and also due to late marriages, as girls prefer to study and settle in their careers first and then marry. If in that process they find a suitable partner, their parents also do not object as they think that with education and employment, they are quite mature to decide for their future.

Kayastha girls and parents are more liberal in their attitude toward girls making their own choice to some extent with parental consent and marrying outside their caste, but not when a boy is from a very low caste. They also favor girls' higher education. An increase in love marriages was noted to be on account of greater freedom for girls accorded by their families where previously there were lots of restrictions with fewer opportunities to interact with boys. With education, girls are able to speak for themselves, whereas earlier they hesitated to speak even to their parents. The Kayastha caste does seem to lean toward status attainment in marriage through the performance of modernity rather than wholly through traditional gender performance.

Girls of OBC castes seem to experience greater patriarchal power within families because of the strong bind of social disciplines. A girl of the Ahir caste on being asked about her father's reaction if she wanted to marry someone of her choice, said her father would kill her. A girl of the Patel-Kewat caste said if she were to have friendships with boys, her parents would beat her and throw her out of the house. A girl of the Pal caste said her parents would not accept anyone outside the caste, but they might not object if she chose someone from the same caste and accept him happily. She hardly discusses anything with her father and so is unaware of his views on love marriage but has heard him criticize and condemn people involved in love marriages. Girls of these OBC castes abide by the gender scripts of traditional socialization with restricted individual freedoms, even as they are aware that editing their personal gender scripts toward a marital life with fewer compromises of an arranged marriage, although desired by them, poses challenges in its attainment.

Among the Rajput girls, the gender script of socialization of traditional gender ideologies is constantly assessed and rewritten with edits in their personal gender scripts of identity and self-constructions, making obvious the contradictory pulls of tradition and modernity. They want to marry according to their choice, giving due regard to their parents' views, prefer to marry outside the caste, and are critical of patriarchal dominance in their caste. They critically assess their parents' marriage and resent the compromises entailed in arranged marriages. The personal gender scripts they write include more freedom as well as the right of children to make their choices about their life and future. One girl said she wants to marry according to her choice but with the consent of her parents, as she thinks it is important to understand the nature of a person before entering into a lifetime relationship, though she did not have a boyfriend. No one has married outside the caste in her family. She, like other girls, is of the view that one does not compromise much in a love marriage. A Rajput girl with a doctoral degree is against arranged marriage, where a girl has to compromise a lot. Although her siblings had arranged marriages, they would still support her if she wanted to marry someone of her choice. Another girl noted that her parents had an arranged marriage and are not compatible with each other, and so hardly talk to each other or go for outings together, with no fun in their lives. Her father, being a doctor hardly has time for her mother, but they do not fight with each other as her mother has adjusted well. Her community folks are very conservative and think that women are inferior to men and should stay at home. Her mother observes *purdah* in front of the elders and is not allowed to talk in front of them, and her uncles beat their wives. Almost all her friends have boyfriends with whom they wish to settle, although it is doubtful if they will succeed. Love marriages are on the rise, they said, because of increased interaction with boys, whereas previously, parents did not allow girls to move out of the house or talk to boys, and also because of the influence of Western culture. While parents think their children are too immature to make their marriage decisions by themselves and impose their choice on them, the children think that they also have the right to make decisions and parents should not underestimate them.

In other communities too, the attempt to write the personal gender script in the direction of modernity, such as granting choice and freedom, is balanced by retaining to an extent gender socialization through traditional gender performance. A Punjabi Khatri girl said that she does not know whether she will marry according to her choice or her parents' choice but would like to marry within her caste only, for she feels that both love and arranged marriages can be successful or unsuccessful. Although it has become a fashion to have an opposite-sex friend, very few mature into marriages as many are just friendships for fun that break up when the relationships get serious.

For most girls, their ability to script their life for a love marriage is constrained by their traditional gender socialization, which makes them prefer the security of an arranged marriage even if it entails compromises. Such gender socialization instills in them a lack of self-confidence in making such a choice, corroborating parental views that they are not yet mature enough. Love marriage outside their caste is further constrained by the impossibility of caste hypergamous relationships for castes like Brahmins and members of those castes perceived by society as being too low in the caste hierarchy, especially if they lack possibilities of upward economic mobility. Girls whose parents had a love marriage felt less constrained in choosing their partner for a love marriage.

PARENTS' VIEWS ON LOVE MARRIAGES

Parental views of love marriage would clarify the extent to which parents of different castes are enabled or constrained either to status attainment through traditional gender performance or through the performance of modernity. A Gupta girl's mother observed that girls are opting for love marriages these days as they are becoming financially independent. They are also more capable of making their decision and when parents oppose them, girls may still go by their choice and parents would be helpless in having to succumb to their decision. She thinks children could make judgment errors for they might get attracted by looks without giving much importance to each other's intrinsic values. When parents search for a suitable match, they emphasize family, culture, and other aspects that may affect their daughter's life, besides education and employment of the boy.

A Brahmin mother complained about the rising cases of love marriage as she noted that the environment these days is not good as children are getting affected by television and the influence of their friends. They have also started opposing their parents, whereas she, in her younger years, did not have the courage to question her parents nor ever answered them back indicating a decline in parental authority over time. She was so afraid of her father that she never looked him in the eyes. She thinks her daughter is also not mature to decide her future. Another mother said that she is confident that her daughter will never choose a partner by herself because she is very simple, and another remarked that she would turn her children out of her home if they wanted to marry someone of their choice, although she thinks her children are obedient and will marry by parental choice only. A father remarked,

> If my daughters ever wanted to marry someone who is well settled and belongs to our caste, then we would consider. We will never consider anyone who is not from our caste. My parents are still alive, how will I face them, they will not eat with us. We are very rigid about caste.

The father of a Kayastha girl observed that intercaste marriages are not good as there are differences in culture and food habits, making it very difficult for girls to adjust in the marital family. He believed that girls are the ones to make compromises. If boys marry outside the caste, they do not suffer much because it is the girl who has to adjust in the marital family and not the boy.

A Rajput mother observed that she did not even see her husband's photo when she got married. Her father's friend had brought the alliance, and after meeting the family and the boy, her father settled the marriage. Her mother-in-law only saw her. As her parents were very conservative, she was not allowed to even come to the front door. But she does not restrict her daughters to stay indoors and are free to make friends. She has no problem if her children want to marry on their own, but she prefers the boy be of the same caste and earn enough to cater to all the needs of his wife without taking help from anyone. As her family is very rigid on caste, no one in her family will go for intercaste marriage, for "marriage is no game of dolls and one has to look at all aspects before taking the decision." Many people suffer after a love marriage, and so wants her children to be careful in their partner selection. A Rajput father observed that these days one is concerned about the happiness of their children, and caste is not so important, as parents get satisfied if the children are happy in their life. He noted that he has seen many "arranged intercaste marriages" in his friends' circle because when one does not get a good match in one's caste, they look into the possibilities from other castes. Though there has never been a love marriage in his family, if his children want to marry someone of their choice, he would try to convince his very conservative brothers to agree to it. He believes that marriages are a gamble, whether "love" or "arranged."

A Punjabi Khatri mother remarked that if her daughter wanted to marry someone of her choice, she would not object but boys deceive girls by portraying a false picture of themselves and their families to entrap the girls.

Moreover, there is no guarantee of a girl's or boy's character being good even if they are from a familiar family. Divorces have also become quite common because girls do not want to compromise, as girls today are only interested in money and do not respect the boy's family.

Among Brahmin parents, gender performance through tradition in matrimonial matters is very strong even as their modern outlook encourages their daughters to pursue higher education and careers. They overwhelmingly assert the parents' right to marry their daughters and the children's obligation toward parents to not embarrass them socially through intercaste marriage. Parents of all other castes are much less strict on gender performance through tradition in matrimonial matters and, to varying degrees are open to intercaste marriage. Clearly marking a distinction between "marriage by choice within caste" and "marriage by choice outside the caste," they would prefer that it be within their caste, as they point to cultural differences posing adjustment problems in marital homes, especially for the girls. Across all castes, parents, with a few exceptions, seem to think that marriageable-age children are still immature to make their life decisions and are likely to make mistakes, necessitating parental interventions in decisions. There is also increasing awareness among parents that marriages, both "love" and "arranged," could fail, a realization that may likely diminish the stigma of singleness and divorce.

FREEDOMS AVAILABLE TO GIRLS AND THE SECRECY OVER BOYFRIENDS

Societal gender scripts of socialization ensure the performance of traditional gender ideologies. The performance of modernity is oriented toward greater individual freedom in many aspects of personal and social life. The trade-off between the two reflects the extent to which the binds of tradition and the pull of modernity are resolved. From the narratives of girls, it appears that gender scripts of socialization still weigh heavily against the freedoms granted to them, as most observed that friendships with boys were either not permitted or were restricted only to academic interactions, such as group study, but not social interactions, such as going out with boys. Those who had the freedom to go out with male friends had to inform their parents, return home before dusk, and not stay out too late. For college girls, it seems one aspect of the performance of modernity is to have boyfriends. The girls edit their personal gender scripts of identity and self-construction, taking into account the extent of freedom granted to them by their parents.

A Gupta girl observed that she and her sister were not allowed to move out of the house alone and someone always accompanied them wherever they went. Her parents used to warn them that if they had boyfriends, they would throw them down from the terrace. Her parents were not ready to send her out for studies but, on her grandparents insistence they agreed on the condition that she opt only for a girls' college. Her grandparents are more broadminded than her parents as her grandfather is a High Court judge committed to certain values of modern freedom. Some girls with male friends could go out with them only after taking permission from their parents, although some neighbors and relatives do not mind if they go out with male friends. A girl of the Agarwal caste says she has no male friends and does not like to make friends with them either, as her friends who have boyfriends are always quarreling with their friends or always chatting with them on their mobile phones, leaving them with little time for studies. While it has become a fashion to have boyfriends and girlfriends and the one who does not have any is often looked down upon by their peers, she thinks these behaviors are childish and does not involve herself in all these.

A Brahmin girl stated that her mother is very strict about talking to boys and has never allowed her to make friends with them, nor is she allowed to go out of the house alone, as her mother accompanies her daughters everywhere. She was not admitted to a co-ed school either, and is not allowed to have mobile phones or use the internet. But a girl from an engineering program with a job offer stated that she has male friends, and they do come home for group studies which her parents do not mind. However, she does not go out with them to movies or for outings. Her parents know all of them very well, and they have met her parents as well. Another girl, preparing for engineering college says that she does not even talk to boys, as she finds them very stupid, though boys approach her for friendship because she is beautiful.

A Kayastha girl confided that although she was allowed to make male friends, she was not allowed to go out alone with them and whenever she went out on their birthdays, her parents would be informed of it. She had to return home before sunset as her father would get very angry if she ever got late. Her father did not take a cable connection for their television for a long time as he felt that children would get misguided by watching television. Her mother, though friendly was very conservative and always wanted them to wear *salwar/churidar* suits to go out and were not allowed to laugh and talk while walking down the roads. She was the lucky one among her siblings, being the youngest, to get permission to wear Western dresses and do a job. Her father says she will not be happy if the groom's parents pressurize her to stay indoors as she is very social. Another girl who hopes to marry her boyfriend says he has a modern approach and does not impose his decisions on her. He does not restrict her from wearing Western dresses or going out at night, unlike other boyfriends of her friends. A Bengali girl's parents are very liberal and do not object to her having male friends or going out with them. Many of them do come to her home and also help her parents whenever they need any help. Her mother says she has no problems if her daughters have male friends or go out with them but she should know where they are going and with whom and return before sunset. She thinks girls should enjoy their freedom without crossing the limits. Another Bengali girl has male friends at the university, but do not come to her house, nor she does go out with them.

A Yadav girl of the Ahir caste says her father is very conservative and does not allow her and her sister to move out of the house, so they never go for outings or have even female friends. A girl of the Patel-Kewat caste says that she is not allowed to make friends with boys, though she studies in a co-ed school, and even at school, she hardly interacts with boys because her parents would beat her if she gets friendly with them. Her elder brother accompanies her wherever she goes. In her leisure time, she reads comics. Another girl of the Pal caste says she is allowed to make friends with boys and they do come to her house, but she is not allowed to go out with them as her neighbors will speak ill of her if she were to do so. She does not do anything that would harm her parents' reputation and make them feel embarrassed.

A Rajput girl's father does not allow her to move out of the house alone and accompanies her wherever she goes. Although she has male friends, she is never allowed to go out with them and is not allowed to talk to them on the phone for any length of time. She too fears her neighbors will speak ill of her. Another girl said that she is allowed to have male friends and go on outings with them but only in groups and not alone. A girl with a PhD says she has many male friends and also goes out with them sometimes, but as her parents do not like her going out with boys, she refuses them most of the time. Her parents also do not allow her to have long talks with her friends on the mobile phone or go out of the house after sunset, even with her girlfriends.

A Punjabi Sikh girl says she has male friends, and they do come home, and her parents, neighbors, and relatives do not object to her friendship with them. However, she can go out for an outing with male friends after informing her parents. A Bengali ST girl says she has many male friends, but they are just friends, and has not found any of them suitable to marry.

Overall, it is evident that gender socialization is more rigid among the Brahmin caste and the castes of the OBCs. As the former group ensures strict caste boundaries in matrimonial alliances, the socialization of young girls seeks to align with that objective, and so girls are given freedom only for collegial and not for social interaction with boys, while among the OBC castes patriarchal dominance within families enforces strict social disciplines on young girls, restricting their freedoms and mobility.

Many with a boyfriend whom they hoped to marry had not yet revealed the relationship to their parents and were in most instances unsure of the outcome whenever they would reveal it. They could only hope that it would work out in their favor, even as a few parents unaware of the girl's love relationship, are actively searching for appropriate matrimonial alliances within their castes.

A Gupta girl with her classmate as a boyfriend looks forward to marrying him, but her parents are unaware of her involvement, and she does not know whether they will accept him as he is from another caste. A girl of the Kesharwani caste has a boyfriend who is her next-door neighbor and of the same caste; both parents knew of their relationship and had already discussed and finalized the marriage. A Rajput girl with a Gupta boyfriend has not revealed the relationship to anyone but is confident that her parents will accept her choice as they are quite broadminded. A Kayastha girl has a Telugu Brahmin boyfriend whom she hopes to marry, but neither of the parents know of their relationship. Her mother, unaware of her daughter's boyfriend, observed that her daughter will not marry by her choice, but if she does, the boy should be of their caste only and had even started looking for a groom for her, though not very intently, pending completion of her studies. However, if they were to find an eligible groom, they will not let go of the match. Her father also preferred a groom from their caste only and will not accept someone from outside their caste, no matter how good the boy may be. A Bengali Kayastha girl says she has a boyfriend who is a Baniya, and although her parents are quite broadminded, she does not know how they will react when she discloses her boyfriend to them.

The secrecy over boyfriends and lovers is indicative of the tensions in the societal gender scripts of socialization and the personal gender scripts of the girls. While gender-caste socialization in families is based on societal gender scripts with its emphasis on caste endogamy in marriage, the personal gender scripts of girls in the direction of modernity tilt in favor of companionate marriage based on their choice.

MARRIAGE AGE AND EMPLOYMENT BEFORE AND AFTER MARRIAGE

Yet another domain where the tension between gender performance of tradition and the performance of modernity is evident is the appropriate age at marriage. Age at marriage gets pushed up with modern aspirations of higher education and financial independence through employment. While girls with lesser education across castes thought the appropriate age at marriage was between twenty-one and twenty-five years, those with higher education were of the view that twenty-five to thirty years would be the appropriate age for marriage. Parents of all castes, though, were concerned with the difficulties of finding an appropriate match for a girl after she crosses twenty-five years of age, as many families still prefer younger-age brides even though higher education and girls' employment before marriage have become quite widespread. Some girls were allowed to pursue higher studies only because parents were unable to find a match. Girls' responses to the appropriate age for marriage were noticeably marked by their personal gender scripts of self-construction. Many felt that the appropriate age is when they become financially independent after completing their studies, as financial independence was important. It also depended on whether the parents wanted her to study further or settle her in marriage to be freed from their responsibility soon enough. Mature responses also indicated that any legally permissible age is appropriate when a girl begins to long for companionship.

A Gupta girl says she would definitely want to work after her marriage as it is necessary for girls to be financially independent. Her mother thinks her in-laws may let her work after marriage, as most girls in her family are working after marriage and those who are not working do so by their own choice. A Brahmin girl wants to do a course in beautician and open a beauty parlor. A Brahmin engineering graduate prefers to work in a city away from her parents, while her father is on the lookout for a groom in the software industry so that she does not have to leave her job. He hopes that she continues working after her marriage as she has worked very hard for it, but he says it all depends on her husband and her in-laws. A mother who had obtained her M.Ed degree could not do any job as her grandmother and father did not permit her, but she wants her daughters to study and become financially independent before their marriage.

The mother of a Bengali Kayastha girl preferred to marry her daughter to someone who would let her pursue studies or a job further. Another Kayastha girl who had worked for a few years insisted that financial independence is important for both girls and boys. A Bengali girl was confident that her boyfriend would get a good job after completing his MBA and that they both would work and earn for their smooth life. A Rajput girl seeking admission in an MBBS program after her graduation wants to complete her MD and would like to carry on her medical career even after her marriage, as her father who is a doctor, has his own hospital. A Punjabi Khatri girl looks forward to joining some private bank as she specializes in Finance. She prefers to work for a few years and only then think of marriage. A Punjabi Sikh girl pursuing her MBA says that if she does not get a good job, she would join her family business. The two Yadav sisters want to take up teaching after completing their graduation, but their parents are not ambitious about the careers of their children and hardly take any interest in their studies. A Bengali Tribal girl doing her MBA says that these days everyone wants to be employed in addition to doing household work, but it is a big challenge to tackle both activities simultaneously. If husbands are supportive, then it becomes quite easy to do both. Many of her friends had to leave their jobs after marriage to look after their family and children. She says it is quite depressing to sit at home attending to children and the family after spending many years studying. People these days still expect convent-educated, professionally qualified girls to sit at home and do household work.

For girls across all castes, scripting modernity in their lives implies primarily their preference for education, employment, and financial independence. In the construction of their modern selves, their focus is on enhancing their capacity to open up their minds to the world through education, seeking employment outside so as not to be confined entirely to the domestic sphere, and greater autonomy in financial decision-making in the families they hope to build. They also negotiate to extend their freedoms in the arenas of friendship and marriage to the extent possible, which is in overall compliance with their caste-based societal scripts of gender performance through tradition. These findings are somewhat similar to those of Scott (2021), who conducted interviews with college students in the Garhwal region of the adjacent state of Uttarakhand a few years after my fieldwork in Allahabad (Prayagraj). Although the culture of the hill people and women's status are popularly understood as being different from the people in the Gangetic plains, the importance of education as perceived by the girls is similar. She found girls to be more serious about their college studies than boys, although the newly opened opportunities of a neoliberal globalizing India are unlikely to reach them anytime soon. The young students, both males and females, seem to largely reinforce and legitimize the dominant patriarchal constructs, which must be a reconstructed one of the patriarchies of the hill people along with the dominant elite constructs of patriarchy of the Hindi heartlands through cultural contacts and transactional relations. The importance given to girls' education and the simultaneous reinforcement of patriarchal constructs is a general, countrywide phenomenon indicating the conundrum of modernity and tradition.

GENDER CULTURE AND MEN

So far, the analysis sought to draw insights from the responses of young women and their parents. As marriage involves both men and women, men's perspectives must sync and go in tandem for the marriage to be a success. Hence, it is necessary to understand marriage choices and marriage issues from male perspectives as well. Although my fieldwork interviews did not include men, an ethnographic study conducted by anthropologist Steve Derne (1995) in the neighboring city of Banaras (Varanasi) provides deep insights into men's roles as active agents in the construction and reproduction of Hindu gender-culture that bolsters male power and subjugates women.

Exploring the reasons why his predominantly young male respondents embraced arranged marriages, joint-family living, restrictions on women's movements outside the home, and limitations on interactions between husbands and wives, Derne argues that men believe these practices help maintain male privilege by making women docile and obedient servants in their husbands' families. According to the Hindu gender-culture of North India and probably elsewhere too with varying intensities, a husband is considered superior to his wife and must always be her boss. If a woman wants to take up employment outside her home, her husband has to give permission to do so. When women move outside, they are expected to be shy, ashamed, and docile and often wear a veil as a head cover. Arguing that women need protection, the joint-family living effectively controls women. Restrictions on interactions between the conjugal couple limit the ability of a wife to influence her husband, and men clearly perceive that such restrictions advance their own interests.

Men prefer arranged marriage as they are distrustful of individual choice and, like women, men too fear the loss of parental support if they were to make their own choice. They fear that equality of relationship in love marriage will lead to a marriage failure as it is uncontrolled by social and familial pressures. Their emotional life is shaped by a collectivist understanding of action. Derne observes,

> Because men emphasize social guidance, they have an elaborated notion of social fear as an exemplary emotion. Because they de-emphasize individual characteristics, they see love as based on duty rather than on the specialness of the beloved. Because they de-emphasize the singular person, they demand that love be extended toward many in a family. Because men distrust individual desires, moreover, they often see love as a dangerous emotion that might tempt people away from joint-family guidance. Men's elaborate understanding of love make them alert to the charm of their wives. But because they emphasize social fear and the goodness of love that extends toward many in family, men often try to limit love that pulls them toward their wives. The dominant understanding of which emotions are exemplary and which emotions are dangerous is consistent, then, with Hindu men's collectivist framework for understanding action. (Derne, 1995, 80)

Societal gender scripts are framed within this collectivist framework of emotions and action, and both boys and girls are socialized in it. When women do not accept or resist the internalization of this collectivist framework, they seek to rewrite their personal gender scripts in the direction of greater freedom and an individualist framework of emotion and action, emphasizing the singularity of conjugal love. Women might adopt a range of stances to express their skepticism toward cultural messages of the societal gender scripts under conditions of modernity. The socialization of girls in Hindu families in their natal homes is based on this understanding of men's collectivist framework of understanding action, and girls are brought up to fulfill the cultural expectations arising from these male perspectives in their marital homes. Although women's oral culture stresses "the desirability of disrupting patrilineal unity in favor of a stress on conjugality" (Raheja and Gold, 1994), women's strategies for advancing their interests often reinforce the gender-culture propagated by men, as patriarchal bargains are set within concrete constraints.

CONCLUSION

Modernity and contemporary globalization impact the lives of young urban women across all caste groups in their marriage and self-construction as modern women. One way to understand this phenomenon is to explore how the contending pulls of tradition and modernity are resolved in the construction of their selves. An approach that considers both the culture and socialization of girls in families and girls' attempts to access freedoms through modernity is explored here through the approach of societal gender scripts and personal gender scripts. As families can seek status attainment through marriage either by the performance of traditional gender ideology or through the performance of modernity, this study examined the dynamics of intergenerational decision-making of parents and daughters on a range of marriage issues, particularly the most important one of young girls' choice of marriage partners across different castes. Brahmins and the OBC castes had a strong tendency for status attainment through gender performance of tradition, even as Brahmins also pursued gender performance through modernity by encouraging girls' higher education and careers that resource-constrained OBC families found difficult. All other castes sought status attainment through gender performance of tradition in some modified form on certain marriage issues and to varying degrees across castes and families in the performance of modernity. Girls wrote their gender scripts of modernity by negotiating for more freedoms in friendship and voice in marriage choices within the societal gender scripts of socialization, even as they sought to construct their modern selves for greater autonomy through education and financial independence.

Overall, the strong preference for within-caste marriage, dowry payment to a limited extent, arranged marriage with the girl's consent, freedom for girls in their pursuit of education and careers, limiting social interaction with boys, and the parental hope that their investment in their daughter's education would not go waste are pointers that the pulls of status attainment are resolved in favor of combining both gender performance through a modified traditional gender ideology and the performance of modernity.

Chapter 4

Diasporic Marriage Alliances among the Tamils

Contemporary globalization has added a new dimension to the reckoning of middle-class social status with increased opportunities for outmigration to foreign countries for employment. Today, middle-class families seek to enhance their social status through the emplacement of their children in foreign countries through employment or marriage, which has diminished the status associated with the Indian Administrative Service (IAS) that was earlier considered prestigious for the middle class. Marrying a daughter to an IAS officer considerably enhanced the family's social status then. Today, for middle-class families whose children are settled abroad, migration to countries like the United States, Canada, Australia, the UK, and European countries accords higher social status than to other countries.

This chapter explores the way in which diasporic opportunities are sought-after and rendered possible through matrimonial strategies with a specific focus on Tamil Brahmins as "America *varan*" marriages became very popular among them. It also provides insights about how second-generation children of immigrant Tamils settled in the United States find their marriage partners. As outmigration of Tamils of all castes and religions has increased significantly recently, it also explores, through recent matrimonial advertisements, the partner-preferences of people of various castes and religions and the discernible social changes prompted by the more globalized context today.

"AMERICA *VARAN*" AMONG THE TAMIL BRAHMINS

Studies on diasporic marriages have been rather few in the Indian context despite being a popular theme for Indian commercial films. Exploring the internationalization of the middle-class family, Uberoi (1998) studied the problem of cultural reproduction in transnational locations through a critical reading of two popular Hindi films that thematized issues of courtship and marriage. Matrimonial strategies have always been an important component of kinship studies but was largely preoccupied with the older debates on the decline of the joint family and largely ignored the diasporic terrain. The study of evolving community-specific matrimonial strategies in what are generally understood as "arranged marriages" is not merely interesting in itself but indeed essential for understanding how habitus constructs gendered identities and how diasporic opportunities redefine social status within cultural groups through the acquisition of both symbolic and economic capital.

Through ethnographic methods, this study explores the widely prevalent and much sought-after form of marriage alliance among middle-class Tamil Brahmins, known as "America *varan.*" The sociological literature has underscored the importance of the principle of "alliance" in Indian marriages, whereby "marriage" is construed as a union between two families through the "give and take" of women, rather than just an arrangement between two individuals setting up a new conjugal family together (Dumont, 1983; Uberoi, 1998).

Among Tamil Brahmins, *varan* refers to a prospective marriage alliance, either for girls or boys. This Sanskrit word means a "boon." Marriage is considered a boon, and the marital state a "blessed state" among Hindus, especially among Brahmins, as indeed it is in many other cultures and societies. "America *varan*" refers to a prospective marriage alliance with Indians residing in both the United States and Canada. Although the term "America *varan*" is reciprocal and could be used for finding either grooms or brides, in practice, it refers to finding America-based grooms. Tamil Brahmins rarely find a groom from India for a girl residing in the United States. This is because girls who go to America on their own do so mainly for higher studies; it is expected that a marriage alliance for them would be fixed with a boy already residing in America. Also, unlike Punjabi or Pakistani immigrants, Tamil Brahmin immigrants in America rarely seek alliances from India for their America-born and educated children.

Since the early 1960s, when marriage-induced migration to the United States started, "America *varan*" marriages caught the Tamil Brahmin imagination, shaping and in turn being shaped by contemporary social aspirations. For instance, the then widely popular Tamil weekly *Ananda Viketan*, read largely by Brahmin housewives, serialized for over a year Savi's story called *Washingtonil Thirumanam* (Wedding in Washington). This was about a Tamil Brahmin wedding conducted in Washington in the most traditional way and incorporating some aspects of the American way of life as well. In a sense, this hugely popular story marked the beginning of a newfound aspiration among middle-class Brahmins to fix alliances for their daughters with boys settled in the United States or Canada. This aspiration grew alongside the aspiration to send their boys to the United States for higher education and employment.

In the 1980s, this enthusiasm was to some extent restrained by a widespread awareness of the risks involved in such an alliance. Such awareness was generated to a great extent by the popular Tamil writer Sivasankari's story *"Napathielu Nattkal"* (Forty-seven Days), later made into a Tamil movie. In this story, a girl who contracts a diasporic marriage is severely ill-treated by her husband, but, using her ingenuity, somehow manages to escape the torture and returns to India. Although the story is set in the context of the Indian diaspora in Europe, particularly France, the story's significance in the popular imagination can be gauged from the fact that most of my respondents referred to it in their interviews with me. Today, Tamil magazines like *Kalki, Kumudham,* and *Ananda Viketan* carry innumerable short stories, including some by expatriate Tamil women writers such as Geetha Bennett, who live unconventional lives, depicting assertive expatriate women in the United States who challenge these "America *varan*" arranged marriages to make choices of their own, even transcending the barriers of race.

Diasporic alliances in the 1960s and 1970s, like domestic alliances, were largely settled through personal kin and friendship networks. As it became increasingly difficult to find alliances in this way, personal networks were complemented through impersonal networks, especially matrimonial advertisements, though many Brahmin families shied away from that style of seeking alliances even in the late 1970s. Those that used the advertisement channel were seen as being less traditional and more opportunistic, and, above all, bold and fearless to the extent that they were willing to entertain alliances from families about whom they had no prior knowledge or even a reference. As inhibitions gave way and as more women came to be employed, even the marriageable girl herself would go to the newspaper office to place the advertisement; some took the initiative to use that channel when their parents felt inhibited to do so. Subsequently, a kind of community networking emerged, using the temple as a nucleus. Many temples in Chennai began to offer horoscope exchange services, and a few, like the Mahalingapuram temple, earned quite a reputation for efficient service. Today, advertising in matrimonial websites has added a new dimension to identifying compatible partners. With the increasing number of girls with higher and professional education, "companionate marriage" is on the rise among Tamil Brahmins (Fuller and Narasimhan, 2008). The process of finding compatible partners that matches both the couple's personal and professional goals and with their familial backgrounds, which under companionate marriage have lower weightage, remains much the same as before.

Among Tamil Brahmins, finding and fixing marriage partners entails first gaining access to the horoscopes of potential spouses, a process of matching horoscopes that usually entails consultations with astrologers, and then inquiries, especially on the part of the boy's family, regarding the attainments and status of the girl's family and the likely quantum of dowry or their ability to hold a "decent" wedding along with the gift expectations. In the case of a diasporic alliance for a girl, such inquiries extend to clearing suspicions that the boy might be an impostor, be already married in the United States, or have a "white girlfriend." Generally, the boy and the girl themselves meet only at the last stage of the negotiations to explore further their mutual compatibility and come to their decision. This study explores the matrimonial strategies of Tamil Brahmins in successfully finding and settling an "America *varan*" marriage alliances.

FRAMEWORK AND METHODOLOGY

The strategies of matchmaking in diasporic Brahmin marriages and the outcome of such marriages are here explored in terms of the acquisition and deployment of symbolic capital for the reproduction of class habitus. Matrimonial strategies, as Pierre Bourdieu argues, are "objectively directed toward the conservation or expansion of the material and symbolic capital jointly possessed by a more or less extended group" with a view to reproducing or improving their position in the social structure (Bourdieu, 1977, 70). This explains why marriage practices may be at variance with the customary marriage rules.

Sociological literature on marriage and kinship in India has highlighted the preference for cross-cousin marriages in South India, which are customarily prohibited in North India. However, there has been a shift in Tamil marriage preferences from kin- to class- and status-based alliances. While Karve (1993) noted that Dravidian marriages are increasingly following the North Indian marriage model, Dumont (1993) observed the commonality between the two in terms of the role of affinity, which, dominant in Dravidian marriages, was not altogether devalued in the north. Gough (1993) observed the preference for matrilateral cross-cousin marriages over patrilateral cross-cousin marriages among the Brahmin youth of a Thanjavur village, although she also noted that patrilateral and matrilateral cross-cousin marriages and marriage to the sister's daughter each accounted for only 4 percent of all Brahmin marriages. Trautmann (1981, 1993a, 1993b) quite rightly suggests that we need to explore through rigorous statistical methods the degree to which marriage practices deviate from the rule. According to him, the rule of cross-cousin marriage on the ground is subject to many contingencies, such as the availability of a cross-cousin, the existence of conflicting rules—for instance, the matching of horoscopes and considerations of family and personal advantage, and so on. Kapadia (1996) brings to attention the fact that cross-cousin marriages among Brahmins were never isogamous, as among non-Brahmins, but were hypergamous, much like those in North India. In the Tamil village that she studied in the late 1980s, she observed a shift from cross-cousin marriages among both Brahmins and non-Brahmins to a marked preference for non-kin marriages, suggesting that class and status-based alliances within endogamous groups are becoming more important as a result of the spread of urban cultural values.

With urbanization and economic differentiation, matrimonial strategies are being deployed in the acquisition of material and symbolic capital, along with widespread awareness of kin marriages likely to cause genetic fetal mishaps. The increased preference for non-kin marriages, along with the emergence of nuclear families in urban areas, has enabled families to reckon their success in terms of the symbolic and cultural capital obtained through marriage alliances, judged by various status symbols.

In the scale of symbolic capital, "America *varan*" alliances are exceptionally prestigious. For a boy residing in America, the symbolic capital of a particular alliance depends on the kind of family from which the bride is taken and the girl's personal attainments, reckoned largely in terms of beauty. The prestige of an "America *varan*" itself varies depending on whether the boy possesses a Green Card or an H-1B visa; whether the boy went to the United States/Canada for higher studies and then settled there or whether he went there for employment. In the case of emigration for employment, there is a distinction between employment for a short-term job contract (like the numerous software professionals who are on the global move) and a more enduring job contract with prospects of permanent relocation. The "America *varan*" alliance with a U.S. citizen or Green-Card-holding boy ranks as the most prestigious match. On the other hand, the parents of girls who go abroad for higher studies and then find their mates through some kind of arrangement (not necessarily a "love" match) never boast of having fixed an "America *varan*" alliance. While obviously happy to see their daughter settled abroad, they view "America *varan*" as a simple necessity, taking pride instead in their daughter's scholastic abilities.

This ethnographic inquiry sought to gather data on general perceptions of "America *varan*" by Brahmin families today, its popularity among girls of marriageable age, and the various strategies deployed by families to find and fix such alliances. This entails considering the importance of different kinds of networks, the role and expectations of astrological matchings, and the way in which families seek to gather and present information on attainments and expectations. In today's complex world of diasporic opportunities, including the demand for software professionals, marriage preferences in diasporic marriages appear to be shaped by considerations of the durability of migration and the nature of the boy's employment as well as by the girl's attainments.

For instance, depending on the nature of their work contracts, some software professionals prefer the girl to have acquired similar professional qualifications, while others definitely prefer the wife to remain unemployed. Those with longer contracts on the higher end of the salary scale prefer their wives to be homemakers, while those on short-term contracts are keen that their wives have similar qualifications. This is despite the fact that such short-term contract workers are generally on H-1B (temporary non-immigrant) U.S. visas, while their spouses, on H-4 visas, are not permitted to work. So, despite their qualifications, they remain unemployed, sometimes shifting locales in the United States within short intervals, leading to isolation and vulnerability. There are two main reasons for the insistence on spouses having compatible qualifications as software professionals. First is the subjective calculation that, in case of permanent relocation, a well-qualified software professional could also enter the labor force sometime in the future. Second, after moving around the world on short-term contracts, a time will come when they will eventually settle in India, where a wife qualified in software could easily find a job. As the total period of global moves is not likely to exceed five or six years, most young professionals feel that their wife's qualifications will not become outdated. A young Master of Computer Applications (MCA) graduate, who was interviewed for a job in Chennai after graduation, made the mistake of letting the interviewers know that her parents were on the lookout for an alliance for her. The potential employer was so sure that she would be married quickly to a software professional proceeding abroad and so did not offer her the job. As luck would have it, her marriage was not settled for a year, and the next year she had to compete for a job with fresh graduates.

This study explores, through interviews conducted as part of fieldwork, how the contending pulls of tradition and modernity are negotiated while settling these diasporic matrimonial arrangements among Tamil Brahmins. Two rounds of interviews were conducted: the first in 2003, during which the information gathered forms a greater part of the chapter, and more recently in 2022, to explore the changes and recent developments, as well as the settling marriage alliances of second-generation Brahmins in the U.S. diaspora. In 2003, I had planned to interview at least fifteen families that had recently (within the last three to five years) fixed "America *varan*" alliances, an equal number of families for their general perceptions of the phenomenon, and as many young, marriageable girls. In the end, given certain constraints, interviews of only eleven families were conducted, of whom two were from the non-Brahmin castes; one person submitted the information I sought by email.

In addition, I engaged in conversations with many Brahmin women. One woman, contacted by an intermediary, refused an interview because she was afraid that I might ask awkward and embarrassing questions. According to my intermediary, the woman refused to be interviewed because *Raj,* a Tamil Television channel, had recently screened a play, *Rakkaiya Kattiya Manasu* (A Winged Mind), in which an Indian male researcher from the United States comes to conduct a survey and asks explicit questions about sexuality, causing discomfort to the women interviewed.

The second round of fieldwork was conducted in 2022, both in the United States and in Chennai (India). Three persons were interviewed over the phone in the United States to learn about fixing marriage alliances among the second-generation Tamil Brahmin children when the children do not find their partners on their own. I also engaged in conversations with a few women in Chennai to know about the current popularity and societal perceptions and practices relating to settling "America *varan*" marriages. They brought to my attention that in contemporary times, diasporic opportunities have opened up for a wide cross-section of Tamil society, and gleaning insights on matrimonial strategies across the spectrum would be insightful.

This prompted me to analyze the sociocultural and economic parameters that alliance-seekers, both men and women, expect and specify in their matrimonial advertisements to decipher how recent migrant alliance-seekers in the diaspora navigate through the contending pulls of tradition and modernity. I scanned through three months of advertisements between June and August 2022 in the matrimonial supplement of *The Hindu* newspaper. I analyzed 135 advertisements of diasporic alliance-seekers and compared them with 207 advertisements of non-diasporic alliance-seekers, both men and women. Such a comparison could provide insights into the strength of the contentious pulls of tradition and modernity between the diasporic and non-diasporic alliance-seekers. Although only a preliminary exploration, the interviews conducted in 2003 and 2022 and the analysis of advertisements yielded many insights on matrimonial preferences and strategies.

"AMERICA *VARAN*": WHO ARE THEY?

In the past, Green Card grooms were much sought-after, as this ensured permanent residence in the United States. A striking fact that emerged from the interviews, quite contrary to my expectations, is that today Green Card boys/girls rarely seek brides/grooms from India and even have trouble finding them. This is because the time involved for the girl to get the Green Card to join her husband is now very long, almost four to five years, with no guarantee that it will be issued by the U.S. immigration authorities. Thus, most of the "America *varan*" marriages today are with boys with H-1B or student visas. Even then, most girls do not expect to be able to become U.S. residents and citizens, unlike in the past. Boys with H-1B visas are scrutinized and classified by the girl and her family in terms of their qualifications and the probability of their securing a Green Card for permanent residence. Families are well aware that, while permanent residence would be their first option, many software jobs are being relocated from the United States to cities like Bangalore and Pune in the post-9/11 scenario, and that the H-1B visa itself is being restricted. Parents, and now girls as well, are prepared to stay in the United States for a relatively short time and then return to India. Some told me that with "everything now being available in India," it really did not matter that they might have to relocate back to India after a few years, and that it was actually important to do so relatively early in one's career in order to be absorbed into the Indian software market. In other words, unlike the earlier Green Card marriage migrants, the majority of the "America *varan*" migrants to the United States today must reckon with the fact of impermanence.

But for parents who would like their daughters to settle permanently in the United States, screening the H-1B visa holders in terms of education is important. Many feel that mere software qualifications, like MCA or degrees/diplomas from GNIIT, are insufficient; in their perception, the probability of the employer sponsoring such a person for a Green Card is rather low. Those with engineering or MBA degrees from reputed institutions are preferred.

Nonetheless, the IT expansion and the growth of software job opportunities in the United States have now brought the "America dream" to a cross-section of middle-class Brahmin households of more modest means than the earlier Green Card marriage migrants. This "America dream" has also spread to the non-Brahmin castes among whom technical higher education for girls has caught on. These respondents often remarked that nobody else from their family was in the United States, whereas in the case of girls who had married and migrated permanently to the United States in the 1970s or 1980s, many family members and relatives are now settled in the United States. In some of the latter cases, even the parents of the girls have become U.S. residents and citizens, and have stayed on there.

"America *varan*" marriages among those on student visas are also common. Boys who have gone to the United States for higher studies are seen as brighter and more intelligent, and therefore likely to have better career prospects; sometimes, though not invariably, they are also from the higher economic and social strata of Brahmins. Typically, a boy who goes to the United States to study returns to get married even before the completion of his studies, enabling him to take his wife along with him on a student spouse visa. Many are confident of getting work sponsorship that will subsequently secure a Green Card. Those who fail to get work sponsorship after an MS

(Master of Science) or MBA program of study move on to a doctoral program to extend their stay in the United States in the hope of staying there permanently, though some do not succeed and are ultimately forced to return to India.

With a growing number of Brahmin girls themselves going to the United States for higher studies, it is now common for parents in India to match the horoscopes and come to a general agreement with the family concerned. Following this, they ask the boy and girl in the United States to talk over the phone, and then meet over a weekend at their mutual convenience to come to a decision as to whether to marry. These girls generally prefer to choose among potential Green Card holders or those with student visas, preferring boys with U.S. educational backgrounds similar to their own, and seeking permanent residence. Only when a young woman is sure of work sponsorship leading to the acquisition of a Green Card would she opt for someone with an H-1B visa. Only very rarely does a girl on a student visa come back to India to select a groom for herself; rather, she lets the parents do the screening and introduce her to young men already in the United States. There is also some revival of cross-cousin marriages in this process of finding an alliance which helps to overcome the long wait of Green Card sponsorship. Male and female cousins go independently to the United States for higher education, especially in the science and engineering subjects, and after their education get married in the United States and/or in India (a civil marriage in the United States followed by a religious one in India) when either or both have got jobs and sponsorship for employment-based Green Cards. In these instances, both the families and the cousin couple have a prior understanding of the marriage alliance even before they go for higher education to the United States, clearly indicating the matrimonial strategy deployed by the extended family for upward mobility, social status enhancement, and children's happiness that is anchored both in the tradition of kin marriage as well as companionate marriage.

In the 1970s, when marriages to Green Card holders were common, Brahmin girls from the upper social strata, who had enrolled for their BA degrees in English literature at reputed women's colleges in Chennai, often hoped to find a scientist husband in the United States, Canada, or Europe. Even if at the time of marriage the young men were still on a postdoctoral fellowship, they could eventually expect to find themselves in a scientific research establishment or a university. Such girls already had a good knowledge of Western society and culture gained through reading Western literature and history and were eager to assimilate to the extent possible with their host society. But in today's globalized diasporic world, the young women getting married to H-1B visa holders are often themselves MCA or engineering graduates and have little knowledge of Western culture and civilization except for what is aired on television. Few of them can claim education in convent schools or Christian colleges that, until recently, promoted greater exposure to Western culture through literature, the arts, and history.

Thus, one respondent, living in Houston and visiting her family in Chennai for the first time after her marriage a few years ago, was eager to tell me how she was running her household in Houston and celebrating religious festivals exactly as she would have done in Chennai. When I asked specifically about her interaction as a housewife with people of another race/color/culture, she said that these interactions were more of a casual nature in the apartment building and stores. Not all girls are necessarily content with such a life, however. One parent respondent who was fixing an alliance for her son, then on a student visa but with a high probability of obtaining a Green Card through employer sponsorship, confided her anxiety that young women are becoming more assertive and independent. She was afraid that a young woman, after getting married to her son, might walk out of the marriage on the grounds that she did not like living in the United States. "What if she came back with her suitcase?" was the way she put it. Hence, the parents had decided that they would prefer to select a girl who had already visited the country for a short while, an ultra-precautionary stand, and they ultimately did succeed in finding such a girl. But not everyone insists on such a condition. Also, I heard of no recent case of a Brahmin U.S. citizen coming to India to select a bride. This could be on account of the time required to acquire U.S. citizenship, by which time the young men would have already found a partner. Or, if they were single, their age or their divorced status may have been a disadvantage in seeking a partner through this kind of arrangement.

THE VARIOUS CHANNELS AND NETWORKS

The channels that each family sources to identify potential brides and grooms are numerous and varied. The first stage of the process involves both putting the horoscope into circulation and collecting as many horoscopes as possible. The use of personal networks of family, extended kin groups, and friends, though prevalent, is now of much less importance than it was the case earlier. Correspondingly, there is greater dependence on the impersonal sourcing of horoscopes. Most respondents clarified that they never searched only for "America *varan.*" For one thing, it would be a little embarrassing to be seen as openly aspiring for material well-being. Second, given the uncertainties of finding such a match, it is deemed best to keep options open. All admitted, however, that they were keenly interested in "America *varan*" for various reasons. For instance, they might claim that the girl preferred to live abroad or that the astrologers whom they consulted had indicated such an alliance as more promising. All the same, most interviewees considered that such an alliance was quite prestigious and status-enhancing for the girl's family within their social class.

Personal networks have generally been, and continue to be a productive source when the girl for whom the alliance is sought is strikingly beautiful. The mother of such a girl is generally prodded and encouraged by her relatives or friends to seek a match for her daughter in the United States, even if she had earlier decided against doing so or had been wavering. Otherwise, it appears that personal networks are not a very encouraging source for locating prospective grooms. Nowadays, personal networks function to provide information to the girl's family that a possible match may be found in a particular family whom they may then contact. Among Tamil Brahmins, relatives tend to leave the initial selection of a prospective alliance to the parents themselves, though in many instances family tradition and hierarchies of status within the family oblige them to consult elders in the family before finally settling the alliance. A Telugu Brahmin respondent highlighted the contrast between his community and the Tamil Brahmins by noting that personal networks for finding boys are still the dominant mechanism of matchmaking in their community. This could well reflect the fact that close-kin marriages are still strongly preferred among the Telugu Brahmins, whereas this is no longer so among the Tamils. Indeed, in light of the literature on Dravidian marriage practices, it is a matter of surprise that not a single respondent spoke of the rule of cross-cousin and preferential marriage, nor did they indicate that any such eligible kin person was overlooked in favor of a non-kin alliance. Clearly, modernity and urban cultural values have weakened kinship relations which are now more or less symbolic rather than functional. With non-kin marriage alliances now overwhelmingly common among Tamil Brahmins, the modalities through which alliances are made are therefore outside the kin networks.

Sometimes friends are supportive in passing on horoscopes of prospective brides and grooms that they come across, mostly intermittently rather than on a regular basis. One respondent told me that she and her husband were assisting their neighbor in finding a suitable boy for their daughter by passing on to them the horoscopes that came their way. One day, the neighbor's family asked my respondent why they themselves could not accept their daughter as a match for their son, living in the United States. Although the respondent was not keen to fix an alliance for their son prior to that of their daughter, they acceded to their neighbor's request, as the boy and the girl had known each other for a long time as neighbors, and the boy consented to the alliance. It is usual practice among Tamil Brahmins, and quite generally among all Tamils, that if the age difference between a son and a daughter is not much, then it is the girl's marriage that gets precedence even if she is the younger of the two. This respondent's experience is, therefore, relatively uncommon.

As the role of personal networks has diminished, impersonal networks have emerged. Advertisement in the English newspaper, *The Hindu,* is by far the most popular channel for placing an advertisement, though women's magazines like *Mangaiyar Malar* also carry advertisements. A non-Brahmin *Gounder* respondent noted that members of the *Gounder* caste brought out a monthly magazine that carried matrimonial advertisements. One Brahmin respondent who was earlier employed in a women's organization was critical of the stereotyping in advertisements for brides expressed in keywords like "slim," "beautiful," "fair," "professionally qualified," "preferably working or studying in the US," disregarding aspects that she felt should be given priority in fixing a match. For her, emotional compatibility, not just physical attraction or material well-being, was the important consideration.

Parents of girls also seemed sensitive to gender power asymmetries regarding responses to advertisements. The girls' families are still cautious about placing a newspaper advertisement, and those that did seemed to have done so just once. Many felt that they did not get sufficiently good responses from newspaper advertisements either in terms of numbers or in terms of the quality of prospective grooms, as judged largely in terms of education and employment. Advertisements placed by the boys' families seemed to be more common and have better responses. The shift in the correspondence addresses from post office box numbers provided for the newspaper to email addresses has not always worked well for the girls' families as the families of prospective grooms often do not respond by email or do so very casually. Almost every respondent from the girls' side complained that in most instances the boy's families typically collected as many applicants' horoscopes and photographs as possible and then short-listed them. Those that are not short-listed get no response at all or, if contacted by the girls' families, are not always told clearly that they did not make it to the short-list. This kind of behavior was seen to indicate that the boy's side has the upper hand in the negotiations.

While personal networks are not usually helpful in identifying potential grooms, it is still necessary to network with persons residing abroad in order to verify the boy's character. Such verification of the boy's and his family's background and character is fairly easy in the case of domestic alliances, but when the boy is residing abroad, the risks involved are many. Most families identify a friend or relative in the United States/Canada to initiate telephonic contact with the boy. I heard of a number of cases in which the boy so contacted was unavailable over the phone or refused to return calls several times. In all such instances, the girls' families invariably dropped the negotiations. In many cases, parents in India are eager for their son abroad to get married, but the boy himself shows no interest. Cases were also reported to me of instances when the boy came to India and got married to a girl of his parents' choice, but then never called the girl to join him abroad, and after some years, terminated the marriage.

SELECTION AND REJECTION

The plight of those on the boys' short-list is no better. The girls' families often felt that they were given too much hope about the alliance being settled. As a result, they sometimes put their search on hold, perhaps for eight to nine months, but when the boy finally came from the United States, he saw half a dozen or more on his short-list and picked the one he liked. Of those girls who were not selected, their parents felt not just rejected, but even cheated. One respondent who experienced this quite recently told me that the boy had chosen his bride even before landing in India, having stopped en route in Dubai where he met one of the short-listed girls and decided to marry her.

While rejection and acceptance are invariably aspects of all matrimonial selection, in the case of domestic alliances, this is done on a case-by-case basis. This seemed less humiliating for the girls' families than rejection based on a brief comparison. One respondent who recently got married to a boy in the United States said of "America *varan*":

> They are so quick in the sense that they go see five girls or more and decide on one and reject the others. This was not the case for me however. It's usually hotshot, see today and get married day after tomorrow.

A boy's family observed that they had received nearly 100 horoscopes in response to just a single advertisement placed in *The Hindu*. However, my respondent expressed surprise that many horoscopes had been sent thoughtlessly since the family had even received one or two horoscopes from families of other castes, though they had advertised only for a Brahmin alliance. The family of a Chettiar girl had even approached them personally to assure them that they had no objection to a Brahmin alliance. There were one or two applicants who were much older than her son, which shocked her immensely. Ultimately, the family did not pursue any of the responses to their advertisement. Not only was the rejection rate by the astrologer whom they consulted for matching the horoscopes very high, but they were also dissatisfied regarding the applicants' family backgrounds. My informant claimed that they were only looking for a "traditional" girl, by which they meant religious background and belief in God, an "acceptable" relationship between her parents, and correct behavior of the girl toward elders. Being personally unwilling to embarrass the rejected applicants, she passed on the burden of rejection to her mother, who made the excuse of horoscopes not matching.

Most respondents used newspaper advertisements along with other channels. For example, temples now provide horoscope exchange services. Commercial and voluntary matchmaking services also undertake horoscope exchange. Many of my respondents had heard of the well-established service provided at the Ganesh temple in Mahalingapuram in the Kodambakkam area. Once registered there, the temple mails a list of prospective grooms/brides on a quarterly or bimonthly basis, from which an initial selection may be made, after which the temple or the party concerned could be asked for the horoscope.

One of my respondents claimed that she had fortunately found an "America *varan*" match for her daughter from the horoscopes mailed to her by the Mahalingapuram temple. However, another respondent, who is still seeking such a match, claimed that the temple list contained applicants from a lower socioeconomic class of Brahmins and not quite up to her expectations.

While the Mahalingapuram temple service is preferred primarily by the Iyer sect of Brahmins, the Iyengar sect of Brahmins in Chennai prefer a similar service rendered by the Parthasarathy temple in Triplicane. A recently married Iyengar respondent observed that her mother had registered her horoscope at the Parthasarathy temple marriage bureau called *Geethacharyan*. She claimed that she had not been totally in favor of an "American *varan*" marriage as she wanted to live close to her ailing parents. But the problem was that the horoscopes of prospective grooms living in Chennai did not match, while the horoscopes that matched were of young men living elsewhere, mostly outside the state in places like Mumbai, Delhi or even abroad. One day, her husband's father, who had also registered his son's horoscope at *Geethacharyan*, approached her parents saying there were *nine poruthams* (the horoscopes matching on nine different counts, which is considered a near perfect match). That is how she ultimately got married to a groom in the United States, who is a software engineer on an H-1B visa.

For this respondent's family, horoscope compatibility was deemed extremely important, as it generally is in the case of domestic alliances as well. But another respondent, the mother of a not-so-beautiful daughter whose marriage was fixed recently to a boy in Bangalore, placed a different construction on horoscope matching. She confided that she would have liked to have fixed an "America *varan*" alliance for her daughter. She believed that the family had the requisite social and economic status, but noted that, in reality, the primary consideration for an "America *varan*" alliance is the girl's beauty; if the prospective groom and his family are pleased with the girl's beauty, they can sometimes even overlook the question of horoscope compatibility.

Indeed, many parents of girls were acutely sensitive to the issue of rejection based on the criterion of personal beauty. Many were bothered by the emerging practice of asking for the girl's photograph along with the horoscope right at the initial stage. The boys' families, on the other hand, claimed that such an approach expedited the matchmaking process, especially considering the fact that the boys concerned generally came on a brief three-week trip from the United States. In fact, even temples or other agencies that use the Internet to maintain their databases of potential partner-seekers ask for photographs to be uploaded. Not everyone approves of this.

COMMERCIAL AGENTS

Not only do temples use computerized databases, but other agencies, such as the *Tamil Nadu Brahmin Association,* have also started providing horoscope exchange services and maintaining a computerized database. The Association came into prominence only about two decades ago and seeks to highlight the social and economic problems of lower-middle-class Brahmin families adversely affected by the policy of backward caste reservations in government employment in the state. Many of my respondents also used the services of one Jayarama Iyer of Mandaveli, who facilitated the exchange of horoscopes by maintaining files of prospective matches, throwing his house open for fixed hours every day for clients to avail of his free services. Other respondents, however, felt that his database contained relatively few "America *varan*" cases. An attempt to confirm this directly from him met with a strong rebuff as he refused an interview with me, claiming he was only doing social service and did not seek publicity by giving interviews.

Individuals have also started commercial matchmaking agencies. A respondent claimed he was cheated by one such agency to whom he had advanced nearly eight thousand rupees. The agent had promised his clients that he would give them a set of horoscopes of prospective boys that suited all their stipulations within three months. Although the client did receive some horoscopes during the period, these were neither pre-screened nor did they come up to their expectations, many being simply downloaded from websites like *Tamil Matrimony*.

A respondent of the Gounder caste told me that marriage brokers are very common in their community, charging something like 3–5 percent of the cash and gold dowry that the boy receives from the girl's family, and a certain amount from the girl's side as well. Such brokers are virtually non-existent among the Brahmin community, however.

THE ROLE OF ASTROLOGERS

When the girl's or the boy's family acquires the horoscope of a desirable match, the next step is to check with the astrologer on the compatibility of the horoscopes. In some families, an elder may have acquired the proficiency to read and match horoscopes, but that is relatively rare. By and large, Brahmin families consult an astrologer whom they have known for a long time, or one who has been introduced to them by someone considered reliable. Astrologers commonly charge fixed fees, or they may leave the matter to the client's discretion. As the process of matching horoscopes might involve numerous attempts, the family will generally seek the advice of the same astrologer, effecting a change only when they find the rejection rate is unduly high, if they learn that another astrologer gives more specific or accurate predictions than the one whom they have been consulting, or for one who uses alternative methods of astrological predictions.

That one of the most forward-looking and modern communities in India, a community that has produced numerous men and women of science, still believes strongly in astrology appears to be a puzzle (Ramanujan, 1990), but faith in horoscope compatibility is a distinguishing aspect of Brahmin matchmaking strategies. In fact, many non-Brahmin castes that had hitherto selected partners on the basis of mutual liking have also begun to consider the compatibility of horoscopes, perhaps yet another aspect of the sanskritization process. A Nadar respondent told me that the Self-Respect Movement of E. V. Ramaswami Naicker (also known as Periyar) in the early decades of the twentieth century was very strong in her village and that most of their caste members have adopted what are called "social reform marriages" that do away with Vedic rituals, Brahmin priests, horoscopes, and so on. Even in such communities, changes in matchmaking practices have begun to set in. Nowadays, something like a fete or fair is held in the village area to which all community members on the lookout for partners come to discreetly make choices. Such get-togethers are prevalent among non-resident Indian (NRI) communities in the New York-New Jersey area, but are also apparently there in some villages of South India as well.

EXPECTATIONS AND DOWRY

Once the horoscopes of the girl and boy are matched, the girl's family usually approaches the boy's family to confirm their interest in the alliance. If the boy's family is also interested and finds the horoscopes compatible after consulting with their astrologers, they indicate their desire to proceed further. Astrologers for both parties do not necessarily concur. In some cases, the boy's family comes to see the girl first to decide on her suitability and whether to send her photograph to the boy abroad; others wait for the boy to come and see the girl. In a few cases, I found that the families concerned had already approved the alliance, the girl and the boy saw each other via a web camera, spoke to each other over the phone, exchanged a few emails, and then agreed to get married. Sometimes, when the boy from the United States comes to India to meet a couple of girls before making a choice, he prefers to meet the girl first in some common friend's house, a shopping mall, a restaurant, or, more likely, at another wedding, rather than in her own home.

It may come as a surprise to many that not a single Brahmin respondent in my sample admitted to having given or received any dowry. Until the 1960s and 1970s, it was common for the girls of Brahmin families to give a specified sum of money, called *Vara Dakshana* (dowry) to the groom's family at the time of fixing the marriage, for which a small ceremony is held at the groom's house. It appears that this practice of giving a stipulated cash sum is not as widely practiced as it used to be. In fact, it would be considered inappropriate and shameful if the boy's family were to ask for *Vara Dakshana*. In its place, the boys' families now indicate that both the marriage and whatever gifts of jewelry the girl's family gives to her should be appropriate to the social and economic status of the boy's family. There are also expectations of gifts to the boy, like a diamond or gold ring, and good quality suits.

Most of my informants observed that the general expectation in the "America *varan*" alliances is one of "decent marriage." This involves gold jewelry to the extent of 15–20 sovereigns (each sovereign is 8 grams of gold), the silver utensils generally required for ceremonies and rituals, diamond earrings of nearly 1.5 carats of diamond, and the mandatory four Conjeevaram (Kancheepuram) silk saris. Additionally, the marriage should be solemnized in a nice *kalyana mandapam* or wedding venue and should include an evening reception with a music program and wedding meals served throughout the entire day-and-a-half of the function for an average of 200 guests each time.

Some respondents mentioned that these expectations for "America *varan*" alliances are in fact relatively modest compared to domestic alliances, where more household items, like utensils, mixers, cots, and steel almirahs, need to be given to the married couple to set up their home, and a number of gifts are to be given on various occasions throughout the first year of marriage. Even so, Tamil Brahmin families do not in general demand consumer durables like cars and refrigerators, as often happens in other parts of the country.

In recent times, newspapers have reported cases of "America *varan*" marriages in which the girl is abandoned by her husband on the promise that she would be invited to join him later. In the meantime, his parents make excessive demands for additional dowry, putting the girl and her family through considerable mental torture. It is difficult to determine the caste status of these families from newspaper reports. A few of my Brahmin respondents did tell me that they were aware of such cases of abandonment and that in some cases the girl concerned had sought a divorce and remarried, but these were all cases that had occurred to "a friend of a friend of a friend." Most of my informants were aware of the risks of "America *varan*" marriages, but were willing to take the risks.

The question of who is to bear the airfare for the girl to join her husband in the United States is sometimes a ticklish issue for middle-class parents who find the marriage expenses burdensome, but usually, the girl herself requests her prospective husband to send the ticket. More worrisome is the question of whether or not a visa will be issued to the spouse at all. When the boy is on a student visa, his family may prefer to have a girl who already has a family member in the United States, either a brother or a sister, who can file the necessary papers to get her there first on a visitor visa and change the status later on. One respondent told me that she was compelled to drop a prospective alliance for her son precisely on the grounds that the girl's father had said that he could not ensure that the girl would get a U.S. visa. Many respondents also indicated that software engineers on H-1B visas have a marked preference for girls with MCA or BE (Bachelor of Engineering) qualifications that would enable them to get employment in the same field, while boys studying for MS (Master of Science) degrees in the United States, and likely candidates for Green Cards, are not so particular about the girl being professionally qualified, often giving her the option to study, work, or just be a housewife.

MATCHES FOR GIRLS WHO GO ABROAD FOR HIGHER STUDIES

As a modernized social group, Tamil Brahmins have always sought to outsmart the rest by playing the education card. This was the first community to overcome inhibitions and send girls abroad for higher education, and it is now the first to capture the benefits of the IT opportunities through technical education. While other castes are now catching up with the trend of sending their daughters abroad for higher studies, there is no doubt that the Tamil Brahmins were well ahead of others.

Finding partners for girls studying abroad is also a major parental concern. Radha Mami's only daughter, Nandini, was an exceptionally bright student who had completed her undergraduate engineering degree from BITS, Pilani. After graduation, she worked for a year in a Bangalore-based IT company, and a year later proceeded to the United States on a Research Assistantship for a dual MS degree in science, technology, and information technology in

Portland, Oregon. Radha Mami, recently widowed and with no income of her own, was initially very frightened and reluctant to send her only daughter to the United States, but she was encouraged by friends and relatives to do so. Today she has no regrets. Nandini was fortunate to have her father's cousin living nearby in Seattle, who took the initiative to find a marriage partner, a boy appropriately qualified and working at Intel in Portland itself. Although her uncle knew the boy's uncle and vouchsafed for his character, it was an arranged marriage in which horoscopes were exchanged and matched. The boy's mother and the girl's mother also met with the girl and the boy respectively. Radha Mami claims that she gave considerable importance to the boy being religious, celebrating Hindu festivals, and keeping up Indian cultural traditions, and she is indeed happy that her son-in-law recites *shlokas* and does *sandhyavandanam or gayathri japam* (daily evening ritual and prayers in Sanskrit that marks the Brahminhood of boys). She is happy that her daughter is both well-settled and very supportive. On completion of her program of study, Nandini got a job in Portland, although she did not yet have her Green Card. She had apparently taken an assurance from her husband before their marriage that he should have no objection to her either being employed or supporting her mother in India financially. With her earnings, she also financed her brother's MBA education in India, and more importantly, contributed from her earnings to her own wedding.

Young women like Nandini, who are bright and who graduate with engineering degrees from good institutions, have used their qualifications as a passport to get out of the rut of Indian middle-class living to what appears to them a better life in the United States. Opting for higher education in the United States and jobs there, they use various channels to find partners, often within the framework of what would be considered an "arranged marriage."

On the other hand, Raghupathy's strategy for getting all his daughters married to boys in the United States indicates the great importance that middle-class Brahmin families attribute to a girl's higher education and professional qualifications in conjunction with marriage to an equally educated and qualified man of the same caste and social background. Raghupathy had encouraged all his daughters to go to the United States for higher education—one for engineering, another for optometry, and the third for media studies—while he himself opted for voluntary retirement from a bank in order to finance his youngest daughter's education in the United States. He also encouraged them to find their partners there. The first two girls found their partners through channels like the Internet, but once they had decided that the match was suitable, they passed on the details to their parents in India, who then checked with the boys' families. The girls were keen to select only boys who, like them, had gone to the United States for higher education and had settled there after finding appropriate jobs. Lest there be too many adjustment problems, they did not want to marry boys who were born and educated in the United States to immigrant parents, or those who had gone to the United States only for jobs through employer or family sponsorship. Once the eldest daughter got married through that process, she helped her younger sister in finding a husband in the same way. Only the last daughter had selected a partner on her own through a love affair with a Brahmin boy of a different subcaste, who had first gone to Australia for higher studies and then joined her in the United States. The father told me that he had indicated to his daughters that he would accept a love marriage, but had advised them to fall in love only with Brahmin boys, as otherwise there would be adjustment problems. He then went on to narrate the difficulties of intercaste marriages in his own extended family in India.

Gowri is perhaps an exception to the way girls who go to the United States find their husbands. A graduate of the Indian Institute of Technology (IIT), she was the only child of a middle-class Brahmin family. Despite her mother's reluctance and fear, but thanks to her father's encouragement, Gowri did what every IIT graduate is expected to do, that is, proceed to the United States for higher studies. After her studies, she got herself a job and a Green Card through employer sponsorship. Once settled there, she found herself a partner, effectively a "love match," to a Tamil Brahmin boy who was born and educated in the United States to immigrant parents and could hardly speak Tamil. She married him in the United States with his family members attending the wedding, and then returned to Chennai where her parents organized a wedding reception. Gowri's selection of a first-generation immigrant would be considered a bold and rare step by most Indian girls and their parents wanting to settle their daughters in the United States.

In all the cases cited, we note how diasporic opportunities are realized by the girls themselves through the channel of higher education, and the ways in which diasporic marriage alliances are fixed, most often within the frame of "arranged marriage." Yet these strategies give the girls a much higher degree of autonomy and freedom of choice in matchmaking than is available in India, where parental involvement is much greater.

WHY THE "AMERICA *VARAN*" PREFERENCE?

Explaining their "America *varan*" preference, most parent respondents said that they felt it would ensure a better future for their daughters. One mother, the principal of a well-known school in Chennai, whose daughter was studying in the United States, explicitly pointed to what she thought were immense opportunities for her daughter's intellectual growth in the United States and the possibilities for her to lead a more creative life. She recounted in detail her visits to the parental homes of young men under consideration for her daughter. In many cases, she said, even if the boy was well-educated and settled in the United States, she had been forced to drop negotiations in view of the way his family lived in India, far below their own social status and standards of good living.

Brahmin women who migrated through marriage to the United States in the 1970s have children studying in leading institutions like Harvard or Princeton, and this serves as a role model for many Brahmin families, like the aforementioned intellectually inclined teacher. Typically, such persons endeavor to send their girls for education to the United States and arrange for them to marry boys who are also studying in the United States and are likely to get Green Card sponsorship through employers.

On the other hand, another mother told me that she has advised her daughter, who is on an H-1B spouse visa, not to put up with all sorts of difficulties just to stay on in the United States. She was most welcome to return to India where all opportunities for a good life are now equally available. A Brahmin father, frustrated by all the efforts that he has so far put into finding an "America *varan*" alliance for his only daughter, was frank about his preference for such an alliance. If he married his daughter to a boy living in Chennai, he told me, he would have to worry about the locality and neighborhood where she would be staying. Earlier, the elite and the rich Brahmins of Chennai lived in independent bungalows and a girl married into such a family would live in her in-laws' bungalow in an extended nuclear, if not a joint family. Now, with apartment living becoming more common, young couples living apart from their parental families cannot afford a pricey apartment in a good residential neighborhood in the early stages of the boy's career. This bothers the girl's parents, who feel that their daughter would be better-off in the United States. In all these rationalizations, we note how matrimonial strategies are being deployed in the reproduction of class status.

With newer economic opportunities available to this forward-looking community, there is greater differentiation within the caste. Matrimonial strategies are deployed to ensure class mobility, as in the case of lower- and middle-class Brahmin families whose children become software specialists and proceed on H-1B visas to the United States. Meanwhile, elite Brahmin families, concerned with the intergenerational reproduction of class status in a globalized world, use diasporic opportunities through foreign education for their children and seek to retain their class status through the strategies of matchmaking.

Even after an alliance is fixed, the girl's family has to exert themselves to keep the boy's family happy. While this may be true in other communities as well, Tamil Brahmins do indeed have an exaggerated attitude toward what is called *sammandi mariyadai* (respect for in-laws), a well-known feature of

Tamil Brahmin society. In fact, there is a ritual enactment of this in the Brahmin wedding when the groom gets angry and decides to opt for an ascetic life by pretending to go on a *Kasi Yatra* (journey to the holy city of Varanasi). The bride's father and uncle will follow the groom, persuading him to come back and marry his daughter. A Telugu Brahmin respondent told me in this connection that the girl's and the boy's families in her community relate to each other like friends and family members once an alliance is fixed, unlike Tamil Brahmins, among whom the in-laws' family will "sit on the drumstick tree." In Tamil folklore, only demons sit on the drumstick tree! One can imagine how much the "respect for in-laws" would be in the case of prestigious alliances like the "America *varan*" marriages.

Both mothers and daughters whom I interviewed felt that fixing an "America *varan*" alliance was socially very prestigious: "It's a big thing," as one girl put it. Many of the respondent mothers had availed themselves of the opportunity to visit the United States at least once, most probably at the time of their daughter's pregnancy and childbirth. For many of them, it was not merely the first time they had traveled outside the country, but the first time they had even boarded a flight. All the excitement aside, it greatly added to their prestige in their own social circles. There are numerous jokes and caricatures in circulation about how some parents wear their pride. One girl I interviewed reported that her father-in-law had told her that he was a simple man who did not go about wearing a T-shirt just because his son was in the United States!

At least one respondent's parents were thinking of migrating permanently to the United States or Canada where both their sons were residing. However, many others felt that this was not feasible and had no intention of migrating, perhaps because they themselves were relatively young. Many of the Brahmin marriage migrants of the 1970s and 1980s have taken their old parents either permanently or for long stays in the United States, especially if there are no other siblings in India to take care of them.

MATRIMONY, TRADITION, AND MODERNITY IN THE U.S. DIASPORA

The study so far dealt with families seeking matrimonial alliances as immigrants from India to the United States. Studies on acculturation have examined how Indian-origin families in the United States and Canada balance and trade-off between traditional Indian values in which they grew up and the modern Western values of their host country on issues like the socialization of their children and issues of marriage. Dasgupta (1998) has noted that ethnic identity is a positive self-concept that consciously anchors individuals in particular ethnic groups, and an important aspect of it is a sense of belonging and a commitment to the group's values, beliefs, behaviors, conventions, and customs. Maintenance of their traditional culture is therefore important in their construction of ethnic identity even as they are involved in a judicious acculturation process through their control over what aspects of American culture they accept in their lives. In this process of judicious acculturation, studies have noted that while on the one hand, they come to accept gender equality, yet the gender socialization of daughters is geared more toward their upholding traditional values, exhibiting some asymmetry between the socialization of boys and girls. This is because the burden of maintaining tradition and identity has historically largely been the responsibility of women in South Asia as part of the nationalist resolution noted in Chatterjee (1989). As keepers of South Asian culture and heritage in the United States, second-generation immigrant daughters are more closely monitored than the sons. Fears of exogamy and cultural obliteration through "Americanization" have contributed to the construction of asymmetric gender roles. This anxiety over cultural reproduction that varies across ethnic groups and families is reflected in the intergenerational differences in the attitudes toward marriage, with the parents' attitudes being more aligned with the South Asian values of marriage while the children, with their bicultural upbringing, are more aligned to the American values of marriage.

The Tamil Brahmins in the United States are generally highly educated professionals, with more women combining the roles of homemaker and professional or other employments outside the home. While they are quite particular about instilling traditional cultural values to securely anchor the cultural identities of their children, they are also liberal in their children's mate selection as the numerous instances of interracial marriages, largely with Caucasians, and to some extent with others such as Japanese, Hispanic groups, and Middle Eastern Muslims. These children, both boys and girls, often find their mates either during their college days or while at work, with the relationships first starting out as friendships. For those not finding their mates through this channel, they get to meet compatible partners through various ethnic cultural associations in which the family participates, such as cultural concerts and performances, celebration of festivals, and some temple functions. Families introduce eligible partners to other families, allowing children to meet them as well. In these cases, both parents and children are largely aligned with South Asian values of marriage. Most Tamil Brahmin families, like other South Asian families, with a few exceptions in cases of single parenting or when the parents have themselves had exogamous love marriages, do not overly encourage their children, especially the daughters, to date along American lines. Instead, they have evolved their own dating patterns that is more in consonance with their Indian cultural norms.

While the majority of second-generation Tamil Brahmin children do marry within their community in the United States, marriage to Brahmins of other ethnic groups of South India, as well as to North Indians, is also common. It is rare for a second-generation Tamil Brahmin to choose an exogamous caste mate from among the second generation of the same ethnic group but do so across different ethnic groups of India. Certain ethnic communities, being more numerous like Punjabi, Gujarati, and Telugu, are also able to find partners more easily within their community. Intermingling among various communities in the United States is quite limited, unlike in the metro cities of Delhi or Mumbai. Long-distance marriage alliances of second-generation U.S. Tamil Brahmins to similar second-generation partners of both Tamil Brahmins and other South Indian Brahmins in other countries such as Canada, the United Kingdom, Europe, Australia, New Zealand, and the Middle East is an emergent phenomenon made possible through the internet.

The second generation being bicultural prefers bicultural partners, and one almost never hears of sourcing mates as "America *varan*" from India except for the rare female cross-cousin marriage from the extended family in India, especially if the girl has had some higher education in the United States. One respondent observed that the second-generation Tamil Brahmin children prefer an "arranged with dating" marriage. Children do want their parents to do the filtering process of potential partners using their many criteria on education, family background, and importantly including the traditional cultural norms such as horoscope matching and other prescribed norms relating to *Gotra,* but not necessarily the subcaste grouping among Tamil Brahmins. How far Tamil Brahmin parents are willing to expand their choice beyond their subcaste grouping to Brahmins from other neighboring southern states or beyond depends on the place where they have settled in the United States and their circle of trustworthy Indian-origin friends through whom they get information on probable candidates. While the Hindu temples in the United States generally do not have horoscope exchange services, the priests in many Hindu temples provide Vedic astrology services to match horoscopes that are downloaded by the interested parents from those uploaded on matrimonial sites or dating apps. Children also register themselves on these matrimonial sites, uploading their profiles and horoscopes, and there is a dating app for America-born South Indian Brahmins. A popular matrimonial site *Banyan-Way.com* promotes minimal parental intervention to let the children themselves take over the matter as a way to bridge the gap between traditional matchmaking and modern dating, and there are several others as well. Parents also get to know the availability of prospective candidates through their circle of friends, through their participation and networking in ethnic associations such as the *Tamil Sangam* that has numerous chapters across the United States, through local Chinmaya Mission groups, and through their parental association in the children's Carnatic music or Bharatanatyam dance classes, as these have become an integral part of children's socialization.

Once they get a candidate screened and introduced by their parents, they take over the process of finding compatibility between themselves, often referred as "chemistry," through a period of dating that starts initially with chat sessions over the phone. They usually go out a couple of times and then decide for themselves. This is clearly different from a girl based in India looking for a prospective "America *varan*" who connects through "Zoom" meetings and various internet and mobile apps between India and the United States to explore their compatibility. The current trend for sending out wedding invitations among Tamil Brahmins is similar to how it is now being done among most Americans through the creation of a website that has photos of the couple and the wedding announcement of the date and venue, along with a gift registry to which relatives and friends can make their monetary gift to the couple. This is different from the way it is done by Tamil Brahmins in weddings in India, where gifts blessed by the priests through the recitation of prayers are given as part of the religious ceremony.

This process of dating after introduction is now becoming quite common, and parents begin counseling their daughters for some years beforehand on how not to expect a Prince Charming or fairy-tale endings. They emphasize that it takes effort to meet the proper partner, that it should be an intellectual and not emotional decision, the desirability of cultural compatibility, and the red flags to note in the dating partner's behavior, such as being secretive about his or her family. But it appears that there is no single definitive approach to finding partners for second-generation children, even within a family, as it could vary even between sibling sisters.

This indicates traditional South Asian caste and religion restrictions remain strong even when the second generation makes their own choice of mates that corroborates children are being socialized along traditional South Asian values. Another respondent noted that compared to the previous or parental generation, priorities, mindsets, and lifestyles have changed. The "new normal" age for getting married now appears to be the early thirties, even for girls. Children are also now accessing and obtaining the freedom not to marry. There is no compulsion to find a partner for themselves, and daughters also say they want to be independent and find their own partners.

CONTEMPORARY TRENDS IN DIASPORIC ALLIANCES AMONG THE SOUTH INDIANS

For an understanding of the contemporary situation of diasporic marriage alliances among Tamils and other South Indians, an analysis was done of those seeking diasporic alliances using the matrimonial advertisements for the period of three months from June to August of 2022 that appeared in *The Hindu*, a widely circulated English newspaper in Tamil Nadu and popular for its weekly Matrimonial Supplement of advertisements, even after online matrimonial websites have gained predominance. Not always does the individual who is looking for a marriage partner insert the advertisement in the newspaper. For younger people for whom it is their first marriage, it is a parent, elder sibling, or an uncle who would place the advertisement on behalf of the young person. Whereas a few decades ago it was almost a taboo, especially for girls, to put in advertisements on their behalf, such taboo has now become outdated, and it is not altogether uncommon for individuals to insert advertisements for themselves. These advertisements were analyzed in terms of the social characteristics of those seeking alliances and the kinds of alliances they sought.

There was a total of 135 advertisements for diasporic alliances for the 3 months that were screened, and repeat advertisements were omitted. There were in all sixty-eight male alliance-seekers, and sixty-seven were female alliance-seekers. Five males and six females were seeking remarriage after divorce. While Hindus were the most numerous, there were fifteen Christians and ten Muslims in all.

While most advertisements do mention their religion and caste, it was also evident that they were quite open to seeking alliances from outside their caste, though not outside their religion. Caste here refers to *jati,* as in popular English usage caste is used instead of *jati,* while vernacular languages use *jati*. Sociologically, *varna* refers to the fourfold Hindu caste structure and *jati* refers to endogamous groups within the fourfold *varna*. 30.8 percent of the total stated "Caste No Bar" (CNB) in their advertisements, although 73.8 percent of them were men, and only 26.2 percent of advertisements put in by women stated CNB. Only one Brahmin male had stated "CNB" in the advertisement, while all other Hindus were among the non-Brahmin castes. Only one Telugu Hindu SC of the Mala caste indicated that he is open to Christians as well. Even Christians had stated "CNB" but not "Religion No Bar" except for one, indicating that caste is still prevalent among the Christian converts.

The fact that fewer women indicate "CNB" could only be explained by the caste socialization of girls from a young age within families on account of the marriage rule of "caste endogamy" in Hindu society, whereas the same rule has much less binding effect on the caste socialization of boys. This is essentially a feature of the gender scripts of modernity and tradition, where there is a greater burden on women in households to uphold tradition along with the aspirations of modernity, while men seem to have less of the role of upholding tradition. There is palpable anxiety among girls' parents that there is a greater burden of adjustment on the girls in their marital homes, associated with their roles as homemakers and bearers of sons for the continuation of lineages.

Interestingly, although 30.8 percent of the advertisements had inserted "CNB," only 15 percent had not indicated their caste, whereas all others comprising 85 percent did mention their caste. Of the nearly 70 percent of advertisers who mentioned their caste and did not specify "CNB," a few had indicated "subsect no bar," indicating they were open to alliances of different subsects within their caste. For instance, a Brahmin advertiser of the Iyer subcaste looking for a bride indicated they were open to considering Brahmin girls of Iyer, Iyengar, Smartha, and Madhwa subsects.

Being open to alliances from outside one's caste is not altogether renouncing the social status associated with caste identity; rather, by mentioning their own caste, they leave it to the subjective assessment of those desiring to respond to understand in what ways the respondent's social caste standing would be acceptable to the advertising person. In most cases signifying that social class standing would override social caste standing in such situations. Very few of the Scheduled Castes and Other Backward Classes (OBCs) mentioned their caste.

Clearly, caste endogamy still rules among Hindus in seeking diasporic marriage alliances, but there are also indications that among the non-Brahmin castes, there is a tendency among men to expand their choice set to include possibilities of alliances outside their caste. Only an empirical post-choice analysis would indicate if the choice-set extension is inclusive of all other castes or is limited to a certain range. As the male advertisers have indicated their caste, it is expected that the choice-set extension is most likely exclusive of other caste groups that do not rank high in their subjective estimation. Nevertheless, the fact that 30.8 percent had indicated "CNB," with 73.8 percent of those being men and only 26.2 percent being women, indicates that, to some extent the rigid caste endogamy rule is rendered flexible to an extent among the diasporic groups.

This trend deviates to some extent from the non-diasporic alliance-seekers, as out of 207 advertisements screened for domestic alliance-seekers at random from the same newspapers, only 23.1 percent had indicated "CNB," and the rest wanted a spouse only from the same caste, suggesting caste endogamy is stronger among the domestic alliance-seekers than the diasporic alliance-seekers. Caste still plays a significant role in social life and interactions with extended family in India, while diasporic groups living in multicultural societies are not bound by caste relations, as their interactions with other Indian immigrants in the host country are a matter of choice determined by many other factors.

Many diasporic alliance-seekers do mention that they are affluent with good net worth, indicating their economic status as well. SC alliance-seekers who have inserted "CNB" without mentioning their caste could imply that they are open to both SC and non-SC castes because scaling up their economic status through education would, to an extent overcome the disparities of caste and social standing. As the diasporic population is generally more aspirational, they carry forward these aspirational attitudes in the sphere of matrimony as well.

Another reason for the expanded choice set by diasporic males could be the increasing lack of enthusiasm and desire among girls in India to move to foreign countries as part of marriage migration, given the uncertainties of permanent residence and employment instability due to the downturns in the global economy. Not expanding their choice set beyond their castes would make it more difficult for males of the diaspora to find suitable life partners.

The countries from where the Indian diaspora sought matrimonial alliances were the developed countries of North America, Europe, Australia, and the countries of the Middle East, with the United States and United Kingdom topping the list, indicating that these were educated people who migrated from India because of their professional qualifications as engineers, software professionals, or doctors. More women than men indicated their willingness to migrate abroad to the United States, even if they were not in the United States, or for that matter, to other countries upon marriage. Those who had returned to India after a U.S. university education mentioned in their advertisements that they were open to both diasporic and domestic alliances.

As more people go the United States for higher education and get employed there, there were more diasporic women from the United States seeking suitable alliances than from other countries like Canada, the United Kingdom, and Australia. Diasporic women from Singapore, Germany, the Netherlands, Dubai, Qatar, and Malaysia also sought alliances. Most of these women employed in these countries had gone there after higher education either in India or abroad. Women are therefore not just responding to advertisements of diasporic male alliance-seekers but are increasingly diasporic alliance-seekers themselves. Diasporic women alliance-seekers have taken big strides to be in step with modernity as these women have sought education and employment in foreign countries mostly through their own individual efforts, overcoming many social constraints, but only few seem prepared to break free from the rule of caste endogamy in marriage alliances.

Significantly, none of the advertisements had asked for a horoscope, but only one male alliance-seeker explicitly noted that a horoscope was not preferred. Although a horoscope was not explicitly sought in the advertisement, 30 percent of the Hindu advertisers did mention their birth star, the star assigned based on the exact time of their birth out of the twenty-seven stars of the Hindu Almanac reigning at the time of birth, a crucial feature of any Hindu horoscope. Brahmin advertisers mentioned both the star and the *gotra,* which refers to the lineages of seven mythical sages. These serve as initial screening parameters as certain star pairings are considered unfavorable, and marriage alliances within the same *gotra* are forbidden among the Brahmins. It is possible that as they proceed further with the short-listed candidates, they may or may not do horoscope matching.

Analysis of the contemporary trends in diasporic marriage alliances among the South Indians, the majority of whom, with aspirational goals, live in the heartlands of Western modernity, indicates the extent to which ideas of modernity and tradition are upheld and reworked in their search for life partners. They preferred the channels mostly followed in India and refrained from dating in their host countries. Traditional norms in selection, though still dominant, are going through some discernible changes as some have chosen to widen their choice set by indicating that caste, religion, and language are not significant. Though none asked for horoscopes, they still provided some minimum horoscope information such as birth star and *gotra.* The extent to which traditional norms are followed, even if the practices are modified to suit the changing times, is indicative of how individuals seek the cultural securities embedded in such norms, which makes them feel more empowered in navigating decisions such as marriage partners in diasporic situations involving more risks.

CONCLUSION

Many may wonder what makes this account of America *varan* marriages so unique to Tamil Brahmins when presumably all other castes and communities would go through the same processes to find a match. While we need to have more information on other caste groups, a number of considerations distinguish the Tamil Brahmin community's preference for such marriages. To begin with, the Dravidian movement in Tamil Nadu for much of the last century was a non-Brahmin movement that, in targeting Brahminism for attack, rendered them a socially and politically powerless group within Tamil society. Sidelined from the state's organized sector employment avenues, such as administrative services and educational employment, on account of the state's reservation policies, Tamil Brahmins have shown great agility in grasping opportunities for upward social mobility. Migrating out to other cities in India, and to the United States and elsewhere from the 1960s, it is not surprising that with the Information Technology revolution, this group is once again at the forefront. Not only have the boys and girls of this community been quick to acquire the requisite technical qualifications without much gender bias, they were also the pioneer leaders of the software industry in Chennai (Fuller and Narasimhan, 2013). Whereas the contemporary outmigration of most other castes is a consequence of the new opportunities of globalization of the last two decades, the Brahmin outmigration to the United States started almost a quarter century earlier and the cultural discourse of "America *varan*" can be dated since then.

The analysis of "America *varan*" marriages among Tamil Brahmins indicates the role played by matrimonial strategies in promoting upward social mobility and enhancement of social status. It also indicates both the awareness and sometimes unquestioning acceptance of deep gender asymmetries in matrimonial transactions. Such acceptance arises from prior caste and gender socialization. The class and gender *habitus* that is the outcome of these dispositions facilitates the reproduction of these gender asymmetries, constructing gendered identities that make Brahmin women subjects of patriarchy in one sphere even as they gain the freedom and opportunity to move into the modern world.

Chapter 5

Religiosity among Hindu Women in Chennai

Indian civilization has always been marked by its distinctive Hindu spirituality, but the heightened display of religiosity in recent times requires an understanding. Some would argue that this could be the effect of the civilization's dilemmas over Western modernity and a constant quest, both collective and individual, to constrain modernity's tentacles from reaching the soul of the civilization. This view is analogous to Chatterjee's argument about the nationalists' claims of the spiritual superiority of India over the West, who hence sought to protect it from the influence of Western modernity. As noted earlier, the nationalist resolution marked the private/domestic sphere of culture as women's distinctive sphere and tasked them with the role of defending the spiritual life of the family. The conundrum of tradition and modernity that was sought to be resolved by the nationalists is, however, an ongoing and contentious one. This chapter explores the terrain of contemporary Hindu religiosity in Chennai and the rise in women's religiosity by focusing on certain markers, including the role of the media in religion, and explores its impact on sociocultural and patriarchal norms and changes in lifestyles.

WOMEN AND THE SANSKRITIZATION PROCESS

Sanskritization process has been an ongoing indigenous civilizing process since the early Christian era, marked by the start of temple building and worship in temples, as Vedic religion in earlier times was not oriented toward temple worship. Sociologist Srinivas explained the sanskritization process as the adoption of the rituals, customs and worldview of the upper castes, especially the Brahmins, by the lower castes that has been ongoing for several centuries (Srinivas, [1952] 2003). Recently, scholars have distinguished between the Brahminization process relating to the constitution of Brahminic hegemony in the construction of Vedic Hinduism and sanskritization relating to the emulative process by other castes (Thirumal et al., 2024, 286). In the realm of religion, this has meant the adoption of the features of sanskritized or Vedic Hinduism by the lower castes, who were previously engaged in a mixture of folk religion and Dravidian forms of Hinduism in the Tamil countryside (Mines, 2005). The implication of this cultural phenomenon in Tamil Nadu needs to be understood in the context of the sociopolitical Dravidian movement and its lasting impact on the social groups, especially the pride in Dravidian culture it has fostered. During the heyday of the Dravidian movement, it strongly projected itself as a non-Brahmin movement against Brahminism, and as it gained political strength, it lost out as a cultural movement to the sanskritization process. Women of different castes are aspiring and accepting the sociocultural norms of the sanskritized upper-caste groups. The electoral successes of the All India Anna Dravida Munnetra Kazhagam (AIADMK) party are to a large extent the result of its stance on religion, despite its origins in the Dravida Kazhagam (DK) party, as it was able to attract large numbers of pious Hindu women into its fold.

Forms of pietistic expression have also changed (Kalpagam, 2007). In a fieldwork study of roadside temples in Chennai by Kalpagam (2006), it was observed that many non-Brahmin women of lower caste and economic strata, particularly the Naicker caste, had actively supported the men in their families in their initiative to build roadside temples and continued to support them in temple maintenance activities, even serving as priestesses on occasions. Brahmin women could also be counted upon as steadfast patrons of these roadside Ganesh temples and were often instrumental in convincing the priests, especially if they were Brahmin priests, and temple managers, who often would be autorickshaw drivers, to install other deities in the temple such as Goddess Durga or Navagraha idols. Specific pujas on *Sankatahara Chathurthi* or *Krithigai* days in Ganesh temples have now become important neighborhood collaborative activities in which upper-caste non-Brahmin women and Brahmin women come together for worship of Goddess Durga and the collective singing of hymns on every auspicious Tuesday afternoon.

Group singing of Bhajans, particularly among the Vaishnavites, has been in existence in the city for a long time. Singer (1963) noted sixty years ago that these were predominantly male groups with women observers on the sidelines. Though Singer also observed that Bhajan groups of women were also coming up in the city then, these groups are predominantly composed of men who sing along when the deity is taken out in a procession inside or outside the temple. Women's collectives for the singing and recitation of devotional hymns are more recent. They meet regularly in most of the bigger and many smaller temples in the city. Women who participate in these have pointed out to me that whereas earlier women did not sing or recite certain hymns like *Vishnu Sahasranaman* (hymn dedicated to Lord Vishnu), confining themselves to singing only the *Lalitha Sahasranaman* (hymn dedicated to Goddess Lakshmi, consort of Vishnu), now there are changes as they do recite *Vishnu Sahasranaman*. Such temple groups have emerged only recently. In the decades of the 1970s and 1980s, the popular trend among Brahmin women was to assemble at an individual's home to learn and recite the hymns *Soundaryya Lahiri* or *Abhirami Andaadhi* under the guidance of a teacher. Many of these Sanskrit poetry compositions are attributed to Adi Sankara, who propounded the Advaita philosophy. Some of these women also seek the advice and guidance of the spiritual leader Kanchi Sankaracharya of Kanchi Mutt, who reaches out to them through their religious magazine *Kamakoti*.

Increasingly, non-Brahmin women are forming informal groups for the regular singing of hymns in the temples which were earlier mostly Brahmin groups. While the Brahmin women sing Sanskrit hymns, the non-Brahmin women recite and sing hymns in the Tamil language composed by the Tamil Shaivite and Vaishnavite saints, the Nayanmars and Alwars, comprising the corpus of early medieval Tamil literature. On a recent train journey from Chennai to Tirupati, I was in a coach that had a large number of women singing loudly as a group some of the Vaishnavite hymns in Tamil as they were headed to visit the famous Tirumala temple. These women's groups have grown remarkably in recent years with the mandatory addition of temple worship services in the Tamil language, whereas earlier it was conducted only in Sanskrit. Legislating the recruitment of priests from all castes, including Dalits, and more recently of women in government-managed temples may have also given impetus for these women's groups.

AMMAN WORSHIP AMONG WORKING-CLASS WOMEN

Goddess Amman, a non-sanskritic goddess, is primarily worshipped by women of the non-sanskritized lower castes and classes. There is a class divide in the patronage and participation in roadside Ganesh temples. While many of Chennai's roadside Ganesh temples are put up by autorickshaw drivers, the women of their households do not participate in the women's collectives in these temples, both on account of the class divide as well as their affiliation to their traditional deities. These women are more involved in the worship of Goddess Amman in varied personified deities. Women usually initiate putting an Amman deity, initially in the form of a stone shaped like a rolling pin, at the foot of any Peepul (sacred fig) tree. Sometimes it is just close to their homes or is the site where they vend their goods if they are vendors. They develop it as a passionate hobby. In the course of time, many have evolved into built temple structures either small or big, sometimes with the woman acting as a priest and/or manager along with her husband or other family members. Some of these women serving as priestesses in their Amman temples have also acquired the skills of folk astrology known as *Kuri* and some form of faith healing. They attract clientele seeking their advice and solace on certain days of the week.

Brahmin women rarely visit these temples, though on occasions they propitiate these deities, sometimes through intermediary women who worship at these temples. These are occasions such as children's affliction with chicken pox or measles, as there is a traditional belief that not appeasing the deity was perhaps the cause of the affliction. Most Brahmin households did have a tradition of offering an annual *pongal* (jaggery sweetened rice and lentil) offering to the Amman deity, which is done in collaboration with and through the help of a non-Brahmin woman, often their domestic help, and the Brahmin women will sometimes visit the temple on this occasion. Among the non-Brahmins, it is customary to make a *pongal* offering at least once a year, generally in the Tamil month of *Aadi,* and/or offer *Koozhu* (millet gruel) both as offerings to the goddess and to the neighborhood community. Sometimes this involves an elaborate process of taking a symbol of the deity in procession, as these ritual practices have evolved in local contexts as local traditions. While women accompany the procession, they are often not the ones to carry the deity, although there are no restrictions in doing so if they comply with certain requirements of the ritual.

POPULARITY OF PILGRIMAGES

Pilgrimage is very popular among the Tamils, especially since the region is dotted with many big temples dating back to the sixth or seventh century CE. Women take vows to visit a particular temple and offer prayers for the welfare of their family. For non-sanskritized women of the working class, pilgrimages are limited to the local and surrounding areas of the city, and for those under the fold of sanskritization to some extent, a visit to the Tirumala temple in Tirupati, the richest temple in the country, in the neighboring region, usually before or after a wedding in the family, is quite common. Women from economically better-off households do undertake long-distance pilgrimages to the famous temples all over the country, even those situated in the Himalayan mountains, while retaining special ties to the *Kula Deivam* or family deity located close to their ancestral village.

Pilgrimage tours have recently become all too popular with an almost insatiable demand for them. While the Tamil Nadu Tourism Department has for decades organized tour packages to the leading temples of the state, they have added in recent years local tours to Amman temples in the vicinity of the city. The Railways too have started running special pilgrim trains to many pilgrimage towns, with tour operators facilitating group pilgrimages to various temples across the country. Plans to build replicas of famous temples are on the anvil, anticipating the future rush with the growth of the population in the country. This upsurge of pilgrim traffic is also a marker of an increase in religiosity.

RELIGION AND THE MEDIA

The print and television media play significant roles in popularizing religion to the masses, which has led to some religious commercialism. This is a pan-Indian phenomenon, as evident in Babb and Wadley (1995) and Mankekar (1999). That religion makes good business is apparent from the spectrum of enterprises, from flower vendors near roadside temples to the upscale shops selling religious artifacts, religious cassettes, and videos. Pilgrimage tourism is part of this religious consumerism.

Devotional books and magazines have become tremendously popular among women. Some years ago, young and elderly women who were literate in Tamil read magazines like *Ananda Viketan* and *Kalaimagal* that carried an assorted bunch of articles on romance and marriage, politics, culture and societal matters, and a little on religion, keeping housewives just informed of what is happening without burdening them with details, and with a plentiful amount of humor by way of cartoons and jokes. Today the print magazine sphere is dominated by religious magazines. A visit to a magazine store in Chennai revealed the existence of numerous magazines such as *Aanmikaalayam, Abhirami, Adigalulagam, Ammandarsinam, Bhava, Deepaaradhanai, Gnanaalayam, Gnanabhoomi, Gopuradarsinam, Jyothidaboomi, Jyothidakalai, Jyothidamurasu, Kadavul, Kamakoti, Kumudham Bhakti, Kurudhan Jyothidam, Om Sarana Aanmigajyothi, Rajayogam, Sakti Viketan, Subayogam,* and *Sriramakrishnavijayam.* The shopkeeper mentioned that there were probably some more that his shop did not stock. Some magazines like *Gnanabhoomi* try to retain a loyal clientele by clipping sachets of *Kumkuma prasad* (vermilion used in worship) from different temples every month and sometimes the special issue *Deepavali Malar* even carries sachets of *Gangajal* (consecrated water from the holy river Ganges) as the ritual bathing on Deepavali morning is known as *Ganga Snan*, the equivalent of taking a dip in the holy river Ganges, which is of significance to the sanskritized Hindus. Religious books too are in good demand. Nearly half the floor space of the oldest bookstore in Chennai, *Higginbothams*, is filled with spiritual books of the Tamil mystic Ramana Maharishi, while the Ramakrishna Mission bookstore has not only Vedantic literature but comics of mythological stories for young children that mothers enthusiastically buy.

These religious magazines and books have a voracious readership among women. Part of the reason for the likely shift in reading habits among women is on account of the television soaps that now substitute for whatever romance and other stories they had earlier craved to read in the magazines, even as television channels air religious programs. These religious magazines cover details on the religious, cultural, and historical significance of various temples in the state, which knowledge the Tamil literate people have always considered an important aspect of Tamil cultural literacy. Women take great pleasure in showing off this knowledge to the younger kith and kin in the family. The advertisements in these magazines on pilgrimage tours and astrological services are also suggestive of their increased popularity. Belief in astrology exists across the spectrum, and so do the varieties of astrological services ranging from folk astrology to *Nadi Jothidam,* where predictions for each person are supposedly written in palm leaf manuscripts held in the possession of certain families in Vaitheeswaran Koil village of Tamil Nadu who are proficient in the interpretive reading of these manuscripts through many generations. The predictions are considered potent as to their accuracy. More and more women across castes and classes consult astrologers on matters relating to marriage, jobs, and health.

The Television, Cassette, and CD Effect

Various television channels cover many of the temple festivities. A popular channel, *Jaya TV* starts early morning everyday with devotional programs such as the Tirupati *Brahmotsavam* worship, followed by discourses of spiritual leaders. In keeping with fast-paced metropolitan living, what was once a practice of upper-caste women to visit the temple early in the morning for worship has now changed to watching television shows. With the television shows aired inside homes, women of other castes have also become regular viewers. A similar situation prevails for religious discourses. Decades ago, the bigger temples in the city used to organize *katha* (storytelling) sessions in the late evenings attended by large numbers of upper-caste women, especially Brahmins. In these *katha* sessions, ethical and moral aspects from various Hindu mythologies as well as scriptural literature would be discussed and analyzed in ways that could be comprehended by non-literate persons. Some *katha* exponents have rightfully become much-admired historical figures of the city, like the late Sengalipuram Anantarama Dikshitar, whose eloquence and mastery in *Upanyaasas* (discourses) or *katha* sessions became famous. Today, these temple *katha* sessions have almost disappeared, replaced by discourses over the television in the mornings or online that can be heard anytime. Whereas the *katha* sessions attracted elderly Brahmin women who considered the evening sessions a great relief after a tiring day of household chores, the television shows have democratized this discursive sphere by bringing in a wide cross-section of viewers of different castes and younger women. Religion-themed dramas and films are now a feature of regular home entertainment for women, much like the way cricket matches are for younger men.

The cassette and CD culture of devotional hymns has become popular also on account of the global Tamil diaspora. The rendition of Hindu devotional songs in Tamil by renowned singers like Yesudas and Ilayaraja makes them even more popular. Ilayaraja even produced a CD on *Thiruvachakam* with a Western symphony orchestra, elevating Tamil classical poetry into a world classic.

The shaping of a distinctive Tamil identity has always been associated with the knowledge of the immense classical tradition of Tamil literature, especially of Tamil poetry, both religious and secular. Tamils with a strong Dravidian consciousness are brought up learning to appreciate the tremendously rich corpus of Sangam literature (Sangam period 300 BC–300 AD). The religiously oriented Dravidian consciousness seeks out the rich Tamil devotional hymns *Tirumurai*, which are the outcome of early Saivism in the Tamil region and the later Bhakti poetry from the fourth to the eleventh century CE. The medieval period devotional hymn *Thirupavai* of the mystic poetess Andal is also very popular. These and other devotional hymns promoted through cassette and CD culture were much sought-after by women until they could all be downloaded and listened to from the internet. Women especially find it easy to recite these hymns with cassette tapes or online audio, whereas earlier they were bound by the timing of the radio broadcast.

DALIT GODDESSES, DRAVIDIAN CULT OF WORSHIP, AND SANSKRITIZATION

The worship of Amman is the cult of the worship of the mother goddess in various personifications and appears to span across the Dalit/Dravidian to Vedic Aryan practice of worship in Tamil Nadu. Elsewhere too, the worship of the mother goddess in the Vedic tradition is widely prevalent (Sharma, 2005). It is generally believed that the original folk religion of the Tamil country comprised heroes and heroines who at one time had valiantly defended the Tamil countryside (Jarzombek, 2009). Village goddesses were generally seen as such women and girls who had made exemplary sacrifices for village protection. Many of the folk gods and goddesses that existed in recent popular memory are, however, fast vanishing. Such village goddesses were, in the course of time, transformed into various Amman deities with their different genealogies located in local contexts.

The village goddess, seen as the guarding deity of the village, was often called *Ellaiamman*, as *Ellai* in Tamil denotes colony or territory. Even today, streets leading to Dalit hamlets will often be called *Ellaiamman* street, with possibly a small *Ellaiamman* temple. In the course of time, *Ellaiamman* was reconfigured through mythological borrowings from the *Puranic* story of Parasuram and Renuka and came to be endowed with the body of a Brahmin lady and the head and face of a non-Brahmin lady. But the Amman was only idolized without the body. In the Vedic version, her name was changed from *Ellaiamman* to *Renuka Parameswari Amman*.

Another well-known Amman among the Dalit goddesses is *Maariamman* who is even today widely worshipped by all Dravidian folk, she being considered the protector from afflictions like smallpox, chickenpox, measles, and other such diseases. Certain characteristics mark the features of Dalit worship, the most important being spirit-possession and trance-dancing. These features are also carried over into the wider Dravidian cult of worship that includes infliction of bodily pain like tongue and body piercing, fire-walking, hook-swinging, and so on. Some of these practices, like hook-swinging were banned under colonial rule as barbaric practices. Both female and male devotees continue many of these practices even today. In the context of Amman worship, it is difficult today to distinguish between the Dalit and the Dravidian cult of worship.

One facet of the process of sanskritization is the transformation of Dravidian gods and goddesses into Vedic gods and goddesses. A similar transformation of gods and goddesses has been noted in Bengal as well (Nandy, 2001). Guarding deities of village and tribal communities have also, in the course of time, undergone such transformation (Valk and Lourdusamy, 2007; Jarzombek, 2009). Such transformation in the gods and goddesses is acknowledged as a transformation of the personality attributes of the gods and goddesses themselves.

Whereas the earlier presiding goddesses in each village are shown to possess the attributes of anger and vengeance in their dispensation of justice to evil-doers and are considered malevolent, needing constant appeasement, these attributes undergo a change in their Vedic personifications in which the goddesses shower grace, love, and are considered benevolent. They also become consorts of the trinity of Vedic gods Brahma, Visnu, and Siva marking their admission into the patriarchal fold, for earlier these independent goddesses had no male spouse. With their inclusion in the Vedic fold, they become embodiments of virtues such as devotion and chastity. Vedic goddesses are often depicted in the presence of their spouses, but not so the Dalit/

Dravidian goddesses. Dalit/Dravidian goddesses induced fear in the believers of their capacity to inflict harm if they were displeased, but not the Vedic goddesses.

Today, the numerous Amman temples put up on roadsides and in slum settlements retain features of the Dravidian cult of worship, even as other Vedic sanskritic features, such as the performance of the *Abhishekam* (the ritual bathing of the idol), are incorporated in some. Idols that were once made of sand and clay are now replaced by stone-chiseled ones to make the ritual bathing of the idol feasible. Amman temples have also begun to sport the *gopuram* architecture that is typical of traditional South Indian temple architecture and are also performing the *Kumbhabhishekam*, a Vedic ritual for the installation of deities. However, many Amman temples initiated by individual women remain small and do not incorporate these features. Given this genealogy of the Amman temples and their affiliation to the Dalit/Dravidian cult of worship, these temples are still more popular among the women of non-sanskritized castes.

Big Amman temples like the *Maangaadu* Kamakshi Amman temple on the outskirts of the city attract young Brahmin women in hordes, as worship at this temple is considered to fulfill matrimonial expectations. The genealogy of this temple is also a more sanskritized Vedic version of the powers of the goddess, as it is believed that Adi Shankara, the propounder of *Advaita* philosophy, visited the temple many centuries ago. However, other big temples like the *Periapalayam* Bhavani Amman temple, where animal/bird sacrifice is practiced, are avoided by women of sanskritized groups. In contrast, women of the non-sanskritized castes of the working class make regular pilgrimages to the temple.

Tamil women's expressions of piety are along the lines of sanskritized Vedic Hinduism and forms of worship that still retain features of the Dalit/Dravidian cult of worship, though in the process of being sanskritized. The spectrum consists of forms of Amman worship with greater elements of folk religion and those under greater influence of Vedic Hinduism, elements of early Saivism that have given a distinctive Dravidian cult of worship, Saivism and Vaishnavism influenced by the two early *Bhakti* movements under the Nayanmars and Alwars that conferred a distinctive Tamil identity as well, to the later more sanskritized forms of worship in the post-Adi Shankara and Ramanuja periods and the rise of Brahmins thereafter in the ritual domain to the present-day modernity of Hinduism of the guru cult and a small segment of politicized Hinduism.

Predominantly, lower-caste women are worshippers of Amman, while upper-caste women are more inclined toward the more sanskritized forms of worship or the more modern trends of Hinduism. A large segment of intermediate castes has assimilated aspects of sanskritized Hinduism, even while consciously striving to maintain a distinctive Tamil religious identity by including features of the Dalit/Dravidian cult of worship. Some castes of the new rich that have not been able to covet political power may likely come under the influence of politicized Hinduism, even as it undergoes a sanskritization process.

Political Hinduism combines both religious and nationalist or regionalist fervor, such as the deification and construction of temples for *Bharat Mata* (the mother goddess of the nation) and *Thamizh Thai* (Tamil mother), and other activities of religious organization. While there exist *Bharat Mata* temples elsewhere in the country, such as the one in Varanasi (Banaras) that has existed for more than a hundred years ago and was even visited by Mahatma Gandhi, there is a recently consecrated one in Neelamangalam village close to Chennai. At the *Kumbhabhishekam* ceremony, RSS chief Mohan Bhagwat observed, "Bharat's Amrit Kaal is before us. We must believe in it. Also, *Akhand Bharat* is true and eternal. We just need to waken our consciousness to understand this truth." (Deccan Herald, May 5, 2023). The *Tamizh Thai* temple, inaugurated in 1993 in Karaikudi in Tamil Nadu, hosts the leading legendary founders of the Tamil language and renowned secular poets of the region. Although there are no worship services as in other temples, the iconography of *Thamizh Thai* leans heavily on the iconography of the goddess Saraswathi, the Hindu goddess of learning.

THE POPULARITY OF TAMIL RELIGIOUS FILMS

The Tamil film industry has long been influential in keeping alive the memories of Tamil folk religion and its transformation among the vast illiterate masses. *Sakthi* worship has been an integral part of Tamil culture right from the days of early Saivism, which accounts for the predominance of roadside Amman temples. It has been the favorite theme of popular Tamil films like *Aadi Paraasakthi* (1971), which starred Jayalalitha, who later became the chief minister of Tamil Nadu and the AIADMK supremo, whom the multitudes of women affectionately called *Amma* or mother. Many other Amman films have since been produced, like *Paalayathu Amman*, *Rajakali Amman,* and *Sri Bannari Amman,* to name a few. In yet other films, the goddess Amman would figure even if the theme of the film is different. The genre of Amman films is now being discussed for its impact on women's empowerment even in film and cultural studies (Ondrich, 2005). Hordes of lower-class Tamil women throng the theaters even today to watch these religious-themed movies and recount with relish the stories to others. The film *Aadi Paraasakthi* influenced many working-class women to initiate putting up an Amman temple, invariably narrating that the deity or a serpent appeared in their dreams and asked them to do so. Tamil movies popularized religion-themed films and have also cast some temple *puranas* (legends) as films. By keeping alive memories of popular Hinduism and Tamil folk religion, Tamil films promote increased religiosity and *Sakthi* worship among women of lower castes and the working classes.

CHANGES IN CULTURAL NORMS

These markers of religious upsurge signify that the sanskritization process across the spectrum of caste and class has led to changes in cultural norms for women, such as marriage practices. Castes that followed Dravidian marriage norms of cross-cousin marriages are seeking alliances outside the kin group and are also doing so through the matching of horoscopes with the help of astrologers, a practice that was earlier restricted largely to the Brahmins and other upper castes. *Nombhu,* or ritual penance such as observing *Vrat* (ritual fasting), usually either to obtain a good spouse or for the welfare of a spouse, generally undertaken by young girls and women, is becoming more widespread. The Tamil month of *Margazhi* (December–January) includes days meant to observe *Paavai Nombhu* by young girls to obtain good husbands by singing in the temples. *Thiruvempavai* (a poem composed by the ninth-century Tamil saint-poet Manikkavasakar) among the Saivites and *Thiruppavai* (a poem composed by the ninth-century Tamil saint-poetess Andal) by the Vaishnavites are the hymns sung by the girls. There are attempts to identify the practice of *Paavai Nombhu* in the Sangam literature both to claim antiquity as well as to make it an authentic Dravidian practice that pre-dates any sanskritic influence. Today, young girls in Chennai visit temples early in the morning in the month of *Margazhi* to sing these devotional songs and also make ritual commitments to visit the *Maangaadu* temple on seven consecutive weeks and/or observing *Vrat* and so on to achieve the same ends. Most non-Brahmin women observe *Nombhu* on *Deepavali* (festival of lights) day.

The claim of the antiquity of *Paavai Nombhu* to the Sangam period also antedates the patriarchal ideology. Given the fact that Amman worship coexisted with elements of Tamil folk religion and the Dravidian cult of worship, many lower-caste women, especially Dalits, who are used to worshiping the independent goddesses without spouses, had never practiced the observance of *Nombhu*. Nowadays, more women are doing so. This is a marker of the origins of patriarchal ideology in the regulation of women's conduct. In the early forms of *Sakthi* worship, these goddesses were in fact projected as independent without the presence of male consorts. Under early Saivism, Siva himself was portrayed as half-male and half-female. It was under the later Vedic influence that goddesses were represented along with their spouses, although in most of the older Siva temples, there are separate shrines within the complex for Siva and his consort, with a late-night and early-morning ritual *Palliarai puja* accompanied by the recitation of hymns with the god being taken in and out of his consort's chamber. Interestingly, the god Murugan, who in the Vedic tradition is the son of Siva, is mostly represented in the temples with his two wives; one married through Vedic rituals is the daughter of God Indra, and the other is a common-law tribal wife, as Murugan also has a pre-Vedic identity as a son of a tribal goddess. Murugan is the most popular god of the Tamils, and his representation with his two wives is not culturally read and deciphered as a religious sanction of bigamy but serves more as a cultural reminder of the hegemony of Vedic Hinduism over the preexisting religious beliefs of Tamil culture.

The transformations in the attributes of gods and goddesses in the religious practices could have changed subjectivities, gender and family relations, and social relations of the Tamil people themselves over the centuries. Hence, this process of sanskritization could be cognized as an indigenous civilizing process toward a patriarchal culture that pre-dates the much later colonial civilizing mission and the project of modernity. For various castes and communities, this could have induced changes in their sociocultural norms and values, often imbibing patriarchal values such as the emphasis on the complementary roles of the sexes that sanskritized castes prescribed and practiced, which arguably over time could have undermined women's autonomy and independence.

RELIGIOSITY AMONG HINDU WOMEN IN CHENNAI

Contrary to earlier theories that suggested the decline of religion with modernity, social scientists are now grappling to explain the worldwide resurgence of religion. Some sociologists think that with multiple modernities, there occurs religious pluralism offering people choices in their religious beliefs. Religious fundamentalism and identity politics are also on the rise, increasingly challenging ideas of secularism and secular society. There is also an ongoing interrogation of the common sense of secularism regarding both the state's neutrality between all religions and freedom of the public sphere including education from religion; a common sense induced in the subjectivity of the people by political forces who have been either promoting or contesting this idea. All these factors, along with the rise of the Hindu nationalist party, may have contributed to an increased display of Hindu religiosity, which is also evident in Tamil Nadu even where the political influence of Hindu nationalism is quite minimal. Other contributing factors are the consequences of globalization, growing disparities and newer uncertainties.

Religion, too, has emerged as a growing sector boosting incomes and profits. Here, we examine the impact of such trends on Hindu women's religiosity in Chennai, a city that is fast globalizing.

Even as the city makes its strides as a global city with swanky office structures and global companies, its landscape is marked by numerous temples, both old and new, and big and small. But the number of temples still appear to be grossly insufficient, judging by the crowds, if one were to visit a temple on a Friday. The police, private security, and voluntary organizations are all engaged in crowd management and traffic regulation in many temples on auspicious days that attract huge crowds. Even the smallest roadside temple has a regular clientele and gets crowded during peak hours, putting pressure on vehicular traffic movement. By all accounts, there is a tremendous upsurge of religious devotion publicly expressed through temple construction, temple attendance, and other activities. This is perhaps true across the country, though it may vary to some degree.

All too often, this flourish of Hindu religiosity is seen more as the outcome of a successful *Hindutva* agenda of the Hindu nationalists for a Hindu *rashtra* (state) as opposed to the secular state, and so has yielded to them a far greater space of Hindu consciousness than what the *Hindutva* forces have so far hegemonized. The considerably larger non-hegemonized space of Hindu consciousness needs to be understood sociologically in terms of social structures, social relations, and social dynamics in their local contexts. To think that *Hindutva* mobilization is taking place without at the same time changes taking place in the structure and organization of the Hindu religious community is as erroneous as to believe that all such changes everywhere are in fact motivated by *Hindutva* forces.

Congregational Hinduism is on the rise in northern India, and crowds that assemble to listen to Hindu religious leaders are quite incredible. In some instances, *Hindutva* forces have indeed mobilized women to participate in these, as evidenced by the late BJP women leader Sushma Swaraj addressing a huge assembly of largely women, who had assembled in Karnal, Haryana, to listen to Baba Ramdev, a popular Hindu yoga and spiritual teacher. But to think the same for the crowds that assemble to have a *darsan* of *Ammachi* (Mata Amritanandamayi), a pious woman from a fisherman community in Kerala, or for Sathya Sai Baba, who had built a global empire of his faithful, would be erroneous.

Recently, governments have started taking advantage of such religious upsurge irrespective of political ideologies. In Tamil Nadu, the Dravida Munnetra Kazhagam (DMK) party, which at one time projected itself as a rationalist party of atheists like its parent organization, the Dravida Kazhagam (DK party), sought the assistance of Sathya Sai Baba's benevolence for an environment and development project, while the Maharashtra government sought the guidance of Sri Sri Ravi Shankar and also received a bountiful sum from Mata Amritanandamayi to handle its problem of farmers' suicides. Presently, a huge state-of-the-art multidisciplinary hospital is being constructed near Delhi, funded by Mata Amritanandamayi. These suggest a synergy of religiosity and Hindu modernity's efforts to scale up charity and philanthropy to a larger focus on development.

Issues in Focus

The location of women in this emerging urban-scape of religiosity needs to be identified and also explored from a feminist standpoint. The task is, therefore, to decipher from this flourish of religiosity the markers that indicate the trends and forms of women's piety and to understand the reasons for the increase in piety. Importantly, whether the increase in women's piety is a pointer to a possibly more regressive move of fulfilling patriarchal norms and how women negotiate between tradition and modernity alongside this flourish. Of particular interest is whether women seek to change religious practices to suit modern times, and the impact of these changes on cultural norms as they affect women. The implications of women's piety for the cultivation of secular sensibilities and the emergence of democratic citizenship among women, and the ways in which women's expression of religiosity and their religious dispositions accord with the project to refashion selves into modern subjects. The flourish of women's piety may also be a pointer to an emerging religious modernity within Hinduism that accords women a greater sense of social and ethical responsibility, which also requires exploration. The validity of the conflation of increased piety with the anxieties of a political mobilization around religious identities needs to be investigated as well as the anxieties that arise as a consequence of the undermining of the certainties of modernity.

This study is not a mere cultural curiosity highlighting aspects of belief and behavior of urban Hindu women but has wider significance for the configuration of feminist cultural politics in the nation and the role of religion. However, this is only an exploratory endeavor and not all the issues are addressed in detail.

Markers of Women's Piety

The markers of increased religiosity are now more diverse, including not just the increase in the number of temples, churches, and mosques, and the attendance at these institutions or the communality in the celebration of religious festivities. The markers also include the proliferation of religious media and the reformation and expansion of a religious public sphere. The religious media includes print media that, at least in some regions, have witnessed a spurt in the publication and circulation of a wide range of religious periodicals, the increased number of television channels airing religious programs, with some devoted exclusively to such programs, the popularity and increase in the cassette and CDs of religious content, internet and web-based media and technologies that are not limited to just the transmission of religious information, devotional videos, and songs hitherto available in cassette and CD formats but have also enabled the virtual access and participation in temple worship. For a long time, the radio and the film industry were the main media channels to popularize religiosity through devotional songs and religion-themed movies.

In Tamil Nadu, Hindu women's piety is very much differentiated along broad caste lines, and the forms of pietistic expressions and practices are differentiated as well, based on the extent of sanskritization that the group has attained. But even these differentiated orientations of piety point to an increase going by the visible evidence in Chennai city.

A distinguishing feature of North Indian Hinduism and the Hinduism in Tamil Nadu is the absence of the *Guru* tradition, although many spiritual leaders from Tamil Nadu have acquired tremendous national and international popularity, like Sri Sri Ravi Shankar. However, the North Indian practice of seeking out a *Guru* by a devotee-follower is not common and one almost never sees mammoth crowds assembled to meet a Guru, but similar large crowds in the temples on festive occasions are all too common. Tamil Nadu has a strong tradition of temple worship dating back to the seventh century that still continues. Most women limit themselves to the direct propitiation of their household deities, marked by frequent and regular visits to temples. Having a *darshan* of the deity in the temple on an auspicious occasion is considered a blessed encounter.

Temples and Attendance

Attendance at temples, big and small is marked by the large presence of female devotees. For a long time, days of temple festivals, especially the ten-day annual festival called *Brahmotsavam* and the accompanying *Thirunal* (carnival), have been occasions that brought together a large number of devotees, including those groups that were only at the peripheries of sanskritic/ Vedic Hinduism. Much like the *Magh Mela* and *Kumbh Mela* festivals of North India, these were occasions for the non-sanskritized groups to come together under the umbrella of sanskritic Hinduism, as these festivals were considered occasions to propitiate the local deities. Although Vedic Hinduism is the dominant form in these large Shaivite and Vaishnavite temples, more and more castes that had earlier worshipped Dravidian/Dalit gods and goddesses are being brought within the fold of Vedic Hinduism. In Chennai city, this is evidenced not only by the mushrooming of roadside temples of both Lord Ganesha of Vedic Hinduism and Goddess Amman of Dravidian/ Dalit Hinduism, but also by the enthusiasm for the performance of the Vedic ritual of *Kumbhabhishekam* for these temples (Kalpagam, 2006). The increasing popularity of Lord Ganesha has simultaneously obliterated many of the gods and goddesses of the Dravidian culture worshipped until recently, such as Sudalai Madan and Munishwaran. This sanskritization process is both cultural and religious.

STRENGTHENING OF PATRIARCHY

It is a moot question whether the upsurge of women's religiosity is accompanied by a strengthening of patriarchy both in ideology and in practice. While religiosity has always been associated with tradition, contemporary religiosity, which also gives primacy to familial values, is taking place in the context of a modernity accompanied simultaneously by a search for authenticity. Among the sanskritized groups, married women are granted a status of auspiciousness and considered as *Lakshmi*—the household goddess of wealth who is supposed to bring wealth and prosperity to the family, especially by bearing sons who carry on the lineage. These notions have not changed and may indeed have strengthened among the groups undergoing the sanskritization process, as such notions have never existed among the lower-caste Amman worshippers. Under modernity's self-construction, women may also be striving to be autonomous and/or seek social mobility in either or both the secular and religious domains. As Chatterjee indicated regarding the nationalist resolution that tasked women to defend the cultural and spiritual domains in the domestic sphere, in almost all families, it is women who resolve or commit to make *prarthana* (a ritual commitment) to gods in fulfillment of certain desires or familial goals, almost as if women were entering into a contract with their favorite boon-granting god or goddess. Men never question women on that even if they do question them on other household matters. It is almost as though it is the women's privilege and prerogative to pray for the welfare of the family, reinforcing once again the family values. Many women also use this privilege as a way to manipulate and control their husbands.

Hancock (2000) discusses the making of Tamil womanhood through domestic rituals and the public culture of religion, wherein her analysis largely centers on upper-caste women and the bigger temples of Vedic Hinduism in Chennai. The worship of Amman is very popular among the lower-caste women in Tamil Nadu. Feminist cultural theorists have explored the implications of the role of the mother goddess in the constitutive role of Hindu women (Lakshmi, 1990; Ganesh, 1990; Sunder Rajan, 1998). Lakshmi shows how motherhood and mother-community are valorized in Tamil political discourses, wherein motherhood endows women's bodies as sites of divinity, sanctity, and purity, and their wombs become "lairs of tigers" that produce men of valor for the Tamil nation (Lakshmi, 1990, WS 72). Although she does not explicitly deal with Amman worship, she shows how mother goddess worship was politically revived. Ganesh observes that the mother goddess can be interpreted as expressing ideas of power, autonomy, and primacy in the widest sense of the term as "she conveys not so much the idea of physical motherhood but a world view in which the creative power of femininity is central" (Ganesh, 1990, WS 58). Sunder Rajan (1998) argues that the claim for the progressive potential of the mother goddess for women's liberation is to be located in three sites of discourse, namely South Asian studies in the Western academy, radical Indian feminism, and Gandhian secularism, while the discursive sites that urge caution in the recuperation of mother goddess feminism are the left in general, the left feminist, and the Dalit movement, which argues that Hindu goddesses as role models have had a pernicious effect on upper-caste women. More recently, Diesel (2002) in the context of Hinduism of the South Indian diaspora in South Africa argues that the worship of Amman offers a feminist theodicy and a post-patriarchal spiritualism.

RELIGION-THEMED FILMS AND WOMEN'S SUBJECTIVITIES

In keeping with the prevalent practice of Amman worship in Tamil Nadu, religion-themed movies or devotional films draw their resources, ideas, and appeal from the vast repertoire of folk culture, history, and religious beliefs, especially the tradition of Amman worship. In 1944, the devotional film *Raja Rajeswari* was produced and screened with the legendary actor N. S. Krishnan playing a role. Since then, the appeal of Amman movies has grown. In 2002, the film *Sri Raja Rajeswari* was produced with an altogether different storyline. Two years later, the hugely successful TV serial *Raja Rajeswari* was aired, which had yet another storyline. Many Amman films have since been produced, such as *Aadivelli, Aayiram Kannudayal, Badil Solval Badrakali, Bhadra Kaali, Devi, Deviyin Thiruvilayadal, Durga, Kai Koduppal Karpagambal, Maatha Gomathaa, Magamayee, Melmaruvathur Arputhangal, Nagathamman, Nageswari, Namma Veettu Dheivam, Paalayathu Amman, Pottu Amman, Rajakali Amman, Samayapurathale Satchi, Saraswathi Sapatham, Sarvam Sakthi Mayam, Sri Bannari Amman, Thaaye Neeye Thunai, Velli Kilmai Viratham,* and so on, or Amman figures in other films even if the theme of the film is different.

Religion-themed films and TV serials are also projects of subject transformation with certain intended effects on audiences that seek to reshape subjectivities. The genre of Amman movies, apart from bringing to popular awareness the uniqueness of the Dalit/Dravidian cult of goddess worship and the religious-cultural transformations that have occurred in Tamil society, is also a project that continues to carry forward the indigenous civilizing mission and hence of subject transformation that can only be understood in the context of the local Dravidian culture of Amman worship. Tamil films and television serials have picked up the theme of the personality transformation of gods and goddesses to form their theme stories in this genre of Amman movies. The popular television serial *Raja Rajeswari* is one such suggestive and imaginative account of this religious-cultural transformation among many others.

THE GENRE OF AMMAN MOVIES

Mythological films have been produced since the start of the film industry in the early twentieth century, captivating the audience's imagination as they seek to narrate stories of morality, virtues, and ideals. While the genre of Amman movies in Tamil Nadu is distinctive for its integration of the themes of Dalit/Dravidian worship and the sanskritization process in the shift to Vedic Hinduism, films of Hindu goddesses are popular all over the country. Their influence is so strong that a 1975 mythological Hindi film, *Jai Santoshi Ma,* even started the ritual of Friday fasting by women in North India to express their devotion to Goddess Santoshi Ma (the goddess of satisfaction or happiness), who, being the daughter of God Ganesha, belongs to Vedic Hinduism (Das, 1981; Joshi, 2024). An analysis is done here to identify the key elements that constitute the genre of Amman films. Limitations of space necessitated the analysis to be restricted to just two films: *Aadi Paraasakthi,* produced in 1971, and *Sri Bannari Amman,* produced in 2002.

Aadi Paraasakthi (1971) is a narrative constructed of anecdotes drawn from Hindu mythology, temple myths, and folk cultural and social practices. Its hugely successful mass appeal among Tamil women, particularly the lower classes, is on account of its story's message, the cinematic effects of color, sound and graphics, and its lyrics. Even with different stories, a common denominator of Amman movies is the cinematic effects of sound and graphics combined with lyrics and music. *Aadi Paraasakthi* recounts the story, largely a string of anecdotes, of what befalls the world of *devas* (Heavenly beings), *asuras* (power-seeking beings who fear the Devas), and humankind when gods Visnu and Siva are separated from their respective spouses, Lakshmi and Parvati, when a curse took effect as Visnu and Siva did not treat their spouses properly. Their separation brings about various calamities that are in each instance resolved through the benign intervention of *Aadi Paraasakthi.* In the Sakthi mythology, the trinity Brahma (creator of the universe), Visnu (protector of the universe), and Siva (destroyer of the universe) all derive their powers and potency from *Aadi Paraasakthi,* considered the primeval or primordial energy, the source of all life and being. Such energy is perceived as akin to the feminine energy, the procreative and nourishing powers. The imaginative portrayal of *Aadi Paraasakthi* in a feminine form lends itself to the very creative use of the form in Amman movies.

Aadi Paraasakthi is portrayed in the film as a fulsome woman clad in a sari in the manner that middle-class Tamil women do. She is bedecked in all the jewelry that marks her as a distinctly South Indian woman. On her head, she wears a high-rising crown, much like the way kings and queens do, that associates her with rulership. She has four arms, in each of which she holds various weapons, the same weapons that are held in portrayals of Visnu and Siva. Her most conspicuous weapon is the *Trishul,* a sharp-edged long weapon that forks into three at one end. She also sports a conspicuously large red dot of *kumkuma* (vermilion) called *pottu* on her forehead, placed over three horizontal ash marks. The *pottu* signifies her powerful third eye, from which lightning-like streaks and electrical waves emanate when she sets out to destroy evil, usually preceded by her anger. Light and sound effects of thunder and lightning accompany the moment when she destroys evil, making it a cathartic experience in the narrative plot as well as for the viewers. This portrayal of *Aadi Paraasakthi* as Amman remains mostly the same in all Amman movies, creating a distinctive genre.

The themes and scenes of the film give an idea of the dominant messages of the movie. In the opening scenes, a male priest who claims to be an ardent devotee of *Aadi Paraasakthi* gives a wrong answer to a question posed by the king while he is in deep meditation. The king wants to know if the day is a full moon or a new moon day and the priest answers wrongly that it is a full moon day. Not seeing the moon rise that evening, the king orders the priest to be burned at the stake. At this crucial moment of death, the priest prays ardently to *Aadi Paraasakthi,* who appears to the priest as though descending from heaven, removes her bright sparkling diamond ear studs, and throws them toward the sky, causing it to appear as a full moon. The astonished king releases the priest from the stake and his life is saved. This anecdote is the temple legend or *Sthala Purana* of the Amritaghateswarar-Abirami temple in Thirukkadaiyur in Tamil Nadu, originally built in the eleventh century. The moral is that benign divine intervention by *Aadi Paraasakthi* for the ardent and true devotees is guaranteed in times of crisis. This is a recurrent theme in all Amman movies. In another scene, a fisherman of the Dalit community asks the priest of a big Amman temple, where Vedic-style rituals are performed, while doing penance by the riverside in order to have a glimpse of *Aadi Paraasakthi* as to how he too can have a glimpse of the goddess. The priest initially tells him that a man of his class is unlikely to get such a glimpse but later relents on the fisherman's insistence, saying that if he is willing to sacrifice his life for the sake of the Goddess, then he can have a glimpse of her. The fisherman immediately jumps into the river and is carried away by the swift current. Just as he is about to drown, *Aadi Paraasakthi* appears and saves his life and he is able to have a glimpse of the Goddess, but the priest is unable to see the Goddess. The fisherman invites the Goddess to his house and she agrees to come if they prepare sweet *pongal* (a dish made of rice, lentil, and jaggery) for her. She keeps her appointment and partakes of the *pongal* prepared by his young wife. At that time, the fisherman tells the Goddess of his perceived discrimination, that he had to almost sacrifice his life for gaining her vision, while his wife was able to meet the Goddess with much less effort. The Goddess answers that she appears quickly to a wife who is a householder and who is devoted to her husband as well as to her, the Goddess. This is a strong message of the film, of steadfast devotion to the husband and a family way of life, and the possibility of speedy spiritual enlightenment through this path even for the poorer classes. The fisherman then tells the Goddess that the priests at the big Amman temple where Vedic rituals are performed have prepared offerings, not just *pongal* but a variety of dishes for her, and they too are waiting for her arrival. He accompanies her to the temple and finds to his shock that the upper-caste priests are all feasting well on the offerings without waiting for the arrival of the Goddess. The Goddess then tells the fisherman, mockingly, that they knew that she would not be appearing and that is why they had such a grand feast. This is a strong social criticism of the Brahminic ideology of Vedic Hinduism, in contrast to the popular Hinduism of *Sakthi* worship that is constitutive of Dravidian culture. The power of *Sakthi* worship is made clear when a foreigner, dressed as a colonialist, enters an Amman temple and the priest tells the foreigner that the water drops on the deity's cheeks signify her healing power. The white man criticizes all the superstitious beliefs as well as the polytheism of *Sakthi* worship, in which Amman is called by various names at various places. Immediately, the white European man is afflicted with pox marks all over, and only by praying ardently to *Aadi Paraasakthi* can he be cured of his pox and his vision restored, and the white man undergoes a spiritual conversion. Interestingly, in the European's narration of the incident to his wife, a white woman, he likens *Mariamman* to the figure of Mary in the Christian religion. The story that began with the gods being separated from their spouses ends with their reunion.

Sri Bannari Amman, produced in 2002, thirty years after *Aadi Paraasakthi,* testifies to the popularity of Amman movies even in later times. This film too has all the ingredients of Amman movies: a number of dance sequences in which groups of men and women dance *karagam* with neem leaves, and a scene of a fire-walking ritual; practices that are still prevalent in some Amman temples of Tamil Nadu. The film narrates the story of an ambitious young man who wants to succeed in politics. He approaches a sorcerer for help, who first advises him to rebuild the dilapidated *Angaalaparameswari* Amman temple in the village and perform the temple *Kumbhabhishekam* (a Vedic Hindu ritual for the consecration of the deity and the construction of the temple top called *gopuram*.) The aspiring politician collects the money for the temple renovation by cheating and looting the village folk. Not surprisingly, he does not win the election. The story thenceforward revolves around the pursuit of all his ambitions under the guidance of the sorcerer, who invokes supernatural powers through his devotion to an evil spirit (an *asura*) who was once annihilated by Bannari Amman, the goddess. Once the sorcerer unleashes the power of the *asura*, Bannari Amman enters the village in the guise of a woman healer. All her efforts are directed to the destruction of evil and to save people from evil designs.

The evil-scheming political aspirant marries a young woman who has befriended Bannari, the woman healer in the village, and begins to consider Bannari her mentor, even as she is also an ardent devotee of Sri Bannari Amman. Every evil scheme of her husband is thwarted by Goddess Bannari Amman, who is residing in the village in the guise of healer Bannari. As his designs are foiled, the marriage runs into great difficulties, and he begins to torture his wife. Interestingly, in the prelude to the torture, the young wife invites healer Bannari to her house for the *Golu* celebration at the *Navarathri* festival. *Golu* is the stepwise arrangement of painted clay figurines of gods and goddesses depicting mythological stories, perhaps meant for children to learn the mythologies, and is usually done in Brahmin households. *Golu* celebration in this non-Brahmin village household in the company of other non-Brahmin women is an attempt to demonstrate the sanskritization process. During the *Golu* celebration, the young wife sings a song about devotion to the husband until death (the song lines when translated read "Until one becomes a stone, it is the husband; Until one becomes grass, it is the husband"). The singing turns into a duet with healer Bannari joining her in singing her lines ("A wicked man is not a husband").

Although the assembled village women have all received good deeds from healer Bannari, they refuse to accept from her hands the ceremonial offerings given out to married women after worship on the grounds that they do not know anything about her husband, disqualifying her on grounds of inauspiciousness to make the offering to other married women. This again is a prejudiced sentiment of auspiciousness and inauspiciousness that is absorbed as part of the sanskritization process.

The sorcerer realizes that Bannari the healer is Goddess Bannari herself when she performs a miracle by making an illiterate woman read a letter written in English. Thereupon, he, along with his politician disciple, connives to frame Bannari on charges of theft in order to expel her from the village. Once Bannari is charged with the theft of jewelry from the Amman temple in the village, the politician's young wife joins the rest of the village in driving her out. While leaving, Bannari promises to return to the village only when she hears the cry of *Amma* (mother) from the young woman's body, meaning only when she gives birth to a child. Soon thereafter, the politician begins to torture his wife, inflicting on her all kinds of violence, especially as she is pregnant and the sorcerer has brainwashed the politician that his progeny may hinder his evil designs. During the annual festival at the Bannari Amman temple in the village, the politician forbids his wife from going to the temple and locks her up in the house. She, being an ardent devotee of Bannari Amman, performs the *karagam* dance and other bodily movements of supplication in a frenzied way while in confinement, leading to a premature delivery of her child. Soon thereafter, Bannari Amman keeps her promise and appears before her. It is at this moment that the young woman realizes that Bannari the healer is Goddess Bannari herself. The Goddess sets out to destroy her husband, he being an evil person who caused horrific torture to his wife. At that moment, the devoted wife pleads with the Goddess not to kill her husband, as that would make her child fatherless and herself a widow. In the end, the Goddess listens to her pleas and spares her husband.

Apart from the usual personification of Amman as the destroyer of evil, the film also carries the usual messages of benign intervention and protection to the ardent devotees of Amman, who also at the same time are truly devoted to their spouse. This of course does not imply blind devotion to the husband as Bannari's song line "a wicked man is not a husband" indicates. While the moral message is devotion to the husband, it urges women to cognize and destroy evil through building strength following a spiritual path of devotion to Amman, the primordial female deity who grants power to the male deities of the Hindu pantheon. While the primordial deity, Amman as *Sakthi,* appears without a male spouse, all the other male and female deities of Vedic Hinduism appear alongside their spouses, establishing a patriarchal cosmic order that is supposedly desirable for the human world to follow.

Drawing Feminist Insights

Aadi Paraasakthi (1971) appeared at a time of sharply polarized Dravidian politics in the state. The DMK, the political party offshoot of the cultural movement Dravida Kazhagam (DK), strongly committed to instilling a Dravidian identity on a rationalist basis, decried *Sanatan Dharam* or Vedic

Hinduism as promoting superstition and social inequality. The DK and the DMK were against Brahminic social hegemony and instilled a sense of insecurity among the Brahmins. It was in this general state of intolerance and insecurity that the All India Anna Dravida Munetra Kazhagam (AIADMK) leader M. G. Ramachandran, himself a renowned actor on the Tamil screen, broke away from the DMK to start his party, the AIADMK, and the new rebel party projected itself as more tolerant, inclusive, and yet rooted in Dravidian culture. This tolerant face of Dravidian politics sought to revive Dravidian culture and identity not by criticizing religion as irrational but by exposing irrational beliefs and superstitions, highlighting the unity of Vedic Hinduism and the popular Dravidian *Sakthi* worship, and projecting the sanskritization process as an indigenous civilizing force.

Dravidian identity was thus sought to be re-scripted on different lines from the DK and the DMK. Whereas the self-respect movement of DK under the leadership of Periyar projected women as equal partners in marriage, initiated self-respect marriages that did away with Vedic rituals in marriage ceremonies, and harped on women's equality (Lakshmi, 1990; Geetha, 2004), the AIADMK sought to re-script Dravidian identity as Tamil identity not on utopian ideals of equality but based itself on social realities and the ongoing social processes subsuming the sanskritization process. Noting that M. G. Ramachandran, the founder and (late) leader of AIADMK, revived the popularity of mother goddess (Amman) worship, Lakshmi (1990) writes, "How effective this mother goddess revival and how deeply it had penetrated became obvious when women's association in smaller localities took up group learning of verses on mother goddesses as one of their major activities" (Lakshmi, 1990, WS 82).

It also needs to be noted that the late DMK supremo Karunanidhi rose to political fame with his script of the film *Paraasakthi*, produced in the early 1950s when he was barely thirty years of age. Although bearing a close resemblance in the title to *Aadi Paraasakthi*, the film *Paraasakthi* is not a devotional film as it deals with the plight of a refugee Tamil family coming from Burma (now Myanmar) during the Second World War and the reunion of the family in Tamil Nadu, which is shown in many ways as a corrupt society. The film, considered a DMK manifesto film, shows how the popular belief in *Sakthi* could be transposed to secular narratives with secular goals. Lakshmi (1990, 1995) argues that the goddess symbol in *Paraasakthi,* as used by the unscrupulous to cheat the gullible, is presented as a DMK viewpoint on religious exploitation. She notes that in a figurative way, "it forms the right symbol for the entire film, for the women characters in the film are used to present a particular view of life and to act in particular ways and restrain from particular actions" (Lakshmi, 1990, WS 80).

Certain feminist insights can be drawn from this genre of movies that has a tremendous appeal among the lower classes, the marginalized, and subaltern groups of women. Dickey (1993) has shown in her ethnographic study of poor South Indian film viewers that the popular reception of Indian films is based on the making of personal connections between viewers and their relationships with the characters and the relationships shown on the screen. The melodramatic nature of Tamil cinema, she points out, is merely the form in which such identification takes place.

Amman movies generally suggest how women, through spiritual devotion that gives them strength can overcome evil. Almost always, it is the men who perpetrate evil and women who undergo a lot of suffering both on account of the evil and also on account of the attempts to overcome it. The Amman of Dalit/Dravidian worship, symbolized by the many forms of *Aadi Paraasakthi,* is an independent and autonomous woman who wields much the same power as male gods, who can be both benign and an embodiment of grace like the Vedic goddesses, but unlike them, she can also be revengeful and destructive when it comes to dealing with evil. For the lower-caste women living materially deprived lives and for whom singleness is a non-viable option, the need to maintain conjugal harmony is an important yet challenging goal. Das (1994) portrays this with extraordinary sensitivity in her biographical sketch of a poor working-class family in Delhi. The relationships of power and evil form a complex web in many of their lives that requires them to cultivate the virtues of tolerance, endurance, and strength to overcome problems of family and community life that are invariably complex to resolve.

The genre of Amman movies generally shows the complexities of the problems they face, even if often in exaggerated forms, and urges them to cultivate such virtues that these women, through socialization in their lives, have been trying to achieve. There is a resonance here between the film's messages and the culture and socialization patterns of their lives. While the Amman movies show the unity of Dalit/Dravidian *Sakthi* worship with Vedic Hinduism as an ongoing process of sanskritization, they also retain their distinctiveness, thereby always constructing a distinct Dravidian identity as well.

SOCIALITY AND COMMUNITY

Yet another question is whether this new religious upsurge promotes greater sociality and community. Certainly, the rhythms of everyday urban life in Chennai revolving around roadside temples in certain residential localities have caused a greater intermixing and cooperation among women of various castes but not necessarily across class. A feeling of community is fostered when women encourage and contribute to certain activities of temple life. As women are the ones who make *prarthana*, they sometimes resolve to contribute silver articles and jewelry to the roadside temple gods on the fulfillment of certain desires like a daughter getting married or a son getting a job abroad and so on. Middle-class women working in banks have also indulged the initiators or priests of roadside temples with their passion-filled obsession of putting up *pucca* (permanent) temple constructions, expanding the temple, or the performance of the *Kumbhabhishekam* by making generous monetary contributions for the realization of their objectives. Roadside temples have thus intensified the degree of cooperative relationships, and middle-class women have played leading roles in that. While contemporary Hindu modernity seeks to rebuild on the ethics of selfless service on a much larger scale in terms of development work rather than just acts of philanthropic service, these are only marginal in the religio-scape of Chennai and do not involve women. Moreover, these large-scale philanthropic development works are perceived as attempts to constitute a homogenous pan-Indian and global Hinduism that erases local traditions, local histories, and the constitution of distinctive regional caste identities.

CONCLUSION

The rise of religiosity, as indicated by various markers, suggests that it is a consequence of the new economic prosperity as the city makes over as a global city, competitively reaping the benefits of globalization. Such economic prosperity has quickened the process of evolutionary cultural change that has been long underway. The debates on globalization and religion should therefore expand its scope from the politicization of religious identities that it has so far largely confined itself to include the broader issues of religion and cultural change as well. Contemporary trends in Tamil women's religiosity signify the impact of such cultural change. The differentiation of forms of piety among Hindu women by caste and class is in consonance with the differentiated worship practices of Hinduism in Tamil Nadu. Upper-caste housewives participate in temple worship and actively sponsor worship, and women employed as teachers and bank employees donate liberally for the construction of roadside temples, even when they are aware that these temples will be demolished if they are seen to obstruct traffic or for street-widening. Women subscribe to religious magazines and are prolific readers of religious books in the Tamil language. Owing to popular demand, there are television channels dedicated to religious programs, with women's home entertainment preferences leaning more toward religious programs than sports, politics, or others.

From a feminist standpoint, the increase in women's piety may be seen as a pointer to a possibly more regressive move of fulfilling patriarchal norms. It appears that this phenomenon across the social spectrum is more a pride-filled assertion of cultural practices and identities and does not destabilize patriarchies at home. Brahmin and other upper-caste women, tasked with the roles of protecting the spiritual domain of the family, seem to propriate gods and goddesses more frequently on various occasions, either seeking blessings or for thanksgiving. Such boon-seeking propitiation of the gods is far less among the poorer working classes, who are only keen to perform an annual propitiation of Goddess Amman in the Tamil month of *Aadi*.

While these practices do not challenge domestic patriarchies, women do have to negotiate between tradition and modernity alongside this religious flourish, especially since employed housewives need to accommodate the religious practices along with their work schedules. Certain festival worships conducted in homes by visiting priests in Brahmin households have been abridged or done by playing cassette tapes rather than having the priest come to the home, but not entirely given up. Apartment décor with religious artifacts and ritual gift-giving to friends and neighbors on occasions such as Navaratri puja have been upscaled as new and attractive goods come onto the religious artifacts market, which in recent years has become a thriving business with the rise in middle-class incomes.

Some Hindu religious practices have changed, such as women singing hymns to God Vishnu, which was not done before. However, cultural norms based on notions of auspiciousness and inauspiciousness as they affect women still remain in principle, although practiced in diluted forms. For example, widows being forbidden to mark their foreheads with red vermilion or make an appearance at weddings. These practices have, by and large, been left to the individuals concerned to observe or not, based on their subjective assessment of the sentiments of others, rather than being compelled to do so. Modern apartment living in circumscribed spaces has also meant reworking supposedly religion-sanctioned cultural practices, such as observing menstrual seclusion for girls and women. This involves adjusting distances and spaces as well as the length of time for seclusion. As Narasimhan (2011) has shown, this also applies to other kinds of polluting states after birth and death in the household.

Tamil women's religiosity seems to have not adversely affected their cultivation of secular sensibilities and their emergence as democratic citizens. This could largely be attributed to the non-Brahmin movement of the twentieth century that later became the self-respect social reform movement of Dravida Kazhagam (DK) with its atheistic and rationalistic outlook. The two Dravidian political parties, offshoots of the Dravidian movement, that alternately hold electoral power in Tamil Nadu are the atheistic-inclined DMK and the more religion-tolerant party of AIADMK, with both being credited as secular parties unlike the current ruling party of BJP at the national level whose secular credentials most Tamils are skeptical about. This fact, along with the state's secular stance of equidistance from all religions, meant that Tamil women did not face any conflict with their religiosity and secular sensibilities except for Brahmin women and men who for long faced social criticism of the Brahmanical ways of life unleashed by the Dravidian movement.

Women's expression of religiosity and their religious dispositions are in accord with the project to refashion themselves into modern subjects with secular and democratic agentic capabilities, along with their making of their traditional self inscribed by their religiosity. Given the continued dominance of Dravidian politics in the state, the rise of religiosity is not conflated with the anxieties of a political mobilization around religious identities. Rather, the rise in religiosity signifies an increase in middle-class incomes in the era of globalization as well as the precarity of the contemporary situation with the undermining of the certainties of modern life such as stability of income, social security, employment, marriage, health, and peace among others. While religious modernity within Hinduism is on the rise with the scaling up of charity to large development projects in the fields of education and health, these are still not so numerous nor do they give women a greater sense of social and ethical responsibility as the donors are predominantly wealthy men, and women are only on the fringes of these endeavors despite the enormous popularity of some women spiritual leaders nationally and internationally.

The major fieldwork for this study was done as part of the Sarai/CSDS Independent Fellowship in 2004. It was subsequently followed up on an ongoing basis.

Chapter 6

Tradition and Modernity in Clothing and Dress

Clothing styles are connected to ideas of being traditional or modern, as modernity offers clothing choices to refashion one's exterior self to present one's body in appealing ways and thereby also assert one's individuality and affirm or reject one's group identity through one's choices, especially in contexts of cultural change caused by transnational and national cultural flows. Since clothing and accessories are markers of social and cultural identities and women make statements of self through such practices of embodiment, it is relevant how, in the contending pulls of modernity and tradition, women make statements through gender scripts of their being as modern or traditional. In the realm of clothing too, there are two ways to status attainment, namely status attainment through performance of traditional gender ideology and status attainment through modernity. The clothing choices for women are not a seamless one without constraints as they have to constantly negotiate with norms of modesty, cultural practices, peer pressures, and status issues.

Drawing theoretical ideas from Bourdieu's significant work *Distinction* relating to social and cultural capital, taste, and structure of lifestyle, this chapter explores the ethnographic terrain of fashion and clothing in Chennai to understand how women negotiate through the multiple contestations of modernity, tradition, modesty, identity, and social class distinctions. The data were garnered through conversations with friends and children of friends, as well as with strangers in many places such as clothing shops, while attending cultural programs or weddings. Conversations on clothing and attire may appear as casual conversations, as it is a common topic to connect with friends and even strangers in certain situations, but as I was going to turn the information into a social-science article, I became more focused while collecting information on the clothing styles of the young as well. While such focused collection took place in the summer of 2014, this chapter also reflects the deep learning of the cultural nuances over the years until the present time as part of my experience of living a greater part of my life in Chennai.

FASHION, CLOTHING, AND CULTURE

Fashion is one of the visible cultural flows that has intensified under contemporary globalization, and as a flow in the global cultural economy, it reveals both disjuncture and difference (Appadurai, 1996a). While fashion signifies the speed of change, it does impact clothing styles that are more enduring within a culture (Hansen, 2004). Imaginaries of possible new urban lifestyles are a consequence of these cultural flows that have inculcated taste for products that define these lifestyles, which varies across social class positions. This chapter examines changes in clothing styles in Chennai, a city known to be a traditional city that is in the process of becoming a global city.

Fashion shows are now regular events in countries where they were nonexistent a few years ago and are spreading as an emergent cultural flow causing the geographic displacement of international fashion from the West, resulting in decentering the hegemony of Western fashion along with the rise of plural fashions (Narumi, 2000). Even Middle Eastern countries like Iran, with their strict dress codes, have fashion shows, and it is reported that when *Yves Saint Laurent* first opened a boutique in Jeddah and *Christian Dior* in Riyadh, their high fashion products were sold out quickly (Rabolt and Forney, 1989). Designer clothing companies in Paris have started showcasing fashion for Muslim women in France, whose attire is markedly different from Western attire.

In India, fashion as a cultural flow is not all derived from the West, though that remains a factor, but is also an emergent Indian one attuned to the local cultural context and often represents some kind of hybridity of both Western and Indian elements. Multicultural societies of the West like New York also hold "Indian" fashion shows where Indian and Western models showcase Indian (considered ethnic) and Western attire, while American fashion shows like the Met Gala have in recent years had at least one Indian participant showcasing hybridity that perhaps "meets with the approval of the Orientalizing gaze" (Narumi, 2000, 311).

Although beauty pageants for women have been in existence in India for the last fifty years (Hoad, 2004), fashion shows started only a few years ago and have been made popular through televised coverage of models walking the ramp both in Indian and Western dresses, often the sari worn as a fashioned outfit. Whereas in the early years the *Lakme Wills* Fashion show was the single most popular annual show, now Western clothing companies like *Vero Moda* also organize fashion shows. Simultaneously, there is increased coverage of fashion in daily English newspapers and magazines, with Western and Indian models posing on the same page, and a multiplication of fashion designing schools and programs of study (Kalpagam, 2019). Perhaps the high point of this cultural flow is the publication of the Indian edition of the popular Western fashion magazine *Vogue,* which includes both Western and Indian fashion models (Kopnina, 2007). Fashion shows are not just aesthetic pleasure or entertainment as they are meant to inculcate taste and stimulate desire, especially in a context of a "mass fashion system" going commercial (Jirousek, 1997).

The intense global and regional cultural flows in the domain of fashion and clothing are marked by increase in the variety of clothing, an expansion of individual choices, and a market-induced democratization of clothing styles and use. While folks in showbiz remain fashion trendsetters, South Asian individual women's choice of clothing is circumscribed by ideas and norms of modernity and modesty that are in constant flux (Bahl, 2005). The manner in which the cultural politics of the "male gaze" over female bodies plays itself out in women's clothing conventions and choices determined by age and class is distinctive to this culture, yet represents a more universal predicament across cultures (Tarlo, 1996; Tyner and Ogle, 2007; Lynch, 2007). As elsewhere, here too clothing is a marker of social identity, and women demonstrate their selfhood through clothing or refashion their self through fashion statements on their bodies (Reischer and Koo, 2004; Wadley, 2008). The embodiment of identity and self as an everyday ongoing practice takes place in the realm of clothing and adornment, a practice that is determined by age and social class, entailing a constant negotiation between modernity, tradition, and modesty (Budgeon, 2003; Klepp and Storm-Mathisen, 2005; Thapan, 2006, 2009; Wolputte, 2004).

The changing clothing styles as a consequence of globalization's effects on lifestyles can be insightfully analyzed by drawing from Bourdieu's ideas on the structure of symbolic space. In his work *Distinction*, Bourdieu (1984) attempts to provide a model of the relationships between the universe of economic and social conditions and the universe of lifestyles in an effort to further understand Weber's distinction between class and *Stand,* which is assumed to connote "status." Faulting economists for ignoring the question of the economic and social determinants of "taste," he urged to

> move beyond the abstract relationship between consumers with interchangeable tastes and products with uniformly perceived and appreciated properties to the relationship between tastes which vary in a necessary way according to their social and economic conditions of production, and the products on which they confer their different social identities. (Bourdieu, 1984, 100–101)

For Bourdieu, a complete definition of a product ought to include "the differential experiences which the consumers have of it as a function of the dispositions they derive from their position in the economic space" (Bourdieu, 1984, 101). He further observes that the habitus "enables an intelligible and necessary relation to be established between practices and a situation, the meaning of which is produced by the habitus through categories of perception and appreciation that are themselves produced by an observable social condition" (Bourdieu, 1984, 101). Hidden under the diversity and multiplicity of the set of practices performed in fields governed by different logics lies a unity, which is the structure of lifestyle characteristics of an agent or a class of agents. The whole set of these structured practices, all the distinct and distinctive lifestyles which are always defined objectively and sometimes subjectively in and through their mutual relations, mark out the structure of a symbolic space. Bourdieu's ideas set up a differentiated analysis of consumers based on their position on the social scale and the associated structure of lifestyle characteristics and their differential experience of the product.

Clothing has always been used by individuals as a way of expressing themselves, be it the colors, the fabrics, the prints, the outfit, and the fashions. While individuals are conscious of what they wear and when they wear what, and know that it is a form of self-expression, they realize that in so doing, they are actually acting out the social scripts of the construction of cultural identity and the contestations of identity; the social scripts that are pre-given for an individual, but in which they can choose their roles. Clothing has been an arena to define cultural tradition, nativity, ethnicity, nationality, modernity, and cosmopolitanism. As Bahl (2005) notes, it is in the choice of clothing styles that one comes to realize that these categories of classification are shifting and not fixed. What had appeared modern in the recent past could well become traditional even in the near future—this is as much a saying fashions change. But there is more to it, as the subjects who are clothed are perceived by others and perceive themselves or think that others perceive them as modern, traditional, and so on. In many cultures, clothing styles are also determined by the social class position, and the subjectivity of the individual is shaped by and shapes the choice of what one wears (Chan, 2000).

Moreover, women's and young girls' clothing are ascribed meanings of modesty, vulgarity, and indecency. Thus, what one wears invites more than classifying a person; it involves reactive behavior and social regulation as well. While what one wears is largely an individual choice, social classes or groups largely conform to certain clothing styles that are determined by the manner in which group identity is sought to be affirmed in the cultural contestations of identity. Both men's and women's clothing are bearers of culture and cultural contestations, but the stakes in the contests over women's clothing are spiked up by patriarchal and political notions of appropriateness with respect to various factors, not excluding the ways in which it is supposed to stimulate and contain male desire.

CLOTHING CULTURE AND THE CITY

Tracing the changes in Indian clothing styles over a long historical period, Chaudhuri ([1976] 2008) observes that the interaction between Indian and the European costumes is immensely more powerful than that which exists up to a point among the Indian forms. This has made the clothes in the cities even more motley than what they would have been if they had evolved by themselves. According to him, there was in all the Indian cities an aggregation of all costumes worn in the country, although in some, the range of specimens was less wide as in Madras (now called Chennai) than in others like Calcutta and Delhi.

The Western influence on clothing in India, according to Chaudhuri, was of two kinds: first, that in which a Western garment had been added to the Indian costume and had become a part of it; and second, that in which there had been mutations of Indian garments on Western lines. This reveals that Tamils in the colonial period were negotiating between tradition and modernity and resolving the conflict in different ways, which is further evident from his description of how the lawyers of the Madras High Court dressed during the colonial era by combining traditional attire with the Western attire introduced by colonial modernity. He notes,

> In Madras people wore a tie even when they put on the coat over the dhoti. The elaboration was not obligatory, but it was usual for formal occasions. For instance, the advocates of the High Court in Madras and others, too, were seen in a costume which, taken in the foot-to-head order, consisted of the following: bare feet; the dhoti on the lower limbs; the shirt, tie, and coat on the torso; vermilion or other caste mark on the forehead; and an immaculate turban on the head. (Chaudhuri, [1976] 2008, 7)

Today, photographs of ancestors in such clothing hang on the walls of elite upper-caste homes, indicating that their high social status was of an older vintage when their ancestors had served in important positions in the colonial government.

Chaudhuri ([1976] 2008) also notes women's extraordinary capacity to absorb Western influences in a far more subtle and penetrating manner, once again resolving the dilemma of tradition and modernity by retaining both in parts. The sari, considered most stable and supremely Hindu garment typical of an Indian woman's clothing, according to him, is undergoing a progressive de-Hinduization. In the cities, the sari is rapidly approaching an all-India norm among Westernized Hindu women while regional variations abound in rural areas. It is arguable whether it is due only to Occidental fashion influences, as Chaudhuri suggests, or to a cultivation of middle-class Indian femininity in the public domain through the presentation of a national dress for women in the twentieth-century modern nation as women increasingly combine their duties in the domestic sphere with roles outside their homes.

The clothing culture in the city has recently seen a noteworthy change, perhaps due to its consciousness as an emerging global city and in part on account of evolving pan-India patterns of clothing culture. Known as a traditional city, perhaps because it neither had the Bollywood aura of Mumbai nor the diplomatic cosmopolitanism of the national capital Delhi, Chennai has sought to graduate itself to a global city largely on account of its intellectual capital of software engineers, the state's proactive role in urban infrastructure development, and political power that for long had a progressive vision of equality overthrowing traditional hierarchies and making it more adaptive to emergent cultural flows.

Men and Boys Attire

Men's attire appears to have changed much less in recent times than women's attire. The upwardly mobile young men, those in the emerging new sectors like Information Technology, who have sizeable cash incomes often because their spouses are also in similar employment with comparable salaries, are keen to buy a car and a home, and enjoy exotic vacations that are more often company-sponsored than to transform their personal images to that of the metrosexual man which many of Mumbai or Delhi's young men seem to do. This despite the numerous billboards of the metrosexual man alluring the young men of the city for various brands of clothing and other commodities. Yet the outlets for branded men's wear in the various shopping malls that have come up indicate the aspirational needs of the upwardly mobile young men. These are the high-end brands. Men buy these brands mostly to wear on their trips abroad that have now increased with globalization's new opportunities. However, for the majority of men whose lives are untouched by the dreams and glamour of globalization, the traditional attire of *Veshti* and *Lungi* holds strong but in most outdoor working situations excepting manual work like digging, construction and a few informal sector vending activities, men especially the young prefer the modern pant and shirt. Tamil men's wear within the homes is predominantly white *Veshti* (unstitched garment) or a colored *Lungi* (where the two width ends are stitched together) across all classes except the youth who may wear pants or shorts. Brahmin men wear two-piece unstitched and unbleached *Veshti* and upper cloth for all ritual occasions which is followed even today and the manner of wearing these vestments are stipulated in the scriptures of Hinduism. This accounts for why the traditional garb was never given up fully for the modern Western attire of pant and shirt. If the attire of the colonial lawyers of the Madras High Court appears ludicrous even while reading about it today, it simultaneously raises the question as to why the Tamil male politicians' attire today do not appear so ludicrous, who wear white *Veshti* along with a white shirt and a white towel over one shoulder, once again like those lawyers combing both traditional and Western attire. The Western shirt has been fully naturalized as an Indian garment while the pant not being fully naturalized is avoided by politicians who seek not to alienate themselves from the poorer working masses who still predominantly wear only *Lungi*.

Men's wear outside their homes can be divided into two segments based on social and class distinctions. Young upwardly mobile men, educated in English and outward looking, that is, those who perceive opportunities accessible to them in the corporate sector catering to global markets, go for clothing from high-end global brands. The other segment of young men who are educated and employed, though not in the global sectors but aspiring to move up the scale of modernity, increasingly opt for ready-made garments, especially shirts, and they too have their favorite brands among the proliferating local brands. Such local-brand ready-made shirts are the popular "Madras shirts" made in the numerous garment factories that dot the city's suburban landscape, drawing young women workers both from the city and the rural hinterlands. Tailor-stitched shirts for young men have almost given way to ready-made shirts, although pants are still largely made to individual order specifications. Surprisingly, it is the T-shirt that has captured the imagination of the youth more than even the blue jeans, widely perceived as an American clothing style. T-shirts too are distinguished as the branded ones sold in malls and the unbranded ones sold on the sidewalks of streets, and these have varying status connotations for the young men, more often confirming their status in the social hierarchy. For the youth, the signature T-shirt, the one with a unique statement or emblem, remains a prized memento of certain occasions. Youth often sport a T-shirt with a striking or surprising statement more to assert their individuality, although young women wearing T-shirts avoid the same as it would provoke jeers and hoots, or men staring lasciviously at their breasts. Although T-shirts and jeans are a rage with a section of youth, precisely because they have the aura of Western modernity, the same T-shirts with shorts and sneakers when worn by a senior citizen going on a walk would invoke a joking comment that he is "America returned," as someone who must have spent some time recently in the United States with his children settled there. Among the very young, the boys' dress has not undergone changes from shorts and pants/shirts, though among the upper middle class, the tendency to dress up children like the way the American non-resident Indians do is an obvious trend. So young boys are often seen wearing loose jeans and T-shirts, an image much flashed in television advertisements too.

Women and Girls Attire

Women's attire has undergone quite a remarkable change. Traditionally, women, generally over twenty-five years of age and most often married, wore a sari and a blouse. Young girls between puberty and marriage wore a half-sari, which is a shortened sari draped over a full skirt. The earlier one got married, the quicker the shift to the sari. So, as the average age at marriage in earlier decades was around eighteen years or even less, most young women transitioned to the sari by that time. In the late nineteenth century, when orthodox Brahmins got their daughters married around the time of puberty, these young girls wore the traditional nine-yard sari every day; archival photographs even show them playing Squash or Tennikoit in that attire. As it was not worn over a petticoat and was divided and wound around the two legs that made free movement possible. A modified way of tying the sari is still prevalent among Tamil women working in the rice fields. Today, Brahmin women wear the nine-yards sari only at the time of their wedding or other auspicious events within the home, as the six-yard sari has become the norm nationally.

The traditional attire for young girls is the *Pattu Pavadai*, the full skirt made of Conjeevaram (Kancheepuram) silk that still remains a cultural compulsion to socialize a Tamil identity in children. Most families, except the poor, do manage to get at least one such silk skirt for the girl despite the cost, although cheaper look-alikes are available in plenty. But even among the well-to-do, the girls now have fewer *Pattu Pavadai* than before. Young mothers say that there are now fewer occasions for their girls to wear the *Pattu Pavadai* both because nucleated families now have fewer religious celebrations with members of the extended family, and for other occasions, they have switched to other dresses.

A Clothing Style Becomes National

Girls below the age of fourteen wore full skirts considered a South Indian dress or sometimes even a half-skirt that is considered Western. The very young were allowed to wear Western-style frocks until the age of eight or nine. Distinctions of class were identifiable from the quality of fabrics they wore, and individual tastes were expressed through colors and designs. Nearly thirty years ago, the contestation over "tradition" and "modernity" in the realm of clothing for young teenage girls was expressed by their preference either for the half-sari or what was then common, the "Bell bottoms and *kurta*/shirt." Families that were then open to modern ideas freely allowed the young girls to wear "Bell bottoms and *kurta*/shirt," while in more traditional families, the half-sari was the unquestioned attire for young girls after puberty. "Tradition" and "modernity" became an everyday contestation in many households when young girls who preferred to wear "Bell bottoms and *kurta*/shirt" waged battles with mothers, grandmothers, and aunts who held firmly to the traditional dress. Sibling rivalries between older and younger sisters were aggravated if the younger one sought to become more modern and if the older one was brought up more traditionally, with elder brothers having opinions on how their sister should present herself before their male friends.

All this has now changed with the heightened pan-India cultural flows. Today, the *salwar-kameez* that for long was seen as a North Indian dress, more specifically Punjabi dress, which Pakistan made its national dress and had, for some time, even forbidden its women to wear the sari, as being the Indian national dress, is all pervasive in the southern states as well. Introduced into India by the Muslim rulers and worn largely by Muslim women and the women of Punjab, it has now become a contemporary style among the Muslims of South India as well (Osella and Osella, 2007). Among Hindu women, while older women still wear the sari, more upper-middle-class women delay their switch to the sari as everyday wear, preferring the ease of the *salwar* suit, which undergoes frequent changes in fashion.

In and around the home, married women except the very old wear a long robe called a housecoat by some and a nightie by others. Considered to be the most casual, convenient, and intimate wear, many young working-class women from slums venture outside with a *dupatta* or stole (the veil-like cloth worn over the *salwar-kameez*) over the housecoat as a sign of modesty, to pick up vegetables or groceries from the neighborhood stores, or drop their children off at the school or at the bus-stand. Each woman decides for herself the limits and bounds of the private space around her wherein she could move clad in the "housecoat with the *dupatta*." While some schools have prohibited mothers from entering the premises in such casual attire, they continue to move in such attire in the narrow streets and alleys, hopping around neighbors' homes with ease. These changes signify both a greater defiance of the social norms of clothing on the part of women and a greater acceptability by wielders of patriarchal power to allow married women to dress according to convenience and ease, and to push the boundaries of the domestic space to adjoining areas.

Among younger women, most have switched to the *salwar* suit where earlier they had worn the half-sari. Now the half-sari is worn only on family occasions like festivals or wedding. Those still holding on to the half-sari as their daily wear are likely to be perceived by their peers as being traditional vis-à-vis the ones wearing the *salwar* suit, although the half-sari has transitioned to become a marker of a distinctive Tamil identity for young girls amid the onslaught of the North Indian *salwar-kameez*. Tamil films regularly portray young girls clad in traditional half-saris, performing group dancing that Tamil adults find aesthetic and pleasing. Citing from Brenda Beck, Wadley notes about dancing by young Tamil girls, "Their playfulness and unconscious sexuality are viewed as a kind of power which can be transferred to brothers and fathers in the family in the form of increased prosperity" (Wadley, [1980] 1991, 156). There are also television shows featuring young boys and girls in Western attire playing the violin to Tamil and Western music, much like the Western orchestras, suggestive of a happy blend of tradition and Western modernity.

As large numbers of young girls seek employment after a high-school education as salesgirls in shops or in garment and other factories, the *salwar* suit has become the preferred dress of convenience and ease. Across the entire cross-section of caste and class, the adoption of the *salwar* suit among young girls is an indication of the extent to which this mode of dress has been naturalized as an Indian dress. Whereas the half-sari still distinguishes one with a regional and ethnic identity as Tamilian, the *salwar* suit with its pan-Indian acceptance as an Indian dress helps one overcome the regional identity markers in the increasingly cosmopolitan city.

The naturalization of the *salwar* suit in Chennai city was in part aided by the fact that many schools that earlier had school uniforms as either half-skirt, full skirt, or half-sari switched over to *salwar* suit in the last two decades. As a uniform, the *salwar* suit makes it possible for the school to ensure uniformity of dress, for earlier they had to permit girls after puberty to switch over to the half-sari from either the half or full skirt abiding by Tamil cultural norms. Schools that had as a uniform either the half skirts or the Western-style pinafore maintained strict watch over the length of the skirts. Girls who wore them too short were pulled up and asked to remove the hem lines to let the skirts get longer, sent back home for the day and their parents duly informed, or otherwise suitably punished. Even the English-medium convent schools considered to be at the forefront of modernity did not compromise on the cultural expectations of modesty.

The makeover from school uniforms that had distinct markers of regional and ethnic identity to one that secures a more national identity is noteworthy. Such shifts are evident in varying degrees in other cultural realms of food, music, religion, and education. Thus, regional, ethnic, and national identities are constantly jostled by collectives of individuals to redraw boundaries and borders as institutions, opportunities, and desires keep changing.

TRANSNATIONAL INFLUENCES

Contemporary transnational trends are also absorbed and reworked in the realm of clothing culture in this city. While many young women have adopted the *salwar-kameez*, some others consider it traditional, with their preference marked in favor of jeans and *kurti* (short *kurta* worn like shirts) as being a hybrid of Western jeans and Indian *kurti*, which is perceived as more modern. College girls, among whom the tendency for group formation is based upon status factors such as whether one had English-medium or Tamil-medium school education or whether one commutes to college by public transport or gets dropped off in a car driven by a chauffeur, father or brother, or, in earlier days, between the so-called half-sari types or the bell-bottom types, have now changed into the jeans-*kurti*-short hair types and *salwar-kameez* types. Even those modern girls who would have worn jeans-*kurti* avoid doing so when they travel to college by the public transport system as crowded buses have always been sites of groping and molestation of young women. Few girls resist by raising their voices, and most suffer silently as it would be considered immodest and shameful to do so. This culture of eve-teasing is the gender war of patriarchal violence in everyday life.

While modern girls wear jeans/pants or even sometimes the skirt on most occasions, the special occasions that compel them to be in Indian attire would make them wear *salwar* suit or sometimes saris. These *salwar* suits are not the ordinary ones worn by the rest; rather, they are in fabric, design, and cut made according to the latest fashion trends from Bollywood. These custom-designed *salwar* suits and similar custom-designed North Indian attire popularized by Bollywood as wedding attire are catching up among the cosmopolitans, even in Chennai through pan-India franchise outlets that advertise and cater to such styles. These are distinctively traditional garments styled in new Indian fashions that compete to expand into regional and global ethnic markets.

Indeed, it is not surprising that the division between those wearing *salwar-kameez* and those wearing jeans and *kurti* coincides with social class divisions. Upper caste and class individuals, who are more often English-speaking and educated in elite schools and colleges, are those sporting jeans, while those outside that social class, the girls from the lower caste and class backgrounds, who are perhaps first-generation college entrants in their families and educated in non-elite schools in the Tamil medium, wear the *salwar-kameez* and sometimes even the half-sari, as a visit to the elite and non-elite women's colleges would reveal.

Neither can the jeans *kurti* group of young girls be considered homogenous if measured on a scale of modernity in clothing. Individuals distinguish themselves as more modern than the rest through varying style statements that range from cut, fit, and design, and accessories like shoulder/hand bag, jewelry, watch, mobile phone, and footwear. The varying styles among those wearing jeans/pants have also concomitantly led to the evolution of norms of what would be considered appropriate and inappropriate dress modes in different social contexts. Some women's colleges in the city have imposed a dress code that forbids girls from wearing hipster jeans and tight short tops/T-shirts or tops with just shoulder straps, just as a sleeveless blouse or a fancy cut blouse with a hipster sari worn in social settings at parties would be considered inappropriate and not permissible in the college setting. If colleges are enforcing norms of modesty in women's attire, the temples are enforcing norms of tradition by their insistence on dress codes considered culturally appropriate in Tamil society. An overwhelming number of Hindu temples are strictly enforcing dress codes and have put up boards on dress codes for girls stating short dresses and tight and torn jeans are not permitted and *salwar* suits have to be worn with *dupatta*, while *Veshti* with shirt and sari are the culturally appropriate ones for men and women.

The absorption of Western dress norms, even by those aspiring to contemporary modernity, is not a seamless act of changing attire. In clothing, as in other realms, the issue is how best to adopt Western mores and yet strike and retain a distinctive Indian identity. This is most evident in the mode of dressing of young newsreaders on the numerous English television channels, who are role models for many of the young girls of that social class. Most of these television personalities these days appear in Western suits, and all have short hair or, if long will let it to flow loose while some have dyed their hair from black to brown and have given up the Hindu identity marker of *Bindi* (red color mark) on the forehead. But their assertion of a distinctive Indianness is to wear the nose-ring that both Hindu and Muslim girls of the larger North Indian society sport as a cultural norm. While in Chennai city, many upper-class girls have discarded the nose-ring as being traditional, they too, while adopting Western dress, mark their Indianness or even the Hindu-ness by retaining the *Bindi* or by wearing ethnic jewelry. That the idea of "traditional" and "modern" are subjective connotations of individuals and groups is evident if we note that while pants worn by a young woman would tend to mark her as modern, the same pants worn by a policewoman would not necessarily mark her as being modern, although women being recruited into the police force is in step with modernity. But these subjective connotations are now overtaken by the most striking objective fusion of modernity and tradition in the contemporary style of the *sari*-pantsuit in which the ensemble consists of pants and a long coat with a sari drape, now becoming the new couture of the *Air India* cabin crew and imaginatively designed by one of India's top couturiers.

The transition from frocks and full skirts to either *salwar-kameez* or jeans and T-shirt among young girls results in fewer frocks on the shelves of the shops. Although *salwar* suits have flooded the market, many with ethnic designs and styles, even the child's notion of being modern has shifted to jeans and short tops. Except for the very poor girls clothed either from donated clothes or cheap frocks sold on street pavements, there has been an across-the-board preference shift to jeans and tops. Many of the parents who cannot afford to buy them feel the pinch and the pressure when children ask for jeans as a birthday gift that is more expensive than a *salwar* set or skirt and blouse. Middle-class children too want their parents to buy them jeans/ tops from branded stores in shopping malls.

VARIETY, CHOICE, AND MARKET DEMOCRACY

The variety in textiles has multiplied manifold in recent times. Cotton textiles, such as handloom, power-loom, and mill products, along with the variety of blended fabrics with polyester yarn and silk, provide the fabric base upon which designs, prints, and colors mark out their distinctiveness. While cotton remains the staple with a wide and affordable range of choices, polyester fabrics are now cheaper, making it a decent option for all. Whereas earlier, women college teachers generally thought that starched cotton saris made them appear smart, today with the busy urban life, they too have switched over to the blended fabric. This is also quite obvious among working-class women like cooks and domestic maids for whom the Nylex/Polyester sari is a boon. Polyester has now made clothing so cheap that it is no exaggeration that for the middle-class family, it is cheaper to buy these clothes for the family than to go for a family dining experience in the somewhat upscale restaurants of the city. The dress norm of the sari remains unchanged in many of the older employments for women, such as teaching in schools and colleges, with few schools permitting primary class teachers to be in *salwar* suits.

A distinctive Tamil identity to the handloom and power-loom textiles has been made possible through various designs and color combinations not replicated elsewhere. With the *salwar* suits gaining popularity, the region's textile industry has been quick to seize the market opportunities. Knowing the preferences of Tamil customers, their cultural and class habitus, the market has been flooded with *salwar* suits with distinctive designs and colors not available in North India, considered the natural home of the *salwar* suit.

The revolution in the textile scene in the city of Chennai and much of Tamil Nadu is the influx of poly-silk saris that are close imitations of the much culturally prized Conjeevaram silk saris with *jari* (gold-threaded) borders and *pallu* (the flowing width end of the sari). While the authentic Conjeevaram silk saris would range in price from Rs. 10,000–100,000 ($100–$1,000), the poly-silk sari could be bought for anywhere from Rs. 600 ($10) onward. Some of the occasions for which middle-class women wore the Conjeevaram silk sari are now passed off with the poly-silk sari, while the number of occasions for which a grand poly-silk sari would be worn has also increased simultaneously. Whereas earlier women visited nearby temples in a cotton or nylex sari and on occasions even the Conjeevaram silk sari, now they wear the poly-silk sari for its grandeur for all temple visits.

This is not to suggest that the Conjeevaram silk sari has lost its pride of place in the Tamil cultural sensibility. In fact, as more and more people move up on the economic scale and graduate into the middle class, the greater is the demand for these silk saris. For these graduating sections of the population, the traditional markers of social status are still very significant. Whereas earlier, the upper castes, largely the Brahmin women, were the privileged customers for the Conjeevaram silk saris in the city's leading stores like *Nalli Silks* and *Rasi Silks*, the newly graduated customers, mostly of the non-Brahmin middle castes, have shunned these leading stores for the newer ones that cater to their taste, perhaps due to their association with Brahmin clientele for too long. This trend for textiles is also true for gold jewelry, suggestive of both growing affluence and widespread consumerism in the city. In this emerging consumerism, traditional markers of social status for women have not been dislodged, although new markers have situated themselves in the new social spaces of lifestyle changes brought by transnational cultural flows such as preferences for certain clothing styles and the brand aura.

Most women, except perhaps informal sector workers, appear fairly well-dressed today unlike in earlier times. While women wear grand saris for temple visits, abiding by the traditional cultural norms, churchgoers dress in more modern ways during their church visits. My carpenter told me recently that he visits the church wearing well-ironed black pants, a white bush shirt, and well-polished black shoes as his pastor instructed him to do so as a mark of gratitude to Jesus. Overcome by curiosity, I visited the famous Velankanni shrine, dedicated to Mother Mary in the city, to see how women dressed when they went to the church. While women wore the same grand poly-silk saris as those visiting temples, the colors were pastel shades and not as gaudy. But girls and young women, even past their teenage years, were all in Western-style long gowns that is paired as a set with short stole in shiny fabric and colors, embellished with intricate work of beads, glass crystals, silver and gold threads, laces, and embroidery, with many with their hair let loose, lipstick and minimal artificial jewelry. The mass production of Indianized Western gowns in the numerous garment factories around Chennai has made such non-branded gowns sold in retail stores quite affordable for the lower middle classes. However, it would be a rarity to see a teenager or young woman in such a gown in Hindu temples where the culturally appropriate dress code means ethnic *salwar* suits or half-saris for them.

These Western gowns are also worn by very young girls without the stole, as the frock worn earlier has now receded in fashion. Whereas the earlier frock's length was only up to the knees, the one-piece gown extends far below, almost to the ankle, much like the full skirt or *Pavadai* with all the glitter of the embellishments, the frills and the shiny fabric. The current fusion of Indian and Western clothing styles has brought a revolution in clothing culture in many ways. It has led to the spread of retail franchises for these factory-made ready-made garments of which the two leading ones are the Industrialist Ambani's venture *Reliance Trends* and the Tata Conglomerate's called *Westside,* with the fusion of the Indian and Western elements varying between the two. While *Reliance Trends* veers more toward Indian, and so considered somewhat as ethnic, the Tata venture is unabashedly tilted to the West as its name suggests. A visit to the *Westside* showroom revealed the clothing fusion of the Indian *salwar-kameez* and the Western pant-suit in mind-boggling combinations of styles and designs. The garment industries supplying these retail giants employ thousands who graduate every year from the numerous fashion technology institutes set up in recent years even as the traditional small tailors are rendered redundant as the younger generations shift fully to ready-made garments. While young girls in employment till recently wore the *salwar* suits in the emerging globalized sectors such as airlines, hospitality and IT services, with some wearing Western pant-suits as a uniform requirement, today the bulk of the urban young women employees in the service sectors opt for these fusion ready-made garments from these two retail giants and others. Plans are on the anvil of these two retailers to expand to smaller towns and refashion the entire younger female population. Social change and education are changing the clothing styles of young rural women as well in many parts of the country (Wadley, 2008).

For the youth wearing jeans or pants, the ready-made garments offer a variety ranging from branded products to fake ones on street sidewalks with prices that suit all budgets. The youth mark differences in social status among themselves based on whether one is wearing a high-end brand or not, and this status marker has also given rise to the proliferation of fake brand labels for jeans and sneakers. While brand aura signifies distinction and social status, aura busting through counterfeit and fake clothing and fashion accessories is a social and class challenge as it seeks to both emulate and disrupt the distinction aspired to by the richer class (Ha and Lennon, 2006; Kalpagam, 2008). Branded clothes from famous brands are no doubt catching up in this city as elsewhere, but the majority of the young wear unbranded jeans or knock-off ones. Transnational clothing designs enter youth preferences as garment manufacturers dump consignments that fail to meet importers' standards in local retail outlets. While the youth of the richer social class find the shopping experience in luxury shopping malls selling global brand products attractive for it tries to replicate the Western or Singapore shopping experience, those shopping on street sidewalks get the exhilaration of a bargain deal with counterfeits and fake labels.

SHOWBIZ, MODERNITY, AND MODESTY

Clothing fashions are widely disseminated through films, advertisements, and magazines. Although Tamil and other regional films are never the national fashion trendsetters like Bollywood films, the clothing styles of Tamil film stars evoke considerable interest and emulation. Sari designs and blouse cuts have gone by the name of the film wherein the heroine had worn such attire that subsequently gained popularity. Although Bollywood fashions do not have a significant influence in Chennai as much as in Mumbai or North India, there is, in recent times, a more liberal attitude in clothing styles of young women actresses who now appear in pants/jeans, Western dresses, or *salwar* suits. What is remarkable is that while greater body exposure on the reel is acceptable as more in keeping with changing aesthetic norms, there is a strict demarcation between what is permissible in "reel life" and in "real life." Recently, a very popular young actress came in for criticism for appearing skimpily clad at a public function that celebrated the success of one of her films, and she had to offer a public apology for offending certain sentiments. A small group of the Hindu right-wing was articulate in their criticism of the actress's attire at the public function, and soon a political party took it up for discussion in the state's legislative assembly on the desirability of a dress code to be brought in by the state to protect the distinctive Tamil cultural identity. While culture policing by certain political and fundamentalist groups has been on the rise in the country in recent years to curb the seemingly negative influence of Western cultural mores that are likely to corrode Indian culture and moral values among the youth, Chennai had so far been outside their sphere of influence.

As culture has now become a highly contested terrain, the adoption of Western-style clothing becomes a tactful negotiation of local cultural norms; ethnic, religious, regional, and gender identity-making processes that are underway; expectations of modesty; and disciplining processes of enforcing social norms at the family and social levels; and the newer demands and requirements of being in step with global modernity. Not long ago, expatriate Tamil women coming from abroad, especially the United States and Canada, would change into Indian attire en route either in London or Frankfurt so that they did not create a culture shock for their family and kin who would be at the airport to welcome them upon arrival. Some even complained in those days that Indian immigration and customs officials, both men and women, were quite rude to them when they saw them in Western-style clothes. Today, hardly anyone changes attire en route as local clothing styles have also changed.

Historically, clothing in India has been invested with meanings associated with the making of a "national culture" amid the politics of anti-colonial nationalism over colonial modernity. While middle-class urban men adopted Western pants and shirts, women's saris remained unchanged. Women's transgression of this dress code was associated with loose morals, bad character, or being too much under Western or Anglo-Indian influence. All this has undergone change among younger urban women, as clothing is now being invested with new meanings of being forward-looking and keeping pace with the nation's progress of modernity, yet retaining its cultural authenticity.

While the change to Western clothing styles such as pants/jeans are a pan-Indian urban phenomenon, there are regional differences in the pace of change even within metropolitan cities. Some smaller towns in the North Indian Hindi belt appear enthusiastic in inculcating such a cultural change among the youth as is evident from the major English-language newspaper *Hindustan Times* (Allahabad/Prayagraj edition) featuring every single day a full-page of fashion news with color pictures, gossip and all about the stars from showbiz and fashion models. Often the pictures of Indian icons of fashion are juxtaposed with the Western, mostly American showbiz personalities (Kalpagam, 2019). Such juxtaposition carries multiple meanings. For one, Indian fashion has come of age and can be made comparable with the fashions of high society, and secondly as Indian fashion models pose in Western dresses and styles, it seeks to instill confidence in the Indian youth to overcome their inhibitions of body images that rarely fit the Euro-American standards.

The current popularity of fashion modeling has almost overshadowed the beauty contests and beauty pageants that were a rage some time ago. Although Chennai does not host high-profile fashion shows as Delhi or Mumbai and its beauty contests were always a low-key affair, the striking change in recent years is that many girl's schools now conduct fashion shows to train the youngsters in both design skills and walking the ramp that signifies a shift in perception from the body as a symbol to the body as an agent.

WOMEN, CLOTHING, AND SELFHOOD

Selfhood is as much interiority as exteriority and as much performative and individualistic as it is relational and interactive with significant others. If gender is performative, then the act of clothing and adorning is a performative practice in the construction of gender. Through fashion, men and women refashion their selves, making clothing a statement of one's self. Women use colors, fabrics, designs, cuts, and dress forms to make these statements of their selves. While fitting into cultural norms in clothing styles is one way of affirming one's cultural self, striking out one's individuality in clothing style is to express one's unique self. Clothing is a way to affirm one's membership in a cultural community and one's individuality.

Women seek recognition and identity through practices of embodiment such as clothing and adornment and hence become subjects of regulation and discipline by others. Married women often reject sari colors that their husbands do not like, while a few reject colors on account of certain cultural sentiments. Elderly Brahmin women for instance never like to wear saris with black color thread woven in them, as black is considered inauspicious. Many such cultural sentiments, like the bride wearing a red-color sari signifying "auspiciousness," are still held on to and are only slowly undergoing changes.

Young women wearing pants/jeans are the most conscious of body image, and the jeans size becomes a regulator of body changes. When they begin to put on weight, they transition to looser outfits like *salwar-kameez* or sari as a cultural compulsion. Their anxieties over their body image are in part due to male expectations and demands in the matrimonial market, where slimness and fairness are at a great premium, more especially if the boy is likely to go abroad, as also the new desire for a cosmopolitan look, spurred by new opportunities of transnationalism. But most of the young women give up wearing pants/jeans after marriage, stating that their husband does not favor the dress. Equally young husbands these days do not prefer their wives to be donning a sari at all times for all occasions, making *salwar* suits the only viable option. Women's bodies portrayed in sculpture, with a slender waist and full pointed breasts that adorn the walls and pillars of all the temples of Tamil Nadu, are today more a cultural ideal than a statistical median.

Tamil women have a strong and an almost insatiable preference for gold jewelry that also serves as insurance in less fortunate times. Those who cannot afford pure gold jewelry adorn themselves with imitation jewelry known as "covering gold." Chaudhuri (1976) makes the perceptive observation that in Hindu society, adornment of the person ceased long ago to be an intersexual affair and became as nearly as possible wholly asexual. The motivation of being well-dressed for the sake of giving aesthetic or emotional satisfaction to men does not exist in their minds. Adornment of jewelry by women is both to make them look beautiful to all and, importantly, as a marker of their social status, as high-priced jewelry of gold and diamonds enables social snobbery over others in the competitive social status games.

FEMALE BODIES AND THE MALE GAZE

The relationship of female bodies to male Others is a complex one as it entails both retaining male attention and warding off male attention, as female clothed bodies are associated with the symbolism of beauty and sensuality.

Women with alluring bodies are known to use it as an asset to attract men, yet women do not always seek to allure all men and at all times. Keeping off unwanted male attention at unwanted times is an issue of concern to women, and cultural norms of modesty regarding body exposure factor this issue into account.

The traditional sari can be worn to cover or reveal the body. Women with good body shapes wear the sari low on their hips, revealing the belly button and encouraging navel gazing, but most women refrain from what is considered an immodest way of wearing the sari. What is considered a provocative way of dressing is associated with the limits of sensual arousal that it induces in the viewer, for excessive sensual arousal would be nothing short of sexual arousal.

Young women learn early on about this duality of sensual arousal and containment of male sexual desire when, upon attaining puberty, they transit to wearing the half-sari. The half-sari allows the viewer to enjoy sensuality in ways non-threatening to the young girl, safeguarding her modesty as the breasts are draped by the half-sari much like the sari. The half-sari, the culturally accepted clothing norm for young Tamil girls, keeps the stimulation of sensual arousal and the containment of sexual desire in balance. Although many young girls have now switched over to *salwar* suits, the half-sari is still the popular costume for young girls on the Tamil screen, as male viewers of Tamil films enjoy the half-sari-clad dancing girls for the sensuality and innocence that it signifies.

These meanings and significations change when young girls either wear *salwar* suits or pants/jeans and T-shirts/tops. The *salwar* suit, being a loose garment and covering the whole body, is considered modest and functional and, at the same time, a de-eroticizing garment quite unlike the half-sari. The widespread acceptance of *salwar* suit as a school uniform in Chennai, worn by girls and women, suggests an assimilation of norms set by North Indian society into Tamil society. While the *salwar* suit is marked as an Indian attire, pants/jeans are distinctly viewed as Western. Tight jeans and tight T-shirts/tops are considered provocative, while a looser fit and longer top would be more acceptable. For the Tamils, to wear a *salwar* suit is to be modern and national, to be in pants/jeans and T-shirt is to be Western and cosmopolitan, and to wear an ethnic *kurti* (short but not too short top) over jeans is to be somewhere in between the two—modern-national and cosmopolitan. By all accounts, there is a greater acceptance than before to young women wearing pants/jeans. Perhaps this attitudinal change is due to the media and increased transnational movement of people.

Yet the stark contrast between what is permissible and acceptable in "reel" life and in "real" life does call for some explanation. "Reel" life enters the "real" life of young men through posters for gazing and fantasizing in private, in the intimacy of one's room or home. Skimpily clad female models who bare their beautiful bodies are accepted in films as producing sensual arousal and aesthetic satisfaction and are soon transformed into poster girls pinned behind doors or pasted on walls. Posters of Bollywood icon Aishwarya Rai wearing jeans and sleeveless tops or as a leggy female model lying on top of a car roof against the backdrop of the Mumbai or Singapore skyline are quite commonly sold on street pavements in North India for a small sum of Rs. 10. Former Tamil actress Sreedevi was widely believed to be a success for her "oomph," that is, the bodily endowments, body exposure, and bodily movements that contribute to male sexual arousal even for a poor young rickshaw driver. "Reel" life permissiveness in female attire and body exposure is on account of its ability to construct a world of fantasy, and in this intimate space of imagination and dreams these reel models who are otherwise sexually inaccessible to the men can be enjoyed in the realm of fantasy. When "reel" life permissiveness enters into "real" life, it threatens to destroy the fantasy world of many men for the sexual inaccessibility of these reel models would now have to be confronted as a brute reality. Such a realm of fantasy appears essential in the male self-construction of masculinity according to the changing cultural norms. Male models also find their spots in this fantasy world of young men and their bodily practices in the construction of masculinity. The socialization of young girls in the patriarchal caste society takes account of this libidinal politics by preventing women from constructing such a world for themselves and seeks to destroy such constructions by them. Young women are by and large socialized into expecting less in terms of lovers and husbands because they are unlikely to be lucky in getting the kind of person they desire and are taught to refrain from asking for the moon. Such disciplining of the female imagination plays a greater role in the construction of femininity than women's realm of fantasy.

Chapter 7

Culture, Consumption, and Women's Subjectivity

The immense range of commodities produced by Capitalism requires simultaneously the construction of consumer-subjects. The technologies to produce these consumer-subjects have made creative leaps, keeping pace with capitalism's innovativeness in the production of commodities, as these are two entangled social orders—the order of production and the order of consumption. For Baudrillard, the order of consumption is constrained by two levels, namely the constraint of signification and the other where the constraint of production is operant (Ritzer, 1998, 7). Commodities are therefore defined not by their use alone but by what they signify, which, being interrelated to the entire system of commodities and signs, produces an infinite range of difference available in this system (Ritzer, 1998, 7). As people seek in consumption not so much a particular object as difference, the search becomes unending as people are never able to satisfy their need for commodities, for difference. For Baudrillard, analysis of the social logic of consumption should therefore focus on the production and manipulation of social signifiers, according importance to the social logic of differentiation. "Consumption" for Baudrillard is multifaceted. As Ritzer notes,

> It is not merely a frenzy of buying a profusion of commodities, a function of enjoyment, an individual function, liberating of needs, fulfilling of the self, affluence, or the consumption of objects. Consumption is an order of significations in a "panoply" of objects; a system, or code, of signs; "an order of the manipulation of signs"; the manipulation of objects as signs; a communication system (like a language); a system of exchange (like primitive kinship); a morality; that is a system of ideological values; a social function; a structural organization; a collective phenomenon; the production of differences; "a generalization of the combinatorial processes of fashion"; isolating and individualizing; an unconscious constraint on people, both from the sign system and from the socio-economic-political system; and a social logic. (Ritzer, 1998, 14–15)

While Baudrillard has analyzed commodities and the role of consumption through structuralism, broadening the Marxian focus on production, anthropologists and critical consumption theorists have noted that the commodity is just one identity of objects among many others. Appadurai's (1986a) edited volume *The Social Life of Things* moved the anthropological focus on cultural objects from museum studies to theoretical perspectives on material culture to show that the social world was also constituted by materiality as much as the reverse way. While Appadurai (1986b) highlighted the trajectory of things as a process of commodification and decommodification with the commodity being only one of a wider range of identities of the object, and the accompanying changing regimes of "value," Kopytoff (1986) noted the social biography of objects in its move in and out of its commodity status. Anthropological research has also noted the contradictory and shifting meanings of objects for different constituencies.

This chapter, in three sections, explores aspects of the social logic of consumption in India in the contemporary neoliberal exuberance of commodity prosperity shared by women as consumer participants, as well as the enthusiastic strides taken by upper-caste Brahmin women in the earlier modern era, some fifty years ago. The first section examines how advertisements draw from or redraw patriarchal discourses in their messages in the era of global consumerism that competitively seeks to construct women as consumer-subjects. The second section recounts the influence of modernity in the reorganization of the domestic space of the kitchen, which is preeminently seen as women's space. It thereby demonstrates Brahmin women's construction of their subjectivity through their desires for newer gadgets, conditioned by cultural patriarchy, as the nationalist resolution explained earlier had tasked women to defend the spiritual culture in the domestic sphere. The last section deals with the habitation of "counterfeit consciousness" in modernity and expands the idea of authenticity to the material sphere of postcolonial modernity. Globalization has witnessed both the rise of "brand aura" with Western goods becoming a craze among the new middle classes, and the desire for the emulation of lifestyles in the social spaces of disparities propelling a counterfeit consciousness through the counterfeit commodity culture of "aura busting," in which women participate as consumers under the allure of high-end fashion.

BILLBOARDS, LANGUAGE GAMES, AND FORMS OF LIFE

Advertising discourses draw upon cultural ideas of tradition and modernity to entice women to desire goods and thereby construct them as consumer-subjects. Ritzer observes that by creating a simulated intimacy between people doing the advertising and potential customers, as well as between the latter and the products being advertised, advertisements have become the most significant arena of significations, a gigantic simulation model of such reciprocal human relations in contemporary modern societies, the generalized game of human relations (Ritzer, 1998, 13). For Baudrillard, the locus of consumption is "daily life," which is not merely the banal sum of daily doings, as there is a social dynamic of needs because models of competition and conformity are brought in, drawn from the group context or from grand cultural models from society at large or from history.

This analysis draws upon advertising discourses from about a hundred billboards installed on the roads of Chennai. The messages and images from billboards were gathered in April 2006, a time when the outlook of the global economy was optimistic with its corresponding effects on advertisement spending. Although the billboard messages were collected in 2006, they still represent the contemporary era of globalization and liberalization of the Indian economy and the consumerism of the new middle-class lifestyles that have since set in.

The collective unconscious of a nation consists of a set of specific human experiences, which constantly accumulate and build new forms called archetypes. These archetypes are what people in a given culture share. It is such archetypes that underlie the advertisements of brands and luxury goods. Brands use them to create associations in the collective unconscious that make people feel positive when they think about a particular brand. The perception of a brand advertisement is also based on these shared archetypes and beliefs that the members of the culture hold.

The terrain of producing women as consumer-subjects in India is one where cultural patriarchy and capitalist patriarchy operate in tandem to produce such subjects. Both these patriarchies configure women as dependent subjects with their primary roles in the domestic sphere. Advertisement being a point of mediation between the local and the global, and culture and capital, it draws from the discourses of patriarchy that circulate in society at the time, even as it contributes to increasing the density of preexisting discourses and create new ones that could, at times although not frequently, even seek to undermine the patriarchal order. Goffman (1979) has noted that advertisements do not depict how men and women actually behave. Rather, they serve the social purpose of convincing that this is how women and men are, want to be, or should be. Such an orientation accomplishes the task a society has of maintaining order, in this case, a patriarchal order.

Billboard advertisements in Chennai city are considered here as a site of representational politics, much like the other media representations. The portrayal of women in images and their utterances in written words impose a consensus on potential viewers to decipher it and subscribe automatically to the code contained in it despite the viewers' varying sociocultural positions, age, gender and experiential factors, as those engaged in the representational task seek to convey a dominant message to an imagined community of consumers of advertisements, a simulated consumer totality. These messages seek to shape the subjectivity of the viewers in certain desired directions.

The dominant messages conveyed by billboard advertisements in the contemporary consumer culture of globalization are examined for the contending pulls of tradition and modernity to construct women as consumer subjects.

The Amul billboard at Spencer's junction on Anna Salai has a kind of permanence as it seeks to make the regular traveler on that route a philosopher of sorts through the common sense of politics and life purveyed through the messages that keep changing constantly. But most other billboards seek to instill a new common sense, the common sense of globalization as a new form of life. The discursive and visual logics normalizing this new form of life are quite remarkable.

Wittgenstein and Bourdieu (2000) as also Lyotard mention that "forms of life" are sites of language games. Considering these billboards as invented language games, one can consider them as performatively repetitive forms of action whose conventions are relative to the circumstances, places, and times of their occurrence. The hoardings' visuals and messages seek to interpellate subjects as globalized cosmopolitan subjects, even as in so doing, they momentarily erase the reality of the local context of their location; being in the midst of a cluster of hutments and a hungry destitute lying uncared for under the hoarding.

The new screen-printed technology of billboards offers an altogether different world as these capture photographic images, making it appear as though those imagined worlds are just within reach for anyone, just waiting to be grasped. When the *Reliance RIM* advertisement for prepaid mobile claims "*Ini, Ulagam Ungal Kayyil*" ("from now on, the world is in your hands") and the young curly-haired girl in that advertisement says "*Ennal Mudiyum*!" ("I can!"), it means exactly that! The imagined world, and possibly the real one, is within one's grasp, especially within her (the young woman's) grasp. This is an optimistic message for young women about the prospects of globalization and how global connectivity has rendered it possible.

Choice as Reality

The hoardings advertising mobile phones are all too numerous, each reinforcing the importance and availability of choice. UniverCell, a firm selling mobile phones, offers over ten brands and fifty models to choose from on easy installments at zero interest and partners with AirTel Connect. Viveks, the most popular chain store selling consumer durables, claims to have the "widest range of mobile phones" even as it advertises models of air conditioners from Voltas, Carrier, Hitachi, Whirlpool, Samsung, LG, National, and Premier. It appropriately defines itself as "The Unlimited Shop." While early capitalism creatively disciplined firms and investors with the corporate structures of "limited liability," today globalization exhorts firms to bring to the forefront of collective consciousness the fact of the "unlimitedness of commodities," what Marx held in the opening statement of *Das Kapital* as the defining feature of capitalism, thus making available an infinite range of difference that is never able to satisfy the consumer in search not for objects but for difference, as Baudrillard noted. No doubt, the easy-to-calculate and remember EMI (equated monthly installment) payments advertised for durables, cars, insurance, and housing transpose the liability to the consumers in less discernible ways.

Power with Pleasure

The seductive logic of "power to the people" that Hyundai's bright red car of Accent brand promises makes it clear that today "power with pleasure" gains over mere pleasure. But "power with pleasure" is realizable only by yielding to the "new temptations" of a red Maruti Zen and equipping oneself with "fitness solutions" at home from Acme Fitness Private Ltd. that sells fitness machines. For smaller vehicles like a Honda mobike, "power with pleasure" is equated with "Karizma, Jet Set Go" as the male model in a black cap and black hand gloves seems ready on a meadow and blue hills picturesque background of what seems like an airstrip. Max Weber taught us long ago that charisma was a form of power embodied in a person. A red Hero Honda mobike embodies such charismatic power on the rider. But not all commodities can endow one with charismatic power, not even the other products of Honda such as the Dio Motoscooter even if it is "From India to the world. And to you." If aboriginal and tribal people favored some objects as talismans endowed with magical properties that brought them good luck, the commodity under globalization, at least some of them, can bestow charisma on those who possess them.

Male Goods and Female Goods

Goods today can be classified as male goods and female goods, depending on which gender uses them most. It is invariably a male good like mobike that has this charisma-endowing capacity, while female goods like diamond and gold jewelry are to "fire the passion," as the Lalitha Jewelry hoarding with pictures of diamond necklaces, diamond earrings, and diamond bracelets indicates.

The question of whose passion is answered appropriately by the hoarding of Sri Palsani Jewels, depicting a picture of a thick and broad gold chain with a diamond-studded pendant, worded "Make Others Go Breathless." Mark the barely concealed value of contemporary times, where one wears jewelry not to adorn oneself and please oneself but to make others "breathless," either on account of envy or a surge of passion. Whether these diamonds "fire the passion" or not is beside the point when the GRT Thangamaligai advertisement of a black-and-white photo-quality drawing of a girl's neckline with a thin chain and a diamond-studded earring of Maya Collection reads "So close to Solitaire, So far from the Price." Diamonds they may be, but they are relatively cheap and are now available in many varieties like Arisha, Asmi, and GRT diamonds, much like mobile phones and air conditioners.

The number of jewelry hoardings suggests that traditional yearnings have not been fully supplanted by postmodern desires. Most jewelry messages reinforced the values of tradition, dedication, and trust and that of Kanishk Jewelers featured a woman in a traditional red bridal sari heavily decked in jewelry to make its statement on tradition. But the one jewelry hoarding that made a statement far exceeding the others was LKS Goldhouse that claimed its existence since 1925. It showed a picture of Rabindranath Tagore seated on a cane sofa with the backdrop of the national anthem in faded letters with the wording, "when he was drafting our anthem . . . we were crafting your aspirations in gold." Here, feminine aspirations are not only contained within gold jewelry but the nation's aspirations and feminine aspirations are linked, albeit in a perverse way. A statement of consumerism such as this, let us call it nationalist consumerism, is at odds with global consumerism that tantalizes one with jet-set cultures.

In strongly containing women-as-consumer within the fold of tradition, nationalist consumerism inserts itself as a guardian to regulate global consumerism's construction of woman-as-consumer. The hoarding of ICICI Prudential Life Insurance has the picture of a North Indian bridal couple, with the man putting the auspicious kumkuma (vermilion dot) on the woman's forehead, accompanied by the Tamil wording that means, "In your protected life, we will stand by you in all your difficulties." Despite ICICI's tie-up with an American insurance company, its advertisement strongly reinforces Indian cultural values and not any new American value, for the Indian woman still needs the protection of a man, marriage, and life insurance!

Step Out of the Shadow!

The hoardings on men's and women's clothing reveal the tension of conforming to tradition or breaking away from it in much more explicit ways.

Raymond, the textile company for men's clothing, appeals to the males to be "The Complete Man" with the picture of a man in a dark suit and red tie. His Indian (ness) is a matter of ambiguity, for he looks more like a Caucasian with dark hair, and the advertisement exhorts men to "Step out of the Shadows." The apparent incongruent modernity of the Indians, who have for long cast their men in the shadows of the white man as the somewhat incomplete "double" striving to become but yet not the same, can do so by dressing like him, even with Raymond Suiting, an Indian textile firm that has been in existence since 1925.

Perri Alley Natural Cotton Shirts not only claimed unabashedly that it was "crafted for the executive class" but the advertisement, with a picture of two green pods signifying nature, stated quite boldly, "In the beginning mother nature gave everyone birthday Suits. Then for the privileged few she spun another yarn." If exclusive privilege and inequality are no more something to be hushed up out of guilt but to be proclaimed and flaunted, then an obsession with Parisian fashion is altogether understandable. As the family clothing store *Sellers* hoarding disclosed beneath a picture of red pants, "haute, real haute." Even though T-shirts have become iconic of a global culture among the youth, a hoarding advertisement for "No Sweat T Shirts" by *Basics* asks you to "just be yourself." But truly, the *Sting* advertisement for a shirt was "Like nothing else" which had the picture of a man with an indigo-colored checked shirt through which the body painted blue could be seen through, and the words read "Some shirts color the soul." Generally, pictures of Hindu gods like Ram, Krishna, and Siva are colored blue, making one wonder if the shirts by coloring the soul also confer divinity to the men who wear them. Gone are the days when clothes just made a man; now in the age of postmodern identity crisis, with the self losing fixity, and getting fragmented and free-floating, even a shirt can penetrate deep to refashion him and reshape his soul!

Traditional or Modern—Still Undecided!

Whereas in the case of men's clothing, the pointer is in the direction of change and modernity, in the case of women's clothing advertisements, the tensions between traditional and modern are all too apparent to escape the viewer. The new Lifestyle clothing store, a rage among Chennai's teens and youth, has in its hoarding the picture of a young girl in pants and a scarf over her top, with the words reading "Stay True/ Don't Blend In." This is much like the "No Sweat T Shirt" for young men that told them "Just be Your Self." For the young, modernity, it seems, is their true natural self. The sari too has become polysemous, for it is all too often used to make statements on tradition, modernity and all.

The sari hoardings that are many in Chennai convey a range of meanings. The hoarding of *Rangachari Cloth Store* is the most explicit in upholding the value of tradition. With a drape of a blue sari with silver worked embroidery, it has the picture of God Venkatachalapathi and pictures of a garland of flowers, Kumkuma powder (vermilion), turmeric powder and turmeric plant, all objects associated with Hindu ritual. The words next to the picture of God and the other objects read "She Needs" and at the bottom is written, "Women know the Best." On top it states "Rangachari for charismatic saris." Not only does the advertisement define feminine needs in terms of the symbolics of religion and Hindu culture, but claims that feminine "ways of knowing" have granted women the capacity to know what is best. This advertisement resonates with Chatterjee's argument of the nationalist resolution that the domestic realm of culture and religion was to be defended from colonial modernity and women were to be responsible for it. Some scholars have noted it as the domestication of cultural patriarchy, which is continuously reproduced in its primary site of the domestic sphere and which the semiotics in the public domain reinforce. In an interesting contrast to the mobike advertisement discussed earlier, where charisma was associated with power and mobility, here in the world of tradition that enwraps women, it is the symbolism of religion and saris that lend charisma.

Invariably, when the sari is made to make a statement on modernity, the model on whom the sari is draped has short hair, a sleeveless or more often a bra-type blouse (*choli*) or even suggestively none at all, and the sari drapes only below, leaving the top uncovered. All these are somehow statements of the modern Indian woman. When the model wears a sari in an ethnic style, like the Gujarati style, and has short hair, it means Indian women can be modern in a variety of ethnic ways; that, in fact, there is no singular modernity for them. But even such an ethnically modern woman in the sari hoardings has to be seen around some objects that convey the sense of tradition. *Nalli Silk Sarees* is a famous Kancheepuram silk sari shop that has been in existence since 1928, with shops spread all over Delhi, Bangalore, Mumbai, Hyderabad, London, the United States, and Singapore. In two of its hoardings, the sari model with short hair was either surrounded with *Diyas* (oil lamps) or was seen painting red pots with a few painted pots lying around, which are ritual symbols of auspiciousness. But Shree Krishna Collections, a sari shop with "23,000 square feet of fresh ideas," had a short-haired model with sari draped only below the waist and was worded "a good reason to break with the traditional." In two other cases, when the sari made a statement that was ambiguous, neither modern nor traditional, the sari became a "poem" or an "ode."

Such ambiguity about the sari's status as modern or traditional was best resolved by *Textile India*, a family clothing store. Its hoarding had pictures of two tall young women, one with pants, a short jeweled top, and a *dupatta* (stole) in her hand and another draped in a sari from below the waist only, with a string *choli* on top. Not only were the two women supposed to each represent the modern and the traditional, but the tension between the modern and the traditional revealed in the attire of each is all too evident. The woman in pants needed the dupatta only as a symbol of modesty, for it was in her hand, and the woman in the sari did not have it draped on her upper part. But both promised "A New Look" and "A New You." Remaking the self through clothing and dress is indeed a strong theme in these advertisements.

The Apartment Complex

With the new "apartment complex" mentality, homes and interior décor have become the way of expressing one's aesthetic judgment or just the ability to live smartly. The messages of trust and building lasting relationships in the advertisements of many real estate firms are very striking. Akshaya Homes advertisement had a picture of a cat and a dachshund dog seated close to each other with the word "Trust" written on top. A reputed builder of luxury apartments had a message with the picture of a pretty girl seated on a sofa cuddling a brown poodle that read, "Some relationships last a lifetime." The promise of a lifetime relationship is also, at the same time, an acknowledgment of the condition of non-permanence and ephemerality that marks the present in many ways.

Targeting young couples to minimize their pain of waiting, strategized by HDFC Bank, is in keeping with the evolving social norm of immediate gratification rather than deferred pleasure. The advertisement says "We understand your world" and features a picture of a young couple on an open balcony against a misty background, with the young man looking at the ring on her finger. The words read "Don't wait to express your love." Another advertisement for the same bank had a lake scenery with hills in the background and a loving couple in a boat with its oars resting, and the message "Don't wait to escape," apparently an enticement to go on a holiday. With global destinations on the preference list of many vacationers, the hoarding of a *Eurail* advertisement that in an earlier time would have appeared incongruous on a Chennai highway is now naturalized into the setting.

Cultural Hybridity and the Cosmopolitan Subject

The advertisements sought to construct globalization's cosmopolitan subjects through cultural hybridity and fusion. Lifestyle Expos are now all too common an occurrence. Furniture dealers used their hoardings to make a statement on style. A dealer of stylish furniture phrased the advertisement,

"Your fantasy, Our furniture," and a picture of a loveseat with a tiger-skin cushion and a modern lampstand with a brown rugby ball in one corner was meant as a statement on style and worded, "Accessories that surpass intrinsic innovation." Fusion as a lifestyle statement is evident in the advertisement of Apartment Hotel floated by Star City, which is a leap in the imagination of Chennai, with its suite done up like a drawing room and banquet halls displaying sherry glasses and cherry-stuffed chocolate balls!

The advertisements revealed varied ways of "going global," as when a group of global companies jointly sponsored an advertisement showing a picture of Singapore waterfront at night, worded "When global companies and organization meet, they choose one destination/ Make it Singapore," while L&T Concrete, claiming to be behind "India's Finest Landmarks," had photographic quality pictures of Chennai's landmarks. But going global also meant the possibility to "Add the sparkle of Blue-Chip Equity to your investments" and to be "Bullish on life," as the hoarding of DSP Merrill Lynch stated, while Principal Global Opportunities Fund, claiming to be India's First International Equity Fund, says, "How easy it is to invest in global stock markets." But United India Insurance Co. Ltd. which claimed that at United India "it's always U before I," indicated the collapse of boundaries by having pictures of the flags of Pakistan and India with the words reading "Relationship beyond boundaries," leaving scope for assigning an alternate meaning of "United India."

Vernacular Subjects

Only one hoarding had used a didactic folktale of a crow sitting at the edge of an earthen urn throwing pebbles in it to make the water rise. This advertisement of *Sri Ram Chits* in Tamil was meant for a vernacular viewer who perhaps is yet to be interpellated as a subject of this new form of life and whose common sense and dispositions, therefore, still respond to the didactic tales of earlier times. But there were, on the whole far fewer hoardings in Tamil, which makes a point that the vernacular subject still rooted in local spaces, local times, and local cultures is not the imagined subject of globalization.

Nor are the hoarding messages a mimicry of global culture, for they do require cultural sensitivity on the part of the viewers and demand a sense of belonging to the place. In an interesting analysis of billboards on Taipei's MRT Mall, Liao (2003) argues the same about the use of linguistic hybridity and feminine sentences in the advertisements as being important in the narrative construction of identities and that the advertisements are part of the lifestyles emerging in Taiwan that help distinguish them from others. There were only a few hoardings that conveyed alternate meanings and sought to reshape dispositions against the current, as all the advertisements that were examined sought to instill a common sense of globalization as a new form of life, but one in which cultural patriarchy still assigned women to safeguard tradition and culture in the domestic sphere even as they are free to imagine and aspire to modern lifestyles that shape their modern subjectivity.

GADGETRY, SUBJECTIVITY, AND THE MAKING OF THE TAMIL BRAHMIN SELF

The theoretical interventions in studies on material culture that followed from Appadurai's (1986a) compilation overlooked the relationship between objects and individual subjectivity, as well as the relation between objects and gender or personality (Hoskins, 2006, 75). The following exposition on gadgetry and subjectivity and the making of the Tamil Brahmin self, dealing with the women's domestic sphere of the kitchen, can be located within the theoretical discourses on material culture, as there is little focus on the study of cultures of complex societies in India either within Indian sociology or Indian anthropology. But media and communication studies in India are now exploring the culture of materialities and the materialities of culture to highlight elite comportment to technologies through the invocation of auratic pasts to reconstruct elite hegemony in all contingent contexts that "disallows the agential power of technology to extinguish the spirit of the Indic auratic past" (Thirumal and Chintakunta, 2024, 299). Venkatesan (2009) explores the agency of persons and things, and Joy and Dholakia (1991) discuss attitudes toward possessions among the Indian diaspora in Canada. Studies on Critical Consumption theories by Euro-American scholars have engaged with the dormant collections of things lying around the domestic spaces of homes, clothing in wardrobes, and photography collections that enable women "to enact, construct, or even dismantle everyday relationships" (Hoskins, 2006; Woodward, 2015, 218).

Martin Heidegger noted that in the modern world "things" become "objects." In distinguishing "objects" and "things," Heidegger clarified that the "thing" is inherently relational, opening relations with the world beyond it. Its essence lies in the relations it maintains throughout the world around it, being inextricably bound to it (Mitchell, 2015). The "object stands before us as a fait accompli, presenting its congealed, outer surfaces to our inspection," while "the thing, by contrast, is a 'going on,' or better, a place where several goings on become entwined. To observe a thing is not to be locked out but to be invited in to the gathering" (Heidegger, 1971, 167; cited in Ingold, 2010, 4). Heidegger's fourfold of the "gathering" that comes to constitute the thing disaggregates the thing by releasing it from the bounds of an encapsulated self-identity into the streams of relation (Mitchell, 2015). Thus conceived,

Ingold suggests that the thing has the character not of an externally bounded entity, set over and against the world, but of a knot whose constituent threads, far from being contained within it, trail beyond, only to become caught with other threads in other knots (Ingold, 2010, 4). The thing, however, is not just one thread but a certain gathering together of the threads of life; one may call it a "haecceity" (referring to the quality of a thing by virtue of which it is unique). Drawing ideas of "practical identities" and "cultural identities" from Magid (2015), one could say that it is this gathering together of the threads of life by things that constitute a "lifestyle" and a "culture," wherein collections of things acquire intelligibility through cultural identities. As things become objects in the modern world, the fourfold gatherings together of the threads of life change, and the collections of objects acquire intelligibility more through practical identities rather than cultural identities, with loss of meaning, significance, and cultural difference to some extent. Authenticity is based on this cultural intelligibility of things.

Baudrillard's classification of objects in modern consumer society introduces gadgets as a useless, impoverished object which simulates a function without having any real practical referent and is part of a broader process of growing numbers of useless simulated objects affecting society as a whole. Consumers act with gadgets in a ludic manner or combinatorial playfulness rather than in a symbolic or utilitarian manner. Baudrillard notes that it is "a game with combinations or combinatory modulations—a speculation in the varieties or technical potentialities of the object, a game with the rules of the game through innovation, and a game with the ultimate combination of life and death through destruction" (Ritzer, 1998, 12). Modern consumer society being dominated by simulations, such ludic activity with gadgets may give the appearance of being a passion, although being always a combinatorial investment, it precludes passion.

In what follows, I have explored some of these ideas through biographical sketches of things in Brahmin kitchens, even as it is written in an anonymous autobiographical mode with insights gained through my life experience in this community. The focus of my exploration was to unravel the webs of social relations encompassing things as modernity ushers in changes. More insights on the social relations of people and things could have been garnered by focusing on issues of comportment. The collection of things in the Brahmin kitchen keeps changing as modernity offers newer material objects, and women's aspirations for lifestyle modernity make them negotiate the contending pulls of modernity and tradition.

Women whose primary site of action is considered the domestic sphere, with culturally assigned tasks of family nurturance, engage with kitchen appliances in a ludic manner, participating in collecting things with playfulness and passion that constitute their modern self-fashioning. Upper-caste men and women being socially privileged, take the lead in their strides in modernity both in the domestic and public spheres. Written in a fictional first-person account of a Tamil Brahmin woman, this section explores the construction of women's subjectivity through the revamping of domestic spaces with newer gadgets and goods, based on my observations over time of Brahmin women.

Can we deny that food is not constitutive of the self? I don't mean fat or slim and the varieties of slimming diets that are offered these days for a good price. That too does make our self; the fact that America is so obsessed with obesity that they give tax-breaks for joining slimming programs or buying exercise gadgets is enough of an indicator. Nor do I mean vegetarian, non-vegetarian, dairy-free, sugar-free, salt-free, and so on, the kind of menu indicators you often forget to tell the travel agent while booking flight tickets, only to find an overworked and unfriendly in-flight attendant serving a pack of steak, and you wake with your Brahmin sensibilities all shaken, saying to yourself "Shiva! Shiva!" and hope the smiling stewardess in the other aisle will show some kindness and give you a vegetarian food pack. We never entered the flight caterers' kitchens and don't really know whether the chef used the same knife to chop both the meat and the vegetables. Such mistakes of ritual pollution do not generally occur in the kitchens of Brahmin households. For that matter, they do not occur, or so we believe, in the numerous Udupi hotels of Chennai, or the numerous other vegetarian restaurant chains like Saravana Bhavan and Sangeetha Hotel that have left Udupi hotels trailing far behind. In smaller towns of North India, which really do not offer much by way of cuisine other than *Chai-Samosa*, one often wondered what makes those Chennai hotels tick, and it did not take long to figure that out. It's unarguable that *Idli* and *Dosai* have more culture and commerce than *Chai-Samosa.*

We can argue whether culture precedes commerce or commerce precedes culture, but we do know for sure that whatever the commerce of *Idli-Dosai* in North India, its culture lies wholly in the heart of the South. Rather, the heart of the Tamil Brahmin, even if Chettinad *Aatchis* raise a few objections and the Kancheepuram *Iyengars* staked claim to an independent identity long ago on the basis of their *Conjeevaram Idli.* The fried *Idli* of North India is an unwelcome intruder, which seeks to dislodge both *Idli* and *Vada* from their cultural heights through the power of vulgar commerce. But how did *Idli-Dosai* become the quintessential feature of Tamil Brahmin culture, at ease when juxtaposed with Carnatic music? For that matter, why did *Idli-Dosai* as an aspect of Brahmin culture spread and find acceptance among the Tamil subalterns who had for long eaten millets and *Idiyaappam*, while Carnatic music suffered elite containment within the Mylapore Music Academy? These perennial questions can preoccupy the new breed of cultural theorists, but one thing is for sure: when culture and technology meet, the filter coffee that distinguished Brahmin culture in South India loses out to *Idli-Dosai.*

Filter coffee, the Brahmin specialty, remained technologically stagnant, not giving way either to Starbucks culture or the commerce of coffee percolators. Not for us the Cafe Latte, Cafe Mocha, Cappuccino, Turkish coffee, Brazilian or Colombian coffee. Not even Nescafe or Bru for that matter. Not for us the filter papers and electric coffee makers that compete with each other in American department stores; even liberalization and duty-free imports have not brought those coffee makers to Chennai's recent fad, the shopping malls. Although coffee filters may not have much to offer as a story, the small black coffee grinder from Brahmin kitchens of some thirty or forty years ago has now become a museum artifact. In those days when there were no television cartoons, the coffee grinder helped mothers discipline naughty children in the afternoons. They filled it up with roasted beans and made them grind it all. Coffee filters made little progress; only the brass ones were replaced by stainless steel. And therein lies the little-known story of the stainless-steel modernity of Brahmin kitchens.

Stainless-Steel Modernity

Traditional Brahmin kitchens took pride in their collection of brass, bronze, and copper utensils. Shining brass and bronze vessels like *kuja* (screw type flask), *kudam* (water pot), and *shombu* (small water pot) were cleaned meticulously with tamarind and ash every day by the non-Brahmin domestic servants of Brahmin households, while the Brahmin women themselves spent considerable time acquiring them and comparing their collections with others. A considerable part of the collection was part of the dowry and part of the heirloom of the family. But no utensil dowry, known as *paathra sheer*, was considered complete without the *Adhirasam* containers—*thooku, sampadan,* and *adhuku*, and the long traditional brass lamp called *kuthuvilaku,* which still remains in many Brahmin homes as the sole relic of the era of brassware. The replacement of these brass and copper vessels by "ever-silver" (stainless steel) was mainly on account of the "ever-silver" quality. Brass and bronze vessels tended to get tarnished, and their cleaning was a complex process done by domestic servants. As urban poverty made survival increasingly difficult for poor households, most domestic servants had to take up work in more than one home. They were the first to resist brassware, as cleaning took a lot of time, which they could not afford. Also, as absenteeism among maids became routine, the task of cleaning was often left to grown-up daughters or daughters-in-law of the house.

Brahmin mothers of the 1960s and 1970s collected "ever-silver" vessels with a passion, but were still attached to the brass and bronze that had symbolic value as they brought them along as dowry or heirlooms. Now the daughters took up the cudgel against brass and copper ware, and either through tactful persuasion or aggressive initiatives compelled their mothers to take them to the utensil stores that ran profitable businesses in repurchasing old brassware. For days after, mothers were still to reconcile parting with them, and the few hundred rupees in their handbags concealed in the steel trunk were a poor substitute for the lost wares. They said to themselves and to other family members that they had not used those brass and copper vessels for ages but had a store of memories associated with each of them, such as how their mothers had got them, from where, how her other sisters wanted them but that they were lucky to get them from her mother, and so on.

The physics and chemistry of why a particular utensil was made of bronze and not of brass was common knowledge to women. It had to do with both heat regulation and chemical reaction of the particular food that was to be cooked in it, and almost every food item had its own special utensil. To this day, there is consensus among Tamil Brahmins that *Rasam* (a light soup-like dish taken with rice almost daily) tastes best when made in a non-toxic lead jar called *Eeya Shombu*, which has now disappeared from all Brahmin kitchens. As Brahmin women generally observed pollution taboos and seclusion during their menstruating period and kept themselves away from the kitchen, the young daughters, often five years old and above, were sent inside the kitchen and forced to learn cooking. It is often remarked that no girl learns to make *Rasam* without melting away at least one *Eeya Shombu* in the process. The *Eeya Shombu* was popular when charcoal fire was used in a small iron stove called *kumuti*. It started going out of use when kerosene stoves replaced the *kumuti* in the early 1960s, and by the mid-1970s when gas stoves entered most Brahmin kitchens, the *Eeya Shombu* vanished, as gas fires would melt it much faster than slow charcoal fires.

Among the vessel collection, the *Appam Kuzhu* and *Idli Paathram* stood out, the one for slowly deep-frying balls of jaggery and flour in ghee (clarified butter) and the other for steaming rice and lentil cakes. There was of course more than one *Idli Paathram* in every Brahmin kitchen. The smaller one was for family use, making between seven to twelve *Idlis* at a time, and the bigger one, which could steam up to thirty-six *Idlis,* was used for ceremonial occasions like marriages, when there were many guests. Every few months, the artisan who specialized in coating brass vessels with an alloy of lead would be called in. That was perhaps the first lesson in metallurgy that children learned, enthralled by the rubber billow being pumped to keep the fire going on a small tunnel-like stove dug in the ground. For days after, children went to that spot, where some ash still remained, and wondered how it was all done.

Those artisans are rarely seen these days in cities; like many others, they probably took to selling vegetables or something else. However, while the alloy-coating artisan has vanished, the knife-sharpener still comes around the streets of Chennai. Generally, he sharpens fewer regular knives, but more of a special type of knife known as *Aruvamanai*. This is a broad metal knife with a base and a coconut grater at its head, which allows women to cut vegetables while squatting on the ground. Like a good typist who never looks at the keyboard, the expert in cutting vegetables worked very fast, without even looking at the *Aruvamanai*. Their hands alone moved in rhythm while they engaged in serious gossip about the *Moolam Nakshatram* in a girl's horoscope or the *Maham Nakshatram* in a boy's horoscope, as their favorite pastime was often matchmaking. The *Aruvamanai* remains in some kitchens these days, if not for cutting vegetables at least for cutting sugarcane into small pieces on *Pongal* (the Tamil harvest festival). But the coconut grater on top is rarely used, overtaken as it is by a modern gadget, which is faster, less strenuous, and can be used while standing; it also fits on both the granite platforms in the kitchen or the sunmica laminated dining tables. As Brahmins are vegetarians, not so much by choice but as a caste compulsion, it being a prescriptive virtue in the Hindu s*astras* (scriptures), their kitchens have only a single fruit-cutting knife and are not stacked with varieties of meat-cutting knives or the new electrical gadgets of meat slicers and grinders advertised on online stores in the United States. Even today, utensil stores in Chennai do not carry such gadgets or knife sets even if most others are non-vegetarians.

In the 1990s, as apartments became more common in Chennai and elsewhere, women preferred to do most kitchen chores standing, although it was the increasing use of dining tables in the 1980s that began dispensing the habit of squatting on the floors. Eating at dining tables became a status symbol just like the possession of refrigerators, although both severely compromised Brahmin notions of *Pathu* (pollution taboo associated with cooked food), and young girls were strictly kept away from the dining table during their menstruation, it being considered *Theetu* or polluting. But in many ways, the replacement of brass, bronze, copper, lead, aluminum, and tin vessels by stainless steel was the more significant change in terms of constituting an indigenous domestic modernity. All other modern status symbols in the realm of cooking and dining came later.

In the early phase, the 1950s, stainless-steel modernity in Chennai distinguished Brahmin households in terms of those that possessed locally available "ever silver" vessels and those who could procure the utensils available in Poona (Pune) and Bombay (Mumbai) through kin networks. The passion to collect stainless-steel vessels found many Brahmin women spending their afternoons either in utensil stores or haggling with the vendors who brought utensils home in huge round baskets. Today there are only a few of those vendors in Chennai, with many selling plastic buckets and plastic containers. Surprisingly, the reason has more to do with developments in the textile industry than a lack of buyers, for such utensil vendors now dot the roadsides much like vegetable or fruit sellers.

Vendors, Chits, and All

Stainless-steel utensil vendors who came home did not sell their wares for cash, but exchanged them for old clothes. They collected all kinds of clothes that were worn out but not soiled, be it cotton, silk, nylon, or polyester. But the most prized items were worn-out Conjeevaram silk saris with *Jari* borders; the thicker the *Jari,* the greater the customer's bargaining power, as in those days *Jari* borders were made with gold-plated silver threads, which had resale value for the precious metal content that was melted and recovered. Now such *Jari* borders set the price of saris so prohibitively high that consumer preference has shifted to synthetic *Jari*, or what is popularly called "Japan *Jari*," and gold-colored thread work. The clever vendor was one who could tempt buyers with a particular utensil and induce them to part with clothes they had not considered ready to give away. Many women gave away a sari or two in anticipation of the next Deepavali purchase because they just could not resist a particular utensil; more often women judged the utensils by the thickness of the sheet metal and the finish. With silver *Jari* going out of vogue, such vending practices have been rendered unprofitable, forcing vendors to start selling plastics to an altogether different clientele of slum and low-income households. Analogous to the stainless-steel modernity of Brahmin households in the decades of the 1960s and 1970s, the 1990s saw plastic modernity enter the slum households. They too replaced their few brass water pots with plastic ones, as these could be left unattended near public water taps and hand pumps when acute water scarcity hit many urban centers. Also, as more water had to be carried home, plastic vessels were less heavy. Most people had also probably pawned their brass utensils and were unable to redeem them.

Apart from this kind of barter trade, many Brahmin women acquired more utensils by enrolling themselves in "utensil chits," known as *Paathra* chits. Stainless-steel utensil stores first acquired pre-eminence in the two Brahmin localities of Mylapore and Mambalam in Chennai, and subsequently set themselves up in other localities, as all other well-to-do folks too joined the stainless-steel modernity. All the well-known utensil stores had schemes of monthly *Paathra* chits. These were like a recurring deposit account into which monthly payments of a fixed amount were made for a certain number of months and at the end of a specified period, one could buy any utensil of one's choice. Invariably, the shops also had a lucky draw every month, and if one were lucky enough to win, one could pick up the utensil without making any further payments. Generally, most non-working Brahmin housewives do not have bank accounts, and most of the household finance is controlled by the male head. Women generally save a little every month out of the money they are given for household expenses, which they use to join the utensil chits. These women rarely buy utensils as outright cash purchases, except when they buy for marriages in their homes. Many begin collecting "ever-silver" utensils for their daughter's marriage when she is just two or three years old. For women who could not make trips to the shops, most shops had a team of mostly Brahmin women of lower economic strata who would go around enrolling women for the chits and collecting their monthly payments as well. In the 1960s and 1970s, stainless-steel modernity had caught on most particularly among Brahmins, and the Brahmin women who went around enrolling women in the utensil chits did more than just that. They often helped women exchange horoscopes of boys and girls and carried the neighborhood Brahmin families' news and gossip from one house to another. They acted as marriage counselors for young married women, advised them on pregnancy-related health care, could be counted on to come and receive betel leaf and betel nut during religious ceremonies like *Mangli Pondugal*, and shared with the women the secret powers of the deities in various temples, like which goddess to propitiate on which occasion.

Today, utensil chits are not as popular as they once were, and many stores no longer offer the chit facility; nor do women attach themselves to any particular utensil store as regular customers. With the Salem steel plant's production of sheet metal, utensil prices have become affordable, while cooking sets of saucepans and copper-bottom utensils of the Butterfly brand have become the heartthrob of many. There are far more stores around and an equally large number of roadside vendors of stainless-steel vessels doing good business these days. Brahmin women who gifted cotton blouse pieces with the plate offering of betel leaf and betel nut on every auspicious occasion to other Brahmin women find that giving a small utensil is more affordable now. Women of non-Brahmin households too have adopted this practice.

Cooker, Gas Stove, and Smartness

The most remarkable consequence of utensil chits was that most middle-class Brahmin households acquired their first pressure cooker through them. The pressure cooker was probably the first contemporary gadget to enter the Brahmin kitchen, and almost simultaneously, the gas stove followed. To have acquired both was then considered by women as worthy of news among one's kin and friends' circle, and it was said over and over again how cooking time was considerably reduced and how fast the *tur dhal* (pigeon pea lentils) got cooked. Before the pressure cooker, one is inclined to believe that rice was cooked in bronze pots called *vangala paanai*, if not exactly over a wood fire, at least with the help of the kerosene stove. The 1960s saw the introduction of a variety of kerosene stoves, but the Primus stove introduced much earlier was preferred. The Primus stove inspired some awe among women, for it was a gadget whose principle they did not quite understand. Before lighting, the stove had to be pumped to bring the kerosene up from the base, which was a delicate job as one might pump too much kerosene and let it spill over, causing fire. This was when nylon/nylex saris had just been introduced, and there was the perennial fear that they might catch fire. It is also possible that many deaths due to kitchen fires, today probed as being dowry deaths, were then written off as accidents caused by the Primus stove.

Although wick kerosene stoves were considered safer, changing the wicks in a ten-wick stove was tedious. The gas stove, in comparison had far too many plus points. The only problem was the long wait to get a new connection. In many Brahmin homes, young girls were asked to register themselves after matriculation at the nearest authorized dealer for a new gas connection in their name. They got their gas connections just after postgraduation, a good five to six years later, when their marriages were being arranged. A gas connection thus became part of the girl's dowry. There was a time when a family was considered smart if it secured two gas cylinders to ensure uninterrupted supply. Some homes strictly enforced the rule that the cylinder suppliers should wash the cylinders in the bathroom or the nearest available tap before bringing them inside the kitchen, and the suppliers generally obliged for an additional rupee or two as tips.

For a long time, the pressure-cooker contest in Chennai was between the Prestige brand manufactured by the TTK House, a Chennai-based industrial concern, and Hawkins. For many Brahmin households, the choice was over-determined. The Prestige brand won out, though not on account of Brahmin loyalty to a Brahmin industrialist. Rather it was considered more convenient because of its high-raised lid that allowed one to pile up the family's requirement of rice over *tur dhal* to be cooked simultaneously, which was not possible with Hawkins with its flattened lid. If a woman had a line of lunch-carriers to be packed in the morning all at the same time, these were serious considerations. Women soon learned the basics of steam pressure cooking; they knew that if the Prestige cooker gasket was new, they should allow the steam to release three to four times for the rice and lentil to cook, and that as the gasket became old and slightly loose, they should let the steam release a few more times. The pressure cooker too underwent progress from aluminum to stainless steel, but unlike stainless-steel utensils, these were less popular. Nor has the recent rice cooker, an electrical appliance, caught on, remaining only a showpiece for enthusiastic window shoppers because it can only cook rice alone and not rice and lentils simultaneously.

Despite its daily use, the pressure cooker never became the pride of the kitchen; nor, for that matter, did the refrigerator. The refrigerator became a marker of social and economic status along with the television, both often standing in the same living or drawing-cum-dining room. And these days, if the apartment is small, sometimes you will find the washing machine there as well. In an era of competitive consumerism, families are eager to possess and display these items to let the world know their worth. But the pride of the kitchen for every Brahmin woman is the *Sumeet Mixie*. What did the Mixie do to acquire this status? If we recall our earlier observation that *Idli* and *Dosai* have more culture and commerce than has hitherto been acknowledged, then the mystery of the *Sumeet Mixie's* status in the Brahmin kitchen is easier to decipher. Long before American and French nutritionists came up with their theories of how the ratio of carbohydrates and proteins had to be maintained for a healthy diet, the Tamil Brahmin had already figured it out in his *Idli* and *Dosai*.

Grinders, Mixie, and Subjectivity

Idli and *Dosai,* made of rice and black gram lentil, one steamed and the other fried like a pancake, require the dough to be ground after soaking the ingredients in water for several hours. For centuries, women ground the rice and lentils in a stone grinder called the *Aatukal*, used for wet grinding. It is by all accounts a back-breaking job and was usually an afternoon chore. The *Aatukal* usually stood close to two other grinders: one, a flat stone surface with a pestle known as an *Ammi*, and the other, a *Yendram*, a grinder with two round flat stones, the one on top to be rotated and used to grind dried cereals and lentils. Of the three, for some unknown reason, the *Ammi* acquired a ritual status and was obligatory near the *homam* (sacrificial) fire in Brahmin weddings. Marriage ceremonies at the auspicious *Muhurtham* time required the bride to place her foot on the *Ammi*, and the groom to wash her feet. For most women, it is symbolic of bondage to kitchen life and grinding stones.

Perceptions of the extent of bondage varied both between the different grinding technologies as well as the different Brahmin groups. The *Ammi* was used almost every day to grind the spice mix needed for cooking. A quick glance at the English edition of Meenakshi Ammal's *Samaithu Par* ("Cook and See"), the most popular cookery book of Tamil Brahmin food, indicates the extent of grinding, usually with grated coconut, required for the different kinds of food. *Kootu, Avial*, *Sambhar* and sometimes even *Rasam,* the staples of a Brahmin meal, all required the use of the *Ammi* for grinding. Even though grinding on the *Ammi* was never considered as tedious as grinding on the *Aatukal,* many Brahmin households with office-goers whose lunch times varied from 7:30 to 10:30 in the morning found even the limited time for grinding on the *Ammi* so bothersome that women often came up with abbreviated versions of cooking. Grinding on the *Aatukal*, however, was definitely a drudgery and considered unavoidable at least twice or thrice a week. It is said that a Thanjavur Brahmin would never like to get his daughter married into a Palghat Brahmin household as in such households, grinding on the *Aatukal* was a daily compulsion. The Palghat Brahmin's fondness for a special variety of lentil pancakes called *Adhai* required grinding every day, although in recent years their claim to it has been undermined by the Udupi hotels in Chennai that offer it on their menus as *Malabar Adhai.*

After centuries of cultural adaptation and many decades after electrical and mechanical inventions had caught on, *Aatukal* grinding became mechanized, with larger versions of the present wet grinders. In the late 1960s and early 1970s, wet-grinding shops sprang up all over Chennai, often managed by Brahmin-looking men who wore their sacred threads prominently as markers of caste status. Despite the Brahmins' fussiness about matters of ritual purity and pollution, they took their rice and lentils to these shops to be ground into dough while complaining endlessly of possible cheating. Scientifically minded Brahmins—there are many like that—resorted to theories of physics and chemistry to suggest that electrically operated machines tended to heat up quickly, leading to quicker fermentation of the dough. This process, they believed, reduced the dough. But entrepreneurial talents were soon to outwit everyone, and the grinding shops hardly knew that theirs was a very short life indeed.

If today, Coimbatore remains on the industrial map despite the secular recessionary trend of its long-standing textile industry, it is largely due to the wet grinder industry. Much as computers shrank in size from IBM mainframes to desktop PCs, laptops, and palm tops, wet grinders too kept shrinking. First to fit into kitchens, replacing the traditional *Aatukal.* Then they became sleeker and tilted, to fit on top of the narrow kitchen platforms of new apartments. With electrically operated wet grinders, the long-standing practice of having *Idli* and *Dosai* thrice or so a week, what elderly Brahmins used to call *Palagaram* (variety food), continued. Wet grinders may have reduced the drudgery of the *Aatukal*, but women found that washing the grinder was still an unavoidable chore. Entrepreneurial acumen once again blossomed in the sale of ready-made dough in plastic pouches; appropriately, the most popular pouch was called *Thayar*, meaning "ready" in Tamil. Mixes for instant *Idli* and *Dosai*, even those of the famous MTR brand, lost their market share to the wet ready mixes. The sleek, bright blue and red wet grinders now stand unused but remain an important marker of consumer status in most Brahmin kitchens.

In contrast, the *Sumeet Mixie* that replaced the traditional *Ammi* still remains the heartthrob of Brahmin women. No marriage *paathra sheer* or utensil dowry is complete these days without one. Its versatility for both wet and dry grinding makes it possible to retain the authenticity of Brahmin cooking. Working women especially find that it enables them to balance their working and familial roles to prepare the preferred but complicated combination of *Kootu* (vegetable gravy dish with coconut) and *Thogayal* (chutney with roasted spices) early in the morning. Even in households where NRI children bring back an *Osterizer Mixie* bought from Jackson Heights in New York City, the *Sumeet Mixie* stands next to it, unruffled by foreign competition, though presently it has been overtaken by other domestic brands.

Behind the story of the *Sumeet Mixie* lies the little-known story of the "entrepreneur of the masses," V. G. Panneerdas, or VGP, a Nadar Christian whose life moved from rags to riches. On Chennai's famous Mount Road (Anna Salai) is the VGP showroom, stacked with consumer durables. VGP can be credited for truly understanding the links between gadgets, desires, and money much more than the firms producing the durables, who thought that advertising alone was enough to create demand. Before the days of credit cards, VGP realized that desire alone was creditworthy. Many middle-class homes purchased their first ceiling fan in the 1960s under the installment scheme started by VGP, with VGP men coming home to collect the monthly installment.

Much the same happened to the *Sumeet Mixie* in the seventies. Once again, the VGP installment scheme got the *Mixie* into Brahmin homes until there was no looking back. It moved from there to refrigerators and black-and-white televisions. By the time it came to color televisions, most salaried Brahmin households had the advantage of a few pay-scale revisions, and outright purchases of color televisions and washing machines became the norm. With more and more cash and credit-card transactions, there are more festival discounts in the year. Not just for Diwali or Pongal festivals, which was the practice till recently, but newer ones like *Aadhi Thallupadi* during the Tamil month of *Aadhi* that merges temporal modernity with temporal tradition.

An "entrepreneur of the masses" could make the masses dream and transform their dreams of modernity into reality, with even a beach resort in Chennai for people to dream in comfort on weekends, not just about gadgets but also their Singapore holidays and Dubai shopping. It is an altogether different story why his astute understanding of gadgetry and subjectivity has recently failed. Contemporaneous trends seek to bring in a tech-tonic shift to the Indian kitchen, from gadgetry to automation, with all modern appliances integrated into the design of open kitchens that can be operated through the touch of a button or remotely through the smartphone. Providing multiple functions, these appliances have become "minimal, sophisticated and highly functional," and like hybrid cars, cooking ranges and ovens come with dual fuels like gas and electricity (Kale, 2023). Such a luxurious lifestyle of contemporary modernity is only within the reach of the privileged classes and, for most remains a fiction as the huge investments required for such a lifestyle cannot be brought within the fold of installment purchase, EMIs, and credit cards. Desire alone cannot now be creditworthy the way VGP thought decades ago.

COUNTERFEIT CONSCIOUSNESS AND THE JOY OF ABANDONMENT

Baudrillard suggests that as the passion for objects ends up as pure jealousy, the joy of possession of objects derives from the value that objects can have for this end and from the fact of depriving others thereof, leading to the production of "sequestered" objects (Baudrillard, 1996, 98). Brands and brand aura go into the making of "sequestered" objects that, by granting "bespoke" and "luxury" characteristics with unaffordable high prices, deprive many of it. This is one of the reasons for their continued multiplication.

While Kitsch multiplies in ever greater quantities because of its weak valency, "classy" objects at the top of the social ladder become fewer in number by increasing their quality and are revived by becoming rare (Baudrillard, 1998, 111). Baudrillard notes that Kitsch's

> aesthetic of simulation is profoundly linked to its socially assigned function of translating social class aspirations and anticipations of expressing the magical affiliation with a culture, with the forms, manners and markers of the upper class—an aesthetic of acculturation resulting in a subculture of objects. (Baudrillard, 1998, 111)

Kitsch as counterfeit still only works on substance and form, not yet on relations and structures as the "classy" objects imitated are not legally protected, although it aims at control of a pacified society by diluting social distinction. It is with the entry of law and protection by brand names, trademarks, and patents that sequestering objects acquires punitive dimensions to protect social class privilege. In this context, Baudrillard calls,

> We will never defeat the system on the plane of the real. . . . We must therefore displace everything into the sphere of the symbolic, where challenge, reversal and overbidding are the law, *so that we can respond to death only by an equal or superior death.* (Baudrillard, 1993, 36. Italics in original)

As the system thrives on symbolic violence deduced from a logic of the symbolic, it can be defeated by violence or counter-violence through "reversal, the incessant irreversibility of the counter-gift and, conversely, the seizing of power by the unilateral exercise of the gift" (Baudrillard, 1993, 36).

For Baudrillard, the sociological study of consumption must move from the superficial level of conscious social dynamics to understanding the unconscious social logic of signs and the code. In other words, the key to understanding lies at the level of deep structures. The usual sociological approach to the issue of individual differentiation or personalization is to think of individuals as consciously seeking to distinguish themselves from others. However, in Baudrillard's view, it is the code or the order of differences that causes individuals to be similar to, as well as differ from, one another. In the very act of particularizing themselves, they are reading and conforming to the code (Ritzer, 1998, 8). As the commodification of culture leads to the erosion of the distinction between high and low culture through massification and reproducibility, the objects of high and low culture are evaluated in a relative manner within the same system of objects. Baudrillard notes that while the upper classes are seen as having some degree of mastery over the code, the lower classes, who lack such mastery, fetishize objects and seek to prove themselves and find salvation in the consumption of objects (Ritzer, 1998, 8).

While neoliberal globalization has introduced a whole range of lifestyle goods for the new aspirational middle class, it has also simultaneously provoked desires from other social classes for these high-value goods, especially Western branded products, whose unaffordability has enabled a thriving market for counterfeits in which women participate as consumers of fashion products. Exploring the domain of counterfeits and counterfeit consciousness through the illustrative Indian context of counterfeits, it suggests that the seeming disorder of postcolonial societies is a challenge through reversal of the neoliberal accumulation strategies that are enabled by legal structures of states.

A predominant discourse that was instrumental in part for the demonetization of Five Hundred Rupee currency note in 2014 was that counterfeit Indian currency supposedly produced in the Pakistani city of Quetta was being funneled into India in large quantities to fund terrorist activities and destabilize the economy. Citizens were informed that banks passed on the counterfeit losses to customers, as withdrawing the currency from circulation would involve significant losses for the banks. Unwitting customers sometimes even got counterfeit notes from ATM machines. Walking into a bank branch that had counterfeit-currency detection machines with a wad of notes to be deposited, many anxious thoughts raced through my mind while being under the scanner of suspicion as a potentially subversive citizen. A sense of relief came over me when it turned out that there was no counterfeit note in my pack. But when a shopkeeper refuses to accept a currency note from me, and when I do not have any other note to offer for the transaction and I quit the transaction, the suspicion cast on me remains permanent.

Soon, economists may flag open economy macroeconomic models that include counterfeit money intended to destabilize the macroeconomy. Disorder is now being factored into the analysis of systemic risks and acknowledged not as an aberration but as a norm of everyday life in contemporary modernity and in postcolonial contexts. Even the current practice of electing representatives with criminal records is a way of normalizing disorder through democratic processes. Like the criminal representative, the simultaneous presence and absence in law have come to represent the figure of the postcolonial subject-citizen who has realized that it is like going through a revolving door to cross thresholds of inclusion and exclusion from law. A little effort or push by her can ensure entry into either zone.

Postcolonial Disorder

The standard juxtaposition of "law" and "order" is a matter of liberal faith which insists that where there is law there is order, and vice versa. However, in the postcolonial disorder of the Empire, disorder does not signify the absence of law (Comaroff and Comaroff, 2006). Rather, as Agamben (2005) observes, it is a situation of law being in force without significance. Some theorists have argued that law being in force without significance is perhaps on account of the illegibility of state-writing, or on account of an insufficient socialization within the parameters of law, especially of those at the margins of the state (Das and Poole, 2004). That the signified, the concept that law expressed as the language of rules, rights and regulations fails to signify is not on account of an interpretive deficiency of the hermeneutic community from which law as the signifier emerges, and toward whom signification is directed. The originary condition of modern law within colonial disciplinary power itself created its counterfeit consciousness, as the serial significations of law spin the myth of modernity; a myth that refers to the possibility of realizing the community of rights-bearing and reason-endowed self-governing individuals who believe in the telos of progress and material well-being.

Through colonial and postcolonial state power and force, modern law continually seeks to transform its counterfeit status, even as the myth of modernity renders it as forever counterfeit. The citizen-subjects of the postcolonial nation-state are forever reconciling the troubled trace of memories of historical injustice buried deep in their collective consciousness, memories that convince them of the counterfeit status of the law that governs their conduct as citizens, even as they are constantly beckoned and ordered to its obedience in their making as citizens. Herein lies the conundrum of the constantly fluctuating borders between legality and illegality based on oppositional perspectives of the state and of those governed, and simultaneously, the powerful and equivocal longing to cross the borders, to claim the zone of illegality, to dwell outside the reach of sovereignty.

This may be read as the transposition of Michel Foucault's analytic of finitude and the doubling of man in the colonial/postcolonial context that Bhabha (1994) has brilliantly elucidated in his essay on colonial "mimicry." Foucault shows how modern thought as the analytic of finitude produces the figure of man as an "empirical-transcendental doublet," an entity capable both of achieving objective self-knowledge in a causal and anthropologically determined way, and of surpassing the bounds of such understanding to justify claims to autonomous selfhood and free-willed ethical or speculative thought. Foucault (1973) also asserted that the unveiling of the "Same" produces the "Double" as other. Following this insight, Bhabha noted the critical potential of the space opened up in the recursive mirroring of the "Same" and the "Double," observing that "colonial mimicry is the desire for a reformed, recognizable Other, as a subject of difference that is almost the same, but not quite" (Bhabha, 1994, 86). Bhabha noted that this ambivalence produces both "mimicry" and "mockery," "resemblance" and "menace," and fixes the subject as a "partial" presence. Mimicry, mockery, and menace are similarly produced in the domain of modern law and the constitution of the legal "subject." The "subject" figures as a partial presence in law, and makes a mockery of the rule of law via its partial presence outside of law. The Hobbesian state of nature as a pre-state condition prevails at the margins of the state—except that it is not "nature," but very much a part of "culture."

Counterfeit consciousness is thus the mode of being of the postcolonial modern, who is constantly aware of both the counterfeit status of law and of his counterfeit status as partial presence. Bending a rule or finding a loophole in law is thus ingrained in the habitus of the postcolonial subject, for whom law or rule, legality and illegality, are factors that one could skillfully negotiate to one's advantage. For the postcolonial modern, the law-abiding position is equivalent to the vantage point of the loser. Socialization in law is therefore always incomplete, and its processes always include "how not to" and "why not to" abide by the law. Therefore, even if state-writing were fully legible, it would not only be read in different "languages," but its performativity would also become context-dependent, and contingent upon subject positioning.

Postcolonial disorder is thus the congenital condition of our coming into being as the postcolonial citizen-subject, embodying a difference as well as a "differance" relative to Western modernity. Adhering to classical strictures in a conceptuality, Derrida notes, "'differance' would be said to designate a constitutive, productive, and originary causality, the process of scission and division which would produce or constitute different things or differences" (Derrida, 1982, 8–9).

As Derrida claims,

> Differance, the disappearance of any originary presence, is *at once* the condition of possibility *and* the condition of impossibility of truth. At once. "At once" means that the being-present (*on*) in its truth, in the presence of its identity and in the identity of its presence, *is doubled* as soon as it appears, as soon as it presents itself. *It appears, in its essence*, as the possibility of its own most proper non-truth, of its pseudo-truth reflected in the icon, the phantasm, or the simulacrum. What is, is not what it is, identical and identical to itself, unique, unless it *adds to itself* the possibility of being *repeated* as such. And its identity is hollowed out by that addition, withdraws itself in the supplement that presents it. . . . And there is no repetition possible without the graphics of *supplementarity*. (Derrida, 1981, 168. Italics in original)

Indeed, we increasingly acknowledge becoming a nation-state with a counterfeit imagination of the nation and an equally counterfeit imagination of Western modernity, as Chakrabarty (2000) has asserted, that in the postcolonial disorder of the Empire, the pragmatic, resilient counterfeit has finally and fully, arrived.

Authenticity is no doubt a concern of European-style modernity. Its association with individuality is linked with the historical processes of self-fashioning as a "modern" individual, observed since the time of the European Renaissance. Bhabha (1994) has usefully highlighted the crucial difference in the constitution of man as a "doublet" in the European and colonial/postcolonial contexts. In the former, the splitting of subjectivity into the empirical-transcendental doublet was to enable the modern European man to find ways to reconcile with his essence, his "authentic" being. In the latter context, the splitting of colonial discourse articulated an interdictory "otherness" that, along with processes of mimicry and performance of the "other," foregrounds "counterfeit-ness," thus rendering the search for authenticity an inherently dubious exercise.

Counterfeit Consciousness

If modernity, the imagined nation, and modern law are marked as counterfeit, the contemporary is marked by a counterfeit consciousness. The condition of living in the realm of the counterfeit, and the joy of abandonment found therein, gives a new meaning to the idea of the "sovereign consumer/citizen" of postcolonial disorder. Here we explore the varieties of counterfeit consciousness in the contemporary by drawing from an array of examples such as imitation jewelry, Chinese Rolex watches, fake labels of Levi's Jeans and

Nike shoes, fake drugs, pirated software and DVDs, counterfeit legal tender, forged documents and passports, replicas of antiquities and art, counterfeit selves, and so on. What differentiates those living in abandonment from those within the embrace of law is explored in terms of the varieties of counterfeit consciousness and states of being that hover at the thresholds of duplicity and offer compelling possibilities of habitation.

Counterfeit consciousness marks the threshold between the "original" and the "fake." The "original" is marked as "authentic," and the "fake" is the counterfeit, the inauthentic. While the "original" allegedly has the sanction of the legal and licit, the "fake" is consigned to being outside the legal, inhabiting the domain of the illegal, the illicit, and the exception. Counterfeit then becomes a way of mocking the rule of law.

Postcolonial counterfeit consciousness articulates the contemporary disorder of the repercussions of Empire through the subversion of globalization, law, and surveillance, articulated via subtle as well as overt strategies of counterfeiting. The fetish of the commodity induces in the postcolonial subject both "desire" and "shock"; the desire to possess things the way he imagines the Western subject does, and the shock that is experienced upon realizing that despite all attempts to mimic the Western subject, the postcolonial subject is never able to achieve fulfillment through sufficient mastery; in other words, the shock of existing in a mode of "lack."

In his essay on Baudelaire, Benjamin (1968b) discusses these two sensations, desire and shock, as intrinsic dimensions of the European experience of modernity. Drawing upon Freud, Benjamin suggests that in the effort to cope with these sensations, modern man seeks to protect himself from his intense fear and lack by creating an epistemic shield. This is the function of counterfeit consciousness for the postcolonial subject; it is also a defense against the power of the state monopoly of coercion. Baudrillard observes that when a "savage" pounces on a watch or fountain pen, as a Western object, he "voraciously appropriates it in an infantile relation and as a phantasm of power" (Baudrillard, 1990, 41). But it is not so with the postcolonial subject, whose relation to things and the law becomes the ground for an elaborate and intricate staging of counterfeit consciousness in which desire, fear, and duplicity constitute a complex ongoing experience of modernity.

Aura Destruction as Subversion

Some time ago, "rolled gold" or "covering jewelry," when worn at a social event such as a middle-class Tamil Brahmin wedding, would be noticed but accepted as the requisite form of entry into a gathering that had certain expectations of participants wearing gold jewelry. This was contingent upon the ornamentation being within limits and the economic standing of the wearer being already known to the other participants. Duplicity here is minimal, restrained, and permissible. Over-ornamentation with "covering jewelry" indicated one had cheap tastes and was limited to the expression of counterfeit desires. But at lower-caste and working-class weddings, where everyone wears "covering jewelry," there is no attempt to camouflage this fact or pretend to the rest of the group that it is real gold; there is no duplicity at all, even if the product is imitation gold. Unlike modern cultural goods produced and consumed in the West, these traditional cultural goods are not experienced "auratically."

If an "aura," as Benjamin noted, consists of the associations that tend to cluster around the object of perception, then the aura of Western goods for the postcolonial Indian is that it signifies Western modernity, even if it is only a counterfeit modernity that is part of the postcolonial's *memoire involontaire.* Brands have the ability to draw from existing cultural archetypes or create popular archetypes in the collective unconscious, which allows them to control and manipulate consumers by tapping into the human desire for meaning and belonging. Luxury brands sell not only a material object but also emotions and a sense of self-identification. Brands also create a shared experience that connects people across countries, continents, and generations.

The recent entry into India of high-end fashion brands in men's clothing such as Zegna, Dunhill, and Canali, and women's accessories such as Louis Vuitton, Chanel, and Gucci, is on account of the captivating power of brand aura and the thrill of becoming the "global modern." Protecting the aura is thus necessary for the successful signification of modernity, status, and social distinction.

Equally, the destruction of the aura then becomes a strategy of subversion. Social distinction becomes a class-contested terrain with "aura backers" and "aura busters." Levi's jeans for the youth of the urban upper class, the highly performative "mimic" class, were till recently the ultimate symbol of being modern and Western. Aunts, uncles, and siblings living in Western countries were routinely asked to bring a pair along so that its wearer could show off among his/her college mates. Soon, even pavement stalls in big cities started selling jeans affixed with the Levi's label. Ironically, many youths who bought these had no attraction to the designer label, nor were they deceived into believing that the product was original; some were unaware of the Levi's aura altogether. In and of themselves, the jeans to these young consumers were a powerful and dominant symbol of being modern. The production of fake designer jeans is an example of the "massification" or vulgarization of "haute" couture.

Many more examples from everyday utilitarian objects can be cited, such as cheap travel bags and suitcases labeled "Samsonite" or "American

Tourister," with the manufacturer's address in some Indian small town. Most users of these products would not even know that an original with such a name exists in the United States and with production in India under some licensing arrangement as these now cater to a global market. Such vulgarization is seen, in the West, as a way by which new forms/goods enter a culture, but one in which the value of the original would eventually be redeemed unscathed. Such is not the case in postcolonial societies in which counterfeit culture produces a fake modernity and a fake trajectory of globalization that exists as a subversion of the imitation modernity of the contemporary mimic man, the "global modern" (Chang, 2004). For many people around the world, the idea of being able to afford a luxury item is more important than actually owning an authentic one. Subversion here is the joyous possession of the fake and the production of the counterfeit.

Counterfeit Profits

Maintaining product and brand authenticity is, however, not just a struggle over aura and related social distinction. It is also a competition over market shares and profit. The "logic of capital," the "logic of culture," and the "logic of counterfeit" conjointly determine the fluid articulations of the regimes of value in the circuits of production and consumption of the real and the counterfeit (Jamieson, 1999). Jha (2005) observes that 30 percent of the counterfeit products worldwide are being produced in China. Chinese Rolex watches are now as famous as the Swiss ones. India, though lagging behind China, has its hubs of counterfeit production. About 70 percent of Indian counterfeits are produced in Delhi, and FICCI (Federation of Indian Chambers of Commerce & Industry) estimates a sizeable revenue loss to the exchequer of approximately Rs.10,000 million each year. Not so long ago, it was a pan-Indian joke to point to the Made in USA inscription on fountain pens or similar objects, and to be told that "USA" stands for Ulhasnagar Sardar Association. Today the counterfeiters are not only those in Ulhasnagar, but also the innumerable small and big manufacturers spread in metropolitan cities and elsewhere.

The International Anti-Counterfeiting Coalition estimates that in the United States alone, trademark counterfeiting robs the country of $200 billion a year. The loss to the EU from counterfeiting and piracy is reportedly £250 billion. The *New York Post* reported on November 16, 2023, that the FBI seized $1 billion worth of fake handbags and shoes from a New York City storage unit in what is considered the largest counterfeit bust in U.S. history. A sprawling collection of phony "designer" merchandise of 219,000 faux items, such as knock-off designer goods, counterfeit high-end handbags of every color and design, fake shoes, clothes, and other accessories, would be the envy of any socialite aspirant. It claimed that this crime actually harms legitimate businesses, governments, and consumers and carries ten years in prison as conviction.

A month later, Swiss info.ch claimed, "New achievements in the fight against counterfeit Swiss watches." Claiming that most counterfeit Swiss watches come from China and Hong Kong, the Federation of the Swiss Watch Industry reported that 1 million counterfeits were confiscated worldwide in 2023, of which the sizeable hauls of counterfeit Swiss watches were from Saudi Arabia, Turkey, and Egypt. While on the one hand, the Federation constantly monitors the market for fake "Swiss Made" watches, on the other it offers training courses, both virtual and face-to-face classes, for customs and police officers in various countries to identify counterfeit Swiss watches.

Dumping counterfeits in the Western markets where high-end brands originate and cutting their profits is what Baudrillard exhorts as a way to defeat the system when he writes,

> We must therefore displace everything into the sphere of the symbolic where challenge, reversal, and overbidding are the law, *so that we can respond to death only by an equal or superior death*" and it can be defeated by violence or counterviolence through "reversal, the incessant irreversibility of the counter-gift and conversely, the seizing of power by the unilateral exercise of the gift. (Baudrillard, 1993, 36. Italics in original)

According to Mehra (2001), counterfeits in India are reportedly rampant in the FMCG (fast-moving consumer goods) sector, software, automobile, book publishing, music industry, movies, packaged water, and garment sectors, as these report the highest number of IPR (Intellectual Property Rights) violations. In many village markets in India, there is a complete absence of branded FMCG products such as soaps and detergents, and duplicates that are look-alikes with or without spelling errors abound. Popular products used in almost every household, such as Lifebuoy soap and Vicks Vaporub, are equally familiar to illiterate and semi-literate rural folk by way of their appearance and function. This counterfeiting is not subversion via "aura" destruction as much as it is an appropriation of the value of a product that has become familiar and acceptable through usage. These are then used by their producers to grab a share of the market, where most rural consumers would not even know that they are being duped.

Some years ago, a Brand Protection Committee of MNC players in the FMCG sector, such as Proctor & Gamble, Hindustan Lever, Colgate, Marico, GlaxoSmithKline, Coca-Cola, Pepsico, Gillette, Britannia, and so on, was apparently set up to deal with the problem of counterfeits. The companies preferred the legal option to curb the menace but found themselves in a position of double jeopardy. First, it created negative publicity, and consumers began to shun the products, thinking they might be spurious. Second, counterfeit producers were intractable, and when arrested could easily be released on bail as "faking" is a non-cognizable offense, and resume their production after a temporary halt. Fake drugs are as common as *jhola—chaap* (quack) doctors, even as the "real," near-identical version of most drugs made by foreign drug companies are manufactured and sold by leading Indian pharmaceutical companies at much lower prices. Waiting for the patent time to elapse for those held by foreign companies is to accept the trade-off between imperialist profits and third-world deaths. In this instance, subversion through counterfeiting has a crucial ethical component that forces the law into retreat.

Authenticity and Ambiguity

"Counterfeit" and "original" are not binary opposites but involve a mode of continuity and heterogeneity wherein techniques and motives of camouflage are both within and outside of the law, and correspondingly, duplicity is both social and/or legal. Counterfeits could be outright fakes, non-functional look-alikes, functional but inferior items, and fully functional items illegally manufactured without paying copyright fees. Known variously as counterfeits, knock-offs, fakes, replicas, imitation, bootleg, and so on, in appropriating the real, the culture of copying occasionally achieves the zenith of simulation, makes the fake *itself* into the real, "perfectly indistinguishable and doubly authentic," an original that is made to appear as a counterfeit, as in the case of Chinese Harry Potter fakes analyzed by Henningsen (2006). It is increasingly being realized that while authenticity may be adequate and valid as a concern of cultural integrity in the West, it has only limited validity elsewhere (Vann, 2006). Near the city of Cologne in Germany is the *Museum Plagiarius*, dedicated to "innovation contra imitation," with the purpose of shaming those invested in counterfeit culture for profit, aesthetics, or economic survival. Ironically, even as museum replicas, the "exact replicas," become a collectors' fad and a money spinner in the West, "counterfeit replicas" are sold by underprivileged ethnic minorities and immigrants on Manhattan's sidewalks; elsewhere, and in the developing world, the proliferating "fake" entity becomes ubiquitous, and subversion both a fact of life and a celebration.

The counterfeit has now defiantly entered the zone of ambiguity, its negative associations subsumed within the global phenomenon of outsourcing. Interestingly, Chinese tourists are now wary of picking up outsourced souvenirs, even as Chinese producers continue to engage in rampant counterfeiting (Notar, 2006). A cartoon that evoked much interest some years ago in the United States depicted the figure of the "outsourced" Santa in place of the "real" one in traditional red garments, who, seated in his office in Bengaluru, was taking orders from American children to dispatch to them stockings filled with Chinese toys. The "place affect" of an object that marks its authenticity has once again been divested, much as mechanical reproduction detached art from its embeddedness in tradition and redesigned it for reproducibility (Benjamin, 1968a). "Even the most perfect reproduction of art is lacking in one element: its presence in time and space, its unique existence at the place where it happens to be" (Benjamin, 1968a, 222). Through reproducibility, art prints and photographic prints became possible even without the original. Now, with image software such as Adobe Photoshop, a click of the mouse can effortlessly alter photographs to produce unblemished counterfeit images. Technology has also made possible the "counterfeit person" or "counterfeit self." The art of impersonating a person is no longer the exclusive privilege of a confidence trickster or an actor but the mandatory self-refashioning of agents in Call Centers, now indispensable in global business, when every twelve hours a "Sita" becomes a "Cherrie" or a "Claire." Cosmetic and plastic surgery can redo a person's face, just as a photo image can be altered or touched up with the help of a computer.

It is in the realm of human cloning, though, that the ambiguous politics of counterfeiting meets its real challenge. The "empirical-transcendental doublet" now has to be rethought along two altogether different axes: gene politics and the ethical limits of man's meddling capacities.

Living in the Joy of Law's Abandonment

As counterfeits and their possibilities multiply and reproduce in all domains of everyday life, some lawful and others unlawful, the postcolonial citizen-subject as consumer and producer develops a new mode of perceiving the world—through tactile appropriation, through a habit of knowing and willing, through understanding when to make her presence and absence felt within the terrain of law, when and how to live in the joy of law's abandonment, and when to be repressed in law's unyielding embrace. A person who would not buy fake drugs or would not use them if she knew them to be so would not hesitate to buy a counterfeit printer cartridge if it were a few hundred rupees cheaper than the original, and would look the other way when her co-passenger on a train bought fake bottled water. A counterfeit consciousness enables her to move back and forth between inclusion and exclusion by agents of state security; to manifest or to recede in the domain of law, or to rest content in the zone of indifference.

Through the same mode of tactile appropriation, the postcolonial citizen-subject knows the duplicitous face of the state as its double. She understands how state sovereignty itself wields counterfeit power by producing the "homo sacer" (Agamben, 1998) by rendering bodies "killable" even within the presence of law, or deciding, in the case of certain bodies, to "let die" through apathy. Her counterfeit consciousness enables her to apprehend what Agamben (2005) notes as the "secret solidarity between anomie and law." It is this solidarity, so well understood by Indian citizens and their sovereign representatives, that even made it possible some time ago for some wives/fiancees to join their "illegal immigrant" husbands/fiances and experience the comforts of marital joy in distant lands by traveling there on forged documents and visas, faking themselves to be the family members of parliamentarians who enjoyed some diplomatic immunity from the law.

Counterfeit consciousness enables those at the margins of the state to move toward it, or equally, to move away from the center. Moreover, these centrifugal and centripetal movements rendered possible by counterfeit consciousness could, in fact, also push the state itself to a margin. This raises the perennial hope and possibility of "a state of the world in which the world appears as a good that absolutely cannot be appropriated or made juridical" (Benjamin, 1992; cited in Agamben, 2005). Agamben too observes, "One day humanity will play with law just as children play with disused objects, not in order to restore them to their canonical use but to free them from it for good" (Agamben, 2005, 64). As "Midnight's Children," we have learned to play this game with counterfeit consciousness. The postcolonial disorder of the Empire is not as hopeless as it seems.

Chapter 8

Life Experiences, Resistance, and Feminist Consciousness

Why do the majority of women in India not identify themselves as feminists even when they perform numerous individual acts of resistance in their everyday lives? Drawing upon Pierre Bourdieu's ideas about habitus and doxa to explain women's internalization of patriarchy and subordinate status, as well as their ways of overcoming it, this chapter examines how women manage (or not) to bring the experience of their subordination from the field of doxa to the field of opinion—a precondition for feminist politics. Feminism must theorize women's experiences as these arise from both the resilient and changing features of tradition and modernity that encapsulate them all through their lives and invoke the entire range of human relations that constitute such experiences.

A feminist anthropologist once made the perceptive remark based on her fieldwork in New Guinea that women do not often resist the way feminists want them to or expect them to (Polier, 1998, 531). In the Indian context too, it is true that certain acts of resistance are valorized in feminist discourse, while most others remain invisible and inaudible. Generally, women's movements valorize not only acts of resistance that are part of organized or spontaneous collective acts but those that also foreground issues of justice, equality, and human dignity. Individual acts of resistance that are isolated and part of the coping strategies of individuals, the weapons of the weak, are not valorized, irrespective of whether such acts of resistance are successful or not.

Here, Vanita's remark that dropping the term "women's liberation" in favor of the term "women's movements" arises out of the emphasis on equity rather than liberation is relevant (Vanita, 1996, 70). For liberation must focus itself at the level of the individual, while equity justifies the emphasis on social structures. Part of the reason for valorizing collective acts of resistance is to ensure an existential situation that would make individual acts of resistance redundant. Apart from being an instance of delusional politics, it also privileges externally sanctioned norms of justice, equality, and dignity rather than subjectively perceived cultural and social norms that vary over time and across communities. There is no a priori reason to assume that, in all instances and at all times, there exists a perfect fit between the two sets of norms.

Feminists' focus on structural factors of gender inequality and women's discrimination in its movement politics has tended to obscure the social and familial issues of male dominance within families as part of constructed gender ideologies effected through emotions, roles, and practices as culture-in-action. An individual act of resistance is in fact proof of the violation of subjectively perceived norms of justice, dignity, and honor; and cultures have intersubjective understandings of these norms, enabling cognizance of when a person violates or is being violated. The Foucauldian insight that there are no relations of power without resistance and that resistance is formed right at the point where relations of power are exercised (Foucault, 1980, 142) means that we can read power from resistance. Foucault provides many useful insights into relations of power that can be of much use to feminist analysis. For instance, he notes:

> Power is co-extensive with the social body; there are no spaces of primal liberty between the meshes of its network; that relations of power are interwoven with other kinds of relations (production, kinship, family, sexuality) for which they play at once a conditioning and conditioned role; that these relations don't take the sole form of prohibition and punishment, but are of multiple forms; that their interconnections delineate general conditions of domination, and this domination is organized into a more-or-less coherent and unitary strategic form. (Foucault, 1980, 12)

Thus, the norms of valorization of an emergent disciplinary practice could be at variance with the norms of valorization set by the individuals for themselves. In fact, we can even say that often the two domains of discourses—feminist discourses and the discourses of women's existential experiences—exist separately. This discrepancy is indeed a serious one for feminist political and ethical practice. However, it is not something unique to Indian feminist studies alone.

Referring to sociological theory, Bourdieu notes, "An adequate model of reality must take into account the distance between the practical experience of agents (who ignore the model) and the model which enables the mechanisms it describes to function with the unknowing 'complicity' of agents" (Bourdieu and Wacquant, 1992, 70). I will interrogate this disjuncture between feminist practice and individual practice to clarify in what ways a more inclusive understanding of resistance may help us reformulate questions of power, dominance, resistance, and subjectivity.

Such an interrogation is particularly important when mobilization strategies of putting family life at a premium are proving successful (Kalpagam, 2000). This strategy, as described in Sarkar (1991), appears to resonate far more deeply with women's emotional needs and is more in tune with (patriarchal) cultural norms than are strategies of highlighting the structural conditions of women's subordination as generally emphasized, which suggests that for a large section of women such a strategy is not objectionable as it is also in consonance with their cultural and emotional dispositions.

Feminism is neither an ideology nor the awakening of a few politically conscious individuals. Being complacent about the non-involvement of the majority of women would be detrimental to the women's movement, especially at a time of increasing domination and authoritarianism in society, from which the family, the most important constituent of society, cannot be immune. In the last few years, we have witnessed how the liberal and democratic idea of secularism was sought to be overturned. For people for whom religious beliefs are integral to their definition of moral selves, the appeal of secularism declined as religion was sought to be politicized. In the contest of ideas at this juncture, it is important to ensure that there are no setbacks and regression for the women's movement. For we must recognize that, like all other notions undergoing change, so too the idea of the "Indian woman" has evolved historically and will be contested in the future.

Ideas such as the valorization of tradition (as though tradition was a singular and unproblematized notion), the preservation of Indian culture against the onslaught of Western modernity, the importance of *Dharmaraksha* (protection of core Hindu religious and moral values) in an era of declining moral values, the spread of high-caste *sanskritic* Hinduism to make it appear as though it were less exclusive and at the same time consolidating a hegemonic Hinduism as ideology over a pluralistic Hindu belief system, the appeal of globalization to the rich and middle-class segments of the population on account of the benefits it offers them, the neoliberal faith in the market and its concomitant flexible labor regimes and state cutbacks in social-sector expenditures, social security and subsidies, all compete with and complement each other today, with far-reaching ramifications for women's lives and for the family as a social unit.

It is therefore necessary to reflect on how the family is to be discursively constituted if it is to contest and clarify the problems of mobilization around family-centered issues, as it is becoming increasingly clear that merely characterizing the family as a site of patriarchal domination or cooperative conflicts is at variance with how women themselves perceive the family. Some feminists would argue that we need to move away from a conception of the family as constituted through heterosexual monogamous marriages and explore other forms of familial arrangements (Vanita, 1996). Although the family everywhere is changing, for a majority of women in India, heterosexual monogamous familial structures are still important. How do we move from a politics of patriarchy at the family level to an ethics of care that involves a mutuality of shared responsibilities and that allows for the full development of women's potentialities?

WOMEN'S AGENCY AND INSIGHTS FROM BOURDIEU

If we follow the trajectory of women's life histories, often through the narratives that women themselves produce, we are likely to encounter the following scenarios of women's own perceptions of their agency, as well as a variety of narrative strategies used by them. Almost all women's narratives of their life experiences are a mix of strategies—of acquiescence, subservience, resilience, resistance, manipulation, domination, pretensions, subversions, simulations, and so on; it is never a linear narration of victimization, even when the women themselves at some point begin to feel that they are indeed victims of male oppression. The passage from personhood, as a being endowed with agency, to victimhood, that is, a person deprived of all resources to exercise any agency—is marked by a profound struggle with power. Indeed, during this passage, the modes of power, modes of struggle, and the subjectivity of the persons involved constantly change and are reconstituted. Absolute victimhood is a terminal state of subjectivity where existence is deprived of all meaning, and when the victim feels it is impossible to exercise any agency.

It is indeed very common for women to declare that they are for greater equality with men or less subordination to men, but that in saying so they are not "feminists." Of course, only a very tiny segment says so, for it is here assumed that those who identify themselves as not being feminists do have some understanding of what feminism is and what the feminist movements are about. It is also not uncommon for that tiny segment to say that feminism is a Western idea. Indian tradition is often viewed as a source of strength for women, for the Indian approach is to emphasize the complementarity of the sexes, and from there, the move to some kind of Gandhian approach is too familiar to bear repetition. My purpose here is not to contest these different views; rather, I would like to suggest that both the feminist "patriarchal" approach and the "complementarity" approach ought to acknowledge dominance, howsoever dominance is understood. While in the former approach there is a clear and straightforward acknowledgment of dominance, and patriarchy is often explained as structural dominance caused by structural factors, the complementarity approach tends to evade the issue of dominance altogether. What is often missed is that complementarity does not in itself contradict a relation of asymmetry, and that the ideal of complementarity is often at variance with the actual relationship of the sexes. Both the patriarchal and the complementarity approaches need to reckon with the fact that life in its everyday aspects are all transactional outcomes.

For almost all women, the family is the single most important institution throughout their lives. Strategies for family-centered mobilization by progressives should acknowledge the diverse family ties that bind women through their entire life cycle and that are crucial to their self-identities and the formation of their subjectivities. The reason why most women privilege the family and the set of ties associated with it over other forms of ties has to be explored to discover why most women do not identify themselves as feminists. Whatever be the cultural and national variants of the women's movements, what is common to all is the call for sisterhood and the solidarity of women. If such sisterhood and solidarity were indeed perceived as natural, then all women would be in sisterhood. But this is not the case. Social analyses have highlighted the fault lines that divide women across class, race, caste, religion, age, culture, education, tradition, modernity, nationality, ethnicity, sexual orientation, and so on. However, we cannot be sure that all potential members of each group would join hands in solidarity, for if that were true, then it would imply that some kind of consensus exists within groups that feminist solidarity is truly liberating. But no such consensus exists even among women within separate or intersectional groups.

Women not only perceive antagonistic differences of goals, needs, strategies, and so on, on a variety of issues that matter in their lives, but they also find that great stakes are involved in such solidarity moves. For too long, feminists have been engaged in a delusional politics, believing that all women subscribe to their perspectives, and that if they do not, they require consciousness-raising and be sensitized to feminist politics. This delusional politics has arisen partly on account of the utopian and visionary ideals of radical transformation. A pragmatic politics of interest-group approach would have made apparent the connection between self-interest and political participation. Today, it is almost a heresy to voice such opinions in feminist groups.

Tharu and Niranjana (1996) have analyzed a number of instances that display the contradictions that emerge within Indian feminist politics today, such as the rise of a militant Hindutva feminism. Women join hands only when there are some perceived advantages for themselves as individuals, and in fact, they may often not perceive such advantages. No doubt, feminism, like all other transformational praxis, has sought to persuade subjects to hold a vision of political struggle that moves beyond such individual calculus. Rajeswari Sunder Rajan, in a personal communication to me, suggested that the problem for feminism is how to conceptualize and mobilize women as a group when neither their self-interests nor their actual existence is predicated on the identity of a group.

Such political and ideological persuasion based on the assumption of a higher common good, that is, some kind of structural transformation benefiting the larger group, has to wrestle with an equally strong and rational pragmatic consideration that adherence to the status quo or individual acts of resistance are more capable of effecting a satisfactory equilibrium in self-other transactions, which is equally important to individuals. The latter may promise greater liberation in intimate family relations, which the attainment of the higher common good does not guarantee. It is therefore necessary for feminist analysis in India, which has so far given considerable importance to acts of collective resistance, to focus some attention on the relatively neglected aspect of acts of individual resistance and on women who do not resist but consent to forms of social oppression either consciously or unconsciously. For there are obviously many millions of women who do not identify with any women's movement, but whose lives are interspersed with acts of resistance and acquiescence. Vanita (1996, 70) notes that today there are many people outside of women's movements who are far more advanced in thinking through and enacting liberatory modes of life, relationships, and community.

To develop a feminist sociological imagination, we need to note that "structure" and "agency" alone do not exhaust all sociological paradigms. In common conversations, women do often acknowledge that they can and are indeed often oppressors of other women, and that men do not always behave as women's oppressors. In my view, such proclaimed truths of experiences are not to be erased as exhibiting a false consciousness on the part of these women. Rather, what is evident is that perceptions of structural asymmetries seem to matter less than striking an equilibrium in self-other interactions that are embedded in everyday transactional life. Women's subjectivities are, in fact, constituted through these self-other interactions rather than through their understanding and/or perception of how social structures constrain or enable them.

Certainly, self-other interactions are not innocent and pure interactions but are generally imbued with power. Structural asymmetries, both social and economic, as well as cultural norms, shape these interactions, though not in the way we expect—not as in the case of understanding causation and determination in social scientific analysis, but rather in Bourdieu's sense of "habitus," that is, "systems of durable, transposable dispositions" (Bourdieu, 1987, 72), or in other words, "a socialized subjectivity" (Bourdieu and Wacquant, 1992, 126).

Bourdieu explicitly notes:

> To describe the process of objectification and orchestration in the language of interaction and mutual adjustment is to forget that the interaction itself owes

> its form to the objective structures which have produced the dispositions of the interacting agents and which allot them their relative positions in the interaction and elsewhere. (Bourdieu, 1987, 81)

He further explains:

> One of the fundamental effects of the orchestration of habitus is the production of a commonsense world endowed with the *objectivity* secured by consensus on the meaning (*sens*) of practices and the world, in other words the harmonization of agents' experiences and the continuous reinforcement that each of them receives from the expression, individual or collective (in festivals, for example), improvised or programmed (commonplaces, sayings) of similar or identical experiences. (Bourdieu, 1987, 80)

Habitus, Bourdieu notes, is

> a system of lasting, transposable dispositions that integrates past experiences, and functions at every moment as a matrix of perceptions, appreciations, and actions constitutes practices. The dialectical relationship between the habitus on the one hand and, on the other, an objective event, which exerts its action of conditional stimulation, provides the conjuncture capable of transforming practices. This conditional stimulation demands a determinate response from those endowed with a determinate type of dispositions, that is, from those who are in direct or indirect possession of a discourse capable of securing symbolic mastery of the practically mastered principles of the "class habitus." (Bourdieu, 1987, 83)

However, on account of the hysteresis effect, that is, a disproportionately greater weight given to early experiences in the constitution of habitus, there is a structural lag between such opportunities triggered by events and the dispositions to grasp them, which retards the responses called for in the transformation of practices.

Although Bourdieu mentions "class habitus" signifying the habitus of groups in a differentiated society, it is possible to extend the same analysis to "gender habitus," as Bourdieu himself has done in his book *Masculine Domination* (2001 [1998]), noting, however, that "gender habitus" would be encompassed within each "class habitus."

He notes that the immanent in everyone's are

> shaped by similar conditions, and therefore objectively harmonized, function as matrices of the perceptions, thoughts and actions of all members of the society-historical transcendentals which, being shared by all, impose themselves on each agent as transcendent. As a consequence, the androcentric representation of biological reproduction and social reproduction is invested with the objectivity

> of a common sense, a practical, doxic consensus on the sense of practices. (Bourdieu, 2001 [1998], 33)

Bourdieu further notes:

> When the dominated apply to what dominates them schemes that are the product of domination, or, to put it another way, when their thoughts and perceptions are structured in accordance with the very structures of the relation of domination that is imposed on them, their acts of *cognition* are, inevitably, acts of *recognition*, submission.

But he also acknowledges, "there is always room for a *cognitive struggle* over the meaning of the things of the world" (Bourdieu, 2001 [1998], 13 Italics in original) as the "partial indeterminacy of certain objects authorizes antagonistic interpretations, offering the dominated a possibility of resistance to the effect of symbolic imposition" (Bourdieu, 2001 [1998], 14).

In fact, much of Bourdieu's ethnographic work on Kabylia kinship and matrimonial strategies deals with gender issues, and he does refer explicitly to them as such. He refers to "gendered habitus" in an interview, and remarks on "the obscurities of the schemata of habitus that are at once gendered and gendering" (Bourdieu and Wacquant, 1992, 172), even footnoting this remark with the statement, "The immediate agreement of a gendered habitus with a social world suffused with sexual asymmetries explains how women can come to collude with and even actively defend or justify forms of aggression which victimize them, such as rape" (Bourdieu and Wacquant, 1992, 172). Only a dispositional theory of practices that acknowledges the embodiment of social structures in dispositions can explain women's collusion with male domination, which is not the result of women's false consciousness. Consciousness-raising cannot therefore be a liberatory strategy and male dominance can only be broken by a radical transformation of the social conditions of production of the dispositions that lead the dominated to take the point of view of the dominant on the dominant and on themselves.

Although Indian feminists do not use Bourdieu's explanatory framework of habitus, they have nevertheless noted the fact that women themselves often legitimize structures of male dominance. Vanita notes:

> The average woman is subliminally persuaded that she has nothing to complain of if her husband does not batter her. The atrocity, constructed as such by media, legal terminology and protestors, functions to legitimize rather than undermine the structures of male-female relationships. (1996, 68)

The effect of habitus in Bourdieu's analysis is to naturalize the arbitrariness of every established order, which ensures the correspondence between social structures and mental structures of the agents, resulting in the most ineradicable adherence to the established order.

Bourdieu remarks: "In the extreme case, that is to say, when there is a quasi-perfect correspondence between the objective order and the subjective principles of organization (as in ancient societies) the natural and the social world appears as self-evident" (1987, 164). He further notes that schemes of thought and perception can produce the objectivity that they do produce only by producing a misrecognition of the limits of cognition that they make possible, thereby founding immediate adherence, in the doxic mode, to the world of tradition experienced as a "natural world" and taken for granted.

He highlights the point that in the case of domestic conflicts in marriage, social groups disadvantaged by the symbolic order, such as women and the young, "cannot but recognize the legitimacy of the dominant classification in the very fact that their only chance of neutralizing those of its effects most contrary to their own interests lies in submitting to them in order to make use of them" (Bourdieu, 1987, 164–65). This experience he calls "doxa," so as to distinguish it from orthodox or heterodox belief, implying awareness and recognition of the possibility of different or antagonistic beliefs.

Any doubts about doxa approaching determinism, as a way of reading off agency from the limits and possibilities of habitus, are only partly valid. For one, all agency is determined by the dispositions of the agents. Action has to be willed; unwilled action is either coercion or an accident and not agency. Habitus, however, strictly refers to durable and transposable dispositions. Non-durable dispositions or transient states of mind could also engender actions. Also, since dispositions are transposable, the same habitus can generate different action responses depending on how dispositions are sequenced. Moreover, the correspondence between the objective order and the subjective principles of organization can vary between individuals in the same milieu, which in turn generates different levels of doxic adherence and hence different agentive possibilities.

The truth of doxa, according to Bourdieu, can only be revealed when negatively constituted by the constitution of a field of opinion, which becomes the locus of the confrontation of competing discourses. Bourdieu writes: "The critique which brings the undiscussed into discussion, the unformulated into formulation, has as the condition of its possibility objective crisis, which in breaking the immediate fit between the subjective structures and the objective structures, destroys self-evidence practically" (Bourdieu, 1987, 168–169).

Whenever the definition of the social world is at stake, the drawing of the line between the field of opinion, of that which is explicitly questioned, and the field of doxa, of that which is beyond question and which the agent tacitly accords by the mere fact of acting in accord with social convention, is itself a fundamental objective at stake in the struggle for the imposition of the dominant systems of classification. He further explains that while

> the dominated classes have an interest in pushing back the limits of doxa and exposing the arbitrariness of the taken for granted; the dominant classes have an interest in defending the integrity of doxa, or short of this, of establishing in its place the necessarily imperfect substitute, orthodoxy. (Bourdieu, 1987, 169)

He defines "orthodoxy" as a system of euphemisms, of acceptable ways of thinking and speaking about the natural and social world, which rejects heretical remarks as blasphemies. Although crisis is a necessary condition for a questioning of doxa, it is in itself not a sufficient condition for the production of a critical discourse.

Bourdieu's analysis of the constitution of a field of opinion with competing discourses to push back the field of doxa is very relevant to an understanding of what ought to be the challenge of feminist politics. According to him, "private" experiences undergo "nothing less than a change of state when they recognize themselves in the public objectivity of an already constituted discourse, the objective sign of recognition of their right to be spoken and to be spoken publicly" Bourdieu (1987, 170). The common feminist cliche that the personal (generally taken as synonymous with "private") is political, never clearly reveals that private experiences are conditioned by habitus or dispositions and can become political only by first being constituted in public discourse. Moreover, even when it is accepted by many in a society that the personal is political, not all private experiences are already constituted in public discourse. Thus, bringing private experiences into public discourse is a perpetual activity of feminist political practice.

In fact, Bourdieu himself remarked on the significance of his analysis of doxa for gender issues when he noted that "the best illustration of the political import of doxa is arguably the symbolic violence exercised upon women" (Bourdieu and Wacquant, 1992, 74). By symbolic violence, Bourdieu refers to the violence that is exercised upon a social agent with his or her complicity. At one point, Bourdieu even acknowledges that one of the tasks of sociology is precisely to examine under what conditions the dispositions to resist are "socially constituted, effectively triggered, and rendered politically efficient" (Bourdieu and Wacquant, 1992, 74).

We may or may not agree with Bourdieu's foundational cause for male domination. For Bourdieu, male domination is "*founded upon the logic of the economics of symbolic exchanges,* that is, upon the fundamental asymmetry between men and women instituted in the social construction of kinship and marriage" (Bourdieu and Wacquant, 1992, 174; Emphasis in original). But his ideas about habitus and doxa are certainly suggestive of theoretical frames for grappling with women's internalization of patriarchy and of their subordinate status, as also of ways of overcoming it.

I use these ideas to explore certain hitherto neglected aspects of women's sociopolitical mobilization in India, in particular the seemingly obvious and innocuous question as to why the majority of women do not identify themselves as feminists or join the women's movement. I agree with Sangari (1995) that a feminist politics must account for women's consent to patriarchies. But she notes,

> It can scarcely afford to give political or theoretical primacy to women's will to consent to forms of social oppression over and above their will to contest these; since such a primacy is already on offer by a standard form of male conservatism. (Sangari, 1995, 3293)

It is important to understand theoretically why women collude in their oppression before they are enabled to contest it, and for women's movements to facilitate the move of women's experiences from doxa to the field of public opinion. One explanation is provided in Steve Derne's ethnopsychology of family life and male dominance in Banaras, which highlights the role of the collectivist framework in shaping men's emotional life and, as a corollary women's socialization from a young age to fit into this cultural framework. Noting that everyday micro-interactions bolster men's power, he observes, "The cultural idea that a family's honor depends on a range of women's actions is just another ace that husbands can play in culture work aimed at controlling their wives" (Derne, 1995, 31). Further, he notes that in the process of the construction of gender-culture, men do not merely mimic dominant norms but often know that these norms advance and maintain their own privileged positions in the family. Women adopt a range of stances toward the norms of gender-culture such as being "True Believers," "Cowed Conformers," "Innovative Mimetists," who mimic adherence to social standards even as they reject them, and "Unapologetic Rebels." The complexities of both women's and men's ethnopsychology regarding the construction, abidance, and rejection of patriarchal gender-culture need far more scrutiny than has been done so far.

MULTIPLE AND OVERLAPPING PATRIARCHIES

Sangari's (1995) insightful formulation of "multiple and overlapping" patriarchies prompts us to think of patriarchy not as a de-cultured and decontextualized category, but as shaped by culture and class, and reciprocally shaping them. She argues convincingly that the plurality of patriarchies in India is a facet of social disparity, which is entangled with as well as produces diversity (Sangari, 1995, 3381). She places emphasis on the totality of patriarchal arrangements, in their differences and overlaps, rather than heterogeneity per se before the question of separate patriarchies governing women of each caste and each religion can be explored. Pointing out that the question of plural patriarchies has been barely addressed theoretically, Sangari notes:

> In the past, caste division, divisions of labor, the coexistence of tribal and agricultural modes of production, of matrilineal and patrilineal systems, and their complex articulation with regional histories including the formation of religious sects, have been significant factors in the crystallization of differing patriarchies. (1995, 3381)

She argues that Brahminization itself could not afford to universalize a patriarchy, and thus different patriarchies coexisted, granting different degrees of sexual access to upper and lower castes, as well as access to remarriage and a public world of work to lower-caste women. As a result, she says, the *Smritis* (sacred Hindu texts) prescribed or allowed for discrete as well as overlapping or intersecting patriarchal arrangements. In their proclaimed distance from customary law as well as in their frequent recognition of different coexisting customary laws, the *Smritis*, according to Sangari, partook in what was effectively at once a practiced and structured diversity. Thus, before the inception of modern law, Sangari notes that there existed social conditions conducive to patriarchal overlaps or mutually congenial patriarchal arrangements. There was little structural difference and often substantive similarities between the elite groups. According to her, elite groups cross-denominationally united in constructing women as status markers. Deep similarities, she notes, also existed between the different lower social groups, for whom there was often a great deal of denominational ambiguity both in nomenclature and social practices.

While the inception of modern class formation produced, according to her, a new axis of political differentiation, it also added to this long history of overlaps. She notes that domestic ideologies produced across denominations under colonial modernity were all combinations of emerging companionate and nurturant bourgeois ideologies with earlier precapitalist ideologies and arrangements. Furthermore, the desire to mark class/caste boundaries and particularize communities through domestic ideologies produced women as similar types of class subjects. The intersection of contemporary political economy with patriarchies also produces new grounds and forms of similarity. Arguably, she notes that particular patriarchal practices are correlated with class, region, and urbanization, and not necessarily on the correlate of community or religion.

These different patriarchal arrangements distribute protection, entitlements, and oppressions differently in terms of class, caste, region, and religion, triggering comparisons that some patriarchies are better than others. According to Vanita, this syndrome of comparative assessments of patriarchies functions both at the collective and individual levels, and within women's movements as much as in society at large, if more insidiously in the former than the latter (Vanita, 1996, 68).

Sangari's analysis of multiple and overlapping patriarchies possesses, in my opinion, only the potential to analyze patriarchies in their systemic features and structuring roles. The experiential dimension of multiple patriarchies must focus more on women as agents. In particular, an exploration of the multiple sets of dispositions embodied by the structuring of patriarchies, along with other structuring principles of caste, class, and religion, at the level of agents, both individual/collective women as agents, is necessary if we are to be concerned with women's ability to both interrogate and resist patriarchies and other social disparities.

At the level of individual and collective dispositions, what matters is women's own identification and affiliation with their perceived communities. At that level, the historical insights into communities matter little as historical consciousness does not wholly possess the agents in everyday life. What matters is that men and women in households have a sense of affiliation to communities, be they kin groups, religious, caste, neighborhood, or occupational communities, which in some ways set norms and shape the dispositions of men and women. Women's everyday transactions with patriarchy are governed by the norms of patriarchal arrangements set by these communities to which they subjectively affiliate. Such affiliations serve functional and emotional needs, although the structuring of society along various axes does not make it possible to choose all the communities to which they subjectively affiliate. The securities of identity and cultural self-worth provided by these affiliations are so strong and meaningful that they shape women's dispositions through androcentric views and schemes of perceptions of the dominant, leading to the naturalizing of patriarchal arrangements and/or sets limits to women's engagement with patriarchal bargains.

In recent times, the question of "difference" has been effectively brought to attention in feminist politics by Dalit women's separate and autonomous organizations (Guru, 1995). Feminists are urged to adopt the Dalit feminist standpoint, much as the Gender and Development debates in the 1980s urged Third World feminists to adopt the vantage point of the poor woman (Rege, 1998). This appeal is fine as far as feminist positioning is concerned, but I am at a loss to understand how a non-Dalit woman would be persuaded to accept that this Dalit feminist standpoint would be empowering to her in her everyday transactions with patriarchy, which, in the context of multiple patriarchies, would be of a different experiential nature if their lives are marked different culturally.

This is not to suggest that women have only a narrow identitarian outlook or politics, or are so obsessed with their self-interest as to be incapable of empathy or solidarity. Rather, what I suggest is that empathy and solidarity with the oppressions of the "other" can arise only after one acquires the agentive capabilities to deal with one's own oppressive predicament. The existence of overlapping patriarchies makes it easier to connect with the "other" than it would be otherwise. Thus, the appeal to non-Dalit feminists to adopt a Dalit feminist standpoint is only a post-consciousness standpoint. An adequate feminist politics ought also to address the possibilities of enhancing the agentive capabilities of all women to deal effectively in their everyday patriarchal transactions.

Not only do patriarchal arrangements offer securities—in fact, they always have to offer both securities as well as control, for otherwise power cannot reproduce itself—but the institutions and networks in which women's and men's lives are enmeshed offer securities as well. It is these securities, both real and apparent—securities that are economic, social, psychological, and cultural—that both naturalize patriarchy and create the dispositions in women and men to reproduce the system of patriarchies. An analysis of how dispositions that are the outcome of structuring principles help to reproduce the system is best explored by considering the network of relations that enmesh women's lives and by exploring both what they perceive as the securities and the liabilities (such as patriarchal domination) of these relations, how the securities and liabilities of one set of relations compensate for the inadequacies, lack or excesses in the others, and how these are perceived to change over the individual's life cycle—in short, engage in a utilitarian calculus of human relations. Bourdieu's economy of symbolic capital needs the same calculus as that of economic capital.

What I am suggesting is that women's tendency to accept or resist patriarchal domination at the level of individual women needs to be explored in the context of the whole gamut of human relations in their lives. Needless to say, the perception of patriarchal domination by women, both individually and collectively, would depend on the transposition of the experience of patriarchal domination from the domain of doxa to the field of opinion. While the field of doxa refers to that which is beyond question, the field of opinion is that which is explicitly questioned. Both "orthodoxy" and "heterodoxy" inhabit the field of opinion. According to Bourdieu (1987, 169), orthodoxy, which is "straight or rather straightened, opinion," aims, without ever entirely succeeding, at restoring the primal state of innocence of doxa. It imposes both a manifest and a latent censorship that delimits the universe of possible discourse, for the boundary between the universe of discourse and the universe of doxa can be interpreted in a twofold sense of what goes without saying and what cannot be said for lack of a discourse. This boundary, in its dual sense, Bourdieu notes, represents the dividing line between the most radical form of misrecognition and the awakening of political consciousness.

Here, too, it is not merely the feminist movement that engages in this transposition, which is of course their political agenda, but the dialogical experience of the whole gamut of human relations can and often does help both to restore and push back the domain of doxa. Patriarchal arrangements may be structurally determined, but patriarchal power is experienced in the minute and dense capillaries of family and social life, requiring a micropolitics of power as well.

WOMEN AND THE TIES THAT BIND

The ties that bind women in their lives provide both securities that impact positively on their personhood, as well as liabilities that are often very oppressive. These ties can be categorized as those of: (a) the family; (b) the sphere of intimacy in which sexuality provides women and men certain affirmations of their selves; (c) the sphere of practical kinship relations; (d) the domain of friendship; and (e) other social ties that are part of everyday life. Unless we explore the trajectories of experience in each of these spheres over the life cycle of individual women and understand what securities and liabilities each offers at each point in time, we will not be able to understand how compliant or resistant selves are constituted. The "self" is constituted in relation to the "other"; and when there are many "others" in each individual's life, the constitution of the "self" can acquire features of game theory, that is, strategic playing based on anticipated responses and outcomes. One can be a compliant self in one self-other relation in order to be a resistant self in another. A simple example: many young women find marriage liberating from parental control! Or equally, a highly repressive and controlled familial environment may make the prospect of marital life appear as such a nightmare that some women may abjure it altogether!

It would obviously be next to impossible for me to list all the different securities and liabilities operating in each set of relations, but I would like to present some of the liabilities that often get discussed in the regular run-of-the-mill conversations of everyday life. Family relations play a very important role in self-constitution. Aspects that would make women reflect on the benefits and costs of human relations and affect their self-constitution as compliant or resistant selves in their self-other interactions include the mother-daughter relation over the life cycle when there are moments that are supportive and at other times competitive; fathers as role models for future husbands; the nature of sibling relations, especially the issue of competition and rivalry between sisters; the norms of brother-sister relations that are culturally defined and the realities that are at variance with these norms; the discursive regimes relating to a woman's body, beauty, and other endowments and achievements that are important in self-constitution and that often shape sibling relations as well; hassles over the distribution of scarce economic and emotional resources; and all the other myriad familial transactions that may at times even appear as, and sometimes are indeed, acts of betrayal.

All these are no doubt related to the process of growing up to be an adult, from dependent to autonomous emotional selves, and self-constitution is really the sum of coping strategies that individuals adopt in these various situations. There is also an enormous price that individuals usually pay if they do not adopt or choose to question the values that a family has adopted as a way of life—the price of being different— when "being different" itself is an act of resistance, and many would have all heard stories of the triumphal acts of resistance of young women opting for intercaste and interreligious love marriages. Many young women would say they wanted to relieve their fathers or brothers from having to pay dowry or wanted to escape the humiliation of the transactions of the matrimonial market, such as inserting an advertisement in the newspaper that they are "slim and fair." These acts of resistance sometimes lead to family and social ostracism for short periods, or even the death penalty imposed by feudal caste panchayats in some regions, or killed by family members themselves as an act of honor killing. Girls could also mistakenly choose a murderer as a live-in partner who would sooner or later kill her, as is being reported in the media these days. Only some acts of resistance figure in feminist analysis.

The sphere of intimacy is another area of doxic silence, even in feminist works, except for issues of domestic violence and economic arrangements. Thapan (1995) is a reassuring piece with a feminist social-science viewpoint regarding how Indian women perceive oppression in the sphere of intimacy. Acts of resistance in the sphere of intimacy by women are an altogether neglected aspect—do angry Indian women deny their husbands food on time, or forget to put salt or put an excess of it in the food served to them? For, as is often remarked, Indians have a way of communicating through food! Or do they deny sex? And how do women resist when men deny them sex?

Vanita (1996) has illustrated some of these, such as women joining some religious groups like the Brahmakumaris or the Jaikishen ashram, that impose celibacy and dietary restrictions, enabling them to withhold both sex and food from their husbands. She notes that fasting and pilgrimage provide women with ways of controlling and accessing familial and individual patterns of life and mobility. Why are these questions not asked at all although we are well aware of these acts of resistance all around us? Are these questions irrelevant to women's lives or to the kind of feminist politics we have configured?

The sphere of kinship has engaged some feminist sociologists and anthropologists, but the understanding of the effects of kinship in practice has not been broadened enough to include issues such as the unequal burden that women bear in maintaining kin relations that requires giving gifts to members of the kin group on occasions such as marriage and birth to uphold the status and honor of the family that men do not show much concern. Just about every woman everywhere is probably bearing this unequal burden of maintaining kin relations. Women may or may not resist, depending on the perceived securities they derive from maintaining such relations. This is just one illustration, and there may be more such issues of kinship politics that need to be explored.

Friendship is an altogether neglected aspect of sociological research in India, although some fiction writers have explored friendships in Indian culture in allegorical terms. It is also something that gets taken for granted. One's own cultural norms and expectations of friendship generally acquire greater clarity in intercultural encounters. Friendship could act as a buffer and serve as a mitigating force for many of the oppressions of everyday life, including the patriarchal, just as much as it can generate them. Often friendship is limited to people from the same social class in the neighborhood, and for women, to bhajan-singing, or temple or movie-going groups. But sufficient space is not available in such friendships to discuss patriarchal oppressions one encounters, for it is generally assumed that an adult woman is equipped with the agentive capabilities to deal with such oppressions on her own. These friendships between women no doubt play a role in altering the domain of doxa, although some women maintain resolute silence when listening to others' experiences. Such strategic silences make it amply clear that even friends have to be as strategically handled as enemies, for friendships need not be devoid of individuals' self-interest. There is much to be explored in friendship in our cultural contexts, such as the jealousies and envies it arouses between couples, competition and envy between same-sex friends, especially women friends, the status of female friendship after marriage, cross-sex friendship, cross-class friendship, friendship possibilities for single women, the tensions in friendship between single women and married women, and the role of age in friendship.

The entire set of human relations in everyday life, including those at the workplace, affords possibilities for breaking the doxic silence on patriarchal oppressions and for forming one's opinion on them. Equally, there are many instances of patriarchal oppression that are difficult to resist either individually or collectively, such as non-verbal, non-sexual abusive behavior. For example, what do you do when men (or even women) around you keep treating you with contempt, such contempt being demonstrated through non-verbal gestures? You have either the option to ignore them, and in effect to accept the abusive treatment, or to retaliate with the same oppressive gesture that you want to oppose! This is not as trivial a point as some might think. All of us are constantly subjected to a variety of abuse, and we often become insensitive to them.

While sensitive feminist novelists portray these unnoticed or minor oppressions in everyday life that are an integral part of human relations, these have generally been ignored in academic works that have largely favored macro rather than micro perspectives. While fiction writing gives primacy to human experience as it seeks to represent the varieties of human experience persuasively and imaginatively, the social sciences, like all other sciences, seek to understand the organizing principles of social life through concepts and categories that are reductive of human experience. No wonder Das (1998, 69) remarked that some realities have to be fictionalized before they can be apprehended. Feminist social scientists are thus caught in an epistemological trap of rendering their activity "scientific" even as they seek to represent the varieties of female experience. As poets and metaphysicians have often reminded us, the recovery of the "whole" experience often forces language itself to confront its own limitations. Feminist social scientists too are forced, in their attempts to recover the whole female experience, to confront both the inadequacies of various paradigmatic approaches in the social sciences as well as the inadequacies of transformational praxis.

It is important to bridge the distance between women's experiences in everyday life and the discourse of feminist politics. Feminist politics ought to recognize the innumerable acts of resistance of women in everyday life and seek ways to enhance their agentive capabilities to overcome their internalization of patriarchy through embodied dispositions. It ought to acknowledge that breaking the doxic silence on patriarchal oppression, owing to women's internalization of patriarchy, can be affected through a whole set of networks of human relations, and not only by feminist groups alone. The media too plays an important role in breaking the doxic silence and enabling women to realize their potentialities. At the same time, once the limits of doxa are pushed, the women's movement needs to ensure that the field of opinion is not annexed and hegemonized by conservative forces, as it would likely be a contentious terrain of conservative and liberatory pulls and pressures. This is especially relevant in dynamic social contexts of the contending forces of tradition and modernity.

HABITUS, TRADITION, AND MODERNITY

It is often noted that even as societies modernize and ideas of modernity in many spheres of life bring perceptible changes, the binds of tradition still remain strong such that women's status is not significantly changed, and women still internalize patriarchal norms, and dispositional practices do not undergo significant changes. The preceding chapters on marriage in rural, urban, and diasporic contexts revealed that despite women and young girls aspire for a change, they are still constrained by moral codes and social and cultural norms, even while changes spurred by education and employment opportunities are evident. The discussion on religiosity and Hindu women's piety has also indicated that even while the sphere of religion is undergoing modernizing tendencies, women's roles and statuses regulated by cultural norms and deemed as religiously sanctioned moral codes are not significantly questioned by women themselves. While sanskritic Hinduism or *Sanatan Dharam* projects androcentric worldviews according primacy to the moral order in familial life that shape women's habitus/dispositions in the domestic sphere and the consequent internalization of patriarchal schemes, the tradition of *Saktism* that coexists and privileges the metaphorical figurehead of the female goddess has also not facilitated such questioning by women; it having been enfolded within the hegemonic fold of *Sanatan Dharam* over many centuries. Cultural norms shaped by moral codes also influence the reworking and innovating of Indian modernity that is constantly underway with its effects also in the material sphere of lifestyles and choices, as discussed in the earlier chapters on clothing and consumerism that reinforce the compatibility of tradition and modernity in women's domestic spheres.

Despite changes brought by modernity and the reworking of tradition, the persistence of embodied dispositions or inertia of the habitus of women that leads to their submission to symbolic violence and the internalizing of patriarchal norms requires further inquiry. Bourdieu suggests that such apparent permanence of patriarchal order, suggestive of essentialism even when changes are evident, is "merely the product of a labor of eternalization performed by interconnected institutions such as the family, the church, the state, the educational system" (Bourdieu, 2001 [1998], viii). Elsewhere he notes:

> A genuine understanding of the changes that have occurred both in the condition of women and in relations between sexes can paradoxically, be expected only from an analysis of the transformations of the mechanisms charged with ensuring the perpetuation of the order of genders. (Bourdieu, 2001 [1998], 84–85)

In India, the family still remains the primary site for the perpetuation of the patriarchal order, and as Bourdieu has explained, it is integral to the economy of symbolic goods. Women's dispositional practices, by applying schemes of perception that are products of male domination, enable the family to acquire symbolic capital such as "honor" and social capital as "social status," which are essential features of matrimonial strategies for building kinship relations through appropriate alliances. In the earlier chapter on marriage among urban girls, we noted that there were two pathways of social status enhancement in matrimonial strategies—either through tradition by abiding by sociocultural norms or through the performance of modernity. Changing the patriarchal order in families, with the concomitant shift in the dispositions of women, could arise with greater exposure to education, employment, and other facets of modernity that could tilt the calculus of gain in the economy of symbolic goods and favor the performance of modernity. But this comes about only through a process of cognitive struggle by women and girls. The sphere of religion too seems to offer much less scope to change women's dispositions to resist androcentric views, as abiding by the religiously sanctioned norms seems more gainful to the family's economy of symbolic capital. While the sphere of modern education seeks to draw more women and attempts to transform stereotypical representations of women, even while opening opportunities for work in the modern sectors, women still need to contest the traditional patriarchal mindset within families when making many of their life choices.

This leaves much of the burden of changing familial private patriarchy to the state. While the state often ratifies and underwrites private patriarchy with those of public patriarchy by subscribing to androcentric views, the post-independent state in India has, since the beginning, made slow strides toward women's equality through legal changes that gained momentum in the later decades on matters of marriage, property, inheritance, employment, political representation, and others. Today, there is a flurry of legislative changes to open up almost all sectors of work for women, and the state of Tamil Nadu has even recently given legislative approval for recruiting women from all castes as priests in Hindu temples, a move that would in due course likely end both caste and sex discrimination that has existed since time immemorial. But much like the nationalist resolution of the women question under colonial rule, there is even in contemporary times an anxiety to defend the core civilizational values against the possible onslaught of Western modernity. In the shaping of Indian modernity, the defense of core cultural values is given primacy in its accommodation with modernity through law, education, and lifestyle choices even as it positions to reap the gains of modernity. This anxiety is clearly evident in the recent Supreme Court ruling on same-sex matters. While ruling in favor of same-sex cohabitation and the non-denial of benefits to the couple, it did not approve same-sex marriage, leaving it to the parliament to legislate on the matter if societal changes deem it necessary, which in an androcentric society is unlikely to happen any time in the near future. Women's acts of resistance in their private lives, a cognitive struggle against androcentric views and its dispositional practices, seem to be an unending one in the contending pulls of modernity offering a potential for liberation, and tradition putting the brakes on it even as it gets revised under modernity.

References

2018. "From Sabarimala to Hadiya: Former CJI Dipak Misra Relives Orders." *Hindustan Times*, October 5, 2018.

2019. Indian Young Lawyers Association & Ors v The State of Kerala & Ors. 11 SCC 1 (India).

2023. "Mohan Bhagwat Takes Part in Consecration of *Bharata Mata* Temple in Tamil Nadu." *Deccan Herald*, May 5, 2023.

2024. "Double Tumbler System: 2 Held for Serving Tea to Dalits in Coconut Shells." *The Times of India*, February 11, 2024.

Abbott, Porter H. 2008. *The Cambridge Introduction to Narrative*, 2nd edition. Cambridge: Cambridge University Press.

Abraham, Janaki. 2014. "Contingent Caste Endogamy and Patriarchy: Lessons for our Understanding of Caste." *Economic and Political Weekly* 49 (2): 56–65.

Agamben, Giorgio. 1998. *Homo Sacer: Sovereign Power and Bare Life*. Stanford: Stanford University Press.

Agamben, Giorgio. 2005. *State of Exception*. Chicago: University of Chicago Press.

Ahuja, Amit, and Susan L. Ostermann. 2016. "Crossing Caste Boundaries in the Modern Indian Marriage Market." *Studies in Comparative International Development* 51 (3): 365–387.

Appadurai, A., ed. 1986a. *The Social Life of Things: Commodities in Cultural Perspective*. Cambridge: Cambridge University Press.

Appadurai, A. 1986b. "Introduction: Commodities and the Politics of Value." In *The Social Life of Things: Commodities in Cultural Perspective*, edited by Arjun Appadurai, 3–63. Cambridge: Cambridge University Press.

Appadurai, Arjun. 1996a. "Disjuncture and Difference in the Global Cultural Economy." In *Modernity at Large: The Cultural Dimensions of Globalization*, edited by Arjun Appadurai, 27–47. Minneapolis: University of Minnesota Press.

Appadurai, Arjun. 1996b. *Modernity at Large: Cultural Dimensions of Globalization*. Minneapolis: University of Minnesota Press.

Arnason, Johann. 2001a. "Civilizational Patterns and Civilizing Processes." *International Sociology* 16 (3): 387–405.

Arnason, Johann. 2001b. "The Multiplication of Modernity." In *Identity, Culture and Globalization,* edited by Ben-Rafael and Yitzak Sternberg, 131–154. Annals of the International Institute of Sociology Vol. 8. Leiden: E.J. Brill.

Aurobindo, Sri. 1970. *The Life Divine*. Pondicherry: Sri Aurobindo Ashram.

Babb, Lawrence A. 1995. "Introduction." In *Media and The Transformation of Religion in South Asia*, edited by Lawrence A. Babb and Susan S. Wadley, 1–18. Philadelphia: University of Pennsylvania Press.

Babb, Lawrence A., and Susan S. Wadley, eds. 1995. *Media and the Transformation of Religion in South Asia*. Philadelphia: University of Pennsylvania Press.

Bahl, Vinay. 2005. "Shifting Boundaries of 'Nativity' and 'Modernity' in South Asian Women's Clothes." *Dialectical Anthropology* 29 (1): 85–121.

Banerji, M., S. Martin, and S. Desai. 2008. "Is Education Associated with a Transition towards Autonomy in Partner Choice? A Case Study of India." *India Human Development Survey Working Paper No. 8.*

Baudrillard, Jean. 1983. *Simulations*. New York: Semiotext(e).

Baudrillard, Jean. 1990. "Subjective Discourse or The Non-Functional System of Objects." In *Revenge of the Crystal: Selected Writings on the Modern Object and Its Destiny, 1968–1983,* edited by Jean Baudrillard, 35–62. London: Pluto Press.

Baudrillard, Jean. 1993. *Symbolic Exchange and Death*. London: Sage Publications.

Baudrillard, Jean. 1994. *Simulacra and Simulation*. Ann Arbor, MI: University of Michigan Press.

Baudrillard, Jean. 1996. *The System of Objects*. London: Verso.

Baudrillard, Jean. 1998. *The Consumer Society: Myths and Structures*. London: Sage Publications.

Baxi, Pratiksha, Shirin M. Rai, and Shaheen Sardar Ali. 2006. "Legacies of Common Law: 'Crimes of Honor' in India and Pakistan." *Third World Quarterly* 27 (7): 1239–1253.

Baxi, Upendra. 2008. "Outline of a 'Theory of Practice' of Indian Constitutionalism." In *Politics and Ethics of the Indian Constitution*, edited by Rajeev Bhargava, 92–118. Delhi: Oxford University Press.

Beauvoir, Simone de. (1948) 1980. *The Ethics of Ambiguity*. New York: The Citadel Press.

Beck, Ulrich. (1986) 1992. *Risk Society: Towards a New Modernity*. London: Sage Publications.

Benjamin, Walter. 1968a. "The Work of Art in the Age of Mechanical Reproduction." In *Illuminations,* edited by Walter Benjamin, 219–253. New York: Harcourt, Brace & World, Inc.

Benjamin, Walter. 1968b. "On Some Motifs in Baudelaire." In *Illuminations,* edited by Walter Benjamin, 157–202. New York: Harcourt, Brace & World, Inc.

Benjamin, Walter. 1992. "Notizen zu einer Arbeit uber die Kategorie der Gerechtigkeit." *Frankfurter Adorno Blatter* 4.

Beteille, Andre. 2008. "Constitutional Morality." *Economic and Political Weekly* 43 (40): 35–42.

Bhabha, Homi K. 1994. "Of Mimicry and Man: The Ambivalence of Colonial Discourse." In *The Location of Culture*, edited by Homi K. Bhabha, 85–92. London: Routledge.

Bhargava, Rajeev. 2008. "Introduction: Outline of a Political Theory of the Indian Constitution." In *Politics and Ethics of the Indian Constitution*, edited by Rajeev Bhargava, 1–42. Delhi: Oxford University Press.

Blanchet, Therese. 2005. "Bangladeshi Girls Sold as Wives in North India." *Indian Journal of Gender Studies* 12 (2/3): 305–334.

Bloch, Francis, and Vijayendra Rao. 2000. "Terror as a Bargaining Instrument: A Case Study of Dowry Violence in Rural India." *Policy Research Working Paper* 2347. Washington, DC: World Bank.

Bourdieu, Pierre. 1977. *Outline of a Theory of Practice*. Translated by Richard Price. Cambridge: Cambridge University Press.

Bourdieu, Pierre. 1984. *Distinction: A Social Critique of the Judgement of Taste*. Cambridge: Harvard University Press.

Bourdieu, Pierre. 2000. *Pascalian Meditations*. Stanford: Stanford University Press.

Bourdieu, Pierre. (1998) 2001. *Masculine Domination*. Stanford: Stanford University Press.

Bourdieu, Pierre, and L. J. D. Wacquant. 1992. *An Invitation to Reflexive Sociology*. Cambridge: Polity Press.

Budgeon, Shelley. 2003. "Identity as an Embodied Event." *Body & Society* 9 (1): 35–55.

Chakrabarty, Dipesh. 1993. "The Difference-Deferral of (A) Colonial Modernity: Public Debates on Domesticity in British Bengal." *History Workshop Journal* 36 (1): 1–34.

Chakrabarty, Dipesh. 2000. *Provincializing Europe: Postcolonial Thought and Historical Difference*. Princeton: Princeton University Press.

Chakrabarty, Dipesh. 2002. *Habitations of Modernity: Essays in the Wake of Subaltern Studies*. Chicago: University of Chicago Press.

Chan, Annie Hau-nung. 2000. "Fashioning Change: Nationalism, Colonialism, and Modernity in Hongkong." *Postcolonial Studies* 3 (3): 293–309.

Chang, Hsiao-hung. 2004. "Fake Logos, Fake Theory, Fake Globalization." *Inter-Asia Cultural Studies* 5 (2): 222–36.

Chatterjee, Partha. (1989) 1990. "Colonialism, Nationalism, and Colonialized Women: The Contest in India." *American Ethnologist* 16 (4): 622–633. Enlarged Version Published as "The Nationalist Resolution of the Women's Question." In *Recasting Women: Essays in Colonial History*, edited by Kumkum Sangari and Sudesh Vaid, 233–253. New Brunswick: Rutgers University Press.

Chatterjee, Partha. 1994. *The Nation and its Fragments*. New Jersey: Princeton University Press.

Chaudhry, Shruti, and Taneesha Devi Mohan. 2011. "Of Marriage and Migration: Bengali and Bihari Brides in a UP Village." *Indian Journal of Gender Studies* 18 (3): 311–340.

Chaudhuri, Nirad C. (1976) 2008. *Culture in the Vanity Bag: Being an Essay on Clothing and Adornment in Passing and Abiding India.* Mumbai: Jaico Publishing House.

Childers, J., and G. Hentzi, eds. 1995. *The Columbia Dictionary of Modern Literary and Cultural Criticism.* New York: Columbia University Press.

Chowdhry, Prem. 1993. "Persistence of a Custom: Cultural Centrality of *Ghunghat.*" *Social Scientist* 21 (9/11): 91–112.

Chowdhry, Prem. 1997. "Enforcing Cultural Codes: Gender and Violence in Northern India." *Economic and Political Weekly* 32 (19): 1919–1928.

Chowdhry, Prem. 2004a. "Caste Panchayats and the Policing of Marriage in Haryana: Enforcing Kinship and Territorial Exogamy." *Contributions to Indian Sociology* 38 (1/2): 1–42.

Chowdhry, Prem. 2004b. "Private Lives, State Intervention: Cases of Run-away Marriage in Rural North India." *Modern Asian Studies* 38 (1): 55–58.

Chowdhry, Prem. 2007. *Contentious Marriages, Eloping Couples: Gender, Caste and Patriarchy in Northern India.* Delhi: Oxford University Press.

Cohn, Bernard S. 1965. "Anthropological Notes on Disputes and Law in India." *American Anthropologist* 67 (6, Part 2): 82–122.

Comaroff, Jean, and John Comaroff. 2006. "Law and Disorder in the Post-colony: Is the World Evolving toward Africa?" Plenary Lecture at the IUAES Inter-Congress. Cape Town: University of Cape Town.

Das, Veena. 1981. "The Mythological Film and Its Framework of Meaning: An Analysis of *Jai Santoshi Ma.*" *India International Centre Quarterly* 8 (1): 43–55.

Das, Veena. 1994. "Modernity and Biography: Women's Lives in Contemporary India." *Thesis Eleven* 39 (1): 52–62.

Das, Veena. 1998. "Language and Body: Transactions in the Construction of Pain." In *Social Suffering*, edited by Arthur Kleinman, Veena Das, and Margaret Lock, 67–91. Delhi: Oxford University Press.

Das, Veena. 2010. "Engaging the Life of the Other: Love and Everyday Life." In *Ordinary Ethics: Anthropology, Language and Action*, edited by Michael Lambeck, 376–399. New York: Fordham University Press.

Das, Veena, and Deborah Poole. 2004. "State and Its Margins: Comparative Ethnographies." In *Anthropology in the Margins of the State*, edited by Veena Das and Deborah Poole, 3–33. Santa Fe: School of American Research Press.

Dasgupta, Shamita Das. 1998. "Gender Roles and Cultural Continuity in the Asian Indian Immigrant Community in the U.S." *Sex Roles* 38 (11/12): 953–974.

Davies, L. 1987. *Pupil Power: Deviance and Gender in School.* Lewes: Falmer Press.

Derne, Steve. 1995. *Culture in Action: Family Life, Emotion, and Male Dominance in Banaras, India.* Albany: SUNY Press.

Derne, Steve. 2005. "The (Limited) Effect of Cultural Globalization in India: Implications for Culture Theory." *Poetics* 33 (1): 33–47.

Derrida, Jacques. 1981. *Dissemination.* Translated by Barbara Johnson. Chicago: University of Chicago Press.

Derrida, Jacques. 1982. "Differance." Translated by Alan Bass. In *Margins of Philosophy,* edited by Jacques Derrida, 1–27. Chicago: University of Chicago Press.

Desai, Sonalde, and Lester Andrist. 2010. "Gender Scripts and Age at Marriage in India." *Demography* 47 (3): 667–687.

Dickey, Sara. 1993. *Cinema and the Urban Poor in South India.* New York: Cambridge University Press.

Diesel, Alleyn. 2002. "Tales of Women's Suffering: Draupadi and other Amman Goddesses as Role Models for Women." *Journal of Contemporary Religion* 17 (1): 5–20.

Dube, Leela. 1986. "Seed and Earth: The Symbolism of Biological Reproduction and Sexual Relations of Production." In *Visibility and Power: Essays on Women in Society and Development,* edited by Leela Dube, Eleanor Leacock, and Shirley Ardener, 22–53. Delhi: Oxford University Press.

Dube, Leela. 1996. "Caste and Women." In *Caste: Its Twentieth Century Avatar,* edited by M. N. Srinivas, 1–27. Delhi: Penguin India.

Dumont, Louis. 1983. *Affinity as a Value: Marriage Alliance in South India, with Comparative Essays on Australia.* Chicago: University of Chicago Press.

Dumont, Louis. 1993. "North India in Relation to South India." In *Family Kinship and Marriage in India*, edited by Patricia Uberoi, 273–286. Delhi: Oxford University Press.

Eco, Umberto. 1986. *Travels in Hyperreality: Essays.* Translated by William Weaver. San Diego: Harcourt Brace & Company.

Eisenstadt, Shmuel N. 1990. "Cultural Tradition, Historical Experience, and Social Change: The Limits of Convergence." In *Tanner Lectures on Human Values,* XI, edited by Grethe B. Peterson, 443–505. Salt Lake City: University of Utah Press.

Eisenstadt, Shmuel N. 2000a. "Multiple Modernities." In *Multiple Modernities*, Special Issue of *Daedalus* 129 (1): 1–29.

Eisenstadt, Shmuel N. 2000b. "The Civilizational Dimension in Sociological Analysis." *Thesis Eleven* 62 (1): 1–21.

Ferrara, Alessandro. 1993. *Modernity and Authenticity: A Study of the Social and Ethical Thought of Jean-Jacques Rousseau.* Albany: SUNY Press.

Ferrara, Alessandro. 1998. *Reflective Authenticity.* London: Routledge.

Foucault, Michel. 1973. *The Order of Things.* New York: Vintage Books.

Foucault, Michel. 1980a. "Power and Strategies." In *Power/Knowledge Selected Interviews and Other Writings 1972–1977*, edited by Colin Gordon, 134–145. New York: Pantheon Books.

Foucault, Michel. 1980b. *The History of Sexuality: Volume 1: An Introduction.* New York: Vintage Books.

Foucault, Michel. 1988. "An Aesthetics of Existence." In *Michel Foucault: Politics, Philosophy, Culture*, edited by Lawrence D. Kritzman, 47–53. New York: Routledge.

Foucault, Michel. 1994. "The Art of Telling the Truth." In *Critique and Power: Recasting the Foucault/ Habermas Debate*, edited by Michael Kelly, 139–148. Cambridge: MIT Press.

Foucault, Michel. 1997. "What Is Enlightenment?" In *Ethics: Subjectivity and Truth, Volume 1 of Essential Works of Foucault 1954–1984*, edited by Paul Rabinow, 303–20. New York: New Press.

Fuller, C. J., and Haripriya Narasimhan. 2008. "Companionate Marriage in India: The Changing Marriage System in a Middle-Class Brahman Sub-Caste." *The Journal of the Royal Anthropological Institute* 14 (4): 736–754.

Fuller, C. J., and Haripriya Narasimhan. 2013. "Marriage, Education, and Employment among Tamil Brahman Women in South India, 1891–2010." *Modern Asian Studies* 47 (1): 53–84.

Ganesh, Kamala. 1990. "Mother Who is Not a 'Mother': In Search of the Great Indian Goddess." *Economic and Political Weekly* 25 (42/43): WS 58–WS 64.

Gaonkar, D. P. 2001. "On Alternative Modernities." In *Alternate Modernities,* edited by D. P. Gaonkar, 1–23. Durham: Duke University Press.

Geetha, V. 2004. "Periyar, Women and an Ethic of Citizenship." In *Feminism in India,* edited by Maitrayee Chaudhuri, 156–174. New Delhi: Kali for Women.

Giddens, Anthony. 1990. *The Consequences of Modernity.* Stanford: Stanford University Press.

Goffman, Erving. 1979. *Gender Advertisements.* New York: Harper & Row.

Golomb, Jacob. 1995. *In Search of Authenticity: Existentialism from Kierkegaard to Camus.* New York: Routledge.

Gough, E. Kathleen. 1993. "Brahman Kinship in a Tamil Village." In *Family, Kinship and Marriage in India*, edited by Patricia Uberoi, 146–175. Delhi: Oxford University Press.

Gross, David. 1992. *The Past in Ruins: Tradition and the Critique of Modernity.* Amherst: University of Massachusetts Press.

Guignon, Charles. 2004. *On Being Authentic.* London: Routledge.

Guignon, Charles. 2008. "Authenticity." *Philosophy Compass* 3 (2): 277–290.

Gupta, Krishna. 1996. *Social Equality and the Indian Constitution.* New Delhi: S. Chand & Co Ltd.

Guru, Gopal. 1995. "Dalit Women Talk Differently." *Economic and Political Weekly* 30 (41/42): 2548–2549.

Ha, Sejin, and Sharron J. Lennon. 2006. "Purchase Intent for Fashion Counterfeit Products: Ethical Ideologies, Ethical Judgements and Perceived Risks." *Clothing and Textiles Research Journal* 24 (4): 297–315.

Habermas, Jürgen. 1983. "Modernity—An Incomplete Project." Translated by Seyla Benhabib. In *The Anti-Aesthetic: Essays on Postmodern Culture*, edited by Hal Foster, 3–15. Port Townsend: Bay Press.

Hancock, E. Mary. 2000. *Womanhood in the Making: Domestic Ritual and Public Culture in Urban South India.* Boulder: Westview Press.

Hansen, K. T. 2004. "The World in Dress: Anthropological Perspectives on Clothing, Fashion and Culture." *Annual Review of Anthropology* 33: 369–392.

Heidegger, Martin. (1927) 1962. *Being and Time.* Translated by John Macquarrie and Edward Robinson. New York: Harper & Row.

Heidegger, Martin. 1971. "The Thing." In *Poetry, Language, Thought.* Translated by Albert Hofstadter, 163–80. New York: Harper & Row.

Henningsen, Lena. 2006. "Harry Potter with Chinese Characteristics." *China Information* 20 (2): 275–311.

Hoad, Neville. 2004. "World Piece: What the Miss World Pageant Can Teach about Globalization." *Cultural Critique* 58 (Autumn): 56–81.

Hobsbawm, Eric. 1983. "Introduction: Inventing Traditions." In *The Invention of Tradition*, edited by Eric Hobsbawm and Terence Ranger, 1–14. New York: Cambridge University Press.

Honneth, Axel. 1994. "Schwerpunkt: Autonomie und Authentizität." *Deutsche Zeitschrift für Philosophie* 42 (1): 59–60.

Honneth, Axel. 1997. "Recognition and Moral Obligation." *Social Research* 64 (1): 16–35.

Hoskins, Janet. 2006. "Agency, Biography and Objects." In *Handbook of Material Culture*, edited by Christopher Tilley, Webb Keane, Susanne Kuchler, Mike Rowlands, and Patricia Spyer, 74–84. London: Sage Publications.

Ingold, Tim. 2010. "Bringing Things to Life: Creative Entanglements in a World of Materials." *ESRC MCRM Working Paper Series* 05/10, Working Paper #15.

Ingole, Anagha. 2019. "Enforced Loyalties: Caste Panchayats and Caste Politics in India." *Social Research* 86 (3): 765–787.

Iwanek, Krzystof. 2016. "'Love Jihad' and the Stereotypes of Muslims in Hindu Nationalism." *Journal of Alternative Perspectives in the Social Sciences* 7 (3): 355–399.

Jain, Meenakshi. 1996. "Backward Castes and Social Change in UP and Bihar." In *Caste: Its Twentieth Century Avatar,* edited by M. N. Srinivas, 135–151. New Delhi: Penguin India.

Jamieson, M. 1999. "The Place of Counterfeits in Regimes of Value: An Anthropological Approach." *Journal of the Royal Anthropological Institute* 5 (1): 1–12.

Jarzombek, Mark. 2009. "Horse Shrines in Tamil India: Reflections on Modernity." *Future Anterior* VI (1): 18–36.

Jeffery, Patricia, and Roger Jeffery. 1996. *Don't Marry Me to a Plowman! Women's Everyday Lives in Rural North India.* New Delhi: Vistaar Publications.

Jha, Ambrish. 2005. "China, Biggest Source of Counterfeit Products." *The Hindu Business Line*, November 15, 2005.

Jirousek, C. A. 1997. "From 'Traditional' to 'Mass Fashion System' Dress among Men in a Turkish Village." *Clothing and Textile Research Journal* 15 (4): 203–215.

Joshi, Namrata. 2024. "The Shifting Shape of Hindu Mythologicals." *The New Indian Express*, January 21, 2024.

Joy, Annamma, and Ruby Ray Dholakia. 1991. "Remembrances of Things Past: The Meaning of Home and Possessions of Indian Professionals in Canada." *Journal of Social Behavior and Personality* 6 (6): 385–402.

Kale, Ridhi. 2023. "How the Indian Kitchen is in for a-Tech-Tonic Shift." *India Today Magazine Insight*, November 18, 2023.

Kalpagam, U. 2000. "The Women's Movement in India: New Agendas and Old Problems." *Feminist Studies* 26 (3): 645–60.

Kalpagam, U. 2006. "Secularism, Religiosity and Popular Culture: Chennai's Roadside Temples." *Economic and Political Weekly* 41 (43/44): 4595–4600.

Kalpagam, U. 2007. "Religiosity among Hindu Women in Chennai." *Nivedini: Journal of Women's Studies, Sri Lanka* 13 (1): 29–52.

Kalpagam, U. 2008. "Counterfeit Consciousness and the Joy of Abandonment." In *Sarai Reader 7, Frontiers,* 90–99. New Delhi: Sarai/CSDS Publication.

Kalpagam, U. (2019) 2021. *Neoliberalism and Women in India: Governmentality Perspectives.* Lanham: Lexington Books. Indian Reprint, Jaipur: Rawat Publications.

Kannabiran, Kalpana. 2021. "Constitution-As-Commons: Notes on Decolonizing Citizenship in India." *The South Atlantic Quarterly* 120 (1): 232– 241.

Kant, Immanuel. (1784) 1992. "An Answer to the Question: What is Enlightenment?" Translated by Ted Humphrey. Indianapolis: Hackett Publishing.

Kapadia, Karin. 1996. *Siva and Her Sisters: Gender, Caste and Class in Rural South India.* Delhi: Oxford University Press.

Kapur, Jyotsna, 2009. "An 'Arranged Love' Marriage: India's Neoliberal Turn and the Bollywood Wedding Culture Industry." *Communication, Culture & Critique* 2 (2): 221–233.

Karve, Irawati. 1993. "The Kinship Map of India." In *Family, Kinship and Marriage in India*, edited by Patricia Uberoi, 50–73. Delhi: Oxford University Press.

Klepp, Ingun Grimstad, and Ardis Storm-Mathisen. 2005. "Reading Fashion as Age: Teenage Girls' and Grown Women's Accounts of Clothing as Body and Social Status." *Fashion Theory* 9 (3): 323–342.

Kopnina, Helen. 2007. "The World According to Vogue: The Role of Culture(s) in International Fashion Magazines." *Dialectical Anthropology* 31 (4): 363–381.

Kopytoff, C. 1986. "The Cultural Biography of Things: Commoditization as Process." In *The Social Life of Things: Commodities in Cultural Perspective*, edited by Arjun Appadurai, 64–91. Cambridge: Cambridge University Press.

Lakshmi, C. S. 1990. "Mother, Mother-Community and Mother-Politics in Tamil Nadu." *Economic and Political Weekly* 25 (42/43): WS 72–WS 83.

Lakshmi, C. S. 1995. "Seduction, Speeches and Lullaby: Gender and Cultural Identity in a Tamil Film." *Economic and Political Weekly* 30 (6): 309–311.

Lambert, Helen. 1997. "Caste, Gender and Locality in Rural Rajasthan." In *Caste Today*, edited by C. J. Fuller, 93–123. Delhi: Oxford India Paperbacks.

Legg, Stephen, and Srila Roy. 2013. "Neoliberalism, Postcolonialism and Hetero-Sovereignties: Emergent Sexual Formations in Contemporary India." *Interventions: International Journal of Postcolonial Studies* 15 (4): 461–473.

Lehman, David W., Kieran O'Connor, Balazs Kov´acs, and George E. Newman. 2019. "Authenticity." *Academy of Management Annals* 13 (1): 1–42.

Liao, Ping-Hui. 2003. "Image Consumption and Trans-Local Discursive Practice: Decoding Advertisements in the Taipei MRT Mall." *Postcolonial Studies* 6 (2): 159–174.

Lynch, Annette. 2007. "Expanding the Definition of Provocative Dress: An Examination of Female Flashing Behavior on a College Campus." *Clothing and Textiles Research Journal* 25 (2): 184–201.

Lyotard, Jean François. 1986. *The Postmodern Explained to Children: Correspondence 1982–1985.* Translated by Don Barry, Julian Pefanis, Morgan Thomas, Bernadette Maher, and Virginia Spate. Sydney: Power Publications.

MacIntyre, Alasdair. 1981. *After Virtue: A Study in Moral Theory.* Indiana: University of Notre Dame Press.

Magid, Oren. 2015. "Beyond the Tools of Trade: Heidegger and the Intelligibility of Everyday Things." *The Southern Journal of Philosophy* 53 (4): 450–470.

Mankekar, Purnima. 1999. *Screening Culture, Viewing Politics: An Ethnography of Television, Womanhood and Nation in Postcolonial India.* Durham: Duke University Press.

Mehra, Preeti. 2001. "Crusade against Counterfeit." *The Hindu Business Line*, July 2, 2001.

Menon, Nivedita. 2009. "Sexuality, Caste, Governmentality: Contests over 'Gender' in India." *Feminist Review* 91 (1): 94–112.

Mines, Diane P. 2005. *Fierce Gods: Inequality, Ritual and the Politics of Dignity in a South Indian Village.* Bloomington: Indiana University Press.

Mitchell, Andrew J. 2015. *The Fourfold: Reasoning the late Heidegger.* Illinois: Northwestern University Press.

Mody, Anjali. 2003. "Where Love Dies First." *Hindu,* Sunday Magazine, November 2, 2003.

Moore, Erin P. 1993. "Gender, Power and Legal Pluralism: Rajasthan India." *American Ethnologist* 20 (3): 522–542.

Mueller, F. Max. 1902. *The Life and Letters of the Right Honorable Friedrich Max Muller: Volume 1.* New York: Longman, Green, and Co.

Nandy, Ashis. 2001. "A Report on the Present State of Health of the Gods and Goddesses in South Asia." *Postcolonial Studies* 4 (2): 125–141.

Narasimhan, Haripriya. 2011. "Adjusting Distances: Menstrual Pollution among Tamil Brahmins." *Contributions to Indian Sociology* 45 (2): 243–268.

Narumi, Hiroshi. 2000. "Fashion Orientalism and the Limits of Counter Culture." *Postcolonial Studies* 3 (3): 311–329.

Netting, Nancy. S. 2010. "Marital Ideoscapes in the 21st Century India: Creative Combinations of Love and Responsibility." *Journal of Family Issues* 3 (6): 707–726.

Notar, Beth E. 2006. "Authenticity, Anxiety and Counterfeit Confidence." *Modern China* 32 (1): 64–98.

Ondrich, Maria-Priska. 2005. "Amman Movies-An Introduction." *The Journal of Religion & Film* 9 (2): Article 5. DOI: https://doi.org/10.32873/uno.dc.jrf.09.02.05. Available at: https://digitalcommons.unomaha.edu/jrf/vol9/iss2/5/.

Osella, Caroline, and Filippo Osella. 2007. "Muslim Style in South India." *Fashion Theory* 11 (2/3): 233–252.

Padia, Chandrakala. 2020. "Resisting Western Critique of Women's Status in India: Reflections on Vedas and Dharmashastras." *Himachal Pradesh University Journal* 8 (2): 3–14.

Parekh, Bhikhu. 2008. "The Constitution as a Statement of Indian Identity." In *Politics and Ethics of the Indian Constitution*, edited by Rajeev Bhargava, 43–58. Delhi: Oxford University Press.

Parsons, Talcott. 1977. *The Evolution of Societies.* New Jersey: Prentice Hall.

Pathak, Zakia. 2014. "Mixed Marriage: Anxieties of Identity." *Indian Journal of Gender Studies* 21 (3): 461–483.

Polier, Nicole. 1998. "True Transgressions: Refusal and Recolonization in the Narrative of a Papuan Migrant 'Bighead'." *Feminist Studies* 24 (3): 511–534.

Rabolt, Nancy J., and Judith C. Forney. 1989. "Contemporary Saudi Arabian Women's Dress." *Clothing and Textiles Research Journal* 7 (3): 22–32.

Raheja, Gloria Goodwin. 1988. *The Poison in the Gift: Ritual Prestation, and the Dominant Caste in a North Indian Village*. Chicago: University of Chicago Press.

Rajasriblog. 2021. "Pudhumai Penn." In *The Modern Women by Bharathiyar*. https://rajasriblog.wordpress.com. July 15, 2021. Accessed July 18, 2024.

Ramanujan, A. K. 1990. "Is There an Indian Way of Thinking? An Informal Essay." In *India through Hindu Categories*, edited by McKim Marriott, 41–58. New Delhi: Sage Publications.

Rao, Nitya. 2015. "Marriage, Violence and Choice: Understanding Dalit Women's Agency in Rural Tamil Nadu." *Gender & Society* 29 (3): 419–433.

Rao, Vijayendra. 1993. "Dowry 'Inflation' in Rural India: A Statistical Investigation." *Population Studies* 17 (2): 283–293.

Raval, V. Vaishali, Pratiksha H. Raval, and Stacey P. Raj. 2010. "Damned if they Flee, Doomed if they Don't: Narratives of Runaway Adolescent Families from Rural India." *Journal of Family Violence* 25: 755–764.

Rawls, John. 1971. *A Theory of Justice*. Cambridge: Belknap Press of Harvard University Press.

Reddy, Chinnappa O. 2008. *The Court and the Constitution of India: Summits and Shallows*. New Delhi: Oxford University Press.

Rege, Sharmila. 1998. "Dalit Women Talk Differently: A Critique of 'Difference' and Towards a Dalit Feminist Standpoint Position." *Economic and Political Weekly* 33 (44): WS 39–WS 46.

Reischer, Erica, and Kathryn S. Koo. 2004. "The Body Beautiful: Symbolism and Agency in the Social World." *Annual Review of Anthropology* 33, 297–317.

Richman, Paula, ed. 1991. *Many Ramayanas: The Diversity of a Narrative Tradition in South Asia*. Berkeley: University of California Press.

Ricoeur, Paul. (1955) 1965. *History and Truth.* Translated by Charles A. Kelbley. Illinois: Northwestern University Press.

Ritzer, George. 1998. "Introduction." In *The Consumer Society: Myths and Structures*, edited by Jean Baudrillard, 1–24. London: Sage Publications.

Sangari, Kumkum. 1995. "Politics of Diversity: Religious Communities and Multiple Patriarchies." *Economic and Political Weekly* 30 (51/52): 3287–3310, 3381–3389.

Sarkar, Tanika. 1991. "Heroic Women, Mother Goddesses: Family and Organization in Hindutva Politics." In *Women and Right-wing Movements: Indian Experiences,* edited by Tanika Sarkar and Urvashi Butalia, 181–215. London: Zed Books.

Sartre, Jean Paul. 1943/1992. *Being and Nothingness: A Phenomenological Essay on Ontology.* New York: Washington Square Press.

Schmidt, Volker H. 2006. "Multiple Modernities or Varieties of Modernity?" *Current Sociology* 54 (1): 77–97.

Scott, Denise Benoit. 2021. "Doing Gender, Class, and Nation in Northern India: Student Aspirations and the New Middle Class." *Sociological Focus* 54 (2): 106–119.

Sharad, Shivantika. 2010. "Being an Authentic Self: Some Insights from the Lives of Sri Aurobindo and Mahatma Gandhi." In *Foundations of Indian Psychology,*

Volume 1: Theories and Concepts, edited by R. M. Matthijs Cornelissen, Girishwar Misra, and Suneet Verma, 223–248. New Delhi: Pearson Education.

Sharangapani, Mukta. 2010. "Browsing for Bridegrooms: Matchmaking and Modernity in Mumbai." *Indian Journal of Gender Studies* 17 (2): 249–276.

Sharma, Arvind, ed. 2005. *Goddesses and Women in the Indic Religious Tradition*. Leiden: E.J. Brill.

Shils, Edward. 1958. "Tradition and Liberty: Antinomy and Interdependence." *Ethics* 68 (3): 153–165.

Singer, Milton. 1963. "The Radha-Krishna 'Bhajans' of Madras City." *History of Religions* 2 (2): 183–226.

Soumhya, Venkatesan. 2009. "Rethinking Agency: Persons and Things in the Heterotopia of 'Traditional Indian Craft'." *The Journal of the Royal Anthropological Institute* 15 (1): 78–95.

Spivak, Gayatri Chakravarty. 1988. "Can the Subaltern Speak?" In *Marxism and the Interpretation of Culture*, edited by Cary Nelson and Lawrence Grossberg, 271–316. Urbana: University of Illinois Press.

Srinivas, M. N. (1952) 2003. *Religion and Society among the Coorgs of South India*. Delhi: Oxford University Press

Stephens, John, and Robyn McCallum. 1998. *Retelling Stories, Framing Culture: Traditional Story and Metanarratives in Children's Literature*. New York: Garland Publishing Inc.

Sundara Rajan, Mira T. 2017. "Adorer of the Feminine Principle." Dasara Special, *The Hindu*, September 28, 2017.

Sunder Rajan, Rajeswari. 1998 "Is the Hindu Goddess a Feminist?" *Economic and Political Weekly* 33 (44): WS 34–WS 38.

Tarlo, Emma. 1996. *Clothing Matters: Dress and Identity in India*. Chicago: University of Chicago Press.

Taylor, Charles. 1989. *Sources of the Self. The Making of the Modern Identity*. Cambridge: Belknap Press of Harvard University Press.

Taylor, Charles. 1991. *The Ethics of Authenticity*. Cambridge: Harvard University Press.

Taylor, Charles. 2001. "Two Theories of Modernity." In *Alternate Modernities*, edited by Dilip Parameshwar Gaonkar, 172–196. Durham: Duke University Press.

Thapan, Meenakshi, 1995. "Images of the Body and Sexuality in Women's Narratives on Oppression in the Home." *Economic and Political Weekly* 30 (43): WS 72–WS 80.

Thapan, Meenakshi. 2006. "Habitus, Performance and Women's Experience: Understanding Embodiment and Identity in Everyday Life." In *Reading Pierre Bourdieu in a Dual Context*, edited by Roland Lardinois and Meenakshi Thapan, 199–229. New Delhi: Routledge.

Thapan, Meenakshi. 2009. *Living the Body: Embodiment, Womanhood and Identity in Contemporary India*. New Delhi: Sage Publications.

Tharu, Susie, and Tejaswini Niranjana. 1996. "Problems for a Contemporary Theory of Gender." In *Subaltern Studies IX: Writings on South Asian History and Society*, edited by Shahid Amin and Dipesh Chakrabarty, 232–260. Delhi: Oxford University Press.

Thirumal, P., P. Narmada, and Himabindu Chintakunta. 2024. "Notes Toward a Theoretical History of Indic Media: On Elite Comportment and Technological Affordances." *Public Culture* 36 (2): 279–302.

Titzmann, Fritzi-Marie. 2013. "Changing Patterns of Matchmaking: The Indian Online Matrimonial Market." *Asian Journal of Women's Studies* 9 (4): 64–94.

Touraine, Alain. 2002. "From Understanding Society to Discovering the Subject." *Anthropological Theory* 2 (4): 387–398.

Touraine, Alain. 1995. *Critique of Modernity*. Translated by David Macey. Oxford: Blackwell.

Trautmann, Thomas R. 1981. *Dravidian Kinship*. Cambridge: Cambridge University Press.

Trautmann, Thomas R. 1993a. "The Study of Dravidian Kinship." In *Family, Kinship and Marriage in India*, edited by Patricia Uberoi, 74–90. Delhi: Oxford University Press.

Trautmann, Thomas R. 1993b. "Marriage Rules and Patterns of Marriage in the Dravidian Kinship Region." In *Family, Kinship and Marriage in India*, edited by Patricia Uberoi, 273–286. Delhi: Oxford University Press.

Trilling, Lionel. 1972. *Sincerity and Authenticity*. Cambridge: Harvard University Press.

Tyner, Keila, and Jennifer Paff Ogle. 2007. "Feminist Perspectives on Dress and the Body: An Analysis of Ms. Magazine, 1972 to 2002." *Clothing and Textiles Research Journal* 25 (1): 74–105.

Uberoi, Patricia, ed. 1994. *Family, Kinship and Marriage in India*. Delhi: Oxford University Press.

Uberoi, Patricia. 1998. "The Diaspora Comes Home: Disciplining Desire in DDLJ." *Contributions to Indian Sociology* 32 (2): 305–336.

Upadhyay, Sparsh. 2024. "Obligatory for Woman to Serve Elderly Mother-in-Law… Jharkhand HC." *Law Live*, January 23, 2024.

Valk, Ulo, and S. Lourdusamy. 2007. "Village Deities of Tamil Nadu in Myths and Legends: The Narrated Experience." *Asian Folklore Studies* 66 (1/2): 179–199.

Vanita, Ruth. 1996. "Thinking Beyond Gender in India." *Seminar* 446: 68–71.

Vann, Elizabeth F. 2006. "The Limits of Authenticity in Vietnamese Consumer Markets." *American Anthropologist* 108 (2): 286–296.

Varga, S. 2011a. *Authenticity as an Ethical Ideal*. New York: Routledge.

Varga, S. 2011b. "Self-Realization and Owing to Others: An Indirect Constraint?" *International Journal of Philosophical Studies* 19 (1): 75–86.

Varga, S., and C. Guignon. 2014. "Authenticity." In *The Stanford Encyclopedia of Philosophy*, edited by Edward N. Zalta. http://plato.stanford.edu/archives/fall2014/entries/authenticity/.

Vatuk, Sylvia. 2013. "The 'Women's Court' in India: An Alternative Dispute Resolution Body for Women in Distress." *The Journal of Legal Pluralism and Unofficial Law* 45 (1): 76–103.

Wadley, Susan. (1980) 1991. "The Paradoxical Powers of Tamil Women." In *The Powers of Tamil Women*, edited by Susan Wadley and Sheryl B. Daniel, 153–170. New Delhi: Manohar Publishers.

Wadley, Susan. 2000. "Negotiating New Rules and Values: Four Generations of Rural North Indian Women." In *Economic Development and the Quality of Life in South Asia,* 189–210. Publication of Scientific Research Results, No. 5, *Institutions, Networks and Forces of Change in Contemporary South Asia*, Japanese Ministry of Education, Science, Sports and Culture.

Wadley, Susan. 2008. "Clothing the Female Body: Education, Social Change and Fashion in Rural North India." In *Widows, Wives, Mothers, Daughters: Women in Northern India*. New Delhi: Chronicle Books.

Wagner, Peter. 2011. "Modernity: From Convergence and Stability to Plurality and Transformation." In *Handbook of Contemporary Social and Political Theory*, edited by Gerard Delanty and Stephen P. Turner, 226–235. London: Routledge.

Wolputte, Steven Van. 2004. "Hang on to Your Self: Of Bodies, Embodiment, and Selves." *Annual Review of Anthropology* 33: 251–269.

Woodward, Sophie. 2015. "The Hidden Lives of Domestic Things: Accumulations in Cupboards, Lofts, and Shelves." In *Intimacies, Critical Consumption and Diverse Economies*, edited by Emma Casey and Yvette Taylor, 216–232. Hampshire: Palgrave Macmillan.

Name Index

Subject Index

About the Author

U. Kalpagam is a former professor and presently an independent scholar. She has authored *Rule by Numbers: Governmentality in Colonial India* and *Neoliberalism and Women in India: Governmentality Perspectives*.